PENGUIN BOOKS

FOREIGN CORRESPONDENT

John Elliott was president of the FCC 2007–09. Formerly with the *Financial Times* in India (1983–88) and elsewhere, he writes from Delhi for *Fortune* and the *Economist*, and has a blog, Riding the Elephant.

Bernard Imhasly is a former FCC president, and was South Asia correspondent for the Swiss daily *Neue Zuercher Zeitung* from 1990 to 2007. He wrote *Goodbye to Gandhi?* (Penguin Books India 2007) and lives in Mumbai.

Simon Denyer was the Reuters bureau chief for India and Nepal till April 2008, when he became Washington bureau chief. Earlier he ran Reuters' Pakistan and Afghanistan bureaux for two years, and was also based in London, New York and Nairobi.

Ryan -

It's been an amazing year getting to know you. Thanks for always opening your door for me and letting me relax at your place. I'm really glad I got to spend my final days in India with you. I hope we always remain friends and our paths cross again on our next adventures.

From your favorite foreign correspondent,

Priya

Foreign Correspondent

Fifty Years of Reporting South Asia

Revised Edition

Edited by
John Elliott
Bernard Imhasly
Simon Denyer

Photo Editor
David Orr

Editorial and Research Assistant
Madhu Chandra

PENGUIN BOOKS

PENGUIN BOOKS
Published by the Penguin Group
Penguin Books India Pvt. Ltd, 11 Community Centre, Panchsheel Park, New Delhi 110 017, India
Penguin Group (USA) Inc., 375 Hudson Street, New York, New York 10014, USA
Penguin Group (Canada), 90 Eglinton Avenue East, Suite 700, Toronto, Ontario, M4P 2Y3, Canada (a division of Pearson Penguin Canada Inc.)
Penguin Books Ltd, 80 Strand, London WC2R 0RL, England
Penguin Ireland, 25 St Stephen's Green, Dublin 2, Ireland (a division of Penguin Books Ltd)
Penguin Group (Australia), 250 Camberwell Road, Camberwell, Victoria 3124, Australia (a division of Pearson Australia Group Pty Ltd)
Penguin Group (NZ), 67 Apollo Drive, Rosedale, North Shore 0632, New Zealand (a division of Pearson New Zealand Ltd)
Penguin Group (South Africa) (Pty) Ltd, 24 Sturdee Avenue, Rosebank, Johannesburg 2196, South Africa

Penguin Books Ltd, Registered Offices: 80 Strand, London WC2R 0RL, England

First published in Viking by Penguin Books India 2008
Published in Penguin Books 2009

10 9 8 7 6 5 4 3 2 1

ISBN 9780143067559

For sale in the Indian Subcontinent and Afghanistan only

Typeset in Sabon by InoSoft Systems, Noida
Printed at Replika Press Pvt. Ltd, Sonipat

Contents

Introduction

Foreign correspondents lead a privileged life. We travel the world, report on people and events as we see them, and have hundreds of thousands (in some cases millions) of readers or viewers who depend on us for news and views. In South Asia we are specially privileged because of the immensity of the story, and the status of journalists and the welcome given (with rare exceptions) to visitors.

We have the awesome task of covering a 'beat' that includes nearly a quarter of the world's population, with wide ethnic diversity and, as V.S. Naipaul put it, 'a million mutinies' in some of the world's most notorious trouble spots. Politics and major events unfold on the streets, not just in closed rooms. Where else does a journalist cover a country in which the ballot papers were printed (before the arrival of electronic voting machines) in so many languages? We are also lucky that the subcontinent shares complex and intense historical relationships with our home countries, which increases interest in our reports.

As foreign correspondents and photographers we try to inform people across the world about the complexities of the region, to expose what is wrong, cruel and criminal, as well as to celebrate what is good and successful. We do not always get it right. It is easy to be professionally seduced by a sudden idea, to jump on to the bandwagon of 'shining India' for example, or be charmed by a military ruler promising to restore order before restoring democracy. We impose ourselves on people, interviewing victims of disaster and taking their stories, giving them nothing in return except a vague promise that their story will be told.

This book, with its collection of reportage, comment and photographs, reflects these ambitions and limitations. It marks the fiftieth anniversary of the founding in 1958 of the Foreign Correspondents' Association of South Asia (FCA)—renamed the Foreign Correspondents' Club (FCC) in 1990–91, when we also moved into our current club bungalow opposite Pragati Maidan on Delhi's

Mathura Road. We have not been too strict about 1958 as our starting point and have included a few articles written earlier (by people who became FCA members) for reasons that we hope are clear: how could one resist Peter Jackson's Reuters scoop report on meeting Edmund Hillary and Tenzing Norgay as they came down from conquering Everest in 1953, or Robert Stimson's 'Goodbye to India', with which the book opens.

We have neither managed to include every major event of the past fifty or so years, though many are here, nor have we covered every country in South Asia evenly. Rather, we have gone for a mixture of good writing and historic moments that give a picture of how foreign correspondents have covered the region.

Significant numbers of foreign newspaper correspondents began to arrive and settle in India only after Independence in 1947, and Delhi became their first home in the third world. Before then, the region was mostly covered by roving reporters who were sent out for a visit or a temporary assignment. Many papers continued to rely on such correspondents, aided by local stringers, till well into the second half of the twentieth century. Business papers like the *Financial Times* and the *Wall Street Journal* only opened bureaus in the 1980s, and foreign photographers began to be based here around the same time. Now there is an ever-increasing number of foreign correspondents. Out of the FCC's total membership of around 400, there are over 200 foreign correspondent members, half of whom have been posted from abroad and the rest are from India. The other 200 include journalists working for the Indian media and other non-journalist associates.

At the beginning of the nineteenth century, news from Calcutta, then the capital of India, took four months to reach the English port of Falmouth. Sketchy reports of India's First War of Independence—'the Mutiny'—which erupted on 9 May 1857 did not reach London until the following month. British journalists established papers here in the early nineteenth century and sent occasional reports back to London, but the first full-time foreign correspondent posted here, as far as we know, was twenty-two-year-old Henry Collins of Reuters who arrived shortly after a telegraph line between Europe and India was established in 1865. His first base was a tent on the esplanade at Bombay. By 1878, just thirteen years after his arrival, the outbreak of the Anglo–Afghan war created such interest in India that Herbert Reuters said 'we cannot afford to let Indian politics drop'. Even so, dispatches were limited to just seventy-seven words a day—brevity, some say, that often generated as much uncertainty as information. There were also men (rarely women) from various walks of life—businessmen, missionaries, teachers, even military officers—who wrote occasionally on what was happening.

In the early years, foreign correspondents were perceived, and thought of themselves, as exclusive observers (if not judges) of India's progress, second only to foreign diplomats. Communication—often by post—was slow. It led many to offer, apart from reporting on the large flow of events, lofty judgements and advice. As Gerald Priestland says in his article: 'It was the agencies' job to belt out the facts and figures; the Specials took more leisurely care of the background, interpretation, interviews and colour.'

Fifty years later, this approach has changed dramatically, partly because of a revolution in communication technology. Post was first replaced by telex and slow, unreliable telephone links. Now we use mobile phones and almost instantaneous e-mail. This forces foreign correspondents today to relay events immediately as they happen, with daily or even hourly updates. There is still plenty of in-depth reportage, which may involve weeks of research and travel, and our collection has such examples. But they flow within a huge stream of news and opinions on multiple channels often round the clock. The news consumer 'back home' is today much better informed—and the Internet means that back home can be the world at large, not just a single country, globalizing the collection and delivery of news.

The job can be dangerous, even life-threatening. We have included two *Wall Street Journal* articles by Danny Pearl, who was kidnapped and killed by Islamic militants in 2002. We know of at least four journalists who have been killed in Afghanistan since 9/11, and there have been more. Yet we have to acknowledge that local journalists across South Asia face far more danger and personal violence than foreign correspondents do.

There are also frustrations. A few of us still shake our heads about the former Bangladeshi press officer who habitually blocked our attempts to get visas, rarely taking our calls and even at times pretending to be someone else when we finally reached him on his mobile. Pakistan demands journalists based in India get special passes for travel outside its major cities. India demands the same for travel to much of its troubled North-East and most of the Andaman and

Nicobar Islands. Minders follow us around India's state of Manipur or Pakistan's so-called Azad Kashmir, in an apparent attempt to influence people we meet.

Access to top political leaders varies widely. Curiously, democracy does not make them more available. Unlike Jawaharlal Nehru, who seems to have been close to several foreign correspondents fifty years ago, later leaders have not always been so easy to meet. Military rulers are much more easily accessible, presumably because they need to conjure up international support. Pakistan's Zia ul-Haq and Pervez Musharraf both ran charm offensives with foreign correspondents—it became a cliché for reporters to recount how Zia came to the doorstep of his residence to bid them goodbye. Indian officials, by contrast, are much more concerned with getting their message across to local reporters.

The FCC decided to produce this book at its annual general meeting in April 2007. The three of us came together as editors in the following months: John Elliott as FCC president; Bernard Imhasly, who brought articles he had collected ten years ago for a similar book project that did not materialize; and Simon Denyer who added the focus of a news agency bureau chief and two years experience in Pakistan and Afghanistan. Madhu Chandra joined us as our hardworking research and editorial assistant, without whom we would have descended into chaos, and David Orr came in to find and edit the photographs.

We decided to collect articles and photographs primarily by inviting past and present members to send work of which they were most proud and would most like to have included. That produced a fascinating mixture of colour writing and big event reportage—see the articles from Peter Kann in Dacca and Barbara Crossette who was with Rajiv Gandhi when he was assassinated. Later we supplemented that by searching the Internet and other sources to fill some historical gaps and journalistic achievements. We finished up with a total of over 400 articles, from which we have been able to choose only the eighty-three that you see here.

We are aware that many of the voices heard in this book have a strong Anglo-Saxon accent. We would have liked to bring in more pieces by colleagues from China, Japan, Eastern Europe and elsewhere, whose presence in South Asia has increased in the last fifteen years or so. But over the whole of the last half century, it has been journalists from Britain and America, plus the Commonwealth and a few European countries, who have formed the largest contingent of South Asia correspondents and who therefore dominate this book. There are also pieces by local journalists who work as foreign correspondents for publications abroad.

Some articles may seem unduly critical of the people of the subcontinent. But it is the duty of a journalist to question and to criticize—to expose corruption and mismanagement (or worse, murders and massacres)—without fear of recriminations. What service would we be doing to be charmed by corrupt officials and ignore the people they are cheating?

It has been said that journalism is 'the first draft of history'—incomplete, momentary, often opinionated, but history-in-the-making nonetheless. We hope that this illustrated anthology of great reportage, analysis, writing—and stories that just demand your attention—will be seen as such a 'draft report', complementing other non-fiction books. We have tried to show the range of what we write about, from politics to tigers, business to inequality, religious fanaticism to fans of P.G. Wodehouse.

We have however only been able to provide glimpses of the many issues that are at work in a region of this size, complexity and rapid change. Not all momentous events or political developments are covered, partly for reasons of space and sometimes because we have not been able to secure pieces that do justice to what happened. We have also had to leave out some of our initial choices—the book could easily have been twice the size—so we apologize to those who are disappointed that they have not been included.

We are very grateful to everyone who has helped us produce the book in such a very short time. We have had support from the FCC committee—Pallava Bagla, Soutik Biswas, Christoph Heinzle, Penny MacRae, Ayanjit Sen, Ashok Sharma, Phil Turner and Raghavendra Verma—and from Kiran Kapur, our hard-working club manager. We have been advised by the club's lawyer, Vijay Shankardass, and by Namita Gokhale, a writer and publisher. Many other colleagues and friends have helped us track down sources.

Above all, editors and publishers of all the newspapers and magazines in this book have generously waived their usual reproduction charges and arranged for us to use articles free of charge.

Our photographers have been equally generous with their images. Finally, the book would not have been possible without the cheerful encouragement and patience—and flexible approach to deadlines—of Ravi Singh, Penguin's editor-in-chief and publisher, and our editor Ranjana Sengupta. Thank you all!

For this paperback edition, we have added four articles. We have filled a gap with one on Mrs Indira Gandhi's assassination in 1984, and also include recent articles on the November 2008 terrorist attacks in Mumbai, and the worsening situation in Pakistan. These help to keep this volume of works by foreign correspondents up to date, though it is sad that all of them have more to do with violence than with the more positive sides of life in South Asia.

Simon Denyer
John Elliott
Bernard Imhasly

Robert Stimson
Goodbye to India

BBC
10 March 1949

A JOURNALIST ISN'T normally encouraged to indulge in personal reminiscence, but one who is leaving India after eleven years may perhaps be given a little licence, especially as there can be only one singing of a swan song.

When I decided to go to Bombay to work on a newspaper, most of my friends—to be frank about it—thought I was mad. 'You can't possibly go to India,' they said. 'Not as a newspaperman. It would be different if you were going into the Indian Civil Service, or even the Indian army. Then at least you'd have some kind of status in a country where the right labels are important. But as a newspaperman no. You'll be an object of suspicion to the Indian. The pukka sahib will look down his nose at you. You'll certainly take to drink. You'll quickly decay in an atmosphere that combines the worst features of one of the drearier London suburbs and some monstrous cloud-cuckooland; when broken in mind and body you creep back to London, looking and behaving like a tropical tramp off a banana boat, nobody will employ you, or even talk to you.'

Nor did the Wimpole Street doctor who prodded and punched me say anything to raise my spirits. He had practised for many years in Bengal and was very much of the old school. He warned me never to be without something called a cholera belt, a swaddling band of flannel worn round the waist and next to the skin. I was to avoid the

**Robert Stimson lived in India for twelve years. He was just five yards away from Mahatma Gandhi when the latter was shot by Nathuram Godse on 30 January 1948. This was his valedictory dispatch.*

sunshine whenever possible, and if I so much as poked my nose out of doors during the day time, I was to catafalque my skull in a pith helmet.

During the first few months in India I did my best to obey the doctor's orders, with the result that, living the life of a unhealthy troglodyte, I was soon covered with boils, which disappeared only when I cast aside my inflaming corselet and ventured into the sun. Boils apart, I found nothing in India to justify the dark forebodings.

Quite often of course, one had to reexamine one's values. I remember a story told quite casually by a distinguished Indian priest who was my fellow passenger on a long railway journey.

One day, shortly after his return to India from Oxford, the priest was in his bungalow writing his first sermon, when he looked up to find a yogi squatting cross-legged on the floor and chuckling over some very delicious private joke. The priest had never seen the yogi before and asked him what he wanted. The yogi said he'd come on a friendly mission, to warn the priest that he mustn't be surprised if, as an evangelist, he encountered a certain mental resistance from the Hindus. And with that the yogi, still sitting cross-legged, rose gently from the floor and went on rising until his head was touching the ceiling. 'Do you see what I mean?' he said. Then he slowly descended and chuckling once more, walked out of the priest's room.

In other ways too, India called for a certain flexibility in the newcomer. None of the English rules of behaviour had taught one how to make the correct reply to an Indian friend who, invited for dinner for the following Thursday, said with the utmost charm that he'd be unable to come because he was about to offer civil disobedience and would be in gaol.

There was the large luncheon party at which I found myself sitting next to an Indian girl so gentle and shy that she had to force herself to cope with the agonies of table talk. After a tremendous effort of will she summoned up the courage to ask whether I liked Indian food. I told her I liked it very much. There was another embarrassed silence and then, rallying she asked me whether I liked Indian food better than English food. So we went on, dredging up remarks of that kind, for I, too, was struck dumb in the presence of such fragility and innocence. Only later did I discover that the girl had once tried to assassinate a famous provincial governor.

It was a new experience for an English man to find himself living among people who were so frankly and volubly critical of the British, or rather of British rule in India. Almost every educated Indian was an avowed nationalist, so that conversation, no matter what its starting point, rapidly developed into a political discussion. It was marvellous to watch the swift adroit transition from, say, racehorses to the Morley–Minto reforms. An Indian employee in the health division of the Bombay municipality came to my flat to wage war on a swarm of mosquitoes. I was telling them how troublesome they were when, with polite solemnity, he pointed out that an enslaved people could not be expected to take an interest in civic hygiene. In a free India, he said, there would be no mosquitoes.

To his credit the Indian nationalist scarcely ever allowed his political convictions to impair his relations with the British as individuals. During my eleven years, I remember only one or two occasions when feeling against the British in India ran high. For a few days for example during the Royal Indian Navy mutiny in Bombay, it was unwise for Europeans to wander about the streets. By ill-luck I was bicycling along a main road when I ran into a crowd of several hundred excited students armed with clubs and hockey sticks. In a rather menacing way the ring leaders told me to get off my bicycle and walk. I pulled up and explained that I was a newspaperman trying to find out what was going on.

Mr Gandhi, I said, was always courteous to newspapermen because he believed that they should have every opportunity of hearing both sides of a question. The mention of the magic name broke the tension immediately. The crowd gathered round and began asking whether I'd ever interviewed the Mahatma, what he had said, what I thought of him and so on. Within a few minutes I was pedalling away trying not to look as scared as I felt.

But incidents of that kind were exceptional. As a rule the Indians were most considerate, partly because they value formal good manners and partly because Mr Gandhi, in his own dealings with individual Englishmen, set a good example. When political differences were at their sharpest, Mr Gandhi—Britain's best policeman in India, as he called himself—made a point of addressing the Viceroy as 'dear friend'.

Very few people met Mr Gandhi without feeling the pull of his disarming personality. He was immensely popular with journalists of all nationalities, because he was so accessible. He didn't always say things that were easy to agree with, but it was a pleasure to interview him because he had an instinctive understanding of news and was a master of simple colourful English. 'I am like a man with a bucket of water,' he said when I asked him what his plans were during the Delhi riots. 'I must try to put out the fires that I find in my path.'

Right to the end, Mr Gandhi was the central figure in the Indian story. But there were others who kept the journalist interested and busy: the elegant, single-minded Muhammad Ali Jinnah, who achieved his Pakistan; Jawaharlal Nehru, brilliant and sensitive, whom one watched develop into what he now is, the greatest figure in Asia; and Subhas Chandra Bose, who thought he could best serve wartime India from Germany and Japan, and today in his own country has a patriot's memorial, not a traitor's.

Mr Rajagopalachari and Sarojini Naidu, Savarkar and Sapru, Ambedkar and Jayaprakash Narayan—all crowded a screen on which princes, mystics, factory workers, agitators, scholars, peasants filled the background.

There were some memorable sequences, such as the Quit India disturbances, with ten thousand people on a dusty common yelling 'Karenge ya marenge'—Do or die.

The Bengal famine with men and women stumbling along the streets of Calcutta and then quite suddenly dropping and dying.

A shower of gold bars over Bombay, as a ship carrying bullion blew up in a great dock explosion.

Independence Day and Lord Mountbatten in a state coach cheered by half a million Indians as he followed with outstretched arm the rainbow that greeted the unfurling of the new Indian tricolour.

And then, a few months later, some shots in a Delhi prayer garden and Mr Gandhi being carried across the lawn, with his own shawl as a shroud.

The story has been a full one: a few shameful chapters, a good many bright ones, and on the whole a happy ending. Between Britain and the subcontinent of India a new friendship and understanding have emerged since August 1947. And since New Year's Day of this year, correspondents have been able to report not only the promise of better relations between India and Pakistan but the fact that the subcontinent as a whole is one of the few relatively stable areas in an Asia elsewhere disfigured by terrorism and civil war.

Most of the British who knew India before the transfer of power and known it since, agree that for them it is now a much happier country to live in; and by India, of course I mean India and Pakistan. One needed to be very insensitive in the old days not to feel uncomfortable in the presence of a vocal nationalism, so persistent a condemnation of things British.

This embarrassment hadn't always a logical cause; one knew that on the whole the standard of British administration was much better than it was painted, that the Indian civil service was remarkably honest and conscientious, that the Indians might have had their freedom earlier if they had shown more unity in negotiation, or even in revolt. But arguments of that kind weren't wholly satisfying; it was difficult to ignore a nagging doubt when Mr Gandhi was detained in 1942 and Pandit Nehru imprisoned. The harsh requirements of war couldn't wholly obliterate the feeling that somehow it needn't have happened; and one of the tragic things for many of the British in India was that they were always slightly on the defensive, rather prickly and so less happy than they might have been. Now all that has gone. Today the British have a much more natural, easy relationship with the Indians. In a very important sense the British in India also won their freedom in August 1947.

One doesn't know what shape the Indian story will take in future, but it's difficult to think of any change that will destroy for one passer-by, the richness of certain memories: the beauty of the nights, with distant strings and drums sliding music across a valley; the Madrassi who walked more than ten or twelve miles a day for many months to talk to a foreigner about the Gita; the exquisite decorum of a Rajput aristocrat; a villager coming forward on a hot morning and shyly offering a newly cut melon; the perfection of rice properly cooked; a young peasant couple walking to the fair and carrying their new shoes so that they'd look shiny when they arrived; a Muslim woman riding a bicycle in a burqua—a thousand things, but especially the quality of an Indian friendship, which once given is given unconditionally and for life.

~

Adrienne Farrell
Indian Government Promotes Tiger Hunting
Maharaja Organizes Shoot in Bundi

Reuters
21 March 1951

New Delhi: INDIA IS BECOMING a hunter's paradise for Americans who want to shoot tigers. Government officials here estimate that between 500 and 1000 tigers could be killed in the country each year without seriously affecting the general tiger population. And they have found that for foreign visitors the word 'tiger-shoot' has more glamour than even the Taj Mahal.

Other big game also abounds in India—elephant, bison, rhinoceros and, up in Kashmir, the hangul deer.

To attract overseas sportsmen, particularly from the dollar area, the Indian government is organizing a network of big game specialists throughout the main hunting areas, from Assam and Bengal to Central and United Provinces, Bihar and Rajasthan. Mostly members of the old Indian noble families, these expert hunters will be responsible for organizing shoots on any scale for visitors from abroad. For an all-in sum of about $1000, a visiting American can spend one month big game shooting in India, with the prospect of bagging not only a tiger or two but also panther, bison, antelope and even bear.

Most of the jungle country is state-owned land; but some is still the property of the former ruling princes who can no longer always afford to hunt on the same scale as before. Part of the government's plan is to enlist the aid of these princes in organizing big game shoots and in helping to provide accommodation for hunting visitors in their palaces, guesthouses or hunting lodges.

Tiger is probably the most exciting of all big game to hunt. With its lightening speed and 18-foot spring, it is the only animal that huntsmen fear to meet on the ground. Shoots are organized on elephant back or from the frail protection of tree-built wooden platforms or 'machans'.

A tiger shoot, however, is necessarily expensive to organize. A body of trained and salaried huntsmen must be permanently maintained.

For days before the hunt they will be watching the movements of the tiger until it is finally enticed into the beat by the lure of a tied buffalo. At least one or two elephants must be maintained, even where machans are used. For if the tiger should be only wounded and not killed, the pursuit must go on by elephant. And an elephant these days will cost Rs 1000 (£75) a month to keep. In addition, on the day of the hunt, 100 or more villagers from the surrounding country will join the trained beaters. If the day's work ends in a kill, they will be entitled to a recompense of about Re 1 (1s 6d) a head.

Part of the attraction of tiger shooting for foreign visitors in India lies in the possibility for even a large party of non-hunters to witness the whole scene. For the type of hunt may vary from the physical arduousness of a shikar in the Assam jungles to the comparative ease of a shoot in one central Indian state, where it is possible for guests to leave the dinner table at the maharaja's palace, cross the lake by motorboat, climb through an underground tunnel and come out into shooting boxes in full view of the tiger at its kill, only 60 yards away.

Typical of a hunt most likely to whet the appetite of American and other foreign visitors was a birthday tiger-shoot recently given by the maharaja of the 2220-square-mile state of Bundi in Rajasthan, to which he invited about thirty American and Brazilian foreign service officers and businessmen. A 22-mile drive from the maharaja's white Arabian Nights palace of Phoolsagar—'Lake of Flowers'—led up to the sandy scrub jungle country where the tiger was reported already in the beat, having made his kill.

More than half the party were mere spectators, but for them, watching from a hillock, the whole scene of the hunt was laid out as in an amphitheatre: the sandy hillside opposite, covered with leafless scrub, slit by the dark gully where the tiger was known to lie hidden; to the right, the still figures of the hunting party ranged, widely spaced, in four tree-top machans along the hill; to the left, the white line of beaters, armed with sticks and forks, creeping across the hillside towards the gully; below, the green dip where the tiger had killed his buffalo.

Then suddenly, breaking the stillness under the blazing afternoon sun, came the first shouts of the beaters and the sound of the exploding blank cartridges. Moments of suspense, as the shouting line moved slowly on, then a wild warning call from the watchers' hillock as the tiger appeared on the lip of the gully. For a moment it paused, tail anxiously swaying, a sandy gold figure against the sandy background of the hill, before heading upwards straight towards the first machan. A single crack from a rifle and the hunt was over, the tiger stretched out in the sand, a crimson streak already beginning to stain the fur across its muzzle.

Good tiger country lies within eight hours' comfortable train ride from Delhi and a night's journey from Bombay—an expedition that has today become quite possible for even a casual visitor to India. One word of advice for would-be tiger hunters. If it is the coat they want, then the best months are from November to March, when the tiger's winter coat is at its best. But if it is the spectacle they want, then the best months are from April to June, when the trees are bare of leaves and the tiger has little protection, while the drying up of pools and rivers cut him down to 10 per cent of his usual beat and makes a kill more certain.

II

India's Wildlife Is Disappearing Indiscriminate Killing by Amateur Hunters

Reuters
25 July 1953

New Delhi: AMATEUR HUNTERS, PROWLING the countryside by night with high-velocity rifles, are massacring India's wildlife. Herds of deer and nilgai (antelope), which used to roam freely through the jungles and fields of northern India, unharmed by the villagers, are being liquidated by poachers from the towns who hunt them down in the headlights of cars and jeeps.

Many of these hunters take no note of close seasons, nor of the sex or size of the beasts they kill, but slaughter indiscriminately for 'sport' or for food. Even the villager, with an ancient muzzle-loader, now joins in the hunt. As the deer vanish, so the bigger game, tigers and panthers robbed of their natural food, begin to raid villages, killing cattle. Some of them become maneaters, so that expeditions have to be organized to hunt them down.

The problem of India's vanishing wildlife is worrying naturalists here and governments in several of the states have already taken action to try to protect wild animals. Some are already extinct. The last report of a wild cheetah in India was several years ago, though in Mogul times they used frequently to be caught and used as 'hunting leopards' to catch game.

Lions, the symbol of India, now survive only in the Gir forest of Saurashtra, where they are carefully protected. They are the last lions in Asia. A census of them taken last year by counting pug marks on a single day, showed that there were only 250 left. The rhinoceros, once on its way to extinction, has been protected for the past forty years by law. There are still about 300 great one-horned rhinos living in the sanctuaries of northern Assam and Bengal, and a few more in Nepal.

Elephants in India are still numerous, despite the shrinking of forest areas. Large numbers of them still inhabit the jungles of Assam or Travancore-Cochin, and the terai jungle area bordering on Nepal. They are also protected in sanctuaries.

But some of the other famous Indian animals are fast vanishing: the musk deer, killed for its scent, the bison, and the wild ass, which now survives only in the desolate Rann of Cutch, on the north-west coast of India.

Some of the famous birds, too, are disappearing. The great Indian bustard is now becoming rare. The pink-headed duck, once common in north-eastern India, has not been seen for several years past anywhere in the country.

Tigers in some states of central India are on the increase. Maharajas who used to organize big shooting parties can no longer afford the cost of large-scale shikar, and tigers and panthers have begun to multiply. But organized shooting parties for tourists, often arranged by members of the princely families in search of jobs, are beginning to take the place of the old big game hunts of Indian princes or British officials. In other parts of India, however, tigers are declining in numbers and it is likely that, unless preserved in sanctuaries, they would die out completely in another twenty-five years.

To preserve the fauna of the country, the Indian government has set up a Wildlife Board, which will study the problems of conserving each species, and drawn up strict regulations against illicit shooting.

Several states have declared large tracts of land as sanctuaries, where no animal or bird life may be taken. Most famous of these is the sanctuary round the Periyar Lake in Travancore-Cochin. A 300-square-mile area of land round the lake has been turned into a vast natural zoo. Visitors coasting the lake shores by boat can get within a few yards of elephants, bison, deer and panther as they come down to the water to drink.

Another vast sanctuary has been made in the wild jungles of northern Assam.

The only kind of Indian wildlife which seems to be permanently on the increase, and for which few have a good word to say, is the monkey. Villagers regard them as sacred and will not allow them to be shot, despite depredations on the country's food supplies which cost India every year thousands of tons of grain.

~

Peter Jackson
Model of Team Work Beat Everest

Reuters
5 June 1953

Thyangboche Monastery, Nepalese Himalayas (by runner): 'I WAS VERY happy—A big effort—I felt damn good.' The men who vanquished Mount Everest after thirty years of vain attempts thus summed up what they felt when they returned to a conqueror's welcome at this mountain monastery.

Colonel John Hunt, leader of the expedition, described the venture as 'an absolute model of team work'.

Edmund Hillary, who reached the summit with Tenzing, said his companion 'threw his arms around me and embraced me' when they reached the hard-won summit, where they spent twenty minutes.

**Peter Jackson sent the first interview with Edmund Hillary and Sherpa Tenzing after they conquered Mount Everest.*

How did it feel up there?

'I felt damn good,' said Hillary.

'I Was Very Happy'

Tenzing, thirty-nine-year-old Tiger of the Snows, whose success came as a climax to more attempts on the Himalayan giant than any other man has made, flashed his winning smile as he told me: 'I was very happy and not particularly tired.'

I met the Everest team in this snowbound Buddhist refuge where they are pausing in their descent to Katmandu on the way back to civilization.

Colonel Hunt said: 'Hillary and Tenzing made the summit with a safe margin of time, oxygen and effort.'

But it was not until the day after that other members of the expedition knew of their victory.

The Signal

'Sleeping bags laid on the snow were to be the success signal,' Colonel Hunt said. 'But after a fine day on 29 May mist obscured the higher camps.

'It was not until the following afternoon that the assault party and support group came down the face of Lhotse [the 27,890-foot sentinel to the south-east of Everest which the party had to traverse to reach the South Col] that we got the tremendous news that they had reached the top.

'We can hardly yet believe that it is true.'

Colonel Hunt said Britons did Sherpa porters' work and heaved 50- and 60-pound loads to Camp Nine, at 27,900 feet. 'The highest ever placed.'

'Weak as Kittens'

'Sherpa Ang Nima went to this height and Sherpa Da Namgyl to 27,350 feet. All who went above the South Col were as weak as kittens for three days but suffered no ill-effects—beyond tiredness.

[The South Col is a ridge between Lhotse and the main massif of Everest and is the route discovered by Mr Eric Shipton.]

'Several of the team spent three nights on the Col and George Lowe [a twenty-eight-year-old schoolmaster, the other New Zealander of the expedition] four nights.'

Sitting relaxed in this monastery, Hillary told me that he and Tenzing stayed 'about twenty minutes on the perfect summit'.

'I took photographs of Tenzing holding a string of flags—those of the United Nations, Britain, Nepal and India.

'Below us the country was like a map—especially interesting to me, as I had climbed over most of it.'

Far over Tibet

'The most impressive sight was Lhotse, followed by Kanchenjunga [28,146 feet, in Sikkim, further to the south-east] and we could see far out over Tibet.'

Hillary said he and Tenzing left Camp Nine at 6.30 a.m. and reached the south peak of Everest after climbing for 150 minutes.

'The final ridge was of high Alpine standard and we finally got to the top at half past eleven,' he went on. 'We had a good look round before starting the descent, but the oxygen was running short and we came down to the South Col in five hours.

'We were pretty tired and I still feel it, but we had a good night's rest and went down to the West Cwm next day.' [The West Cwm, far below the South Col, is a huge punchbowl of glaciers and treacherous icefalls between Everest and its southern mountain sentinels.]

Hillary echoed Colonel Hunt's estimate of the expedition's team work.

'This whole thing was team effort and the success is due mainly to Colonel Hunt,' he said. 'Everything went according to plan.'

Colonel Hunt's Account

Colonel Hunt gave this history of the expedition, whose brilliant achievement came so appropriately at the beginning of the new Elizabethan age:

'We started with two big periods of acclimatization, which paid tremendous dividends.

'At the beginning of May, I myself and Charles Evans, Tom Bourdillon, Charles Wylie and Michael Ward made a reconnaissance of the Lhotse face to decide on our plan and to test the oxygen equipment operationally.' [Evans is a thirty-four-year-old Liverpool doctor; Bourdillon (twenty-nine) a rocket research scientist from Farnborough, Hampshire; Wylie a serving major in the British Army; and Ward (twenty-eight) the expedition's doctor.]

To Prove Equipment

'The plan was for two assaults—the first with closed-circuit oxygen equipment to give it an opportunity of proving itself and the second with the usual open-circuit type of equipment.

'The first assault was also a reconnaissance for the second. I selected Evans and Bourdillon for the first attempt, while for the second Hillary and Tenzing stood far above everyone from the point of view of fitness.

'Each party had a support group—myself and two Sherpas for the first and Alfred Gregory and three Sherpas for the second.'

[Gregory, forty-year-old managing director of a Blackpool travel agency, was, after Colonel Hunt, the oldest member of the expedition.]

'Everything went according to plan and we went ahead with the preparation of the Lhotse face, fixing ropes and establishing the route. Camp Seven was set up on 20 May.

'This was five days later than had been fixed by the original plan, and was due to bad weather and deep snow.'

Sherpas Stopped

'On 25 May the first big party of Sherpas started for Camp Seven on the South Col. On the way the coolies would not go further. Wilfred Noyce went on with one Sherpa.

[Noyce (thirty-five) is a schoolmaster and writer.]

'We could see this from the West Cwm. I decided the build-up must go on and sent Hillary and Tenzing up to boost the Sherpas.

'It worked—we saw the whole party move to the South Col with food, tents, fuel and other equipment.

'The weather was good and the first assault party went to Camp Five on 22 May and moved to the South Col in the evening. This assault was delayed twenty-four hours because of a bad wind and tiredness after the heavy climb.

'The second assault party were forty-eight hours behind. On 26 May the first assault went up.

'Evans and Bourdillon had instructions to go for the South Peak and, if the oxygen was working well and the route good, to make for the top.'

'Brilliant Show'

'It was a brilliant show. They reached the South Peak but turned back because of oxygen shortage and bad weather.

'With Sherpa Da Namgyl I carried loads to 27,350 feet and left a dump for the second support group. As the first assault group came down the second party went up to the Col.

'On 27 May the night was all hell let loose. There is no place on earth so inhospitable as the South Col, and the second party, too, were delayed twenty-four hours.

'On the 28th the morning was lovely. Hillary, Tenzing and the support group went up. One Sherpa, Ang Nima, went to the south-east ridge at 27,900 feet.

'The party carried the rest of the equipment and picked up what I had left at the dump.

'They each carried loads of from 50 to 60 pounds, a remarkable achievement at that height. On the 29th Hillary and Tenzing went for the summit and made it with a safe margin of time, oxygen and effort.

'This was tremendously exciting. It had been a big effort.

'We had a steady build-up and because of acclimatization and diet the expedition enjoyed remarkable health.

'The food was basically army compo (composite rations) with some variations and an assault ration which was nearly the same as the army "snow" ration (a two pound pack).

'It was supplemented by items from luxury boxes, for everyone felt the need for solid food.

'From Camp Four [the advanced base camp on the Western Cwm, 6000 feet below the summit] to the South Col we ate with pleasure food left behind by the Swiss expedition last year—bread, honey, cheese and jam.

'Apart from one Sherpa getting a slightly frostbitten finger, no one suffered from trouble.'

Tenzing Looks at K2

Tenzing, who last November got to within 1000 feet of the summit with the toeless Swiss mountaineer Raymond Lambert [the highest point attained until the final conquest], told me that seven attempts at Everest were enough for him. He would not like to tackle the giant again.

'But now I would like to go to K2, for I think that can be climbed,' the sturdy Sherpa declared.

K2 (Mount Godwin Austen), the second highest mountain—in the Karakoram range, Pakistan—is being attacked this year by an American expedition.

'Thinking about Return'

Tenzing said of Everest: 'I did not have much time on the peak to think about the achievement. When you get there you are thinking about the return—if there is time, if the oxygen will last, and whether the route will still be all right.

'The real moments of happiness come later.

'I am very happy now because the whole party is down and there were no accidents. We are all together. We had a fine view from the summit of Everest over all the Himalayas and Tibet.

'We could see the northern route which expeditions used before the war. It was quite black. No snow, just rock.'

[This route has been closed since the communists moved into Tibet.]

In the first, unsuccessful attempt on the peak Evans and Bourdillon became temporarily the world's highest climbers. Their feat in reaching 28,700 feet had never been excelled.

Evans told me it was 'a great disappointment' not to have reached the top during their bid on 26 May.

Nonetheless, Colonel Hunt said, their climb was a 'brilliant show'.

Evans said: 'It was not a very fine day and my oxygen was not working properly. In addition it was 1.30 p.m. when we reached the south summit and there was not enough oxygen to get to the top.'

Colonel Hunt at Katmandu

Katmandu, Sunday: Colonel Hunt arrived here yesterday, accompanied by Tom Bourdillon and Alfred Gregory, after their 160-mile nine-day trek back from Everest.

Colonel Hunt promised a fuller story of the Everest success at a press conference in a day or two.

Referring to Queen Elizabeth's award of the George Medal to Tenzing, Colonel Hunt said: 'He deserved it and more.'

~

Gerald Priestland
The Delhi Scene

BBC
1954–58

DELHI IS THREE inhabited cities and three or four more in ruins on the plains round about. No other capital in modern Asia, with the possible exception of Peking (which I do not know) offers such a picture book of its own history.

Richard Williams had bequeathed me accommodation in the Cecil Hotel in the Civil Lines. This meant that in order to get to Parliament House or the government offices and embassies one had to drive through the middle of the Old City, which was laborious but instructive. It gave me a daily reminder that India was like a sheet of plywood with a thin veneer of mid-twentieth century glued over layers of the nineteenth, seventeenth and even earlier centuries, all hanging together somehow and forming an amazingly strong and flexible whole.

Jam-packed with bureaucrats and refugees, Delhi had little to spare in the way of private housing, so the international press corps had adopted the Cecil as its professional ghetto and, incidentally, a convenient way of keeping an eye on one another. The Reuter correspondents, Peter and Adrienne Jackson, did have a combined flat and office in the centre of town; and Felix Nagar, the gay representative of the French News Agency, had a classic bungalow hung with tiger skins near the India Gate; but almost everyone else was to be found on the bougainvillea-hung verandas of the Cecil Hotel. There were no lifts or coffee shop or air conditioning; the place was more like what it eventually became, a Jesuit seminary.

At the tables were to be found Louis Heren of the *Times*, Philip Deane of the *Observer*, Colonel Harold Milks and his assistant Gene Levine of the Associated Press of America, Johnnie Hlavacek of United Press, Kenneth Ames of the *Daily Mail* and, from time to time, visiting firemen like James Cameron of the *News Chronicle* and Rene McColl of the *Daily Express*. All the resident correspondents were married and had wives with them, and the pregnancy rate gave rise to the rumour that there was something in the water of the swimming pool that stimulated conception. More likely was the fact that ayahs—nursemaids—were easily come by and everyone was taking advantage of the opportunity while they were in India.

Twice a year we were joined by the Kendal troupe, a family of actors who roved India doing Shakespeare in princely palaces and pseudo-English public schools and were eventually filmed by Merchant and Ivory acting out their own story as Shakespeare Wallahs. There was also a large and amiable man called Ted, with a voice like the Man in Black, who professed to be working for a features agency nobody had ever heard of. He would press his service upon you for nothing—it consisted of stupefyingly dull stories that were not worth paying for—and it did not take long to figure out that its real purpose was to provide cover for his activities as a spymaster, presumably On Our Side. Tony Wigan had implored me not to get mixed up in that kind of sideline (I am a little hurt to report that no one ever tried to recruit me), but so many colleagues had been involved in intelligence during the war that I find it hard to believe that all of them gave it up afterwards.

One advantage of Delhi was that it was five and a half hours ahead of Greenwich, so that if you rounded up the day's events at midnight it would still catch the evening bulletins in London. Press cables were still a penny a word, and twice a week I could broadcast in my own voice by borrowing All India Radio's shortwave transmitter for the BBC to pick up and record for re-broadcasting. The disadvantage of this was that colleagues who knew the wavelength could eavesdrop and steal my stories before London had transmitted them officially.

A routine day in Delhi usually began with a visit to the Lok Sabha, the Indian House of Commons, where most of the business was still conducted in English, South Indians in particular being reluctant to use the national but northern language of Hindi. Nothing much happened in the early afternoon, respected as siesta time, but about teatime I set out on 'the rounds': the external affairs ministry, the Press Information Bureau (which issued a torrent of handouts including something called the Semi-annual Estimate of Rape—about oilseed), possibly the information department of the British Commission, and a few Indian contacts. Some of these you kept on retainer, others were flattered to be consulted for nothing, or even called at your office to deliver their gossip. Among these was the extraordinary Nirad Chaudhuri, who made it his special mission to stop me getting romantic or mystical ideas about Hinduism, of which he was a great debunker.

Above all else Nirad was a Bengali gentleman of letters. No one should miss reading his *The Autobiography of an Unknown Indian.* But his knowledge of English literature was almost as great as that of Bengali and his written use of the English language almost as elegant. When he at last visited England—by courtesy of the BBC and the British Council—he knew exactly what he would find there and when he returned he announced with satisfaction that it had all been as he expected. He took the trouble to visit my parents for tea, perching himself upon a small coffee table which they were too polite to tell him was not a stool. It did no harm, since Nirad was about the size, weight (and chattiness) of a starling. Eventually he quit India for good and settled with distinction in Oxford, dressing always as a Bengali indoors and an English gentleman when out.

To my relief I found that cut-throat competition scarcely existed among my Delhi colleagues. The *Mail* and the *Express* were always trying to scoop one another with increasingly outrageous stories but the rest of us saw little point in adding to the trials of a trying climate and exchanged notes freely. It was the agencies' job to belt out the facts and figures; the Specials took more leisurely care of the background, interpretation, interviews and colour. In a country as alarming as India, company away from base was very welcome; so we tended to hunt the major stories in a pack, usually organized by Colonel Harold Milks of the American Associated Press. Colonel Milks, a portentous figure with a toothbrush moustache and a dead-pan expression, lived in an apartment in the Cecil Hotel entirely surrounded by skins of tigers, noble creatures which he had personally massacred as the guest of various maharajas. He would also career across the Punjab by night, in a jeep, mowing down black buck and blue bull (or maybe the other way round) which he stored in the hotel freezer and issued to friends when they tired of the restaurant's water buffalo. Mrs Milks—Evelyn—did not join him in the killing; she stayed with the air conditioning, playing cards and drinking gin-and-water.

Colonel Milks hated a disorganized rabble. When a press expedition was inevitable he would make all the bookings, buy all the tickets and circulate Roneoed orders, thus: 'Operation Bombay Riots—Correspondents will parade on platform 2 Old Delhi Station at 1800 hrs tomorrow for the Bombay Mail. Equipment to include portable typewriter, bedding roll, two bottles Scotch (NOT Indian), light reading and cash for poker (minimum stake Re 1). NB: DO NOT forget Scotch, Bombay is PROHIBITION TERRITORY.'

It only took me one such trip to learn not to play poker with Americans—and never with Colonel Milks. I had imagined that his dead-pan face had something to do with his sense of burnout, but after three hours in a railway compartment with him I realized that it had become a fixture from years of poker-playing. I never did get the hang of his sudden announcements that 'red threes are wild!' or 'guess I'll sweeten the freakpot!'

II

With Nehru Around India

BBC
1954–58

THE FIRST SUCH outing I went on was to Madras, where the Indian National Congress was holding its annual convention. Madras issued dissolute Europeans with ration books for liquor (it still does), so as the junior correspondent I was dispatched to draw the entire party's supply, returning in a taxi with a month's entitlement which took even us a week's hard drinking to get through. Fortunately there was not much news to be drawn from the convention. These affairs were more like colossal folk festivals arranged for scores of thousands of Indians to 'have darshan' (that is, to bask in the charisma) of their leaders, especially of Pandit Jawaharlal Nehru, Prime Minister and anointed of Gandhi. For the Madras rally a fantastic stadium had been constructed by the Tamil film studios out of old sets of temples and palaces, and around its perimeter various public-spirited organizations had set up pavilions. 'Come inside, dear sir!' cried the man from the All-India Health Ministry, plucking at my bush shirt. 'Come inside for free syphilis test! By tomorrow you will know the worst!'

One of my first discoveries about India was that in spite of being an obviously well-to-do imperialist entirely surrounded by poverty, one was perfectly safe in these enormous crowds. Nobody stabbed you or robbed you or even jostled you—indeed, if you started giving them orders they instinctively obeyed, and if you marched past policemen in order to get where you had no right to be they usually snapped to attention and saluted. Imperial instincts die hard and it was a constant temptation to exploit them. In one corner of Andhra state, eight years after Independence, I came across an English collector with his English police sergeant running their district as if the viceroy were still in Delhi.

After the uproar of Madras I pushed off down the coast to watch Nehru take possession of Pondicherry, the last of the tiny French settlements in India. The French language was spoken widely if not too well and the native police wore gendarme caps, but the only regrets anyone had about changing flags concerned alcohol. I found more serious drinking to be done in the French Club, whose members were polishing off the champagne before the Madras prohibition squad moved in. When Nehru arrived, by train, he was far from pleased with what he found. The reception committee were all tipsy and the police had pushed them to the rear of the platform and were confronting them suspiciously, uncertain whose side they were on. With a little cry of rage Nehru hurled himself at their rear, belabouring them with his swagger stick, crying, 'All I ever see in this country is policemen's backs!' The reception committee cheered happily.

Even so, Nehru was not quite truthful, for he spent much of his time on ornate rostrums, all over India, lecturing the multitudes on the evils they were so obstinately attached to such as astrology, incantations, dowries, cow worship, untouchability and the many unshakable prejudices peculiar to their castes and regions. They listened respectfully, understanding hardly a word of what 'Pandijee' was saying (for he spoke to them either in English or bad kitchen-Urdu), and then went on committing the evils he had just denounced. It could hardly be otherwise, for India is not China and never will be; Indians are not Chinese, to be turned in their tracks like vast regimented armies. Nehru might preach the virtues of scientific socialism and five-year planning, and looking about you at the poverty and squalor you sympathized with him; but it was made endurable by traditional Hinduism, and if anyone was allergic to collectivism it was the Hindus.

That may seem a reactionary stand to take. How can you defend casteism (so much crueller than western racism) or the ruthless exploitation of the poor by rich landlords and moneylenders? The answer is that you cannot justify any single case. But in its own extraordinary way the system works, even though it ought not to, and to break it would take a bloodbath. There were times when I found myself writing: 'This country is doomed; if it does not starve to death or perish of the plague it will surely explode in bloody revolution.' But India has done none of those things.

Contrary to the belief of many Westerners, India is not a profoundly spiritual country but a profoundly materialistic one. The object of most religious practice is to ensure material success. The twist is, however, that nobody has much confidence that material achievements will last or that attempts to interfere with fate will bring anything but trouble in the long run.

The really extraordinary thing about Hinduism is that, far from producing a grim and depressed society, it produces one that is full of music and dancing, brilliant colours, feasts and festivals. When, later, I was posted to the Middle East I was struck by the drabness and dourness of the Arabs compared with the Indians, and by how much more the Arabs complained in spite of their relative prosperity. I would not wish to be a Hindu myself—anyway, they are born, not made—but Hinduism has served India well.

Nehru himself was an old-fashioned Fabian agnostic, really a brown Englishman of the Webbs and Shaw generation. After the death of Sardar Patel there was nobody of his intellectual class left in the Congress leadership (apart from the abrasive Krishna Menon), and Nehru much preferred European company when he could find it. At press conferences he would perk up when, having politely left the first dozen questions to Indian reporters, the foreign correspondents stepped in with the broader issues he appreciated. It never seemed to me, however, that he had a particularly astute political mind. He was no more obviously brilliant than the average English headmaster or Oxbridge don, whom he so much resembled in conversation. But he had other qualities which, put together, made him the leader his country needed in the dangerous early years of her independence.

I suppose the key word is charisma. Some of it clung to Nehru from his association with Gandhi, the Father of the Nation, at whose side he was so often seen. But they believed in two different Indias, the India of the spinning wheel and the India of the power station, and while Gandhi's charisma was that of a rather wily saint, Nehru's was that of a modern prince. For a start, he was strikingly handsome, even in middle age. Nobody looked more debonair in laughter. His fair complexion and Aryan features established him as an aristocrat among Indians (who are terrible colour snobs) and his Kashmiri origins put that beyond question. He might claim to be an agnostic, but everyone knew he was also a pandit, a Brahmin. Nehru squirmed when greeters put dabs of vermilion on his forehead and hung garlands round his neck.

Like the best of the British who educated him, and like his father Motilal before him, he had a profound sense of public service and of duty to his people. I say 'his' people because it seems to me that in a House-of-Windsor way Jawaharlal Nehru developed a sense of royalty that was really the essence of his powers. It was as if he had been born and brought up to the job. He knew that he had to do it, that only he could do it, so he did it with modesty yet authority and never failed to be fascinated by the way it worked with the crowds.

III

Goa Showdown

BBC
1954–58

THE NEXT GREAT expedition was to Goa, the last of the European colonies left in India, for the Portuguese had been there since 1524 and saw no reason to give up just because newcomers like the British and French were leaving. This was awkward for the Indians. Having persuaded the British to quit by (more or less) non-violent means, and being in the business of deploring the use of armed force by everyone else, it would have looked bad for India to turn her army loose on a few thousand Portuguese. The moral argument against colonialism was irresistible was it not? And if the Portuguese really were the monsters they were supposed to be, surely the Goanese (of whom there were many living comfortably in Bombay) would liberate themselves, non-violently, of course.

There were at least two flaws in this argument. The first was that the Goanese rather enjoyed having a foot in both worlds—the Indian and the European—and were in no hurry to see their pleasant Catholic homeland liberated by pagans. The second was that the Portuguese were not cricket-playing Englishmen but nasty fascist policemen, whose motto, constantly repeated, was, 'Authority must be respected, orders must be obeyed'.

The Indian opposition parties, always short of an issue, taunted Nehru for doing nothing about the Portuguese. In the end he agreed that non-Goanese should be allowed to march peacefully across the border to hoist the Indian flag and tell the Portuguese to go home. The Portuguese made it perfectly clear that any such intruders would run the risk of getting shot, whereupon Nehru dithered and ordered his police to make it as difficult as possible for the demonstrators to get through without actually arresting them. There was much digging up of roads, cancelling of flights and confiscation of buses for having defective brakes. Border towns like Belgaum and Sawantwadi filled up with angry and frustrated demonstrators, sweltering in the heat.

Through this confusion I and half a dozen other reporters bribed and bullied our way to the border. There was half a mile of scrubby no-man's-land which the taxis refused to cross, so we heaved out our suitcases and typewriters and staggered off down the track, the Indian army outposts rattling their rifles at us as we passed. Round a bend in the road we saw the border chain and, parked just beyond it, a Portuguese waggon laden with chilled beer. At the sight of this the foreign press corps broke into a shambling trot, pursued by Indian jeers.

The great day was 15 August 1955 when according to the Portuguese more than 3000 *satyagrahis* (or 'moral strugglers') entered Goa at twenty-two different points. Most of them got lost in the jungle and straggled home again; but at six places they got fired on and at four some of them were killed, the nastiest incident being in a railway tunnel where the Portuguese, alarmed by the approach of a chanting mob, simply sprayed the passage with machine-gun fire. Perhaps twenty people were killed altogether. The Portuguese contented themselves with arresting a few ringleaders and booting the others back into India.

I went charging up and down the border in a rented jeep and managed to find three groups of about forty satyagrahis each just after they had been intercepted. The first consisted of militant Hindus who squatted sullen and rebellious under the carbines of the police. The next was a group of communist peasants, poorly dressed and utterly dispirited. Then, herded around the altar of a village temple, I found a batch of socialists from Rajasthan—one of them dead, shot in the back. It was a tragedy of incomprehension: the satyagrahis had been trained to believe that provided they did not use force, no one could resist the rightness of their cause; the Portuguese had been trained to believe that anyone who did not obey the law could, after due warning, legitimately be shot. Neither could understand the convictions of the other. So the satyagrahis marched straight ahead, shouting that India and Goa were one, and the Portuguese after shouting 'Halt or we fire', fired in the air, fired into the ground and then aimed to kill. Each now protested against the stubbornness of the other.

After a few more futile plunges into the jungle, it all petered out. Goa was left alone for another six years; until, goaded on by Krishna Menon who had become defence minister and wanted the exercise, Nehru's patience was declared at an end, non-violence was explained away, and the Indian army rolled ponderously over the colony like a steamroller. Was it worth it, even then? The following year, in 1962, the war with China broke out and Krishna Menon's army was shown to be a paper elephant facing the wrong way.

Menon was a dangerous mixture of charm and malice. As a Westernized South Indian he had a few friends among the Congress establishment, mostly northerners who had gone to jail while Menon was being lionized in London; yet when he sought British company it was usually to vent his spleen against British imperialism. He particularly disliked the BBC—a 'bunch of bloody pukka sahibs'—though he never seemed to miss a news bulletin and was always making complaints to me which, when it came to chapter and verse, he could not substantiate.

~

Arthur Bonner

India's Masses
The Public that Can't Be Reached

The Atlantic
October 1959

I FIRST BEGAN thinking about India's communication difficulties three years ago. I was in the western part of Bihar when Prime Minister Nehru inaugurated one of the major dams that have sprung up throughout the country since Independence. I stopped at a post office and saw, in a corner, a short spear with two little bells attached to the shaft near the head. I recognized it, from descriptions in books, as a spear carried by *dak* (mail) runners. I thought it was a relic of the days when the mail was delivered by runners who needed the spear to protect themselves from robbers and wild animals and who carried the bells just to keep up their courage as they jogged along jungle trails. But the postmaster assured me that he still delivered some of his mail by runners who took three days going out along one route and three days coming back by another.

India is trying to build itself anew, and there are many visible signs of progress. But communications are still needed drastically. Only 18 per cent of the people in India can read and write. Two years ago a research team from Jamia Milia University in New Delhi surveyed 150 villages in selected areas of the four Hindi-speaking states of north-central India. They found that six out of sixty-seven persons selected at random were entirely ignorant of the fact that the British no longer ruled India.

In response to another question, the researchers found that fifty-four out of 314 respondents did not know the name of their own country. Some, however, were aware of the word *Bharat* (India); they said they had heard people shouting *Bharat Mata ki Jai* (Long Live Mother India). But when these same villagers were asked what *Bharat* signified, they said they did not know.

It is difficult to try to communicate the complicated forms of modern democracy to a people who may not even visualize a nation.

I accompanied Prime Minister Nehru shortly before a general election when he attempted just this. The Prime Minister visited the lovely old ruins of Mandu in central India, where five centuries ago there lived a king who, with eight thousand wives, put Solomon to shame. A special effort had been made to gather together thousands of Gond tribesmen, who form the penniless peasantry of the surrounding scrub-jungle-covered hills. Nehru, speaking through a translator, gave a simple lecture in civics. He said there were no more British; they had all gone away. There were no more maharajas; they too were not ruling India. There were just the Indian people, who were ruling themselves. Everybody was an Indian, he said. He was an Indian and the Gonds were Indians. With no more British and no more maharajas, the Gonds like other Indians had the opportunity to choose who would be their rulers. He then went on to explain about the elections and what it meant to cast a vote.

Nehru was careful to speak slowly and to use simple terms that he repeated many times, as if speaking to children, but the entire idea must have been difficult for the Gonds to grasp. Nevertheless, Nehru delivers as many as a half dozen speeches a day during his tours because he knows that the only effective communication with the masses of India must be on a person-to-person basis.

The daily circulation of newspapers in India, with a population of 400 million, is only 3.1 million, and one-third of these papers are in English. The dozen or so English-language papers are extremely important, since 99 per cent of the people are ruled by the 1 per cent who speak English. When I first came to India and heard people say this, I thought they were exaggerating. But my own experience has proved it true. I have talked to thousands of government officials and business, professional, and labour leaders throughout India, and we always conversed in English. An Indian who does not speak English cannot gain authority outside of his own limited circle. But the only persons who can afford the long education necessary to become proficient in English are those who were born with money or property. Thus the feudal system is perpetuated, and thus the English-language papers are so important; they help mould the opinion of the people who count.

But this should not be overemphasized. Newspapers have little impact even on many of those who are literate, either in English or the regional languages. Stanley and Ruth Freed are young American anthropologists who have spent more than a year working in a village only 14 miles from Delhi. About two weeks after the revolt in Tibet began, when the Dalai Lama had just reached the Indian frontier, the Freeds asked several of the more educated people in the village what they thought of the matter. The newspapers were full of news about the Dalai Lama, yet only one of the persons the Freeds asked had even heard of him. The sole exception was a young man studying for his master's degree. Among those unaware of the Dalai Lama's existence was their interpreter, a young English-speaking girl who had completed two years of college.

There is no television in India, and there are only slightly more than 1.5 million radio sets in use, most of them in the four major cities: Delhi, Bombay, Calcutta and Madras. The government has installed about 40,000 subsidized community radios in the villages, but this is just a beginning—there are 500,000 villages in India. It is more than just a matter of poverty. There are no repair facilities in the rural areas, and so an entire system has to be set up to keep the community radios in working order. Besides, many villages do not have electricity and need battery-operated sets, which means that the batteries must be brought into a district centre at regular intervals to be recharged.

Language is a further barrier to understanding. There are fourteen major languages in India, plus a few hundred dialects, and when Nehru speaks in his native Hindustani he is understood by less than half of the people. Unfortunately, the intellectuals who run All India Radio, the government-owned radio network, scorn Hindustani as a polyglot tongue and insist on using a highly Sanskritized version of Hindustani called Hindi, which the government is trying to propagate as the national language. As a result, there are relatively few who understand the Hindi news broadcasts of AIR. The language pattern outside of north-central India is even more complicated. AIR news broadcasts in Bombay and Hyderabad are delivered in five languages, while special programmes for the hill tracts of north-eastern India are spoken in fifteen separate dialects.

It is laid down in the Indian Constitution that the government should try to switch over from English to Hindi by 1965. But there is so much opposition to Hindi that the government recently had to promise that it would not insist on this deadline. It is not that those who oppose Hindi love English more, but they fear that if Hindi becomes the national language their own languages will be neglected. They also fear that those who speak Hindi as their mother tongue would find it easier to get government jobs than those who would have to learn Hindi as a second language. In most of the rest of the world language ties a nation together. In India language separates people and makes them enemies.

India is such a complex country that it needs modern communications to bind it together, yet a great majority of Indians live in the age of the bullock cart. The Indian Airlines Corporation, the government-owned airline that provides all of the internal passenger service and almost all of the air freight traffic, has only seventy-seven aircraft on regular service. More than two-thirds of these are decrepit DC-3s used during World War II. There are only 400,000 telephones, or one for every 1000 persons. Most of the telephones, like most of the radios, are concentrated in the four major cities. There are only 110 pages in the telephone book for the entire state of Kerala, which has a population of fifteen million, or almost double that of New York City. There is only one motor vehicle of any sort, including motorcycles, for every 850 persons. But there are ten million bullock carts, or one for every forty people.

Automobile drivers curse the bullock carts for slowing down traffic, and highway engineers hate them because their narrow, iron-rimmed wheels destroy the surface of the roads, especially in the summer, when the asphalt melts under the baking sun. Yet they are as much a part of Indian life today as they were at the dawn of Indian history. And, judging from ancient temple sculpture, the bullock cart has remained unchanged throughout the rise and fall of countless kingdoms. The cart has two wobbly wheels about 5 feet in diameter and is drawn by two humped bullocks with the yoke resting on the bullocks' necks in front of the hump and cutting into the flesh. The Indian peasant is poor in money and technology; the bullock cart is the only vehicle he can afford or knows how to use.

It is estimated that each bullock cart travels 2000 miles a year and that 70 per cent of the goods in India are carried by bullock cart. The 80 per cent of the Indians who live in villages are scattered as far as

20 miles from a motorable road. When the second Five Year Plan ends in 1961, there will still be but 138,000 miles of all-weather motorable roads, or 1 mile for every 9 square miles of territory. Only 1500 miles of this will be two-lane highways.

India depends primarily on its government-owned railroads for interregional movement. It has the fourth largest railroad system in the world, but it still does not meet India's needs. There are 35,000 miles of track, or 27 miles per 1000 square miles of territory, compared with 74 in the United States. There are only 9 miles of track per 100,000 people, compared with 138 in the United States. The Indian railroads were neglected during the depression in the 1930s. They were badly damaged and overworked in the war years and later when the subcontinent was partitioned between India and Pakistan. Meantime, population has increased at the rate of seven million a year, and there is the new and heavy burden of the industries and projects begun under the two Five Year Plans. Because of all this, the Indian railroads today are less able to meet the demands made on them than they were thirty years ago, even though about 20 per cent of the Five Year Plan allocations are spent for railway improvement.

Travelling in an air-conditioned car on the Indian railways is about as comfortable as travelling Pullman in the United States, but third-class travel, which is what most Indians use, can be sheer horror. About 200 passengers are jammed along with mountains of luggage into a single dirty, hot carriage. The seats are narrow and made of wooden slates. The smell of humanity is reinforced by the odour from the inadequate and seldom-cleaned toilet. There is no drinking water on the train, and the rush for seats is so great that even when the train stops, a person who has a seat does not dare leave it to get a drink of water at the station. Some improvements have been made, but not many. The failure is deliberate. India is trying to build its industries, and freight gets priority over people.

Thanks to this priority, most of the outdated freight cars have been replaced and the total number has increased by 40,000 in the past ten years, but freight capacity is still inadequate. Businessmen complain that they have to wait three months for a freight car to carry their goods and that, at times, when a car is made available they have to wait another month before it can be attached to a passing train. They also complain that the movement of freight cars is so chaotic that even after goods are dispatched it might take a month for the shipment to arrive at a destination only 500 miles away. The shortage of freight cars is a major cause of governmental corruption. Businessmen say that the only way they can get a car is by bribing railway officials.

Governmental inefficiency is the keynote. All of the interstate communications are owned by the Central government, and many of the individual states have nationalized interurban bus and truck lines as well as their municipal transport systems. Yet entering a government office is like stepping back fifty years or more. There are few filing cabinets and paper clips. Papers are attached by a string threaded through a hole in one corner and then wrapped in a folder tied together by another string. A code letter is pinned to the cover, and the name of the file is registered in a ledger. The file is then tossed on a shelf along with mounds of others. The registers are tossed someplace else, and how any file is ever found again is a wonder. The rules for handling correspondence at the district level in Uttar Pradesh have changed little since they were drawn up in 1880. A letter has to pass through forty-one distinct steps and be entered in dozens of registers before it is answered. Throughout India, the government moves so slowly that it is not uncommon for an official to die before his pension is sanctioned and paid.

Fortunately, not all government organizations are so creaky. One of the most promising things in India is the community development programme, which has shown itself receptive to new ideas and methods. It has sent thousands of village-level workers and others into the villages to teach everything from adult literacy to better ways of farming. It emphasizes the person-to-person approach and at times has shown great imagination. For instance, it has organized group tours of India by as many as 500 villagers—tempting them with a chance to worship at the traditional shrines and, in the process, showing them the new factories and dams, which Nehru calls the modern places of pilgrimage. In trying to communicate ideas, the village-level workers have a whole armoury of new weapons. All branches of the Central and state governments are turning out books, pamphlets, and leaflets; special movies have been prepared along with audio–visual aids. There are hundreds of mobile vans equipped with generators to penetrate into the darkest interior, and there are even a few publicity setups mounted on bullock carts.

But an urban Indian intellectual is often as much a stranger to an Indian peasant as an Englishman or an American. Even when they do speak the same language, they do not think the same thoughts. When an educational movie is prepared in a Bombay studio, using actors disguised as farmers, the real farmers will always flock to the mobile van to see it. But they laugh at the wrong places. It is often a parody of their own lives and as such is entertainment, not education.

The problem is greater than just making more realistic films. Ideas not only have to be understood, they have to be accepted; and once accepted, they have to become permanent. The community development programme works intensively in blocks of 100 villages for about four years, after which the area is given much less attention. There are many apparent changes in these blocks. But community development officials have now found, much to their dismay, that the villagers quickly give up their new habits and ideas as soon as the external pressure is removed.

The reason for this is found in the word *dharma*, a religious term roughly meaning 'the Hindu way of life'. But since religion, especially in the villages, is intertwined with man's every act, it means more than the ceremonies of religion. Dharma includes all the ethics and mores of a man's family, caste and community; it determines how a man dresses or plows his field or eats and even how he goes to the toilet. Dharma gives the sanction of heaven to the class and caste structure and lays down that superior authority must be obeyed. Thus a village-level worker, who represents authority, might easily get the peasant to change his habits. But once the village-level worker goes away, other aspects of the dharma—mainly the spiritual pressure of tradition—reassert themselves.

Foreign experts are often discouraged. I met a British nurse whom the World Health Organization had sent to Kerala, where she worked for three years establishing maternity and child-care centres. We had a long talk about all the things she had done, but as I got up to leave she remarked sadly that she would soon be going home and it would probably all be forgotten. I also met an American who came to India under our technical assistance programme. He was sent to an area where another expert a year previously had taught the villagers how to install and use a large number of diesel pumps for their wells. When the second man arrived at the scene, he found that none of the pumps were in use. Some were mechanically defective, others had simply run out of fuel.

Perhaps the best way of getting ideas permanently accepted would be to present them through religious channels. But Hinduism has no established church which can be used as a means of communication. There are only individuals like Vinoba Bhave, Gandhi's disciple, who is collecting thousands of acres of land as gifts for his Bhoodan movement. Vinoba, with his asceticism and his long tours on foot, is operating within the dharma and is easily accepted. The landlords who give part of their holdings to Vinoba for distribution among the landless are the same men who strenuously resist all land reforms proposed by the government. But the Westernized administrators of India scorn Vinoba and his religion-oriented methods.

Nehru often says that he is not 'religious-minded', and government spokesmen take pride in echoing that India is a secular state. After living in India for more than five years and realizing the force of the dharma, I am convinced that there is a direct relation between the de-emphasis of religion since Gandhi's death and the fact that much of the enthusiasm that existed at the time of India's independence has now evaporated.

Many factories and huge new dams spring up, yet despite the best efforts of the government, per-acre yields remain among the lowest in the world, and thousands of ancient minor irrigation works are falling into disrepair. The level of literacy is what it was a decade ago, and the fine-sounding laws banning untouchability or child marriage are seldom enforced. That is, there is a failure of the things that require the active cooperation of the masses. This cannot be accounted for solely by the lack of physical communications. Gandhi showed that despite the absence of roads and post offices it is possible to establish contact with the vast masses and mobilize them for action. But nowadays this spiritual rapport is missing; there is a vast gulf between the rulers and the ruled. This has serious implications. As long as there is no close contact between those at the top and those at the bottom, democracy in India has slender roots.

~

Charles Wheeler
Fast for Chandigarh

BBC
19 August 1961

AT IRREGULAR INTERVALS during the last forty years, the Indian scene has been dominated by the grown-up who refuses to eat his dinner until he gets his own way. As every schoolboy knows, it all began with the late Mahatma Gandhi, who hit upon the 'fast unto death', as he called it, as a way of stabbing the conscience of his followers and of bringing his people together.

Now Gandhi achieved remarkable results, and his weapon survived him. But his motives did not; it's striking that all the great fasts since Gandhi's time have been devoted to creating new divisions. Invariably the issue has been one of language. Before Independence the Indian national leaders promised to create a Union of States with their boundaries drawn on linguistic lines. By and large the promise was kept; but where it conflicted with the national interest the map was left as it was; or rather it was left as it was until the government's hand was forced—forced by mob violence, which led to the partition of Bombay state, or by rioting following the death of a man on a fast, which brought about the division of the state of Madras.

Now each time the government bowed to pressure, Mr Nehru has cried: 'Never again'. But another trial of strength is now approaching a climax—this time in the north Indian border state—the Punjab.

The case of the Punjab is complex. Two religious communities live in the state—the Hindus and the Sikhs. The Sikhs form no more than 2 per cent of India's total population. But they're a highly self-conscious, enterprising minority, and in their home state, the Punjab, they dominate the larger but more easy-going community of the Hindus. This has frightened the Hindus, who have reacted by disowning the common language of the Punjab, Punjabi, as a symbol of Sikh communalism, although it's the only language that most of the Hindus speak.

Now the Sikhs regard the preservation of Punjabi as vital to their religion. Their Bible the Adi Granth, is written in the Punjabi script,

Gurmukhi, and they argue that a threat to Punjabi is a threat to the faith. So they are demanding a state or a province in which Punjabi will have the status of an official language. To bring this about, the Sikhs want the government to cut away the predominantly Hindi-speaking parts of the Punjab, leaving them—the Sikhs—in a slight majority in the larger part of the state. But Mr Nehru says 'No'. He argues that the Sikh demand is religious rather than linguistic in character and he insists that the creation of a theocratic state is utterly incompatible with the secular nature of the Indian Union.

Now Mr Nehru's argument in fact goes to the root of the problem. In the past 200 years the dividing line between Hindus and Sikhs has become so thin that any feature that emphasizes the difference between them is strenuously advocated by the Sikh leaders, who are obsessed by the thought of the Sikh community losing its separate identity. So that what the Sikhs are really doing is this; they are asking a secular government to take executive action to help them protect their religion from decline.

On the other hand even Mr Nehru's most fervent admirers cannot say that he has handled the problem with his usual wisdom and tact. One cannot cope with a proud and aggressive people like the Sikhs by simply saying 'No' and by clapping their leaders in gaol, for this is precisely the treatment the Sikh community has thrived on for centuries. Nor does it help matters to question the Sikhs' loyalty.

Up to a year ago it might have been possible to agree on a compromise. Since then, attitudes have hardened all round, and today nobody seems able even to suggest a possible formula. And it's in this state of deadlock that the Sikh religious and political leader, Master Tara Singh, has begun his fast to death in the Golden Temple at Amritsar, where the police cannot reach him without causing frightful repercussions.

Master Tara Singh is seventy-six years old, and he's no Mahatma Gandhi, who was accustomed to a modest intake of things like curds and grapes. The risk that the Master's heart will fail any day next week must be considerable.

Meanwhile the Hindu extremists have staged a counter-fast in Delhi, resolving to die rather than see the Punjab divided, which doesn't make Mr Nehru's position any easier. But the decision is the Prime Minister's alone—whether to acknowledge the obvious, that the Sikhs won't give up until they have their Punjabi speaking state, or whether to allow the Master to kill himself, creating a reaction among Sikhs that may bring bloodshed to the Punjab and Delhi, and which might well bring about the creation of a Sikh state in the end.

~

Arthur Bonner
Tragedy of Tibet

The Saturday Evening Post
9 September 1961

Darjeeling: WE WERE BROUGHT up to think of Tibet as Shangri-La where the Dalai Lama ruled as a living god and monks meditated on the mysteries of eternity. Isolated between the snow-capped ramparts of the Himalayas on the south and trackless Taklimakan Desert in Sinkiang on the north, Tibet was a living museum—interesting to anthropologists and adventurers, but certainly of no concern to the housewife pushing her shopping cart through a supermarket back home, or to the boys around the soda fountain in Dallas.

But Tibet does concern us. It is one of the few places where a reporter can penetrate Red China's Bamboo Curtain. This can be done by interviewing some of the more than 60,000 refugees who have fled from Tibet in the past two and a half years. It is often a painful experience. Grown men begin to cry. Women try to relieve the tension of painful memories by pulling at their clothes or clenching their hands till their knuckles are white. You must promise not to disclose their identity in any way because they greatly fear what the Chinese might do to relatives and friends still in Tibet. It is also possible to pick up many details (again not for attribution) from Indian or Nepalese diplomats with connections in Tibet, or from traders crossing the frontier. Naturally, information is spotty. Everyone is restricted in his movements and spied upon. But the general outline is clear.

Soldiers of the Chinese communist army first marched into Lhasa in May of 1951, carrying a huge framed picture of Mao Tse-tung. The troops constructed barracks and airfields and built up fuel stores. The Chinese promised to respect Tibet's autonomy and allowed the existing social system to remain virtually intact, at least in western Tibet.

Then, in the last half of 1958 Khampa warriors who had been carrying on a private revolt in eastern Tibet were able to spread west, touching off an uprising in Lhasa in March 1959. After the Dalai Lama escaped to India. The Chinese, with their superior weapons, manoeuvrability and trained soldiers, soon took over the major towns and most populated valleys. First they smashed the revolt and then they began to destroy traditional Tibetan culture.

Thousands of monks were swept into concentration camps, and a systematic programme of degradation began. It is when they talk of these events that Tibetan refugees break into tears. They relate how venerated lamas were dragged before 'People's Courts'. There communist agents in the audience—often Tibetan criminals freed to bear false witness—would stand up and shout: 'You murdered my father,' or 'You raped my sister.' The accusers would then beat the lamas, spit on them, pull out their hair and kick them.

Other Tibetans told me how the Communists put the monks in long pits. They stood on the edges and urinated on them and told them to pray for their food. After the victims were weakened by hunger they would be exhibited to the townspeople as evidence that there is no God. In other places Chinese soldiers with their boots on would sit on altars, smash clay images and tear up sacred manuscripts. 'If there is a God, why doesn't he destroy us?' the soldiers would demand.

Before the communists came to Tibet there were 20,000 monks in three main monasteries near Lhasa—Drepung, Sera and Ganden, the three jewels of Lhasa. But now, worship in these monasteries is forbidden, and the Chinese apparently intend to turn some of the principal monasteries into museums. However, the most beautiful images and most valuable manuscripts have been taken to Peking.

About 5000 monks and lamas, along with members of what the communists call the 'upper strata'—the former noblemen, landlords and traders—have been herded into the Dhrabchi concentration camp a few miles north of Lhasa, on the road to Sera monastery. It was previously a Tibetan military camp. It is now surrounded by a high fence.

After a hard day's work, sometimes in freezing temperatures, the monks were forced to attend evening lectures and indoctrination classes lasting until after midnight. Subjects for discussion often were: 'Who are the upper strata?' or 'Who is responsible for the feudal serfdom?' They were expected to blame themselves and the Dalai Lama. Very rarely would monks speak against the Dalai Lama, and this did not make their lot any easier.

Lhasa has been divided into four zones, north, east, south and west. Each zone is under a branch of the Lhasa municipal communist party and further divided into areas under local 'people's committees'. But to make controls even tighter, these are broken up into groups of ten persons, each under a captain responsible for all they do. He is either a Tibetan collaborator or a Chinese.

Group captains were ordered to make lists of everyone's possessions. Everything in excess of a bare minimum had to be surrendered. People were allowed to keep only two sets of clothing, one for summer and another for winter. The Chinese wanted to unearth gold, jewellery and religious objects, but most of all they wanted to discover any hidden weapons.

The communists introduced a rationing system early in 1960 and promised everyone about thirty pounds of grain a month. That is a meagre diet, by normal Tibetan standards, but still enough for subsistence. However, all of the many Tibetans I talked to said the full rations were never available.

The lands of the monasteries and the former nobles were distributed to the peasants, who were given title to about half an acre each. But these penniless farmers had neither implements nor seed. The Chinese told them that, since they were the owners of the land, they must find their own seed. The peasants were seen in Lhasa trying to sell their belongings to buy seed.

The Chinese have opened several schools, but the Tibetans have to be forced to send their children. They are afraid that the children will be enlisted in the 'Young Pioneers' and taught to spy on their parents or, what is worse, will be taken away to China. The Chinese repeatedly carry off children from twelve to sixteen years old—about twenty at a time—and they have never been heard of from again. Presumably the communists hope to process a new generation of Tibetans who no longer believe in their culture or the independence of Tibet.

The worst Tibetan criminals in the Chinese view are the so-called 'upper strata'. Many of these have been put into the most dreaded prison of all—Taring House—the former spacious home of a Tibetan nobleman now in India. After perfunctory trials they are routinely sentenced to twenty years in prison, including a certain period to be spent at hard labour. Actually, this is slave labour from which few survive. A Tibetan who escaped from a slave gang working on a mountain road told me his Chinese guards made a practice of setting off dynamite blasts without warning. If a man was injured but could still work, he was put back to work. But if a bone was broken and he was helpless the guards would simply toss him down the cliffside. Prisoners who collapsed or died from hunger or exposure were left where they lay. When about a dozen of them had accumulated a pit was dug and all were thrown in—the partially alive as well as the dead.

Because of last year's formation of ill-planned communes, which left large areas unsown, along with the influx of hundreds of thousands of Chinese soldiers and civilians, and perhaps the food crisis in China itself, Tibet is now experiencing its first famine in history. One refugee who arrived in India recently, pointed to a tin containing fifty cigarettes and said it would serve as a measure of the amount of food a Tibetan now gets for an entire day. 'The famine is so severe that even the Chinese soldiers are reported on short rations.'

The two and a half years since the flight of the Dalai Lama have been marked by frantic, feverish military preparations. In addition to the three earlier roads linking Tibet with the Chinese provinces of Sinkiang, Tsinghai and Kansu, a fourth has been rushed through. It skirts the north-western frontier of India and goes to Yunan province. There is also a circular highway that links all the important towns of Tibet and there are at least eleven branch roads striking south to the borders of India, Nepal and Bhutan. Before the communists moved into Tibet only two automobiles had been seen in Lhasa. Both had been dismantled and carried across the mountains from India on the backs of mules and men. Now the Chinese mass hundreds of trucks for regular convoys. Small tanks have been seen and refugees tell of new airfields under construction. Garrisons of from 100 to 500 soldiers have been strung out along the entire 2500-mile southern frontier. Trenches and underground emplacement have been dug at all strategic points.

'Why all this feverish activity?' I asked an Indian official whose main job during the past ten years has been to keep in touch with events in Tibet.

'They say they are preparing to defend themselves against American imperialism,' he replied. 'But disregard that. Will the Chinese invade India? No, they are not so stupid as to openly involve themselves in aggression. Besides, they known they cannot conquer all of India in one sweep, using Tibet as a base. But a war of liberation? Yes. That is what they will call whatever they do. When they first marched into Tibet they spoke of liberating it. They now claim some parts of India and would like to liberate these areas too. First they liberate one area and then use the local population to liberate the next.

'The Chinese are an ancient nation,' the Indian, who spent some years in Peking, continued. 'They think in terms of centuries. They take infinite pains and have infinite patience. In Tibet they are preparing actions elsewhere, perhaps in Laos or Vietnam. They are sending their technicians to the Middle East, Africa and Cuba. They will plan and wait—and strike when they find a weak point.'

The Chinese openly proclaim that they intend to aim at the entire world. I asked a young man who left Lhasa a few months ago if the Chinese gave any reason for what they are doing. 'They say that until the whole world becomes communist, the agony that is in the world will not end,' he replied.

Tibetans see the advent of communism as an unmitigated disaster. Last year the Chinese hung boxes around Lhasa and asked people to drop in notes with comments or criticism. One Tibetan told me that if someone wanted to injure someone he only had to write the victim's name on a slip of paper and drop it into a box. The person named would be picked up for questioning the next day. Once someone dropped a note into a box at a place called Chapi House. In trying to discover who had written the note, the Chinese disclosed the contents to many of the indoctrination groups. It said: 'During the old government there was a word called "hell". No one knew what it really meant. Now we know what hell is and we know that the old government was heaven.'

~

James Cameron

The Trap! As Soon as Nehru Said 'FIGHT' He Had Lost the First Round

The Daily Mail
22 October 1962

THE SMALL WAR between India and China on Asia's lost horizon is now a brutal deplorable fact, sad and menacing.

For those of us who know and love both countries these are sickening days.

These frontier battles are archaic and absurd. To wrangle in these cosmic years over a meaningless stretch of empty mountainside is explicable only in symbolic terms that have nothing to do with the McMahon Line, or the Namkachu river, or the town of Dhola.

Nobody really gives a damn about these places, and everyone knows it. The trouble is in the heart.

Of all the conflict possible in this imbecile world this is the most painful, exasperating and futile.

Nobody on earth can profit by it. No territory of any value can change hands, no ideology be promoted, no cause be advanced.

The whole situation was engineered to put the Indians on the spot, which has worked.

It is heartbreaking that in the twilight of his great authority Jawaharlal Nehru should be saddled with this intolerable dilemma.

The thing has, of course, been blowing up for years over the truly piffling issue of exactly where, in that enormous Himalayan wilderness, India ends and China begins.

The fact that practically nobody *lives* in this vertical desert seems beside the point. This is nothing to do with a lump of land. This is nothing, essentially, to do with a handful of unhappy soldiers huddling on the snowline.

This operation is to drive India, morally and economically, to the wall. And the fact that the thing has begun at all is Square One for China.

Since the Chinese army first nosed across the line in 1959 the quarrel has nagged away at Indo–Chinese relations, making a total nonsense of the *panch sila*, the famous Five Principles of Coexistence formulated by Nehru and Chou En-lai, which so many of us applauded for their enlightened realism.

There at least, we thought, the Asians could be above the battle.

But all negotiations over this absurd geographical misunderstanding failed, as—it became clear—the Chinese meant them to fail.

The Chinese moved into Ladakh, in north Kashmir, and occupied an area the size of Belgium. Now, moving far to the east, they have driven the Indians back from the Bhutan border.

Mr Nehru was goaded into an announcement that the Chinese must be thrown out by force. He had waited two years before making it, under every kind of pressure, partly because the Indian army was in no shape to take the field.

It is pretty certain that he did not want to make it anyway.

In the event, he had no choice. The people of India were angered, his Congress party was aroused, even the Indian communist party accused the Chinese of aggression and demanded that they be expelled.

But the moment that Jawaharlal Nehru proclaimed that he was ready for war the Chinese had won their first point. Nehru, the apostle of pacifism, had been trapped into bellicosity; the prime mediator of the world's disputes had been manoeuvred into refusing discussion.

Throughout the sensitive and vulnerable Afro-Asian world where China and India compete for influence, India could be represented as solving her disputes by force of arms.

Moreover, Nehru has now been jostled into proclaiming that India's economy must be geared for war, to the immense disadvantage of her current Five Year Plan, to the interruption of the progress she has worked so bitterly hard to achieve.

If the border war goes no farther than sporadic engagements on the high tops, the Chinese have accomplished much, in sabotaging both India's international image and her finances.

Nobody, of course, can actually win this war. The idea of a Chinese invasion of India over these ferocious mountains is a macabre improbability.

I know that north-east region moderately well. I loafed around there for weeks waiting for the Dalai Lama to emerge from the mists.

It is indescribably beautiful, difficult, remote and useless.

It climbs all over the place up to 15,000 feet, torn by ravines, locked in terrible winters. You would have a job to find a more hopeless place to wage a campaign.

But it is there that the whole northern wall of India meets its hinge, at the junction of the peculiar little kingdoms of Bhutan, Sikkim and Nepal, intensely vulnerable to Chinese penetration.

There, too, India has her own troubles with the Naga tribes. Her situation can become politically dangerous as Peking works even harder to isolate her from her other neighbours, Pakistan and Burma.

There is a nice irony, to be sure, in the fact that it is Russia who is now supplying her with military aircraft. But even with these her chances of any kind of swift victory are small. The high Himalaya is no place for an aerial war.

The last time I saw Chou En-lai was in Delhi, garlanded and benign with his arm round Nehru. The only cry then all over India was 'Hindi Chini bhai bhai!'—India and China are brothers, they shouted, and how splendid it sounded and how far away today.

~

Ivor Jones
India Mobilizes

BBC
17 November 1962

BY NOW, A month after the main Chinese attacks began, the majority of Indians know there's a war on. Some primitive tribes and peasants away in remote hills and jungles may not have heard, but that's probably all. Not that the news has spread in the Western way. There are only about a million radio sets here, and the daily sale of newspapers is only about five million. In any case, fewer than a fifth of the people can read.

**The war between India and China began on 20 October 1962. A cease-fire was declared on 20 November 1962.*

The news is passed by word of mouth. It's been heard on communal radio sets in the larger villages, and passed on from there to the outlying ones. On hearing it, people there have walked or cycled to their nearest centre to hear it for themselves—sometimes by the hundreds. They in turn have spread what they know. The village headman may have had business in a town or city and been to a public meeting. On getting home he'd probably call on himself to pass on what Mr Nehru said—or whoever it was. Or he might sit outside his house, smoking a hookah, with his neighbours gathered around him.

So now, men from even out-of-the-way places have been arriving at recruiting centres. These have already been set up in many of the larger villages, and they help to spread the news further. For instance, a centre was opened in a small town some way from Delhi and 10,000 men turned up on the first day. The sole recruiting officer there hadn't a chance of coping with them all. But they were so afraid of not getting into the army that they wouldn't let him go home for the night. They just sat or lay there telling each other about the war, and hearing what he had to say. The same thing's been happening all over the country. There's no doubt about the people's violent wish to fight and work for India. The problem is to maintain and direct it—to shape it into a national effort.

I don't mean persuading people to donate blood or knit scarves for soldiers—which they're doing enthusiastically—but something harder. India is a country of villages—more than half a million of them. The civil service isn't strong enough in either numbers or ability to draw them fully into a total war effort, and it's doubtful whether they can do it themselves. Their basic institution is the village council—the panchayat. It's already been decided—at government and state level—that these should take on such jobs as seeing that more food's grown, getting people to save money, finding labour to repair and improve important roads and bridges, spreading information, and so on. But there are serious doubts as to whether many panchayats are up to this. They may—long ago—have run their villages justly and smoothly. But it seems that this tradition is often lost in apathy, and Indians who should know, say that many of them are now in the hands of ambitious mischief-makers.

Somehow, the panchayats will have to find a new spirit if the mounting national feeling is to express itself through them. But if the problem is a tough one on the land, it may be even tougher in industrial mobilization. There especially, all the enthusiasm and fervour, the demonstrations and the shouting, are no substitute for organization. To start with, there's the difficulty of knowing what's wanted. It's agreed that there's no going back now—that even if the Chinese withdrew tomorrow, the line of the Himalayas would have to be heavily guarded. But it seems that the government hasn't yet made up its mind what's involved, and industrialists certainly don't know what's expected of them.

The Planning Commission has made some general recommendations. The country's administrative machinery must be strengthened; agricultural and industrial output increased; high priority given to clearing such bottle necks as the coal and power shortages; and the present Five Year Plan must be reshaped to favour projects that will show a quick yield. Incidentally, it looks as though national mobilization will sharpen the controversy between the planners and the free-enterprise men. Some details are clear; such as that plants making air conditioners and the like will be turned over to arms, and that idle industrial capacity must be used—and there's a good deal of it.

It will take time, even to do these things. But beyond them seems to lie something larger. To fight a modern war, India itself will have—in its own way—to become more modern. Indeed, if the Planning Commission's targets are met, that will already have begun. And many traditions will weaken in the process—such as the one of hoarding gold and jewellery. It's perhaps this that Indian leaders mean when they talk about the war as a challenge and an opportunity.

~

Neville Maxwell
Tarnished Image of Mr Nehru

The Times
4 April 1963

MR NEHRU HAS been head of his government for sixteen years. He could claim in that time to have set the course, defined the aspirations, for a society of 480 million people, and by an effort that by virtue of his personal predominance often seemed single-handed, to have put his country under way towards the goals he had articulated. Partly as recognition of, partly as foundation for these undeniable achievements 'Panditji' has stood high in the affection, and trust of his countrymen—but lately there has been a change.

Where once his judgments were accepted without question, now they are often mistrusted and even scoffed at. Where once he was accepted as the embodiment of what India should and would become, now the left faction of his party has found it necessary to make an explicit identification of nation and leader and to protect him from criticism by presenting such as treason. Where once the question, 'After Nehru, who?' was asked with despair, now it has become a subject for matter-of-fact speculation. There is the feeling that what must come, must come—and that change will bring its own benefits. What has happened?

Most immediately, of course, China's raid into India and the crumbling of India's defences before it have been an incontrovertible demonstration of the failure and even the folly of policies especially identified with the Prime Minister. But in the grey clear-sightedness that follows emotional shock Indians of the political class at least are looking back now beyond Mr Nehru's China policy and the disasters to which it led to the whole course of his stewardship.

Survival of Unity

The watershed in Mr Nehru's political life may be seen by history to have lain years before the mountain debacles of 1962, perhaps round about 1957. By then the greatest political tasks of the new India's beginnings were done.

Unity has survived the trauma of Partition, Indians had begun, the great majority of them anyway, to share a common view of what sort of nation they should become, and how the transformation should be achieved. India should be a secular state, in which religion should be the concern only of the heart and the temple or mosque, and no longer the seedbed of massacre or the clamp of social oppression. It should be democratic, the people actively participating in the ruling of their own affairs at every level. It should be socialistic, the well-being of the masses its first concern, and impatient of wealth and the wealthy—and it would struggle out of mass poverty by planned effort, helped by whoever would help, unaided if need be. These were Mr Nehru's ideas and they had become India's.

At that time too India's stature in the world was approaching its heady zenith, Mr Nehru's vision of a nation aligned with neither of the world's hostile camps but friendly to both had begun to be accepted, valued and emulated. India's voice carried far in the counsels of the world—and that voice was Mr Nehru's.

About that time the balance must have tipped, and the tasks before India became those of administration, of implementing plans as well as drawing them up, of seeing that social aspirations had their full political expression. Mr Nehru was less gifted for the new tasks than he had been for the old.

Sense of Detail

As an administrator he has the high virtues of humaneness and a sense of the importance of detail, but he lacks follow-through, the determination to see that what has been decided should be done, is done. He lacks the true political leader's gift for bringing into government men who share his ideas and have the zest to put them into force. He lacks—and many of his failings are those of virtue—the ruthlessness inseparable from political leadership. In a famous essay, published anonymously in 1937, Mr Nehru wrote this of himself:

> He has all the makings of a dictator in him—vast popularity, a strong will, energy, pride . . . and with all his love of the crowd an intolerance of others and a certain contempt for the weak and inefficient . . . His overwhelming desire to get things done,

to sweep away what he dislikes and build anew, will hardly brook for long the slow processes of democracy.

Perhaps he feared such tendencies within himself too strongly, and in suppressing his hankering for Caesarism weakened too the power for making hard decisions, against opposition not only external but within himself. He has brooked far too often not only 'the slow processes of democracy' but also the failures and misdemeanours of colleagues, the obstruction or deflection of policies which he has passionately declared to be vital for India.

But to say that Mr Nehru is a man diminished by a just but inhibiting abhorrence of dictatorship is not quite sufficient; there is another facet of complexity. There is one kind of dictator which he would like to be: a leader so beloved, so trusted, so needed that for him to wish a thing done is to see it done—a dictator who needs no dictatorship. Gandhi was sometimes nearly that.

Seeing Both Sides

Another quality of Mr Nehru's may add something more towards indecisiveness, the completeness of his view. In every choice he seems to see so clearly the balancing claims of the two sides that choice between them appears to him injustice. Every utterance of the Prime Minister provides stylistic evidence of a habitual hedging of judgment. There is never a flat statement, even his strongest eloquence is watered down by his compulsive qualifications.

So marked has been this deep awareness of the validity of conflicting claims that it might be said that not one of the great political decisions of independent India has been taken by Jawaharlal Nehru. The linguistic reorganization of the states of India; the imposition of Central rule in Kerala in 1959; the eventual bifurcation of Bombay, the last of the multilingual states; the seizure of Goa—in each of these there were cogent arguments, strongly advanced, on both sides, and in none did Mr Nehru willingly give a clear lead.

The pattern is so marked that it can almost be called a technique, if an unconscious one: unwilling to act, Mr Nehru procrastinates, allowing and even encouraging events to take a course—or to be put on a course by others more purposeful—that works towards leaving him no choice, so that at last he can accede to something that has become ineluctable.

Trusted Figure

Mr Nehru has expressed self-dissatisfaction in the past more than once in announcing that he intended to retire. But here, too, velleity has come in the way—that and the frightened clamours of the political multitude. For Mr Nehru's failings, like his grandeur, have been emphasized by the general paltriness of Indian political life. The people who once begged him to stay may yet become impatient of his going, but there is not one of them, for all his shortcomings, who could fill his place. If there were, Mr Nehru, who no longer bears his years lightly, might gladly go; because there is not, he must stay.

For the village masses Mr Nehru is still the man most trusted, indeed, he is the only remaining national leader who can even claim to be universally known in India. For most of those outside north-east India the defeats along the border last year seem to have meant little, and Mr Nehru's reputation to have been accordingly left unscathed. But now that the opposition parties feel freed to attack the Prime Minister personally his stature in the country must be subject to erosion.

In the past Mr Nehru's popularity rubbed off on to the governing party: nowadays the unpopularity of government policies—its attempt on the gold-hoarding habits of the people and the new budget, for example—seems to be rubbing off on to Mr Nehru. The closing years of the Nehru phase of Indian history are likely to be anti-climactic at the least, and perhaps even tragic as time and circumstance continue to undermine the achievements of one of the great men of the age.

~

Selig S. Harrison

A Fairy Tale Vale Laced by Bullets
'Incidents' Are Commonplace along the Cease-Fire Line Dividing Kashmir

The Washington Post
15 December 1963

Poonch, Kashmir: THE OLD MAN on the stretcher moaned and pulled a blanket over his blood-smudged face to keep away clouds of giant horseflies. Crowded around him were excited villagers telling a jeepload of Indian army officers about the midnight visit of armed adventurers from the Pakistan side of the Indo–Pakistan cease-fire line.

Their story followed a pattern repeated almost daily on both sides of the United Nations-patrolled truce line in Kashmir. Brandishing clubs, knives and rifles, a band of eleven marauders burst into the mud hut of Punnu Mohammed and demanded his valuables. When the old peasant and his son Ghulam fought back, the intruders mauled them and made off across a field to the other side of the cease-fire line with Rs 1247 ($268), eight blankets and a goatskin coat.

Ghulam grabbed the Indian brigade commander by the shoulders and told him the stolen money represented his savings for eight years from his salary as a village watchman. He demanded weapons, cash restitution and a telephone linking Degwar village to the nearest army patrol post.

The Terror Was Real

My first reaction to the agitated scene encountered on our arrival at Degwar was that the Indian authorities had staged the proceedings to breathe life into atrocity charges constantly levelled against Pakistan. But the moans were real and so were the deep gouges in Punnu's forehead and neck.

The faces of the villagers were studies in terror. It seemed clear that violence had visited Degwar the night before and that the only place near enough to serve as home base for the raiders in the desolate

Betar Valley was the neighbouring Pakistan village just across the line. Degwar is 2 miles over the barley fields from the end of the jeep track connecting the Betar Valley to brigade headquarters at Poonch.

What did not seem certain, despite the insistence of the villagers, was that Pakistan had officially inspired the raid. The Degwar peasants argued that the Pakistan-sponsored Azad (Free) Kashmir government singled out the watchman's hut to intimidate the whole village in the hope that the area would be vacated and its rich lands redistributed among peasants living next to the Pakistan side of the line.

The Indian general commanding the brigade in the Poonch area listened sympathetically but did not commit himself. His only firm promise was a telephone. India is not arming the villagers next to the cease-fire line, he maintained, while Pakistan has been equipping 'volunteer' and reserve units of former servicemen. Punnu and two others who had suffered minor injuries were taken to a military hospital.

Incidental Incident

The Degwar incident was not made the basis for one of the endless formal complaints of 'encroachments' made by both sides to the UN observers and was not leaked to the headline-hungry nationalist press in New Delhi.

Privately, Indian officers stationed at Poonch said that their greatest problem lies in sorting out deliberate Pakistani provocations across the cease-fire line from intervillage feuds and conventional decoities (robberies). Like villagers along most disturbed borders, the peasants on both sides of the line are aware of their strategic position and exploit every opportunity for material reward.

The Degwar incident gives the village a claim on the Indian authorities if it is presented as a Pakistan-engineered affair. Ghulam gets more restitution if he reports the loss of Rs 1247 rather than, say 500.

Clash over Water

And yet the incident at Degwar might well have occurred with the encouragement of the Azad Kashmir authorities for one compelling reason. Six weeks ago, the Betar area was the site of the most widely publicized clash on the cease-fire line in recent years.

Pakistan forces fired 1000 rounds of light machine gun volleys at Indian civilian workmen repairing a diversion canal leading to the

Poonch hydroelectric power station. The canal had been breached by Pakistani saboteurs in retaliation for an earlier incident 50 miles away involving Pakistani water sources on the Indian side of the line.

Major Frank Hoeter, an Australian UN cease-fire observer on the Indian side of the line waved a white flag but was fired on three times in the 30 October Betar incident from a Pakistani bunker 575 yards away before the Indian forces fired back. In the last volley, Pakistani bullets missed him by 18 inches. With a bad case of jitters besetting the villagers on the Indian side, the Betar area would offer a vulnerable target for Pakistani-sponsored sabotage activity and intimidation tactics. The fear of sabotage activity was accentuated after a recent helicopter crash near here killing six top Indian army officers, though preliminary evidence has indicated that the disaster was accidental.

Thirty-Four Patrol the Line

The dominant impression you get after a four-day tour over 550 miles of loop-the-loop mountain roads on the Indian side of the cease-fire line is that the truth lies out of reach in assessing a substantial number of charges of truce violations.

Thirty-four United Nations observers roam the front line and do their best, but the UN comes onto the scene after the crime has occurred and must normally rely on local witnesses to judge between Indian and Pakistani claims.

The most frequent shooting incidents occur when villagers appropriate fallow land straddling the line in the sowing season and then stand their ground until harvest time. Cattle rustlers and bandits who flee across the line to dispose of their loot often become the focal point of armed clashes which are downgraded or blown up by India and Pakistan to suit momentary political needs.

Sloshing in an Indian army jeep through Himalayan rivers and over rocky mountain tracks, I visited eight Indian outposts within sight of the cease-fire line. My escort officer, Major V.P. Puri, a veteran of the fifteen-month Kashmir operations of 1947–48, told me that I was the first foreign correspondent who had ever been given a jeep's-eye view of the cease-fire line on the Indian side.

A Military Artery

My journey took me up and down the length of the 157-mile north–south route linking Poonch to Jammu in the plains and off into dozens of lateral jeep tracks running to brigade, battalion, company and platoon headquarters of the Indian army.

You drive up the two-lane Jammu–Poonch road in the midst of convoys of 3-ton trucks loaded with Sikh and Gurkha soldiers sprawled atop tightly stacked gasoline cans. There are occasional coal trucks from the Kalakot mines scuttling back and forth, but the highway is for the most part a bustling, carefully policed military artery.

Along the roadside are woodsmen toting primitive axes, Kashmiri Moslem women shrouded in heavy woollen blankets and an occasional herdsman prodding his goats. The monotony of straw-coloured mud huts is relieved by red chillis drying in the sun on a roof here and there and crude decorations sketched in lime on the adobe walls.

Near army encampments, the military hutments are camouflaged with fringes of pine needles on the rooftops and melt into the landscape. No restrictions were placed on my movements in military areas and I spoke freely with Indian officers of all grades.

There was no visible evidence to support Pakistani charges that American arms aid is being used in Kashmir. The UN cease-fire regulations imposed after the shooting stopped 1 January 1949 limit the defences of both sides to the force levels and troop dispositions as of the moment of the truce.

This means that the Indian outposts flanking the cease-fire line cannot exceed platoon strength and must not send jeep patrols closer than within 500 yards of the line. Border police units, however, can enter the 500-yard zone.

Casualties Are Few

There are continual firing exchanges across the line from bunkers tucked into cliffside crannies and perched on commanding ridges. Much of the firing is necessarily from such long distances that it is aimless and ineffective. India reports a total of twenty-three civilians and no army personnel killed along the cease-fire line since the beginning of 1960.

'We don't return a great deal of their fire,' said Major Gen. S.K.D. Manavati, commander of the 25th Division, who has been killed since our conversation in the Poonch helicopter crash. 'Why waste the ammunition? Most of the fire comes from civilians who have been given arms, you know, and the beggars don't have very good aim.'

At Basuni, an Indian outpost, a Gurkha battalion commanded by Major R.S. Rawat faces persistent Pakistani fire as the result of a dispute over the introduction of an Indian customs post at nearby Balakot manned by police armed with light machine guns. India maintains that the post was necessary to check a smuggling racket but Pakistan replies that the post serves in effect to add a link to the chain of Indian defences on the cease-fire line.

The police were installed inside the post under the cover of infantry fire and Pakistan is now raining retaliatory bullets on the post night after night.

The Odds Are Short

As the hottest spot on the cease-fire line, Balakot is one of the few front-line outposts claiming a full time UN observer. He is Maj. William P. Hall of Australia. I met him inside the mud walls of the Indian army checkpost facing the disputed Balakot village.

The major grabbed my sleeve and pulled me down into a crouch. 'Out here, it doesn't pay to be too tall,' he warned.

Pakistani bullets had been whizzing overhead two hours before my jeep drove up, and there was no telling when the firing would start again. Maj. Hall pointed over his shoulder at a massive boulder towering behind the makeshift fortress. The rock was a disfigured mass of nicks and gouges left by six tense months of intermittent machine gun fire.

As UN assignments in Kashmir go, Balakot is considered rough duty. Most sectors of the cease-fire line are placid for weeks at a time and the UN is content to send men once every three months on routine patrols to check against possible troop build-ups. But mounting Indo–Pakistan tension in recent months has prompted a new policy of front-line assignments to keep tabs on potential trouble spots.

No Time to Root

The UN has divided the responsibility for manning the 360-mile cease-fire front among ten rotating field observer teams headquartered at key brigade centres on both sides of the line. The team offices are connected by radio telephone and confer regularly on suspicious troop movements.

After a week on the windswept hilltop at Balakot with a platoon of Gurkhas, Maj. Hall will be transferred across the line to a Pakistan post. There he will live with Moslem Pathan troops. Shifting the men back and forth is part of a strict procedure designed to preserve their objectivity and avoid one-sided personal friendships.

Life on the cease-fire line has attracted a surplus of volunteers from participating UN armies despite the dangers. Lt. Gen. R.H. Nimmo of Australia, who has headed the group since its beginning, cites the lure of the Himalayas to account for the drawing power of the job.

The snow-capped hills of western Kashmir offer an abundance of wild boar, brown bear, cheetah and the mighty mahaseer, a mountain fish which is considered small if it weighs 40 pounds and measures 3 feet long. Trekking over Himalayan trails and remote outposts, the UN observers may use their hunting rifles so long as they put them away before they reach their destination.

$3650 a Year Extra

Each observer signs up for a year and gets the regular salary of his home military service plus $3650 a year extra. For every month of duty on what is virtually a full-time job, he gets six days off, which he can spend in the Indian and Pakistani capitals of New Delhi and Rawalpindi or in Srinagar, the tourist paradise of Kashmir.

Over the years, 416 military observers have served on the cease-fire line. At present, there are seven Canadians, six Australians, four Swedes and a scattering from Belgium, Chile, Uruguay, Italy, New Zealand and the other Scandinavian countries. No American personnel have served with the Military Observers Group since India questioned their impartiality in 1958 after the start of the United States military aid programme to Pakistan.

Now the tables are turned. Pakistan is suggesting that Canadian and Australian observers cannot maintain a neutral posture in view of Commonwealth participation in Western military aid to India, and hints that these should be replaced with recruits from Indonesia, Ghana and Burma.

Nominally, Gen. Nimmo has the strictly technical military role of investigating complaints of cease-fire violations and making confidential reports to India, Pakistan and U.N. Assistant Secretary General Ralph Bunche. In practice, however, Nimmo and his observers find themselves cast in the role of informal mediators and are often in a position to determine whether an incident is quietly buried or mushrooms into a bigger explosion.

Nimmo recently stepped quietly into the simmering controversy between India and Pakistan over the use of armed civilians to get around the cease-fire regulations. While not pointing the finger at either side, Nimmo has pointedly reaffirmed earlier rulings defining all paramilitary personnel as military within the terms of the cease-fire. This would include the heavily armed policemen now installed in the Indian customs checkpost at Balakot.

India Crowding Line

Behind the Balakot dispute lies a basic political conflict between the Pakistani conception of the cease-fire line as a provisional military delimitation solely intended to separate the two armies pending a Kashmir plebiscite, and the Indian attempt to treat the line as a de facto international border.

The establishment of the Balakot post was a gesture of Indian determination to administer all of the territory, right up to the cease-fire line. Pakistan has responded at Balakot and Chaknot, 150 miles north, with calculated intrusions across the line.

Pakistan cannot respect the cease-fire line as a de facto administrative boundary without jettisoning its claim to Indian-held Kashmir areas and acquiescing for all practical purposes in the perpetual division of the state.

The validity of the 1947 decision by Kashmir's late Hindu maharaja Hari Singh to accede to India has been consistently challenged by Pakistan. After the Rawalpindi-backed tribal invasion 21 October 1947 followed by protracted hostilities in the state, failed to shake India's hold, the battleground shifted to the United Nations and the diplomatic arena.

India took the issue of the tribal invasion to the UN in the first instance and made the initial proposal for self-determination. But New Delhi has progressively backed away from the plebiscite plan and is now standing pat. In the Indo–Pakistan Kashmir talks earlier this year, India sought to get a settlement limited to modifications of the cease-fire line.

Difficult to Defend

The Indian fear expressed here is that Pakistan will now resort to guerrilla warfare tactics in an effort to maintain tension along the cease-fire line without the risks of a clear-cut Kashmir invasion. Logistically, the rough terrain in western Kashmir would be difficult to defend against sustained guerrilla-style raids.

Major Rawat keeps copies of Che Guevara's account of the Cuban insurrection and Mao Tse-tung's guerrilla warfare texts on a shelf in his bunker high on a hill opposite Balakot. At the Burejal Post to the south, the commander is Major R.S. Tyagi, who has just returned from two years as a military observer on the staff of the International Control Commission in South Viet-Nam. 'The topography is different,' he says, 'but the problem could turn out to be something like the same sort of thing.'

Talk of a 'Militia'

And the pro-Pakistan Azad Kashmir regime at Muzaffarabad is talking noisily in terms of a guerrilla-style 'war of liberation'. K.H. Khurshid, President of Azad Kashmir, told his governing Liberation League 23 November that all ex-servicemen in Pakistan held portions of the disputed Himalayan state should be organized immediately into a border militia.

Pakistan does not permit foreign correspondents to visit Azad Kashmir areas adjacent to the cease-fire line and my movements in Azad Kashmir were restricted to Muzaffarabad. A Pakistan government spokesman in Rawalpindi explained that India lets correspondents tour the line because India 'is on trial. It is not up to us to prove anything, and there would be no point in people going there.'

The proposal to call up ex-servicemen holds a special significance in the rough and ready Azad Kashmir environment. In pre-Independence days, the British Indian army drew heavily on the rugged hillmen of the Poonch and Mirpur districts, both of them now part of Pakistan-held Kashmir territory.

Poonch Is Objective

Moslems in the Poonch countryside staged the revolt against Hindu princely rule in Kashmir that inspired the intervention of Pakistan-assisted Pathan tribal raiders 21 October 1947. Their ambition now is to recapture Poonch, which was split from its natural hinterland to the west in 1949 by the UN cease-fire line.

Indian troops fought off a Pakistani assault on Poonch town for a year in the Kashmir war of 1947–48. As a result, the cease-fire line isolates the town from traditionally-linked market centres in what is now Azad Kashmir.

The artificiality of the status of Poonch town is aggravated by the fact that its old road links with nearby Srinagar, now the capital of Indian-held Kashmir, were also cut off by the cease-fire demarcation. A 21-mile loop of Pakistan territory reaches across the Poonch–Srinagar road, and to supply Poonch, Indian army trucks have to make the 157-mile run over rocky Himalayan terrain all the way from Jammu in the plains.

A Desolate Contrast

Although Pakistan controlled most of the Poonch and Mirpur ranges of western Kashmir at the time of the cease-fire, India held the lion's share of the state, including the fairy-tale Vale of Kashmir. The Vale, centring around Srinagar, has thrived as a tourist mecca, with palatial hotels and a busy houseboat trade on flower-lined canals.

Muzaffarabad offers a desolate contrast to the lush prosperity of Srinagar. It is just a temporary stopping off point on the way to Srinagar in the minds of Azad Kashmir leaders, and the thought of making it into a tourist centre or more than a provisional political headquarters runs against the official ideology.

The only place in town to stay overnight is a seven-room government guest house of barracks-like simplicity alongside the cluster of makeshift hutments housing the administrative offices of the Azad Kashmir government. Nearly all of the thirty-eight names entered in the guest book for 1963 are those of diplomats, journalists or Pakistan officials.

~

James Cameron
The Death of Nehru

The Daily Herald
28 May 1964

I HAVE BEEN dreading the moment when I should have to do this, as I knew some day I must, as increasingly over the past few weeks the time drew clearly nearer.

It is the custom of our trade, when a great man dies, to enshrine him in phrases long prepared, the elegiac print, and this I had often thought to do for Jawaharlal Nehru, whom I honoured—the forms of words, the analysis of this complex and graceful person, the true tribute to a long affection. I knew I would not do it well.

Now that the words are needed it seems impossible to say more than that Nehru is gone at last, and we are immeasurably the poorer. Not for the loss of the frail phantom he had latterly become, but of the luminous, elaborate, obstinate, inspirational human being of the brave days when no one denied him his greatness.

How to capture in a handful of words the character of this extraordinary man, compounded of every paradox, himself not one man but many, torn every way between the good and the possible, the real and the imaginary, the triumph and the failure?

I knew him many years—not well, perhaps, who did? He used to say: 'Sometimes I quite baffle myself by my own behaviour.' He shared with Gandhi the long luxurious reveries of self-examination and he could be merciless in his findings.

Long years ago a cutting analysis of the Nehru character appeared in a magazine; it probed every secret corner of his intellectual arrogance, his vanity, his impatience. It was years before it became known that the anonymous writer was himself.

The conflict within Jawaharlal Nehru was more than that of all liberal men who find themselves in a dilemma for which they feel partly responsible and from which they see no immediate escape.

He was too many people within himself—the Indian who became a European, the rich patrician who became a mass demagogue, the Brahmin who became a socialist, the socialist who was sustained by capital, the humanist who tried to weld a secular state from a land of the most tormented religious medievalism.

Seventeen years ago he undertook the incredible task of trying to make a viable democracy out of the most fantastic pattern of ex-Imperial wastelands, kingdoms, princely states and minor satrapies the world ever knew.

Whether he succeeded or not is yet to be determined.

The life and times of Jawaharlal Nehru have been described and defined a thousand times: the elegantly aristocratic background, the strange transmutations of Harrow and Cambridge, the plunge of dedication into the Independence movement, the long years of imprisonment.

Jawaharlal differed from Gandhi in that nationalism was not to be the end, but the beginning: how to build from 400 million mainly illiterate Indians in a land of grinding poverty the first socialist democracy in all Asia?

There the frustrations began that were never to cease.

He was melancholy, irascible, intolerant of lesser men. He seemed to the very end incapable of delegating responsibility; his enemies blamed his jealousy of power, his friends that there was no one else capable of responsibility. However that might be, nothing grew in the shadow of that tremendous tree, with the dire result we see in India today.

But he was once needlessly and gently kind to me. I was returning from the Korean war, deeply and nervously riven by personal conflicts of my own.

Nehru recognized this condition; the half-hour talk drifted into hour after hour of quiet and healing reflection and simple talk. He seemed to me then, and for years to come, to be the only man in the business who clung to the more reasonable values of politics, perversely pursuing the principle of humanity without appearing to mock it.

What he said then about Korea could without changing a syllable be said today about Vietnam:

'When you enter the realm of the military mind there's always that impulse to go the limit, and possibly betray the object for which you're fighting the war.

'War itself is never an objective; victory is not an objective; you fight to remove the obstruction between you and your objective. If you let victory become the end in itself then you've gone astray and forgotten what you were originally fighting about.

'It's *always* wrong to assume you can succeed by pursuing military means to the last; every war on earth has shown that. There may have been soldiers who were great men, but I don't think the military outlook ever solved any major problem in the world.

'And yet—here in India we've spent our lives trying pretty imperfectly to follow the spirit of Gandhi. He talked of non-violence—and here we're in charge of a government that keeps armies and air forces and indulges in violence pretty often. What are we to do about it?'

Years later that disenchantment reached a special depth of hell for Jawaharlal Nehru with the Chinese war, and from then on he flagged and failed and declined. He who was honoured above most men died at last in the dreamy failures of regret.

Once upon a time no man could have believed that the cry 'Nehru get out!' could be heard in the streets of New Delhi—but it was. His deepest and closest friends protested that under a sick and powerless leader, who to his death refused to hint at a successor, India was drifting into a chaos of non-administration.

I think his heart had been broken long before that unhappy yesterday, when it stopped.

I shall never forget him in my life. If he was over-idolized, as he sometimes was, he was equally cruelly outraged at the end. All I know is that somewhere between the excesses and threats that hem us all around there was, for many splendid years, something in politics that put a higher value on principle than on expediency, and that was, like Nehru, very rare.

~

Selig S. Harrison

Servants, Servants Everywhere and Not a Leisure Moment

The Washington Post
27 September 1964

New Delhi: 'BUT MADAM, THERE Are No Fish Knives!' is the title of a memoir written by a local American memsahib and currently going the rounds here in a newsletter put out by the memsahibs to cheer each other.

It is the heart-rending tale of one woman's efforts to live up to what was expected of her by a venerable Indian bearer (butler) who had worked most of his life for the pukka sahibs.

The new American sahibs and their families are generally deplorable from a bearer's point of view.

They don't possess fish knives, and, in some cases, don't know what they are. Their children go riding in jeans, not jodhpurs, and the family eats at six, not ten. They are afflicted with incomprehensible do-it-yourself urges. In time, some of them even manage to get control of their own households.

From a distance the thought of a large staff of cut-rate servants charms the trapped housewife from Washington or Dubuque, who imagines herself without a care in the world, her every whim attended to in one glorious, uninterrupted tropical siesta. But disillusion comes quickly as the implications of a caste-bound society sink in.

The division of labour dictates that a cook cooks but doesn't wash dishes or serve. The bearer serves, dusts and acts as major domo but wouldn't think of cooking or putting his hands in dishwater. The sweeper sweeps and scrubs but disdains the laundry tub.

In our house, it takes seven servants to do the work, and the grand total of the servant population, children included, comes at the moment to fifteen.

Theoretically, the bearer performs the managerial chores, but the theory rarely proves out in practice. Most of my wife's would-be siesta time is spent sorting out feuds, doctoring the cook's sniffles and keeping a kindly eye out for petty larceny.

It is also necessary to play your part as a sort of baronial moneylender, doling out advances to meet perpetual emergencies.

The mali (gardener) told us recently that he would have to sell his water buffalo if we didn't lend him Rs 75 ($15) to help pay for the resurrection of his ancestral hut in a nearby village. Monsoon floods have washed away half of the structure, and Namku, as his family's only urban breadwinner, would lose face if he failed to come up with ready cash. There are also special financial problems of Harpal, the cook, who maintains two wives in his village and thinks we don't know; and Hamid, the bearer, a Moslem whose aging wife's diabetes keeps him constantly in thrall to Hindu quacks.

The problem for the memsahib is that if she lets the quality of mercy rain too predictably, her charges soon get so deeply in hock that we literally could not afford to fire them. This rather offbeat approach to job security is but one of the endlessly unfolding aspects of what we have come to respect as a virtually foolproof system.

There is the story of the man down the street who decided that he did not need a Gurkha chowkidhar (watchman) and that this was a logical place to save Rs 90 per month.

Oddly enough, his is the one house in the block which suffers repeated thefts, arranged, or so some say, by a sort of underground chowkidhars union functioning in the area.

You soon find that your bargaining power with your cook is sharply circumscribed by the fact that relatively few domestics here know any English and that the few who do are in great demand.

The best of these are the Mughs, or Baruas, a tightly knit clan of Buddhists originally from what is now East Pakistan. Legend has it that the 100-odd Mughs in Delhi gather regularly by moonlight beside the tomb of Mogul Emperor Humayun to fix the grocery prices which will be paid by all memsahibs for the week.

The Mughs help each other out when there is a big party by quietly pooling dishes and cutlery. A memsahib friend of ours was astounded one recent evening out to find the salad plates from her best bone china stacked on her host's buffet table.

The clan also blackballs families with one defect or another, and it was our misfortune to offend our Mugh by suggesting that he dust the dining room table. We never got another to apply.

Our present cook is an ex-sweeper who graduated to cooking as the result of a democratic impulse on the part of a former American ambassador, Loy Henderson. He has been passed on from one family of new sahibs to another and defends his new status with a Brahman's hauteur toward the rest of the staff.

The lack of privacy resulting from an outsized contingent of domestics maddens at first but gives way to an awareness that you are living, willy-nilly, in a cosmopolitan species of the Hindu joint family.

For all of your efforts to regulate the movements of the staff, you never know when an unexpected encounter will occur. Kalu Ram, our sweeper, cooperates by coughing and clearing his throat loudly if we are about to enter a room in which he is working.

A particularly delectable young mother of our acquaintance wandered out to the refrigerator in her negligee at four o'clock one morning to get the bottle for her infant and met up with the mali. He was puttering about in the living room, arranging and rearranging his marigolds, and seemed mildly annoyed at the intrusion.

One of the most portentous aspects of the situation in our case has been the impact of fawning solicitude on our children, who have been quick to claim their due as chota (little) sahib and missy sahib.

Hamid, the moustachioed Moslem bearer, acts as a built-in grandfather, delightedly sabotaging parental authority by taking an openly indulgent view of the most heinous offences and treating them to endless snacks delivered with a flourish on a tray. He has nearly persuaded them that it is immoral to pick up and carry anything bigger than a marble with their own hands.

It struck us as strange that he was pushing soft drinks so vigorously until we discovered that our full quota of rebates on the bottles was slowly being whittled down.

It is all very droll until you are suddenly struck across the face with something close to home reminding you of your very tragic surroundings.

Kalu Ram, our sweeper, is a bent, harried untouchable who would be doing most of the other servants' work if it were not for our intervention. He has had trouble supporting four children and would rather not have had his fifth child in August. He shuns what is known here as 'family planning'. Unbeknown to us, his wife Shanti, who works across town as a sweeper, recently decided to deal with the problem of caring for her new son by toting him under arm on her long, daily trudge to work.

When it rained hard one week, as only an Indian rain can at monsoon time, the drenched baby caught double pneumonia and died. We later learned that the child had been left all day with the children of servant friends while Shanti worked nearby. Sweepers, we were told, don't often go to doctors.

The constant presence of poverty and despair on your doorstep imparts an oppressive sense of guilt and frustration to life here which no amount of benevolent paternalism ever fully removes.

One sad story follows another in dismal succession. You can assuage your guilt to the extent that you are able to give your empathy and share financial crises as they arise, and it is precisely this that had never been possible with Kalu Ram. The language barrier had always kept us from entering into his life and world.

He was so near and yet so far, too proud to come to us with his problems through the humiliating good offices of other servants. When the bearer would grudgingly consent to translate, a torrent of paragraphs from Kalu Ram became a sentence and a shrug. And so we have started trying to beat the system, in our way, by enlisting the help of an Indian friend to serve as occasional interpreter.

Though the climax has passed, our lines of communication are now open.

~

Peter Hess
In the Famine Region of North-East India

Neue Zuercher Zeitung (Switzerland)
20 December 1966

THE VILLAGE UNTHOO has a population of around 1500. It is the centre of the eponymous gram panchayat consisting of six other villages and is situated 10 kilometres north-west of the district headquarters Aurangabad in the Gaya district, one of the regions in south Bihar most severely affected by the drought. A feeling of gloom has descended over the people here. Their stocks will soon be depleted. Their fields are lying fallow. The continued drought has rendered the earth as hard as stone.

Under normal circumstances the famous Patna rice should have been harvested at the end of November, the most important harvest of the year. Withered rice plants bear witness to the destruction created by the drought. At the most, the meagre crop can be used as fodder.

Failure of the Monsoon

Between June and November there is normally 150 centimetres of rain, but this year there was less than 40 centimetres. Till now, the Adri canal which flows past the village provided sufficient water for irrigation. Even this canal has been completely dry for months since it is fed by a river that is in turn dependent on rain.

There is only one source of water in Unthoo that does not depend on rain: groundwater. Because of the canal there was no reason until now to invest in costly and doubtful drilling operations. Several small hand pumps installed in the village merely ensure a supply of drinking water. Since traditional sources of water have gone dry this year the government implemented a programme for the construction of irrigation wells. However, no one in Unthoo has received any such subsidy. The block development officer who is responsible for the development plans of the block (consisting of seven gram panchayats) states that there is no money available to help finance these wells. However, he repeatedly encouraged the farmers to build the wells themselves and held out hope for a government subsidy amounting to Rs 600 per well. The farmers, however, contend that there are too many problems. It is possible that there will not be enough water even at a depth of 10 metres.

Recently, when a well was being dug in a neighbouring village the shaft caved in and buried two workers alive. The farmers are also doubtful whether the block development officer will actually arrange for the government subsidy. Electrical pumps, without which the well will benefit only about 0.2 hectares, are not easily available and are also expensive—one with a 5 horsepower motor costs Rs 1800. In addition, there is still no electricity available; there is only the promise of a connection on the condition that at least twenty wells are ready for operation. The high cost of oil, on the other hand, makes the running of diesel pumps prohibitively expensive. Under these circumstances only the two largest landowners of the village, members of the local upper caste of Rajputs, have begun to construct wells.

The battle for the winter harvest, the so-called kharif harvest, is already lost in Unthoo. The question now is whether sowing can begin for the spring harvest in April, the rabi harvest, which consists of some rice, wheat, pulses and potatoes. Dire straits have compelled some farmers to use the seed-corn as food. Hopes were revived recently when there were 2 centimetres of rainfall and some farmers are trying to plough their fields. Everything now depends on whether the winter rains reach Bihar in the days to follow.

Stocks Consumed

Unthoo's cattle population consists of 200 cows, only half of which give 1.5 litres of milk a day, 300 oxen, 150 goats and 100 buffaloes which produce 3 litres of milk daily. Since there is practically no grass, straw from the rice plant is the most important form of fodder, but these stocks will not last for more than four weeks.

The villagers only have meagre reserves of food grains and money. Only the six families who own 20 hectares of land are confident of surviving the crisis on their own. Already some villagers can only afford to eat one meal a day. Kalhat Yadav, a farmer who owns 1.2 hectares of land, eats Sattu once a day—a concoction of pulverized grain cooked with water, salt and chilli powder. Everyone in the village knows that those belonging to the lowest caste (Dalits) eat only once a day. There are no details about the situation among the middle class: members of this group try to conceal the extent of their distress. The landless families who live from hand-to-mouth are severely affected. Normally they work for the landlords, but because of the drought they have not been able to find employment. Many of them therefore resorted to the employment projects initiated by the state. Byas Vyas Dusad, a landless Dalit, did not, however, receive the daily wage of Rs 1.75 allocated by the planners in Patna. He was given only Re 1 and sometimes Rs 1.25. After the recent rains some landless labourers found temporary jobs again with the landlords for which they get 1.5 kilograms of wheat a day.

Unchanging Taboos

Social prestige renders the situation of those members of the higher castes who own a small amount of land more difficult. Ram Jag Singh, a forty-year-old Rajput, has three hectares of land which did not yield a harvest this time. His stocks will soon be depleted. There has been no response to his loan application made weeks ago. The status of his family, however, does not allow him to benefit from the employment programme since it consists of manual labour of the lowest kind. He would rather die of starvation in his hut than lose his honour, he asserts. Social taboos retain their power even in situations of extreme distress. Ram Jag Singh is not aware of Chief Minister Sahay's programme to receive wheat against a kind of promissory note that can be repaid with wheat at the next harvest.

Unpopular Government Shops

Although wheat supplies sent to Bihar could provide for the minimum needs of at least twenty million people through the fair-price shops, hardly anyone in Unthoo buys wheat at subsidized rates from the ration shop. The ration cards, which Patna claims to have distributed, don't exist as yet. The block development officer in charge of this explains that on account of insufficient supplies it has hitherto only been possible to help a small and particularly needy section of the population. The ration cards will be ready next week, he says. It is surprising that even the poorest landless labourers don't go to the ration shop and prefer to buy their wheat in the open market in nearby Aurangabad. This could indicate a lack of faith in the state distribution system. Only one family in Unthoo has been given the red ration card meant for those among the needy who cannot work and which entitles them to free rations.

A Family's Budget

Even if the ration system were to work there are still enormous problems. Another informant, Abdul Khan, lives in Aurangabad where he can buy his provisions regularly from the fair-price shop. He works as a waiter in a government guest-house and earns Rs 66 a month with which he supports the six members of his family as well as his parents. The ration card entitles him to 15 kilos of wheat every fortnight at the rate of 65 paise per kilo. He actually needs double this amount, but he cannot afford to buy the required quantities of extra wheat in the open market where a kilo of wheat would cost him Rs 1.10. Fruit does not figure in his budget. Rice, which he prefers to wheat, is only bought for special occasions since it costs, depending on the quality, between Rs 1.60 and Rs 2.20 per kilo. The daily menu is supplemented with the cheapest vegetable available—generally potatoes or cauliflower. As a Muslim he also eats meat: a kilo of buffalo meat costs Re 1. In addition, Abdul has to pay school fees for his son amounting to Rs 5 per month. Thus, hardly anything is left over for clothes and other occasional expenditure. He saves on rent, however, by living in his simple hut.

A Family's Distress

At present the physical effects of starvation can only be seen in extreme cases that are generally hushed up. Sixty-year-old Munshi lives in a mud hut in Unthoo together with his blind son and his grandchildren. Till now they were able to earn a modest living by farming a leased patch of land. Now, however, they are left with nothing. It is common knowledge in the village that Munshi only eats once in a while. The villagers, who are also experiencing hard times, don't offer any help. Further enquiries reveal that he has not eaten anything for days except Sattu. When he hears that the block development officer has come to the village Munshi approaches him supported by two men and throws himself at the officer's feet. Whether from agitation or weakness he is unable to speak and only babbles khana, khana (food, food) while opening his mouth and pointing to his tongue.

The block development officer says that the mukhia, the head of the gram panchayat, should have reported such cases for the issue of a red ration card; he fails to understand how this family's distress could have escaped the notice of the administration. One gets the clear impression that government officials, who are like demi-gods to the villagers, have very little contact with the poorer sections of society.

~

John Slee
The 'Lion of Kashmir' Resumes His Fight

The Sydney Morning Herald
8 March 1968

FOR WEEKS SINCE his release in January, Sheik Abdullah, the sixty-five-year-old 'Lion of Kashmir' who was given a hero's welcome on his return to Kashmir last Monday week, has been forced into a cat-and-mouse game with the Indian government.

The government is watching the Sheik, waiting for the first false move which will, according to India's view of her interests in Kashmir, require his rearrest and reimprisonment.

Mrs Gandhi and her cabinet colleagues have not wavered from the official stand that Kashmir is an integral part of India and that its future therefore is not negotiable. After fourteen years' almost continuous detention, the Sheik is still fighting for self-determination for Kashmir. He insists that the Indian government has gone back on Nehru's promise of a plebiscite.

The Sheik was arrested first in 1953, again in 1958 and most recently in May, 1965, after his return from Algiers, where he met the Chinese Premier, Chou En-lai. On each occasion the Sheik enjoyed freedom for only a short time before the government rearrested him.

Implications

Over the years, particularly since the 1962 border war with China, Indian resistance to any move to take Kashmir out of the Indian

Union has hardened, because of Kashmir's strategic importance and its implications for the very concept of a unified India.

Across the border, Pakistan, which occupies and administers about one-third of Kashmir, calling it 'Azad' or 'Free' Kashmir, looks to the day when the rest of the predominately Moslem state will be 'liberated' from India and merged with West Pakistan.

Pakistan is probably no less apprehensive than India of Sheik Abdullah's intentions in Kashmir, since what he wants—complete independence from both India and Pakistan—is just as unacceptable to Pakistan as it is to India. But for the moment the Sheik is India's problem.

India says that since Mr Nehru gave his promise of a plebiscite in Kashmir circumstances have so changed—particularly since the state is divided by the cease-fire line—that it is now impossible to hold a plebiscite of all the people in the state.
No circumstance can take away a people's basic right to self-determination. If the government of India now wants to go back on its promises we have no power to stop it. They have their army there and we have no guns. We have been betrayed many times; history is full of betrayals; but ultimately truth will prevail.

After such a long period under detention are you sure you still have the support of the mass of the people in Kashmir?
Quite sure. We must see now just what the political climate of the state is, but there is no doubt that the freedom for which we have been fighting since 1931 is still longed for by the vast majority of the people.

You have often said that in pressing for self-determination for Kashmir you do not want to harm India. Most Indians seem to think your activities very damaging to Indian unity.
We want to do nothing to harm India; but we will not give up our struggle as long as India continues to maintain the attitudes of a colonial master. We do not deny the facts of geography. Kashmir is part of the subcontinent of India in the same sense that Pakistan is. There should be peace between all the diverse peoples living here; but none should be subject to others.

If you achieve independence for the parts of Kashmir now administered as a part of India, Azad Kashmir would also have to be returned to you?

Yes, Jammu and Kashmir includes the areas on both sides of the cease-fire line: all the areas occupied by Pakistan and all those occupied by India.

What about the 2000 square miles of Azad Kashmir ceded by Pakistan to China in the Sino–Pakistan border agreement in 1962?
I spoke to Premier Chou En-lai about this in Algiers. There is a clause in the border agreement which makes the borders renegotiable by the ultimate government of Kashmir. China negotiated with Pakistan only because at that time, as now, Pakistan was in control of the area in question.

Will you meet President Ayub Khan of Pakistan again now that you have been released?
No useful purpose would be served by my going to Pakistan just now.

You seem to have set yourself again on a collision course with the government.
I am not afraid of collisions.

The Sheik said this with a broad smile and rose from his chair to conclude the interview, managing to look a full head taller than his already impressive 6 feet 3 inches height, but unable to conceal an underlying heaviness in his heart, as he set out again on a course which seems certain to bring him new disappointments.

~

John Rogers
China Sets the Pace for India in Space Race

The Hong Kong Standard
29 July 1970

SPURRED BY THE launching of China's earth satellite last April, India is expanding its space programme and hopes to join the space club in 1974.

The start will be modest—the orbiting of a 66-pound scientific satellite the size of a football at an altitude of 248 miles above the earth.

But the Atomic Energy Commission (AEC), which also handles India's space programme, plans a more advanced rocket system able to hurl a 2645-pound communications satellite payload into orbit by the end of this decade.

Not Known

Plans for speeding up the programme—pledged to an angry Parliament by the Indian government after the Chinese space shot—have not been announced.

But after the Chinese launch, AEC Chairman, Dr Vikram A. Sarabhai, proposed a ten-year nuclear and space programme which would increase production to 2700 megawatts of nuclear power by 1980 and see the lift-off of India's first satellite by 1974.

Experts said the programme would enable India to make nuclear weapons at any time she wanted during this decade.

But controversy over whether India should go nuclear has died down—temporarily, at least—following firm government statements that the build-up of atomic energy was intended only for peaceful uses.

Alongside the development of new atomic power stations, AEC scientists are working on the four-stage rocket which will lift India's first satellite into orbit in three and a half years.

After the current static firing tests, the third-stage motor will be test-flown from a new launching site being built at Sriharikota island about 50 miles north of Madras on the east coast.

Development of the Sriharikota complex—whose launching range is expected to be ready by the end of this year—includes a solid propellant plant for large booster rockets.

All facilities needed to handle multi-stage vehicles and satellite systems, such as tracking radar telemetry stations and a rocket control centre, are expected to be in operation by 1973–74.

A satellite tracking station is to be built in the Andaman and Nicobar Islands in the Bay of Bengal.

After the trail-blazing scientific satellite, scientists plan to launch India's first communications satellite with overseas technical aid, to be followed by satellites made entirely in India after 1980.

Launching

The launching of the first satellite will be the product of experience gained in the firing of over 200 low-level atmospheric research rockets from the Thumba launching pad in Kerala state with collaboration from the United States, the Soviet Union, France and Japan.

The first Indian-made two-stage rocket, a Centaure, was launched from Thumba last year, two years after the development of India's own small Rohini rockets.

The cost of India's space programme is relatively low—only Rs 300 million (£17 million) have been authorized for 1969 to 1974—and later developments are expected to send the space budget shooting up.

Late Start

But, says Dr Sarabhai, 'because we have started late in the day, we have been able to draw on the accumulated experience of other countries'.

Apart from its importance for scientific and possible military uses, the space and satellite programme is designed to improve India's communications and bring television into some 450,000 villages.

India's first earth station for the international Indian ocean satellite Intelsat-3, is due to be completed at Arvi near Poona next October and another is to be built in the Himalayan foothills of Uttar Pradesh.

Under an agreement with the United States, India will use a NASA satellite for a twelve-month period around 1973 to beam instructional television to major cities and about 5000 villages.

An Atomic Energy Commission plan now being studied by the information ministry would bring television to community sets throughout the country in about ten years time.

~

Erhard Haubold

Model of a Guerrilla Revolt
How a South Indian Mountain Tribe Is Enticed by Maoists

Neue Zuercher Zeitung (Germany)
24 January 1971

Vishakapatnam: THE DRIVER OF our jeep has put the vehicle in high gear. We are moving forward slowly—maximum speed 10 kilometres per hour—on a dirt road which in stretches does not deserve even this name. On both sides of the road the thick undergrowth of the jungle makes it difficult to see anything; on the horizon the high mountain ranges are barely visible: 'You are the first foreigner on the Indian *Ho-Chi-Minh-path*,' says the official accompanying us, a member of the Indian Administrative Service (IAS) from which the most capable government servants are recruited. There isn't a soul in sight and the few villages we pass through are remarkable only because of their tongue-twisting names: Mondemkhalli, Neelakantapuram and Seethampeta. But, the peace and beauty of the landscape are deceptive: only a few months ago our journey would only have been possible under police protection and at night it is dangerous even today. It was here that a few thousand Naxalites who would like to bring about a revolution on the Chinese model engaged in bloody battles with the police.

The 'Ho-Chi-Minh-path' begins a few hours ride away from the provincial town of Srikakulam and advances inland about 60 kilometres to the north-east. Srikakulam, a previously unknown town situated on the Bay of Bengal in south-east India, became the starting point of the communist guerrilla movement in the union state of Andhra Pradesh. This small city (80,000 inhabitants) will go down in the history of Indian communism like Kerala, West Bengal, Calcutta and, especially, Naxalbari where the first Indian peasants' revolt broke

**The Naxalite movement started in 1967 in West Bengal and quickly spread to Orrisa and Andhra Pradesh. It is still active in many districts of India (See Somini Sengupta pp 367).*

out in 1967 giving the name 'Naxalites' to insurgents in the entire country.

Andhra Pradesh hit the headlines for the first time in November 1969. On Diwali day 500 members of the Girijan tribe armed with spears, axes, knives and a few pistols marched down from the mountains into the plains. Shortly before midnight they surrounded the small village with the unpronounceable name, Banjarayuvarajapuram, on the border between Andhra Pradesh and Orissa. A small detachment crept towards the house of the richest farmer, broke open the door and stabbed him to death. The Girijans, partly still semi-wild nomads and descendants of India's original inhabitants, then cut off the victim's head and hung it up on the veranda. A woman member of the troop, whose husband had been shot dead by the police recently, dipped a finger in the farmer's blood and wrote 'Long live Mao' on the wall of the house.

From then on there was no looking back. A different village was attacked almost every night by the guerrillas. Their preferred victims were landlords, money lenders and policemen. These people were murdered in the most brutal fashion, often along with their entire families, and the women Naxalites proved to be particularly merciless. Afterwards, the guerrillas looted the houses, distributed the plunder among the poor in the village and burnt all statements of debt. By doing this these late descendants of Robin Hood garnered a great deal of sympathy and won over new members. For a long time the police were powerless and didn't dare follow the Naxalites into their mountain hideouts. Law and order could only be established gradually once the central government had sent a 3000-strong detachment of the Central Reserve Police as reinforcements. The big question, important also for India's future, is how mountain tribes cut off for centuries from the outer world could become cold-blooded murderers and, that too, in the name of an imported ideology.

Disadvantaged Tribes

In the reservations of Andhra Pradesh, known as Agencies, there are about 1.5 million members of different tribes: this amounts to 4.5 per cent of the entire population of the state. Dominant among these semi-wild people are the 80,000 strong Girijans who inhabit 500 square miles of land and are divided into different communities of which the Savara, Jatapu and Koya are the most well-known. At a superficial glance the Girijans lead a happy life untouched by the materialism of the plains. The men walk upright and their faces display courage. Apart from a loin-cloth they need no other clothing. They like to drink a lot.

The unmarried girls among the Savara shave their heads in order to appear as unattractive as possible to their suitors. According to an old tribal ritual cohabitation can only take place during the day and only on particular days. Child-marriage is the norm and one finds many widows who are not yet fourteen years old. Re-marriage is, however, permitted in contrast to the Hindu custom prevalent earlier. The women, also almost completely naked, are fanatical cigar-smokers; they can keep the glowing end of a cigar in their mouths for hours which has led to a number of cases of cancer.

If one looks more closely one sees what a miserable life the Girijans have been leading for generations. Their food consists mainly of various roots, mangoes and tamarind seeds. The Koya even eat the bark of trees and lizards. Leprosy and other diseases are widespread. It is superfluous to mention that the rate of illiteracy among them—96 per cent—is the highest in the country. Most of the members of the tribe gather nuts, fruit, honey, flowers and hides and exchange these in the weekly markets in the plains for sugar, salt and other food items. Others hire themselves out as agricultural labour. Before the 'revolt' the daily wage was not even 15 centimes. As a result their debts to traders and money-lenders kept mounting. Those who could not repay the credit and the exorbitant interest on time lost their land.

Although a law of 1917 lays down that the Girijans can sell their land to non-tribals only with the permission of the district authorities, the law is seldom applied. Forest officers and exploitative traders were their only contact with the outer world and no one told the Girijans about their rights. 'The bureaucrats in the state capital knew the region at best through binoculars,' remarks our IAS companion. The Indian constitution provides special privileges for the 'scheduled castes and tribes', for example with a fixed quota of parliamentary seats. Often, however, the petty rulers (rajas) living in the plains were given a seat if they could prove a connection with a tribe, even if it went back many generations. Financial help from the government also flowed into corrupt channels in the plains.

Struggle According to Mao's Textbook

This was the situation at the beginning of 1967 when a teacher from the plains, Vempatapu Satyanarayana, espoused the cause of the Girijans. In order to gain their trust he married a woman each from the two most important communities, the Savara and Jatapu. Very soon he was a recognized leader. Impressed by his success the radical-left communists persuaded him to join their movement. The idealistic teacher's campaign gained an ideological content and Naxalite leaders from West Bengal like Kanu Sanyal (who has since been arrested) and Charu Mazumdar (for whose capture there is a large reward) were frequent guests in Srikakulam. Satyanarayana's demand for the return of illegally obtained land to the Girijans alarmed the big landlords. In October 1967 they attacked a group of tribals on their way to a communist meeting. Two Girijans were shot dead and disaster then took its course. The teacher organized his followers in guerrilla gangs which had about 8000 members at the height of the movement. They were joined by young, politically inspired intellectuals from the villages in the plains, among them many students and sons of rich families. The surgeon Chaganti Bhaskara Rao abandoned a successful practice in Guntur, joined the Naxalites and became 'famous' for the elegance with which he chopped off the heads of rich farmers.

On the whole, the Naxalites in Andhra Pradesh would have commanded a guerrilla army of about 10,000 men and women. The Chinese news agency has often praised the 'red revolution of Srikakulam' and called the district a 'lighthouse for the suffering Indian people'. The Naxalite leaders have made no secret of the fact that the uprising was organized according to Mao's teachings. The terrain with its absence of approach roads also proved very useful. On the 'Ho-Chi-Minh-path' surrounded by jungle every police troop became an easy target. The Naxalites set up a courier system, carried out intensive training in guerrilla warfare and established hideouts. In a short time they had an area of more than 100 square kilometres under their control. For a long time the source of their weapons couldn't be established. In the meantime it has become clear that these didn't come from China. The insurgents plundered the stocks of the rajas and landlords, manufactured simple muskets from water-pipes and also used homemade bombs, spears and knives.

In the long run the Naxalites had to yield to the better-equipped police. The villagers also turned against them after the many brutal murders and with this they lost an important operational base. According to the Indian government 110 Naxalites have been killed so far by the police in Andhra Pradesh, which is not always fastidious in its methods. The murder of their colleagues had awakened feelings of revenge; in addition, large rewards had been announced for the capture of fugitives. The remark 'shot while trying to escape' appeared with suspicious frequency in police reports. According to conservative estimates at least 250 to 300 people have been killed so far in Srikakulam. Around 200 guerrillas have been imprisoned in the nearby city of Vishakapatnam and are awaiting judicial sentence. What will happen to them? 'Hang the communists, but let the innocent Girijans go free,' says our companion.

The Lesson of Srikakulam

The Maoists have shown how a small committed group of extremists can organize thousands of politically ignorant people who feel that the government has neglected them. They are then willing to fight against the 'authorities' and against the 'wealthy'. This is the lesson to be learnt from the revolt which has been put down for now. There are many 'Srikakulams' in India and Asia with impenetrable forests and a desperate populace. The Naxalite-problem cannot be solved by the police but only by quick and tangible economic improvements. Delhi has introduced the first steps for this. Government land lying fallow is to be distributed to the tribals and a senior official has been entrusted with the responsibility of ensuring the return of all Girijan land to the original owners. The government is also considering putting a stop to the role of money-lenders and channelizing credit at low interest-rates through the Girijan co-operative which already has 30,000 families as members and is doing good work. It buys the harvest products from the tribals at a fixed rate and sets up warehouses in regions that are not easily accessible.

The most interesting and, if it fails, also the most dangerous government experiment began three months ago. Since then about 2000 Girijans are living in seven 'regrouped villages' in the plains. They have been brought down from their mountain hideouts, not entirely without force as is to be expected, in order initially to bring the Naxalite movement under control. In the long run, the government would like to have as many families as possible settle permanently in the valley. We had the opportunity to visit a 'regrouped village'. In material terms the 250 families there would never have been so well-off. The government distributes rice, kerosene, salt and sugar free of cost and also runs a school. The Girijans did not object to being relocated, but they complained bitterly about some police methods. They had to transport their huts themselves to the valley and weren't allowed to harvest their fields before leaving. They are particularly concerned about the fate of husbands, sons and brothers who are in prison in Vishakapatnam. Although they are under trial prisoners their families cannot visit them. The latter would, in any case, have to walk three hours to the nearest road and then travel four hours by bus. They cannot afford the fare either. 'They aren't communists' was the common refrain we heard in the mix of tribal dialect and Telugu.

Race Against Time

The 'pensioner's life' that the Girijans presently lead is dangerous. They could lose all initiative in the long run. The government will therefore have to organize irrigation, seeds and technical advisors. The milk-cows that they gifted to the village recently were slaughtered the next day: the Girijans didn't have any water and couldn't keep the cows alive. There will be many such problems of co-ordination and corruption at the lower administrative levels will further delay the process of pacification.

The example of Srikakulam shows that India's dramatic race against time will have to be won in the villages and jungles and not in Delhi. If the country arms itself with patience and perseverance—for physical reasons the Girijans cannot work for more than four hours a day—the government has a small but real chance. The tribes of Andhra have lived for millennia in the bitterest poverty. They are grateful for even small improvements. The senior officials, who, in India, are committed and incorruptible, can make a valuable contribution. Our companion, thirty-six years old, speaks English, six tribal dialects and three south Indian languages; he earns 800 Swiss francs a month. In his house there is neither a fan nor an air conditioner. Despite this, he wouldn't like to change places with his colleagues at their desks in the ministry. After our twenty-hour jeep ride he sleeps for four hours and is then back in the jungles. However, there are only 2000 people like him—that is the extent of the Indian Administrative Service—for more than twenty states and almost 550 million people.

~

Peter R. Kann
Dacca Diary

The Wall Street Journal
14 December 1971

Dacca, East Pakistan: *FRIDAY, DEC. 3*: ENTERING ELEVATOR IN Intercontinental Hotel when another reporter runs up to ask, 'Have you heard the war is on?' It's just before 8 p.m. Happen to notice sign by elevator: Happy Hours 6 to 8 p.m. Except Fridays. Rest of evening spent with other journalists clustered around shortwave radio.

Evidently, fighting broke out along border between West Pakistan and India this afternoon. India says Pakistan started it; Pakistan says India. Who knows? But India has been launching limited attacks on East Pakistan border for past ten days. What are you supposed to do when a war starts and the cable office is closed? Play poker. Go to sleep.

SATURDAY, DEC. 4: Day starts early. About 3 a.m. sky lights up with fantastic fireworks display by Pak antiaircraft batteries out by airport. Indian air raid or jumpy ack-ack gunners? Moot question because by breakfast time, Indian MIGs making regular rocket runs on airfield. Makes you wish you were a photographer. MIGs diving through clear blue sky. Little white puffs from the ack-ack. Even couple of inconclusive dogfights above the hotel. Several Indian planes shot down. But every observer has different count. 'Better than Pearl

**When the Indo–Pakistan war broke out in December 1971, Peter Kann was stranded in Dacca until Indian troops took over the country. Due to the difficulties of transmission he kept a diary of the events taking place. They were reprinted by the* Wall Street Journal *at the end of the hostilities and earned Kann a Pulitzer Prize in 1972.*

Harbor,' one of the television types says. Air strikes continue almost hourly rest of day.

Dacca streets deserted except for few military vehicles with palm leaves and other assorted foliage tied to tops. Policeman down the street also sprouting foliage from his cap. Run into Nepalese consul, dean of diplomatic corps in Dacca. He says he arranged a diplomatic-corps conference on the crisis—but cancelled it because of the crisis.

SUNDAY, DEC. 5: Anticlimatic day. Nothing to compare with yesterday's air spectacular. Lots of rumours circulating. One favourite has Indian army columns only 60 miles from Dacca. Someone consults map and discovers Indian border to the east less than 60 miles away. Western families resident in Dacca congregating at Intercontinental. Rumours of planned United Nations relief flight to Bangkok confirmed by UN officials at evening meeting in the bar. A Gregory Peck scene—distinguished grey-haired UN official talking about women and children first. Some of the men buying out hotel bar's Scotch supply at $35 a bottle. It's a stockpiling sort of day.

'Sartre would dig this place,' one reporter says.

Why?

'No exit.'

MONDAY, DEC. 6: Try a road trip to Sibalay about 50 miles west of Dacca. Impression: Pak army bound to lose East Pakistan if only because of logistics. Small army convoys stalled along roadside. Overheated radiators and other mechanical maladies. When convoy stalls, the Bengali farmers flee from nearby fields. Until now army trucks meant search for Mukti Bahini guerrillas, razed villages, civilian massacres. Army hasn't much time for that now. Irony: Bengalis probably safer now that general war is on.

Back at the Intercontinental tonight. Evening talk at the hotel is of UN plane turning back ten minutes out of Dacca because of Indian air strike at airport just before a temporary cease-fire scheduled to go into effect. And Gen. Rao Farman Ali Khan gave an afternoon press conference in which he said Pak forces facing some supply problems, are cut off from West Pakistan for the time being, and on the defensive for the time being. He said the best Pak defence is to gradually cede some territory to the advancing Indians. Last week his boss, Gen. Niazi, had said the best defence is an offensive. But times change.

TUESDAY, DEC. 7: Dacca seems to be learning to live with war—or, rather, threat of war, because Indians so far bombing only few military targets on city outskirts. But people do keep glancing nervously at sky. UN tried again for mercy flight, but the plane was hit by naval gunfire, presumably Indian, off East Pakistani coast. India not winning very many friends among stranded Westerners here. Some Americans in hotel lobby demanding to know why the Marines don't come in and evacuate them. 'We did it in the Congo,' one says. 'Yeah, but this ain't the Congo,' another says. 'It will be soon,' the first says.

I am out near the airport when an air-raid siren goes off. Run across field and spot a foxhole. So do four Bengali rickshaw peddlers. So we all squat politely around the rim of the foxhole—no one wanting to be the first to hop in. It wouldn't hold more than three. But the planes pass over, and we share a cigarette.

The military situation remains, in the words of a Pak communiqué, 'unclear'. An American diplomat says Pakistan is 'between a rock and a hard place'. Have lunch with a West Pakistani pilot for Pakistan International Airlines who is stranded. 'What do you plan to do?' he is asked. 'Die here,' he says. Almost everyone thinks there will be another bloodbath soon, with Bengalis taking their revenge on non-Bengali minority (Biharis) and other army collaborators. If it's an eye for an eye, there will have to be a lot of Bihari eyes lost.

Rumour that food supply at the hotel is running short. Menu is dwindling a bit, but food is still remarkably good and always lots of butter available. The hotel bought out the stock of a Danish dairy project that folded just before the war. 'But can man live by butter alone?' one foreigner asks.

More Indian air strikes in the afternoon. High-altitude bombing. Now the hotel roof is full of journalists and photographers. One cameraman just up from the swimming pool is still in his bathing suit. Another reporter brings a chair. A diplomat on the roof says Biharis are looting evacuated homes. 'Well,' he adds, 'they can't take it with them where they're going.' General feeling seems to be that Biharis had fun while it lasted. One talks of mass killing quite calmly here. A half-million Bengalis massacred by the army in the last nine months and so on. East Pakistan is like a sponge that soaks up suffering. 'You could drop Biafra into East Pakistan and never find it again,' the diplomat says.

WEDNESDAY, DEC. 8: The breakfast rumour is that Gen. Niazi bugged out last night on a small plane to Burma. Last week he said, 'The more Indians who come, the more Indians to kill, the more I am happy.' Tend to doubt the bugout report, but he may later wish he had.

Military situation still very vague, but reports have Indian advance units about 35 miles south-east of Dacca. 'The military situation is deteriorating faster than we anticipated,' an embassy source says. The Bengalis one encounters seem delighted by way it's going. Independent nation of Bangla Desh probably no more than a week away.

UN mercy-flight plans seem to be in limbo. The UN people are always in conference. Curious how much attention we all pay to the plight of several hundred foreign nationals stranded at Intercontinental. A half-million or so Bengalis probably died in last nine months; another ten million or more trapped in misery of border camps. What makes a few hundred Western lives so valuable?

Rooftop air-strike watcher crowd thinning a bit. Rumour has it one cameraman was nicked in backside by piece of ack-ack shrapnel. Intercontinental filling up with armed West Pakistani civilians, which makes other guests uneasy. Radio news says President Nixon says war broke off sensitive negotiations that could have led to 'virtual autonomy' for East Pakistan. Last March the Bengalis were demanding 'virtual autonomy'. Bit late for virtuals. Television correspondents have secret information that small Pak plane planning to make secret night flight to secret Burma airstrip and pilot willing to take some film and newspaper copy. Film packed in a suitcase and ready to go.

One of week's unlikelier eventualities: in evening we roast marshmallows over a candle on a poker table.

THURSDAY, DEC. 9: 'Only ten shopping days till Christmas,' says an American businessman at breakfast. Kind of crisis conviviality continues. Another American goes off to consulate to pick up his income-tax forms. 'I may be an optimist,' he says, 'but it's something to do.' But there are a few frayed nerves. A grey toy poodle named Baby, stranded in hotel along with 'parents', has been under tranquilizers since war began.

Definite sense that Pak army crumbling. Gen. Niazi rumour still being circulated. Reports have Indian units 20 miles from Dacca. Indian radio says all major East Pakistani towns, except Dacca and port of Chittagong have fallen. Pakistan radio denies it. Pak army elements said to be leaving their cantonment and dispersing to scattered positions around the city. They evidently took over a tuberculosis hospital, evicting patients onto street. We drive around the city and see few soldiers, but we see a West Pakistani policeman beating a Bengali with a stick. Consistent to the end.

Everyone wonders whether Pak army will try to make last-ditch stand in Dacca. Some UN people talking of plan for conditional surrender of Pakistani troops in East Pakistan. Condition would be safe return to West Pakistan. But who could guarantee that?

Visited residential area where three bombs fell last night. Used to be an orphanage here, but now it's just three big craters surrounded by mountains of mud and debris. Watch several small bodies being dug out of the mud. Orphan 'body count' later said to total over 200.

International Red Cross (Geneva) succeeded in having Intercontinental and one hospital designated 'neutral zones'. This evening group of Red Cross officials and journalists moved from room to room confiscating weapons, mainly from West Pakistani guests. Several packets of explosives were found in the women's lavatory. They are moved out to hotel lawn and surrounded by sandbags. Swimming pool consequently closed.

FRIDAY, DEC. 10: The talk at breakfast is about the 3 a.m. air raid during which several bombs landed close to hotel. I slept through it. More Bengalis seem to be leaving the city today for relative safety of villages. Bengali friend, in tears, tells me about continuing army massacres of Bengalis in several suburbs. 'So many children,' he says—and begins to sob. Non-Bengali minority (Biharis) fleeing villages for relative safety of Dacca.

Bengalis in Dacca all seem convinced that the bombs that landed on civilian areas the past two nights, including the one that hit the orphanage, were dropped by Pakistani planes so civilian casualties could be blamed on India. Reliable foreign sources note that the bombs were dropped by propeller planes, not MIGs, and that makeshift bomb rack fell from plane along with bombs. Evidence still circumstantial. All seems incredibly cold-blooded. But one diplomat says 'Anyone who has been here since March wouldn't blink an eye at the Paks doing something like that.'

One rumour is squelched. Gen. Niazi shows up at hotel gate and is very definitely not in Burma. Under new Red Cross rules he is told he cannot enter the hotel with his weapon.

UN still negotiating with Paks and Indians to bring in evacuation planes. Apparent success. Twenty-four-hour cease-fire in air activity in Calcutta-to-Dacca corridor goes into effect 6 p.m. Evacuation planes, at least for women and children, scheduled to fly into Dacca tomorrow morning. But then: they've been scheduled before.

It's now exactly one week since general war began.

SATURDAY, DEC. 11: Midmorning blast at United States Information Service library. Debris scattered 100 yards around. Books lying all over the road, including *The Nuclear Years* and *The Role of Popular Participation in Development*. This is land of popular participation in destruction. Did the Mukti Bahini do it? Librarian says man who blasted it spoke Urdu, language of West Pakistan. Who knows? Within minutes books being looted from rubble. Old man goes by with tome called *Religion and Ethics* under his arm.

Big rumour of the day is that Gen. Rao Farman Ali Khan, deputy martial-law administrator and the 'gentleman general' of Pak forces here, was involved in secret negotiations, apparently with UN, to make conditional surrender of Pak forces in East Pakistan. But—the rumour goes—the commander here, Gen. Niazi, and President Agha Muhammad Yahya Khan in Islamabad found out. All this said to have affected evacuation planes, which don't come in again today. Part of problem with planes is that India, for political reasons, insists they fly to Dacca from Calcutta. Pakistan, for political reasons, won't accept that.

Stranded foreigners sense they have become political pawns. Looks more and more likely that Pak army will make a last-ditch stand in Dacca. Diplomatic sources say more troops being brought into city—or simply falling back here on their own. Gen. Niazi reported to have told a journalist at the airport: 'You will be here to see me die.'

Mood at American consulate very low. Realization America backed losing side and will suffer diplomatic and perhaps other consequences from it. 'The US mucked up this situation perfectly,' a Western diplomat says. This afternoon a curfew is clamped on the city. The streets are deserted. One estimate is that fewer than half the city's 1.3 million people are still here.

Red Cross calls meeting at hotel. Meeting is presided over by retired British colonel, now Red Cross official. Very David Niven. Tells hotel residents to disregard the 'quite extraordinary rumours floating around' but adds that hotel guests on higher floors might want to move down a 'wee bit'. Says hotel security man, Mr Beg, did 'jolly good job' of defusing those bombs in the toilet and says that they have since been buried in a slit trench so the pool is open again. Applause. But cautions that quite a bit of shrapnel from ack-ack guns has been pulled from swimming pool. Dive at your own risk.

Journalists try telephoning various towns around East Pakistan to see whether Pakistani or Indian army answers the call. Most phone lines are down, but we get through to Khulna, town in south-west that supposedly fell to Indian army days ago. Some sergeant answers phone. 'Where are the Indians?' we ask. Good cowboy-movie line. 'Not here,' he says.

SUNDAY, DEC. 12: A full-day curfew is in effect. City completely still as if some epidemic had suddenly wiped out all living things except the black crows hovering everywhere. Of course, the only epidemic in the city now is fear.

We awoke to the noise of C130 transports circling overhead. Looks as if evacuation flights for women and kids really are coming in. If the planes are leaving, this diary may leave with them.

II

Dacca Diary II

The Wall Street Journal 21 December 1971

SUNDAY, DEC. 12: FATHER TIMM OF Holy Cross College arrives at the Intercontinental Hotel to say mass about 9.15, but word has just arrived that evacuation flights are on the way. Foreigners are rushing to get to airport. 'Now I know what it feels like to be a bride left standing at the altar,' the father says. Ride out to airport with elderly American couple booked on evac flight. Man is wearing aluminum hard hat, lady is clutching cage with two squawking myna birds. 'I had to leave my dog,' she says. 'It was terrible.'

At airport British diplomats and other volunteers out sweeping runway with tree branches to try to clear away shrapnel. British Royal Air Force C130s make several passes; finally one risks landing on badly damaged runway. Safe landing amid great clouds of orange dust. Cheers and applause from evacuees. Propellers turning as evacuees run to planes and board. All quite orderly. Women and children on first plane and so on.

Indonesian embassy people try to get massive suitcases on board. 'Ten kilos only' is the command. Amazing how attached people get to belongings; even last passengers for last plane trying to tote valises down runway when extra thirty seconds could mean missing plane. Some tears and frayed nerves.

Scenes like Pakistani army major approaching American official to ask if his wife could please be evacuated. Answer is no, and the Pakistani says thank you and turns away. Soviet consul general is in good spirits. 'I am happy my fair lady is aboard the plane,' he says.

Paks maintain symbolic presence at airport with immigration officer standing amid shattered glass and other rubble of terminal building to stamp passports of evacuees. But it's basically a British show. 'Now I know why you guys won the Battle of Britain,' German television correspondent tells a British colleague. Four C130s finally get off in the four-hour airlift, taking almost all the foreigners who want to go.

Hotel strangely quiet now that evac flights gone. Remaining Westerners, mostly journalists, spend afternoon by swimming pool in pickup games of water polo and soccer and tossing dirt clots at the omnipresent crows. Games break off every hour on the hour for BBC radio news. Indians moving closer to Dacca, crossing rivers, supposedly dropping parachute units. But Dacca under curfew and no one going out to find the war. Someone at poolside reading book, *Six Days in June: Israel's Fight for Survival*. Pak army has so far survived ten days, but betting here is that it won't last two weeks. Pak army still razing neighbourhoods in city outskirts, and fires can be seen burning from hotel.

MONDAY, DEC. 13: A morning paper announces with bold headline, 'Enemy Advance Halted', but longest article in paper is 'Spectre of

Famine Haunts Upper Volta'. From breakfast room, one can watch hotel employee pulling bits of ack-ack shrapnel out of swimming pool with a magnet tied to the end of a rope.

Drive to city centre during six-hour period when curfew lifted. Much of Bengali population has deserted city, but many Biharis (non-Bengali minority) visible on streets and, of course, the rickshaw peddlers. I see fewer Pakistani flags flying today. 'Every sewing machine in Dacca is busy working on Bangla Desh flags,' diplomat says.

Gen. A.A.K. Niazi, commander of Pakistani forces in the East, shows up across street from the hotel and gives curbside interview. How is the battle going? 'As I planned it.' Will you defend the city? 'To the last.' But doesn't that mean Dacca may be destroyed? 'These are the prices of freedom.' What about a cease-fire or surrender? 'The army will die. There is no question of surrender. There will be no one left to be repatriated.' Wonder if his troops share the sentiments.

Small crowd of perhaps twenty-five Biharis standing around Gen. Niazi chanting, 'Pakistan, Zindabad, Pakistan, Zindabad,' meaning, 'Long life, Pakistan'. Several are weeping. Several others jumping up and down screaming madly. Rickshaw passes, and Bihari passenger does wild war dance on the seat as Bengali driver pedals on with head bowed. Biharis going out in kind of final frenzy of the damned.

The press corps, under direction of handful of Red Cross people, now has taken over most of the responsibility for security at the hotel, which has been declared a neutral zone. So there's an early-afternoon security search of all rooms in an effort to confiscate any remaining guns and to try to ascertain how many people are holed up in hotel and who they are. Four more guns found on West Pakistani civilians, some of whom are living six to a room. In the evening, residents meet in a room that used to feature Australian strippers in better days. Rather solemn talk about first aid and fire-fighting equipment, security guard duty, slit trenches.

TUESDAY, DEC. 14: By early afternoon it appears the battle of Dacca is about to begin. Indian MIGs rocket 'Government House'—Governor's office—in central city. Two reporters return from several-hour drive south-east of city. They report Indian troops 7 miles from city and advancing with only one river to cross. Considerable fighting. Indian planes drop leaflets on city calling for all military and paramilitary forces to surrender to nearest Indian unit with guarantee of protection for lives and property.

Red Cross official says food situation in Dacca has become desperate. All foodstuffs in short supply, many shops closed, curfew prevents people reaching open shops, and prices now so high that poor cannot afford to buy remaining food anyway.

Local paper announces that 'due to emergency situation and difficulties of communication, it has been decided to suspend the Get-a-Word Competition in East Pakistan until further notice. The inconvenience caused to the competitors is due to reasons beyond the control of the management and is regretted.' It's midafternoon and there's more bombing close to city.

News of the resignation of A.M. Malik, Governor of East Pakistan, and rest of the civilian government. One UN official who was in the Governor's office about 1 p.m. says Malik wrote out the resignation longhand between the first and second Indian air strikes on Government House. Then Malik washed his feet, knelt and prayed. During brief interlude between the strikes, Gen. Rao Farman Ali Khan, deputy martial-law administrator here, ran down hall past UN man and said: 'Why are the Indians doing this to us?' UN man tells a reporter: 'As we were under direct air attack at the time, I didn't go into political explanations.' Paks really seem to think it's somehow unfair, unsporting for India to be winning the war.

Later, a Pakistani colonel arrives at hotel gate and is asked how the military situation is going. 'Plenty fine,' he says. Will army surrender? 'Of course not.' Will you keep fighting? 'Of course.' Very polite, very soft-spoken.

I spend two hours on door duty searching luggage of arriving ministers of civilian government who are seeking refuge here. Strange role for a reporter, but all rules are fluid here. Some of ministers wait as if in trance as bags are combed. Others try to joke. One says: 'Ashes to ashes and dust to dust; if the Indians don't get you, the Muktis must.' But he can't manage a smile at his own joke.

Several photographers return from site of afternoon air strikes. Say rockets hit civilian neighbourhood, killing at least dozen Bengali civilians. At the site there were two young members of the Mukti Bahini, or East Pakistani guerrillas. 'Why did they (Indian planes) do it?' says one of the shaken Muktis. 'We are their friends.'

WEDNESDAY, DEC. 15: Indian air strike during breakfast. Dining room empties in about ten seconds. Whole roomful of half-eaten instant scrambled eggs.

The chairman of the Dacca Peace Committee, a key collaborator with the West Pakistanis, arrives at hotel gate and is turned away. He argues for a while, finally walks off as if in a trance, like a man walking to his death.

Gen. Farman arrives about 9 a.m. Will the Pakistani army surrender? 'Why should we surrender? The question of surrender does not arise.' Farman is riding around in a Mercedes camouflaged with mud, two general stars on its licence plate. No armed escort.

A few minutes after 10, a British journalist runs by, yelling that Farman is coming to hotel to surrender within the hour. Great excitement. TV types' pleading with one another to get organized, form a line. 'For once,' they say, 'let's not have to photograph each other.'

Farman enters gate on schedule but turns corner and gives TV cameras nothing but long shots. Rumour is that President Yahya gave approval to surrender plan last night, but Gen. Niazi may be balking.

Pak army doctor, a colonel, arrives at hotel. Sad conversation. 'What is honour?' he says. 'How much sacrifice must be made for honour's sake? In the old days we fought duels for our honour. Now a million men must die to satisfy honour.' He says Pak army has taken terrible casualties.

Gen. Farman leaves the hotel. Many surrender rumours still floating. Too many.

Lee Lescaze of *Washington Post* and I now doing four-hour guard duty at gate. Lee stops a mongoose trying to scurry under the gate into neutral zone. We suggest mongoose get Iranian passport.

Evening radio news says dollar being devalued. Seems like pretty distant crisis from here. Japanese consul general remarks that Pak army must surrender 'like Japan at the end of World War II'.

Staggering rush of events these past days. Like watching a pro football team play its whole season in one week.

THURSDAY, DEC. 16: At 10.10 a.m. a hotel official walks up: 'It's definite, it's definite. It's surrender.' Five minutes later, UN aides in the hotel make it official: 'The ultimatum to surrender has been accepted.'

Several reporters hitch a ride out to Pakistani army cantonment to try to see Gen. Farman. No luck but quite a spectacle at cantonment gate. Soldiers now pouring into cantonment in every sort of vehicle—buses, trucks, cars, even rickshaw. Rolling by is a microbus with these words stenciled on back: 'Live and let live'. West Pak and Bihari civilians also trying to enter cantonment. Most of them seem to have deserted all personal belongings except transistor radios.

Pay visit to Paul Marc Henri, UN chief here, who is operating out of another neutral zone at Notre Dame College. Henri in ebullient mood over surrender but stresses his role only as channel of communications. He's walking around college campus with big, black Labrador on a chain. Labrador keeps getting into fights with another dog, interrupting Henri's monologue. Henri still concerned over possible massacres of minorities. One of his assistants puts it plainly: 'Tonight will be the night of the long knives.'

Rush out to airport with other reporters. At 12.45 a Pak army staff car with two stars on plate rolls up. Figure it's Pak general coming to meet Indian helicopter. But a general in purple turban and another in cavalry hat get out; that isn't Pak military headgear. 'Hello, I am Gen. Nagra, Indian army,' cavalry hat says, 'and this is Brigadier Kler,' he adds, introducing turban. They had led Indian column that pushed into Dacca suburbs from north early this morning.

We hear of mob trouble at Intercontinental and return to the hotel. A hysterical Mukti is carried through hotel gate with a light leg wound. Mukti finally is laid out on three hotel chairs. Hotel official arrives, dapper as ever in glen plaid suit. 'He's bleeding all over my damned best chairs, and all the bastard did was stub his damned toe,' hotel man says.

This city is full of panicky men with guns: excited young Muktis, confused Indians and frightened Pak troops who are trying to surrender but who don't know how or where to do so.

This afternoon Gen. Nagra and Pak Gen. Farman come to hotel gate in jeep. Mob begins shouting at Farman: 'Butcher, killer, bastard.' Farman walks towards mob and says, soft-spoken, 'But don't you know what I did for you?' He means the surrender, which saved lives. Maybe the mob knows, but it doesn't care.

It's 5 p.m., and reporters rush to golf course for formal surrender ceremony. Surrender papers are signed in quadruplicate. Takes a while because Gen. Niazi reads the documents as if for the first time. Scene after signing is complete chaos. Mob trying to carry Indian generals on shoulders, Pak generals being jostled by crowds. Gen. Farman is wandering alone, dazed, through milling mob. 'You see, we are beaten everywhere,' he mumbles as two running Bengalis bump into him. Farman continues walking slowly, one hand in sweater pocket. 'How do I get out of this place?' he asks no one in particular before I lose him in the crowd.

FRIDAY, DEC. 17: Chat with the hotel laundry bookkeeper who has emerged as a Mukti police inspector. Turns out he had been Mukti cell leader for Intercontinental Hotel staff during past nine months. He had devised an underclothing code. If an agent handed him one undershirt, it meant four terrorist acts had been successfully completed. Two undershirts meant three successes, three undershirts meant two successes and four undershirts meant only one terrorist success. Nothing seems incredible here any more.

At 5.55 p.m. two Soviet correspondents arrive. 'We are Tass and *Pravda*. We have just arrived. What is the news?' they say.

Two hours later, sipping Scotch in a hotel room, a reporter says, 'Hey, the lights are on.' And so they are. It's the first night in nearly two weeks that's not spent by candlelight.

Later, three Indians arrive to report that 'the city is all quiet now, a curfew has been imposed, we have stopped all this bloody shooting business and . . .' The rest is drowned out by automatic-weapons fire.

But today was quieter than yesterday.

SATURDAY, DEC. 18: Considerable shooting and some killings, especially of Biharis, still continuing. A Bangla Desh victory celebration turns into a bloody spectacle; four West Pakistani sympathizers are tortured and killed. Earlier today Muktis uncovered mass graves of prominent Bengali intellectuals who had been taken hostage by local militiamen and butchered night before last. This is a traditionally bloody society that has just gone through a nine-month bloodbath. Why should the bloodletting suddenly stop?

At the airport, an Indian brigadier wanders around the terminal area trying to organize repair of the runway, which is full of holes. He wants Bengalis, not Indian troops, to make the repairs, which are, of course, vital for any relief effort. 'But the Bengali chaps are just milling around and celebrating all day,' he says with exasperation.

For now shouting 'Joi Bangla' (Victory to Bengal) is more important to the Bengalis than food.

Dacca appears to be calming down gradually. Some men are taking their wives and children for their first stroll in Bangla Desh. One Bengali says his three-year-old son, Aupoo, hasn't been taken out in public for months. The reason is that last March, during the brief period before the Pakistani army cracked down and imposed a reign of terror in the East, the child learned to shout 'Joi Bangla'. But for the past nine months the parents feared that the child might shout 'Joi Bangla' in public and thus get the family killed.

Today both father and son are on the streets, yelling, 'Joi Bangla!'

~

Henry Bradsher
From Law and Order to Revenge

The Washington Star
20 December 1971

Dacca: IT STARTED OFF as a victory celebration by the Mukti Bahini, featuring twin themes of following law and order now in Bangla Desh and asserting the Mukti Bahini's right to a future political role. It ended with four exemplary murders.

It was held on Paltan Maidan, the traditional political meeting ground in the heart of Dacca's commercial area, on Saturday.

The last time many of these same youths had held a meeting there was 23 March—while East Pakistan's elected political leaders were negotiating for autonomy within Pakistan with President A.M. Yahya Khan.

At that rally nine months ago, Dacca University student leaders ceremonially raised the new flag of Bangla Desh, a green and red banner with a golden outline of the region which they wanted to be independent rather than merely autonomous within Pakistan. And they paraded their comic little student guard armed with dummy rifles and old castoff guns.

They said they were prepared to fight for independence. The comic turned tragic two nights later when the Pakistani army made students one of the first targets of their brutal crackdown on Bengali nationalism. Many youths who rallied then were killed.

And those who survived to come back to this victory celebration now returned as hardened guerrilla fighters. They carried modern rifles and submachine guns.

The main speaker Saturday was the 'Tiger of Tangail', a district 50 miles north-west of Dacca. He is Abdul Quadir Siddiqui, a former student leader who became head of the Mukti Bahini—freedom fighters for Bangla Desh—in the area from Dacca north to the Indian border.

Siddiqui was one of the most effective and most feared guerrilla leaders. The Pakistani army put a bounty of Rs 25,000 ($5250) on his head.

It is a head much like Fidel Castro's, with a bushy beard and wild hair set off by a khaki military outfit. The resemblance to Castro does not end there.

Siddiqui is widely believed to be eager to keep and even augment his power gained from guerrilla leadership.

When Siddiqui was introduced to a crowd of perhaps 8000 persons, there was a loud roar of acclaim.

He began speaking in Bengali by telling how, on the way to the rally, he had seen a merchant attacked by youths who tried to grab his money bag. The merchant was called to the platform to hold up the money bag for photographers.

Siddiqui captured the youths and they were now tied up on the ground near the platform, he said. Three men about twenty-five years old sat there with their arms tied behind their backs looking worried. He said they had also tried to kidnap some girls off the street.

They will be turned over to proper authorities, Siddiqui said. Now that victory has been won by Bangla Desh, law and order must be reestablished.

His voice sometimes breaking as he shouted at the crowd, Siddiqui said the Mukti Bahini must not act in a manner unbecoming to regular army troops.

He demanded that West Pakistan release the Bangla Desh nationalist leader, Sheikh Mujibur Rahman, or else the Mukti Bahini will attack it.

Siddiqui then served notice on the government formed after 25 March by Rahman's Awami League political party that intended to have a say in governmental policy.

The Mukti Bahini did not fight the war to set up a society with exploitation and inequality, he said. 'We want to set up a cooperative society and whoever opposes us, we will stand up against him.'

This is the kind of utopian socialism that has long prevailed in Dacca student ranks. The essentially conservative Awami League has been pushed from the left by it, but collision lies ahead when governmental policy starts being implemented.

Siddiqui reminded the crowd that he controls some 12,000 Mukti Bahini guerrillas. They will not lay down their arms until Rahman is free, he said—and there was a hint that his political ideas must also be followed.

The rally ended with Moslem prayers for those who died in the liberation struggle and for the release of Rahman.

As the crowd began going home, several Western and Indian correspondents caught Siddiqui behind the platform for an interview.

He said he was twenty-five years old. Will he become a political leader now? No, he said, he will return to his village in the Tangail district and work for the people there.

This idea of educated youths now going to the countryside to help the peasantry is widely echoed in Mukti Bahini ranks, but not widely believed by observers.

Siddiqui was asked about the murder of Dacca intellectuals just before the Pakistani army's surrender. He estimated the number at between 250 and 300.

As in any civilized country, Siddiqui said, 'We will give guilty persons legal trials when we catch them. We will punish anyone who takes law and order into his own hands.'

While a cluster of correspondents talked with Siddiqui through a translator, 5 yards away a circle of guards around the three tied up youths was beginning to hit them as a few hundred of the disappearing rally crowd gathered around. The fourth youth was being held by the hair and arms on the edge of the circle.

The situation seemed to build its own momentum. Mukti Bahini guards began kicking the three tied youths. By the time correspondents, noticing this was happening, broke off the interview with Siddiqui, guards were jumping with both feet onto the youths lying on the ground.

Siddiqui walked over. The guards drew back. Siddiqui waved his swagger stick at three, then hit two of them with it, and made a brief speech to them in Bengali.

The sickened translator was unable later to recall what Siddiqui said but apparently it was an execution order.

Bayonets on the ends of the guards' rifles were unsheathed. A youth in a white tee shirt who appeared to have been badly injured by stomping was the first to be bayoneted repeatedly.

He said nothing throughout, no pleading, no prayers. He just lay there and was stabbed and bled.

Then the Mukti Bahini went to work on the second youth, bayoneting him on the ground.

The third one, the one in a flowered shirt, was hauled up onto his knees to make a better target. Siddiqui took a rifle from one of the guards and ran at the youth, vigorously thrusting the bayonet into his stomach. Then others struck him.

With those three finished, the fourth youth was thrown into a grassy circle. They were beginning to bayonet him as I walked away.

A single shot rang out that someone said must have been the coup de grâce for one of the four who had not been very efficiently bayonetted.

The rally was over. Youths who had gathered there with such optimism early on a spring morning nine months ago, who had been so eager to tell me then of their hopes and dreams for Bangla Desh, had come back to Dacca.

But a civil war later, things were different.

~

Lewis M. Simons
Mrs Gandhi Turns to Son in Crisis

The Washington Post
10 July 1975

Bangkok: PRIME MINISTER INDIRA Gandhi, distrustful of even her closest cabinet colleagues at this time of grave crisis for India, is turning to her controversial younger son, Sanjay, for help in making major political decisions.

Sanjay, twenty-nine, assisted his mother in deciding who among her political opponents should be arrested. Since then, Mrs Gandhi has imposed a state of emergency and assumed dictatorial powers, and Sanjay is guiding her toward retaining power at any cost.

Although he has no government or political position, he takes part in the daily meetings of her emergency council. Operating from the Prime Minister's office, he gives orders to cabinet members and top civil servants.

One man who had been a member of Mrs Gandhi's so-called 'kitchen cabinet' shortly after she became Prime Minister said: 'Sanjay is calling the shots now. The system is no longer functioning in this country. It's all Sanjay and his goons.'

Sanjay came to his mother's side immediately after a high court judge convicted her 12 June of corrupt election practices and barred her from political office for six years, a verdict that is now under appeal.

Shortly after Mrs Gandhi got word of the court judgment, she went home. Sanjay ran out to meet her on the spacious, tree-shaded lawns and, according to a source who was there at the time, 'he threw his arms around her and cried like a baby'.

According to critics of the Prime Minister and Sanjay, as well as to sources close to the family, Sanjay has become a millionaire in the last few years, not because of what he has done but who he is—the Prime Minister's son.

**The emergency was the only instance in the history of independent India in which the Constitution was suspended. Prime Minister Indira Gandhi imposed it on 25 June 1975 and lifted it abruptly on 21 March 1977.*

Critics charge that were it not for his mother, Sanjay would never have been granted government approval four years ago, when he was twenty-five, to build a large Detroit-style plant for the manufacture of a small car he designed and called Maruti, 'Son of the Wind God'.

Critics also say that Sanjay would never have been able to collect some $10 million to launch the project, in which his own investment is said to be about $1500; nor would he have been allotted thousands of tons of scarce steel to build the plant, or 297 acres of superbly located farmland, at a bargain price, on which to construct it.

The car itself has still not appeared on the roads and there are signs that Sanjay has lost interest in it. Since the start of the current crisis, he no longer goes to the plant and his older brother, Rajiv, an Indian Airlines pilot, has taken his place there.

The question many otherwise informed Indians have been asking for years is why a hard-nosed politician like Mrs Gandhi has allowed the controversy around Sanjay and herself to continue. They note that particularly in the early stages, she could easily have extricated herself.

The answer does not seem to be in the realm of politics. More likely, it lies in the complex family relationship between Sanjay and his mother and, at its roots, in the Prime Minister's marriage to the late Feroze Gandhi and her extraordinarily close relationship with her father, former Prime Minister Jawaharlal Nehru.

Feroze and Indira Gandhi were married in 1942. Seven years later, she left their home in Lucnow and, with Sanjay and Rajiv, moved into the Prime Minister's residence with their father. Feroze tried to live there with his family, but it did not work out and the marriage soon failed.

In her book, *We Nehrus*, Indira's aunt, Krishna Hutheesing, wrote that Mrs Gandhi's living with her father 'was not a good arrangement from a family point of view and that (Indira and Feroze) finally drifted apart'. Feroze's friends said he felt 'shut out' by his wife and resented his 'inferior' status in his father-in-law's home.

Soon after, she became her father's hostess and began rising in the Congress party. Feroze, who was a member of Parliament, could not accept his wife's importance and he apparently resented being referred to mockingly as 'the nation's son-in-law'.

According to several couples in New Delhi who knew Feroze and Indira socially in those days, Sanjay suffered psychologically from the humiliation his father endured. 'He's never forgiven his mother for what he thinks she did to Feroze,' said one of these former friends.

As a result, Sanjay is said to fluctuate in his feelings for his mother. A family friend who attended a dinner party with Sanjay and Mrs Gandhi several months ago said he saw the son slap his mother across the face 'six times'.

'She didn't do a thing,' the friend said. 'She just stood there and took it. She's scared to death of him.'

One of Mrs Gandhi's most hostile critics, author and journalist Rajinder Puri, writing on the automobile plant recently, said 'The scandal surrounding the Maruti small car project of the Prime Minister's son, Mr Sanjay Gandhi, is the darkest blot on the Indian government in the last twenty-five years. Never since Independence has corruption been approved, abetted or practised by a Prime Minister so brazenly as has been done with the setting up of this factory.'

A less vitriolic assessment of the son's role appeared in a biography of the Prime Minister that was published in the United States last year. The late Krishan Bhatia wrote that the scandal over the activities of Indira's son, Sanjay, the official favours he has allegedly received, and the wild, sometimes shocking rumours and gossip that surround him have robbed his mother's name 'of the luster with which it shone in late 1971 and early 1972', after the Bangladesh war.

Over the years since the small car project's inception, Mrs Gandhi has come under frequent fire in Parliament and the press for her involvement and her alleged attempts to whitewash the 'scandal'.

She has always responded by stoutly defending Sanjay saying he won government approval on his own merits and that he was a model for other Indian youth. Through her party's overwhelming majority in Parliament, she has regularly managed to squelch debate.

More than 100 members of Parliament—one-fifth of the membership—submitted a memorandum on allegations against the project. It was swiftly dismissed. When asked about this last March while testifying before the court at Allahabad that convicted her last month Mrs Gandhi said, 'Each item in the memorandum was carefully gone into and found devoid of substance.'

Newspapers have given the Maruti controversy a considerable amount of attention, but the Indian press has done little actual investigative reporting.

Local editors cannot be entirely faulted for ignoring the sensitive matter. Several months ago, when I approached a source who had a great deal of unpublished information on the Maruti, he refused to discuss the issue. 'It would surely get me thrown in jail and you thrown out of the country,' he said.

The most concerted attempt to investigate the Maruti case was made over a period of years by the *Motherland*, the daily newspaper of the right-wing Jana Sangh Party.

Motherland editor K.R. Malkani was apprehended by police in the first wave of arrests on 26 June. He is the only journalist known to be arrested.

In a five-part series entitled 'Sanjay Gandhi's Super Scandals', which appeared in the *Motherland* in March, Mrs Gandhi was admonished: 'The Prime Minister's family must be above suspicion. The sudden wealth of her son Sanjay has roused many suspicions. As a first step toward removing these suspicions, the PM must ask her son to make his assets and income tax and wealth tax public.'

The articles went into considerable detail on allegations against Sanjay. They also traced the role played by the chief minister of Haryana state, Bansi Lal, in evicting 1500 farmers from land in Haryana, just outside New Delhi, for sale to Sanjay.

The impact of the articles was lessened by the fact that the *Motherland*, like the Hindu nationalist Jana Sangh Party, has for years been a declared enemy of Mrs Indira Gandhi. Nevertheless, a large section of the Indian public is aware of the alleged scandal and Mrs Gandhi has undoubtedly been hurt politically by it.

Sanjay, short and slender, with handsome, even features and black, curly hair balding at the crown, gives the impression of being a pleasant, mild-mannered young man.

A few months ago, he married a teenager whom friends describe as a 'teeny bopper'. The young couple live with Mrs Gandhi in the spacious Prime Minister's residence.

Unlike others of his age and class, who dress in the latest European styles, he affects simple white homespun cotton pajamas, even in his office at the Maruti plant.

Yet he is obviously tough-minded. Until he recently began appearing at his mother's side during rallies intended to win popular support for her, he stayed out of the limelight.

A year and a half ago, after I made a dozen efforts to interview him and even confronted him once at his office, an aide finally told me, 'Mr Gandhi does not approve of your writing and he refuses to release any information to your *Washington Post*.'

Friends warned me just before I left India that if I was going to write about him and the Maruti project, I should wait until my family had left India, too.

II

Five Days in June India's About-Face

The Washington Post 14 July 1975

Bangkok: THE CUSTOMS OFFICIALS had just confiscated my notebooks and I was being escorted by a policeman to the plane when it occurred to me with dumbfounding suddenness: How little it took to destroy democracy.

This was early in the morning of 1 July, just five days after Prime Minister Indira Gandhi began locking up thousands of her opponents and locked India into a state of emergency.

India, the world's largest democracy; India, which had never hesitated to lecture the world, and particularly the United States, whenever governments appeared to be infringing on the rights of citizens.

Suddenly this India was little more than a dictatorship, hardly different from the many third world countries run by el supremos whom the Indians had looked down upon with pity and contempt.

To me, the most astonishing part of it was how easy it had all been. In five days, less—overnight—democratic guarantees had been quashed. There were a few war cries of rebellion, a few young people who threw stones and shook their fists. Just about everyone else simply took it. They collapsed in the first shock and never attempted to struggle back to their feet.

For the poor, it was never really a problem. The illiterate 'untouchable' who mowed my lawn and the Rajasthani woman digging a ditch in the road near my house had hardly benefited in any tangible way from democracy. And, they reckoned, they were not likely to suffer very much under authoritarian rule.

But the liberal intellectuals, the editors, the professors, the businessmen with Harvard degrees have done nothing either.

Some say it's just a matter of time, that they are catching their breath. 'We won't allow this to go on,' claimed a brilliant young political analyst I had known for several years. 'We may need six months or so, but we'll get rid of her and get back to normal.'

Maybe.

But for now it is all over. The other night I heard on the radio here in Bangkok that newspaper editors in New Delhi were appealing to the Prime Minister to lift what she calls 'pre-censorship'. In its place they were not proposing a return to a free press, but some unspecified form of self-censorship.

There is no need to look very far to determine what changed the outspoken Indians into silent bystanders in a huge nation ruled by one strong-willed woman. It is fear, pure and simple.

Fear of being arrested. Fear of losing a job. Fear of losing a position of influence. Fear of losing wealth perhaps even fear of being killed.

Fear is palpable in India today. One could almost feel it within hours after the first pre-dawn arrests began. By the time I was forced to leave the country, it had intensified, with the certain knowledge that one could be arrested at home or on the streets, thrown into jail and never have the right to appeal to the courts.

All the little things that had been taken for granted suddenly posed threats. Was the telephone tapped? Was the mail being opened? Could one speak openly in front of a person he had just met at dinner?

The answer to the last question was 'no'. Parties became pointless and boring, with guests discussing health problems, movies, the weather, everything but what was really on everyone's mind.

Were the fears real or imagined?

• A young married couple came to visit my wife the night before she and our children followed me out of the country. They had ignored a warning from the husband's parents, 'you'll have trouble if you go to their house'. A few minutes after they arrived the telephone rang. My wife answered. There was no reply and the line clicked off. The couple stood up and left.

The evening before, a group of close friends, all Indians, came to see my wife, to tell her how sorry they were that I had been expelled and that our family would have to leave. They were speaking angrily about press censorship and the continuing arrests. Another Indian arrived. My wife knew him, but the others did not. The conversation stopped.

• Telephone conversations have become the briefest possible cryptic exchanges. 'How is everything with you?' 'Fine, just fine and you?' 'The same.'

• Two days before I left, a friend came to me and said that the man with a little tin suitcase selling cigarettes on the street corner outside my house was a secret police agent. 'He's writing down the licence number of every car that comes to your house,' he said. After I left, a stream of sympathetic and helpful visitors continued to see my wife, but most came in taxis or parked their cars blocks away from the house.

Mrs Gandhi has learned the lessons of fear well. She has learned from a decade of experience in playing off political colleagues against each other and pressuring vulnerable businessmen for financial support.

The white-haired police official who served me with the expulsion order at the shabby, barricks-like Foreigners Registration Office was a victim of fear. He seemed genuinely embarrassed.

'This is a terrible thing,' I said to him. 'I agree with you,' he replied. 'But what am I to do? She provides my salt. I am a police officer dedicated to obeying the orders of my government.'

At the airport the next morning, my last in India, I appealed to the customs officials who had taken my notebooks to return them. They refused. 'These notebooks contain information harmful to the government of India,' said one white-uniformed official.

'They contain only the truth,' I countered. His reply silenced me for good. 'Don't worry about India. Go away from this place and worry about your own country.'

~

George Evans
Indira Gandhi: 'Why I Had to Clamp Down'

The Sunday Telegraph
12 October 1975

ALMOST FOUR MONTHS *after the declaration of India's state of emergency many political prisoners are still held without trial, and censorship is rigid. Faced with a storm of international protest, India's Prime Minister, Mrs Indira Gandhi, has remained adamant. But last week, in the first detailed interview with a British-based journalist, she gave vent to a deeply felt national sense of grievance. Sitting at the desk once occupied by her father, she talked at length about the pressures that caused the crisis and spoke with icy contempt of her critics.*

Prime Minister three main charges have been made against you in the past few months; namely that in imposing the emergency you lost your temper with the Opposition and overreacted, that you are edging closer to personal dictatorship, and that India is in the process of becoming a police state.
I can only say it is not true. Our legal system is complex and so is the political system. For every appointment there are committees, and they go through various levels.

I would say that the emergency has made no difference to my powers at all. I cannot do any more now than I could before. Sometimes one would like things to move faster. One is exasperated when something has to be done, because some of our methods are very cumbersome.

It was all right when the British were here, their main purpose was to keep law and order. Now the main purpose is development. Law and order, by the way, is essential for you cannot have development if you have chaos.

So there is no question of you having lost your temper?
I haven't. Sharada Prasad [Prime Minister's press secretary] has known me for many years and I doubt if he has ever heard me shout at anybody, in spite of a regular campaign of calumny by the Opposition and every possible kind of insult in Parliament.

What were the external pressures that influenced you in proclaiming a state of emergency? The government claims, for example, that Mr George Fernandes, leader of the railwaymen's union and socialist party, wrote to Chairman Mao soliciting support, and that substantial sums of money were received through a foreign bank.
First, the real reason for the emergency, long before my case came up in the courts, was the developing and deepening crisis. Most of the chief ministers of the states were very worried and were urging me to take some action. I don't think the railway strike itself had anything to do with the declaration of the emergency, though it was clear that it was not just an ordinary strike for a better deal for the workers. Some of the demands were just but others were clearly meant to embarrass the government.

Mr Fernandes said the money was for trade union activities. The money was originally put in his personal account though later he transferred some of it. The cheque came though the Reserve Bank of India from Japan, and we had information that part of it came from somewhere else to Tokyo and then here. Before that a cheque was received from Holland, I think to a party in Orissa. They quickly said it was for agricultural work but the sort of campaign that was going on was obvious. Those who went on strike were being paid. Where did the money come from? Our trade unions aren't rich.

Did extremist elements visit London secretly to seek Chinese advice on forming the Marxist-Leninist communist party?
This is not really a party but a group, because they don't believe in normal party functions. They have always been very pro-Chinese with slogans like 'Mao is our Chairman'. But apart from this, the Chinese have been instigating some of our people on the borders. We have recovered Chinese arms and books from people who have been encouraged to go across, undertake guerrilla training, and come back. This interference has been continuing and, of course, is not limited to India.

Turning to Indian affairs, how many political prisoners are still being held without trial? Are their cases being reviewed? Do you feel the system of imprisonment without trial is repugnant?
Well, I am not for any kind of imprisonment I might tell you. But sometimes the situation arises when you don't know what else can be

done. We have not so far given out the number of people arrested. I can only say that we are reviewing them and people are being continuously released. Initially, several different types of people were arrested. Some were political leaders thought to be involved in the planning and carrying out of this campaign to paralyse the Central government. Apart from that, we left it to the state governments. We also arrested what are known here as 'anti-social elements', who are not at all political.

Estimates, no doubt widely exaggerated, have put the number of arrests at 100,000.
The estimates I have heard have been widely exaggerated. I can only say it's nothing like that at all.

It is reported that some of the arrested leaders, including the politicians are being held in conditions of hardship in over-crowded prisons. Are they reasonably treated as regards access by their families, and are any in solitary confinement?
I don't think there is any deliberate solitary confinement except that there are a couple of people who are kept in houses. They have the whole house to themselves. Most have been visited by lawyers and relations.

Why have the Moscow-oriented communists been exempted from arrest?
Some have been arrested and even some members of our own party have been arrested. Why more have not been arrested is obviously because they are not obstructing our plans or programme in any way. We arrested only those directly involved in the planning of direct action to paralyse the government by preaching insubordination to the army, police and so on. I think we could, perhaps by taking some action earlier on, have held the situation, but we felt we should not arrest anybody so the situation went on slipping until there was just no other way to stop it. Since the emergency we have not used the baton to enforce discipline in any way. In fact, in the last hundred days there has not been a single occasion when the police have had to use force of any kind and nothing of what you call 'lathi-charges'.

Is the Indian army apolitical, or, in spite of its long tradition of accepting civilian supremacy, has there at any time been a threat, a

military coup, and could one happen? What attempts were made to subvert the army? Does any kind of organized underground movement exist?

The army is quite apolitical. They were not involved in this or any other political decision. The Opposition did appeal to them not to obey government orders, though later they backed down, saying that what they meant was that the army should not obey immoral orders to suppress the people. But we have never asked the army to suppress anyone. At the most, if there is a riot or something, we alert them in case they are needed if the police cannot handle the situation. But they have never had to act. I think they remain totally detached from politics. There is no regular underground movement. They do produce some literature but it isn't on a large scale and is diminishing.

On censorship, it is widely said that it is a device to stifle criticism. Otherwise, why clamp down on foreign newspapers which don't circulate in India and therefore can have no influence on public opinion?

To take the domestic press first, for over nine and a half years they wrote what they liked against me and I did not react in any way or lose my temper with them. But in the last months they had begun to undermine the nation's confidence, which is also my complaint against the Opposition. Our very real achievements in the face of tremendous odds, such as reducing inflation from 31 per cent to –2 per cent, were ignored. Day in and day out, anything that was achieved was tucked away on some middle page with all the prominence given to political quarrels, corruption, and inquests into what had gone wrong.

So this was the sort of climate that was created and this is why we had to clamp down on the Indian press. This being so, how could we allow non-Indian journalists who work here to have a different set of laws? As for those who were sent out of India, they had repeatedly broken the word they had given to the minister and boasted about hoodwinking officials here.

Does it disturb you to find that Indian newspapers which have a long tradition of independence and outspoken political comment have become obedient but colourless since their teeth were drawn by the censor. Should there not be dissenting voices in a democracy, particularly in India at this time?

Nobody minds dissent but there must be some self-control. This is why we formed a Press Council. We thought they would control one another. When our railway minister was assassinated a newspaper here started the campaign that I had had him murdered, and none of the other papers was willing to take this up. There must be some limits to which a newspaper can go. Either there must be self-control or they have to be controlled.

Is it the case that Indian newspapers are forbidden to print speeches by Mahatma Gandhi and Jawaharlal Nehru?
I don't think there is any such kind of ban. But I must confess that we have no experience of censorship because we have never had it before. We don't have competent people to be censors. Originally the state governments put in anybody they could lay their hands on and I might tell you that even my own speeches were censored, as were government and official handouts!

Is it the case, Prime Minister, that the newspapers are forced to give favourable publicity to the government, even to the extent of printing your own picture on the front page? Does anyone lean on them in this way?
It is not true. You can see for yourself straight away that they do not print my picture as you suggest.

What are your specific complaints about British television and the foreign newspapers?
That the BBC has been very anti-Indian has been conveyed to me by the heads of other countries for many years, not just now. When I have attended conferences of non-aligned countries and so on, this was drawn to my attention, but we did not do anything about it. But just now the misrepresentation has, I think, crossed the limits.

They seem to feel that anything is fair if it is anti-Indian. For instance, we got information that the BBC had arranged a programme on the situation in India. They selected one person to speak for and one against—both Indians living in England. But when they found out the overall impression was pro-Indian, they just cancelled the programme.

Similarly, they have given a lot of time to one individual who is preaching a separate Sikh homeland. He has no following whatsoever here and hardly any abroad, but he was the one chosen to speak on Indian affairs though he is not at all in touch and doesn't know what is happening here. Then there was an ITV interview in which a writer, now a British subject, said 'Mrs Gandhi is going to be assassinated on such and such a day and I know who is going to do it.' That particular day is long past now! The high commissioner in London and deputy high commissioner have written taking these matters up, but the point is that this is a systematic campaign all over Europe and America, not just in Britain.

So far as newspapers are concerned, take a liberal paper like the *Guardian* which reproduced an article from the *Washington Post* saying that my son was slapping me. Another journalist wrote in an article published in many European papers that I was in the habit of slapping my cabinet ministers in cabinet—all kinds of fantastic nonsense.

Another canard that was spread, and is still being spread, was that this whole decision was taken by my son and one of my personal assistants—who have absolutely nothing to do with it. My family has been very much maligned and of course my son is not in politics at all. An Australian paper represented a picture of a demonstration in our support as an 'anti-Indira demonstration in London'. I must say too that several Indians and Britons who have returned to England have told me that British and American newspapers refuse to print their letters if they are favourable to India.

On relations with the United States, it is widely believed in India that American money has been fed to Right-wing Opposition parties to oppose the government's socialist policies. Do you believe, for example, that the Central Intelligence Agency has meddled in Indian affairs?
This is a rather difficult question. We read almost daily about the CIA's omnipresence and its mysterious operations. We ourselves don't have the resources to collect such information, but sometimes their movements here are a little suspicious and what we glean about their doings in other countries does cause us alarm here. So far as general Indo–American relations are concerned, we have always tried to work for friendship and we have received a considerable amount of economic aid from them. But politically it's not a question of our assessment but the assessment of the United States: what they think about this region and what is our place in their scheme of things.

Mr William Bundy wrote recently in *Foreign Affairs Quarterly* that the United States had got along far better with authoritarian régimes than with democracies and it was considerations of global strategy which prevailed in such matters. India's policy of non-alignment has been a sore point with them which they have mentioned to us. And even in my father's time there were attempts to build up what they call more 'acceptable' leaders, even within the Congress party. We can only hope they will realize that countries don't like being pushed around by anybody—not just by them, but by any country—and that stability in India is a factor for peace in this whole region.

In view of India's economic difficulties, how can her recent nuclear explosion be justified? Are further tests planned?
Surely it's because of our economic difficulties that we must turn to science. We didn't have our experiment to make a bomb but to see whether it could be used for peaceful purposes. The development cost was quite small and came from the regular budget. As to whether there will be more tests, that depends on what the scientists still have to find out.

Is there any intention of equipping the country with a nuclear deterrent?
I don't think so.

~

Suman Dubey
The Indira Express

The Asian Wall Street Journal
31 October 1978

Chikmagalur: AS FOLKLORE HAS it, a local ruler in what is now the Indian state of Karnataka centuries ago assigned a village to his youngest daughter as part of her dowry. The village, the story goes, thereby acquired the name of Chikmagalur, which essentially translates to 'little daughter' in the language of Karnataka.

Now, a real-life version of the tale is in the making as Indira Gandhi travels around Chikmagalur district asking the local people to adopt her as their latter-day 'little daughter'. And instead of a dowry, she wants their votes and the chance to again get into the thick of Indian politics.

Mrs Gandhi chose this constituency after the local member of Parliament resigned to seek election to the state legislature. But political analysts say he resigned to make way for Mrs Gandhi, who decided the time had come to step up her political comeback. Since being swept out of power in March 1977 by the now-ruling Janata Party, she has undergone judicial inquiries for alleged violations of the Constitution during her emergency rule between 1975 and 1977 and is charged in courts with misuse of power.

She chose this location, analysts believe, because the state is ruled by officials from her Indira Congress Party.

Even so, the comeback effort by the sixty-one-year-old Mrs Gandhi is the hardest campaign she has ever fought. In the past, when she ran from Rae Bareli in the northern state of Uttar Pradesh, she usually would concentrate on other constituencies, campaigning for other candidates. Voters in her own constituency would see her for a day or two at most.

How Mrs Gandhi was able to run for office in this controversy has stirred up some controversy in itself. There have been reports that she allegedly made false declarations in order to get her name included as a voter in the district, thus qualifying her for participating in the election. Mrs Gandhi's political team dismisses these claims, but her opponents are contending that she's guilty of contravening election laws.

Still, times obviously have changed. In the Chikmagalur constituency, her campaign started 19 October and will continue, from early morning to late at night every day, until forty-eight hours before polling day 5 November. At that time, by law, all campaigning must end.

By Car and Jeep

As Prime Minister, Mrs Gandhi had ample use of government perquisites to aid her campaigning. Now she must criss-cross this sprawling constituency by car and jeep to reach the remotest villages.

The effort takes its toll, and her face shows the strain of the campaign. On one typical day recently, the campaigning started at about eight o'clock in the morning in a town of perhaps 10,000 people. Wearing a lime green sari of handwoven cotton, she emerges from her room in a travellers lodge to be mobbed by a few hundred women and children who have been waiting since dawn to greet her. She exchanges few words because she doesn't know the local language. Her advisers point out local citizens of importance and she bestows a fleeting, mechanical smile on each. A local religious leader places his palm on her head and says a prayer.

'There's going to be a stampede,' someone shouts as the crowd jostles to allow her access to her car. At the beginning of her current campaign she used an American limousine, but she switched to a smaller car of local manufacture when its flashiness was criticized. As her car moves away there's fierce competition between about thirty other cars vying with one another to get close to her in the convoy. Three or four police jeeps get into the motorcade, and a grey minibus mounted with a large wood and pasteup portrait of Mrs Gandhi moves up front.

Barely a mile down the road, which is decorated with banners put up by the Indira Congress Party and the opposition Janata Party, the motorcade is flagged down. Leaders surrounded by drumbeating and slogan-shouting youngsters insist she drive through their locality. It isn't on the schedule, but Mrs Gandhi obliges, switching to a jeep. Supporters keep up an incessant chant, and a small band blares local music. Groups of children run alongside. Flowers are thrown to her, and she dutifully returns them, usually to women in the crowd.

More Interruptions

The motorcade resumes its journey, but just out of town it is stopped again by a knot of villagers standing beside a festively decorated welcome arch of wood and paper. Women chant a prayer, offer her garlands, and after a minute or two, Mrs Gandhi is on her way again. Villagers interrupt her progress several times more before she makes her first scheduled public meeting almost an hour late. 'How can we keep to schedule when so many people want to see her?' says a harried aide.

The meeting is in a small village, so Mrs Gandhi speaks for less than five minutes. Her first words are of greeting, uttered in the local language. The crowd responds warmly. Then she switches to English

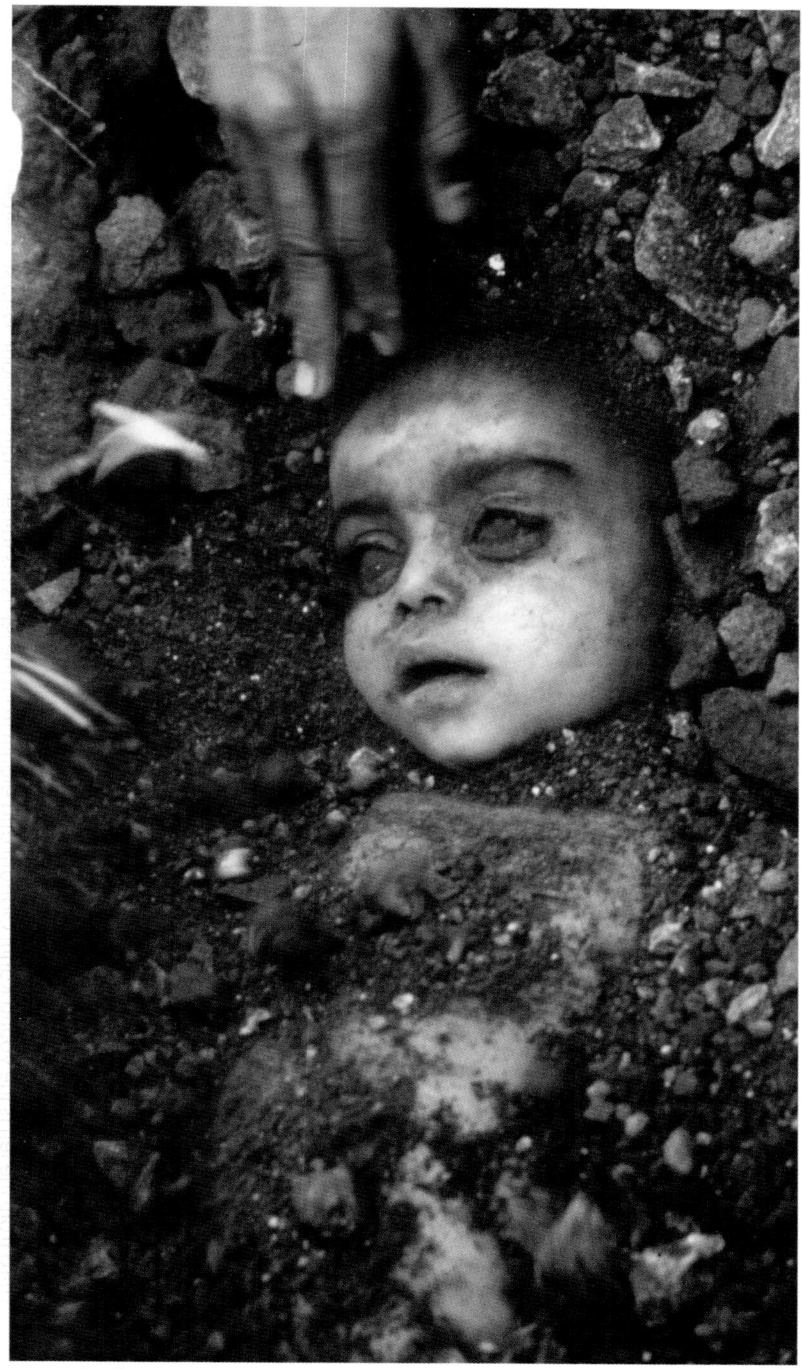

A child is buried after the leak of more than 40 tonnes of highly toxic gas from the Union Carbide chemical plant in Bhopal, India, in 1984. Photograph by Pablo Bartholomew. (World Press Photo of the Year 2004)

Pakistan People's Party parliamentary candidate Benazir Bhutto addresses a crowd while campaigning at a railway station between Lahore and Islamabad in1988. Ms Bhutto was assassinated at an election rally on 27 December 2007 just over two months after returning to Pakistan from exile. Photograph by Robert Nickelsberg/Getty Images.

and tells her audience in five or six sentences not to be misled by Janata Party 'propaganda' and to vote for her. Her speech is translated by local leaders, but the crowd doesn't seem to be impressed. 'They've come to see her, not to listen to her,' an aide explains.

At the next village is a well-known temple so she starts her visit with a benediction and a brief prayer.

Such visits and spontaneous greetings are common place during the day. She will speed through the countryside in her car, pausing each time she meets a group of villagers. But as her schedule slips further behind, these meetings become fewer. Sighting a small town, she will switch to her jeep and drive through it, hands folded in greeting or sometimes waving to the crowds. She will address perhaps a dozen roadside meetings each no more than five minutes. She will attend one or two larger meetings where her speech will be fifteen minutes.

One such meeting takes place just before her break for lunch well into the afternoon. Her speech, which seldom changes except in emphasis here or there, is halting and unimpressive. Her interpreters have to elaborate to make sure her audience gets the message. She speaks in short, jerky sentences and sometimes seems to grope for words.

Typically she will say that she and her party are the real champions of the poor. 'It's quite clear that the Janata Party is taking the country towards capitalism, communalism and casteism,' she says.

If there are Moslems in the audience, she may switch to Urdu and say that they are being persecuted under the Janata government. Skipping the long history of religious conflict during her own years of rule and before, she will recount alleged assaults on Moslem communities by the more numerous Hindus in recent months. If the audience consists of Harijans—'untouchables' as they were know before they became a political force—she will tell them, again ignoring the past, that under Janata rule high-caste Hindus are assaulting and exploiting their brethren in other parts of the country.

'She's relying on these two communities,' says a Janata Party worker 'and she's making capital of our social problems which are not of the Janata Party's making.'

Mrs Gandhi's party has traditionally had the support of these communities throughout India. She lost the March 1977 general elections particularly because her emergency rule angered them throughout northern India.

She doesn't say much about the emergency during her speeches, knowing that in southern India the more repressive aspects of those twenty months weren't that evident. During emergency rule Mrs Gandhi jailed about 130,000 political opponents, and her government practised enforced sterilization of men as well as forced resettlement of slum dwellers. None of these policies was popular. The government of Karnataka and other states in southern India generally tried persuasion rather than compulsion.

Mrs Gandhi tries to cash in on this by telling her audiences not to listen to Janata Party 'propaganda' about her.

~

Dean Brelis

'Dark Clouds and More Blood'
Ethnic Riots Deal a Grievous Blow to a Struggling Democracy

Time
15 August 1983

Colombo, Sri Lanka: FOR THE PAST six years, Sri Lanka's President Junius Jayawardene has doggedly pursued a paradisiacal dream. Inspired by the example of Singapore's highly successful free-market economy, the seventy-six-year-old President was determined to turn his tropical island into a model of democratic stability and prosperity in South Asia. Despite recurring tensions and clashes over the years between Sinhalese and Tamils, the nation's two major ethnic communities, Jayawardene had succeeded to the point where his government boasted to potential foreign investors that Sri Lanka was the 'best bet in the third world'.

Last week that bet was off. After ten days of bloody race riots, the worst in Sri Lanka's history, Jayawardene's hopes lay in tatters, with hundreds of his fellow citizens dead, years of economic gain annulled, and the spectre raised of further upheaval, perhaps even partition.

Civil liberties were drastically curtailed, thousands were left homeless and long food lines snaked around city blocks. Even though the 13,000-man army had restored a semblance of order by enforcing a daily curfew, most government offices remained shuttered. Said Jayawardene sadly, 'All human dreams evaporate.'

The main victims of the eruption were Sri Lanka's Tamils, who constitute 12.6 per cent of the nation's fifteen million people. Since independence thirty-five years ago, there has been tension between the predominantly Buddhist Sinhalese who, with 74 per cent of the population, dominate the government and the military. It was rising Tamil demands for a separate state, backed by a terrorist movement called the Tamil Tigers, that set the stage for the bloodshed. The trigger: the ambush killing of thirteen soldiers, all Sinhalese, by a Tiger hit team. In the havoc that ensued, 267 Tamils, according to government reports, were killed by Sinhalese mobs; unofficial estimates put the figure at three times that number. Some 100,000 Tamils lost their homes; in Colombo, the capital, seventeen Tamil-owned textile mills were gutted and hundreds of small shops lay in ashes. Total damage: an estimated $300 million.

Worse, de facto partition appeared to become a reality as thousands of terrified Tamils made their way toward Jaffna, a predominantly Tamil city on the northern tip of the island. Said one government official there: 'The partition is now complete. Every day more Tamils are arriving here to find a roof over their heads, but they have not forgotten what happened to them. They have been hurt and they want to hurt back. The signs I see signify dark clouds descending over this island and more blood raining on Sri Lanka.'

Under pressure from angry Sinhalese leaders, President Jayawardene moved to suspend indefinitely some fundamental democratic rights. Separatism, he said, was now outlawed—a direct threat to the separatist-minded Tamil United Liberation Front, which has sixteen deputies in Parliament—and anyone proposing Tamil secession would be stripped of civil rights. Censorship was imposed. Sri Lanka's communist party and two other extreme left-wing opposition parties were banned, their leaders ordered arrested. 'They are trying to get rid of me,' said the President. 'I have been forced to impose measures that are not democratic.'

There was indeed some evidence that the opposition exploited the passions that exploded after the Jaffna ambush which was, by all indications, carried out with the tacit support of local residents. At first, the government tried to keep the killings quiet to prevent a Sinhalese cry for vengeance. But word leaked out after the soldiers' bodies were returned to Colombo. Some Sinhalese troopers changed into civilian clothes and began to attack Tamil families, looting their homes. As the violence spread, the government believes, Tamil Tigers used sympathizers to whip up even more Sinhalese rioting in an effort to bring about total chaos. The left-wing Sinhalese parties joined the mobs. At one point, several Tigers dressed in navy uniforms opened fire on soldiers, sowing confusion among the military.

The bitter irony was that Jayawardene has been more liberal and generous toward the Tamils than any of his six predecessors. When he was swept to power in 1977, Tamil was accepted as a national language, in addition to the official Sinhala; through district development councils, Tamils were given a measure of local power. Encouraged by the concessions, the Tamils asked for more, with extremists calling for separate state to be named Eelam. Terrorists activity spread: between 1975 and mid-July, fifty soldiers and policemen, mostly Sinhalese, were killed and thirteen Tamil politicians, labelled collaborators, as well as fourteen Tamil police informers were assassinated. Jayawardene took little action against the escalating terrorism, angering both the military and the majority of Sinhalese. Then came the Jaffna ambush.

The economic momentum that Jayawardene had brought to Sri Lanka now has been jolted to a stop. Unemployment had fallen from 25 per cent five years ago to 14 per cent. The country was becoming self-sufficient in rice, and foreign investment and aid were readily available. But far worse than the loss of Tamil-owned businesses, which accounted for one-third of Colombo's commercial life and at least 30,000 jobs, will be the long-term damage to Sri Lanka's reputation for stability. Said lands minister Gamini Dissanayake: 'What has been attacked is the open economy that was launched by the Jayawardene government.' Dissanayake talked of 'building on the ashes of what was destroyed', but with passions still inflamed, the island remains a political power keg. Said one Sinhalese army colonel: 'It's our land. We win or we die, and there are a hell of a lot more of us than them. When all the dead are counted, the Sinhalese still will be here. We will build again.'

~

Sudip Mazumdar
'It Was Like Breathing Fire'

Newsweek
17 December 1984

IT WAS AN unseasonably cold night in central India. In the shantytowns of Bhopal, thousands of poor families were asleep. At a nearby railway station, a scattering of people waited for early-morning trains. Suddenly, at the local Union Carbide plant, a maintenance worker spotted a problem. A storage tank holding methyl isocyanate (MIC), a chemical used in making pesticides, was showing a dangerously high pressure reading. The worker summoned his boss. The supervisor put out an alert. But it was already too late. A noxious white gas had started seeping from the tank and spreading with the northwesterly winds. At the Vijoy Hotel near the railroad, sociologist Swapan Saha, thirty-three, woke up with a terrible pain in his chest. 'It was both a burning and a suffocating sensation,' he said. 'It was like breathing fire.'

Wrapping a damp towel around his nose and mouth, Saha went outside to investigate. Scores of victims lay dead on the train-station platform. 'I thought at first there must have been a gigantic railway accident,' he recalled. Then he noticed a pall of white smoke on the ground, and an acrid smell in the air. People were running helter-skelter, retching, vomiting and defecating uncontrollably.

Many collapsed and died. Dogs, cows and buffaloes were also on the ground, shuddering in death throes. Saha made his way to the

**Twenty-three years later, the plant has not been dismantled. Several thousand tons of toxic waste remain on the site, polluting local water supplies. Compensation has still not been fully paid to over 500,000 victims. Legal cases against Union Carbide, which was taken over by Dow Chemical in 2001, and against Warren Anderson, have not been resolved.*

railway office, only to find the stationmaster slumped over his desk. For a moment, he thought that an atom bomb had hit Bhopal. Staggering back to the hotel, half blind himself by now, he sat down to write a farewell letter to his wife.

Saha lived, but thousands of others did not escape. For days the body count ticked upward—from 300 to 1000 to more than 2500—in the worst industrial accident in history. Across Bhopal, hospitals and mortuaries filled to overflowing. Muslims were buried four and five to a grave, and Hindu funeral pyres burned round the clock. As many as 100,000 survivors may be left with permanent disabilities: blindness, sterility, kidney and liver infections, tuberculosis and brain damage. There were fears that a cholera epidemic could strike. Breaking off a campaign swing through southern India, Prime Minister Rajiv Gandhi rushed to Bhopal. Local officials ordered a full-scale judicial inquiry—and demanded that Union Carbide compensate victims of the disaster. As a precaution, Union Carbide stopped production and distribution of methyl isocyanate at a plant similar to the Bhopal factory in Institute, West Virginia. But it deflected questions about what caused the mishap until it could complete an internal investigation. The prospects of staggering lawsuits helped drive down the company's stock and forced officials to deny rumours that Union Carbide might have to declare bankruptcy. When Warren Anderson, the chairman of the firm, flew to Bhopal to talk about relief, local authorities arrested him on charges of criminal negligence. Later they released him. Union Carbide offered emergency relief, but refused to discuss outright compensation.

For millions of Americans, the Bhopal catastrophe raised a frightening question: could it happen here? So far the worst industrial accidents have tended to occur in the third world, where population density is higher and safety measures often fail to keep up with the spread of technology. By contrast, the US chemical industry can boast of a strong safety record. But with more than 60,000 chemicals produced and stored in America, government regulators and watchdog groups can't even tell where potential time bombs are—let alone guarantee that they won't go off. 'It's like a giant roulette game,' says Anthony Mazzocchi, an expert on worker safety in New York. 'This time the marble came to a stop in a little place in India. But the next time it could be the United States.'

Most of Bhopal was asleep when disaster struck. After the leak started, as many as 200,000 people ran through the city streets, coughing, screaming and calling out to each other. At about 2 a.m., the pesticide factory's siren went off. Thinking a fire had broken out, hundreds rushed toward the plant—straight into the path of the deadly gas. The train station was littered with the bodies of railroad employees and red-uniformed porters. The junction was paralysed for twenty hours, making it impossible for survivors to flee by train. Those wealthy enough to own cars gathered their families and tried to escape. But many drivers were blinded by the gas, and there were scores of accidents.

City of Corpses

The next morning it looked like a neutron bomb had struck. Buildings were undamaged. But humans and animals littered the low ground, turning hilly Bhopal into a city of corpses. Outside the mortuaries, bodies lay in piles. Those of Muslims were piled on top of each other in hurriedly dug graves. At night the city glowed with the flames of funeral pyres, so many that the local cremation grounds ran out of wood. A fresh supply had to be shipped in overnight before as many as seventy pyres could proceed with Hindu rituals. Three days after the catastrophe, rescue workers still hadn't uncovered all the dead. Teams broke into the tin, clay and wood shacks of the shantytowns, searching for victims trapped by the gas. One group of volunteers came upon an entire family snuffed out in the night. A small ten-year-old boy named Zahir guided *Newsweek*'s Sudip Mazumdar to the gates of the Union Carbide factory. Zahir wiped his swollen red eyes with a dirty rag, then pointed to the faulty gas tank. 'That's the one,' he said. Zahir had escaped from the shantytown on Sunday night, wandered through the countryside until daybreak, then returned to find his neighbourhood deserted and his parents missing. Hundreds of other kids roamed through the streets. Eventually, the government set up a missing-persons bureau to help all the lost survivors.

The city's hospitals came under siege. Hordes of sufferers, many still vomiting, crowded the emergency rooms. The worst off were old people, children and the poorest shantytown inhabitants. Many of them were chronically ill from malnutrition even before suffering the effects of the methyl isocyanate. Many doctors had also been exposed to the gas and were unable to work. Medical students and policemen had to be brought in from neighbouring towns to help out. What the victims needed most, said one harried doctor, were massive doses of anti-biotics and vitamins. But some of the more inexperienced volunteers treated them with anything at hand—glucose, painkillers, even stomach pills. One house painter named Salim arrived at a hospital with ulcerated eyes and burning pains in his stomach. A medical worker gave him a handful of high-potency antacid tablets.

'Keep Calm'

Rumours spread like brushfire. One day after the disaster, a blanket of early-morning fog caused people to speculate that another gas leak had taken place. Policemen had to take to the streets in cars to stop everyone from panicking. 'Keep calm,' they called out through their loudspeakers. 'There has been no new leak.' There was another report that all the milk and vegetables in the food shops had been contaminated. In the end, that also turned out to be false. However, a local official rekindled fear when he told townspeople to wash their vegetables carefully.

The response of Indian officials was mostly slow and self-interested. Local authorities never set up a crisis-management office. There were even rumours that Arjun Singh, the chief minister of Madhya Pradesh, had fled Bhopal during the gas leak. When Singh finally did talk to reporters, he angrily denied the charge. 'If this can be proved,' he said, 'I will resign from public life forthwith.' Later, Rajiv Gandhi showed up briefly, touring two hospitals and talking to relief workers. Then he left Bhopal for a campaign tour of the rest of Madhya Pradesh. For most of a day, Singh dropped his other duties to join the Prime Minister.

In retrospect, the arrest of Anderson also looked like a clumsy political stunt. Earlier in the week, Bhopal police had arrested five senior Indian executives at the Union Carbide factory, including the works manager. When Anderson made plans to visit Bhopal with two other company officials—Keshav Mahindra, the chairman of Union Carbide India Ltd, and V.S. Gokhale, the managing director—he was evidently promised safe passage. But as soon as the businessmen got on their plane, they were arrested and rushed to Union Carbide's guesthouse on a hill overlooking the Narmada river. The arrest order came straight from Arjun Singh. In a written statement, Singh charged Anderson with 'corporate and criminal liability', and accused the Union Carbide management of 'cruel and wanton negligence'.

It quickly became apparent that Singh had overstepped his authority. James Becker, a Bombay-based US diplomat who was in Bhopal to help with relief, arrived at the guesthouse to lodge a protest. 'I'm amazed at the arrest,' he said. For the next six and a half hours, Anderson and his colleagues were detained while a stream of police jeeps carried local Indian officials in and out of the guesthouse gates. Just before 4 p.m., Anderson was released on a Rs 25,000 ($2100) bail. He was taken directly to the local airport, where he boarded an Indian government twin-engine turboprop plane for New Delhi. Later, a US Embassy source hinted strongly that Gandhi himself had intervened to get the Union Carbide chairman released. The source suggested that Gandhi saw the entire incident as an embarrassment to himself and to his government.

After Anderson flew back to New Delhi, authorities in Bhopal finally let a team of Union Carbide scientists into the plant to conduct an investigation. In the United States, two Florida attorneys, Michael Tobin and Jack Thompson, working in association with San Francisco lawyer Melvin Belli, prepared a negligence suit against Union Carbide on behalf of all the victims of the gas leak. The suit, filed in US district court in Charleston, West Virginia, asked for $5 billion in compensatory damages and $10 billion in punitive damages. When Belli made plans to fly to India, a man identifying himself as a former Indian police official called the lawyer's office and warned that Belli might be in danger if he went ahead with the visit. The caller pointed out that numerous Indian businessmen and officials were angry about the negligence suit.

The roots of the Bhopal disaster traced back almost twenty years. In the mid-1960s, India was in the midst of its 'Green Revolution'—the central government's plan to eliminate chronic food shortages. Increased production of pesticides and fertilizers was a vital element of this project. So when Union Carbide approached New Delhi about building a pesticide plant, the authorities were receptive. A feasibility plan for the Bhopal factory was finished in 1969. Three years later both parties signed a letter of intent. In 1975 the Indian government granted Union Carbide a licence to manufacture pesticides. The company was set up with 51 per cent majority ownership by Union Carbide, with the other 49 per cent in the hands of private Indian companies and individuals.

Cronyism

In those days the surrounding area was not densely populated. Bhopal is the capital of Madhya Pradesh state; 900,000 people live there now. But Union Carbide built its factory on the outskirts of the city. Even in 1975, M.N. Buch, a local official in charge of public services, foresaw that the railroad and the plant would attract more people. He tried to get the plant moved beyond city limits, citing a law requiring that factories manufacturing dangerous substances be built at least 15 miles from population centres. But nothing happened. Buch was removed to another post; soon afterward Union Carbide donated $2500 to the city for a park. In the following years, more than 100,000 people moved into north-east Bhopal, most of them settling in the shantytowns of Jayaprakash Nagar and Kali Parade.

As time passed, strong ties grew between Union Carbide and the local political establishment. The pattern of apparent cronyism developed in part because Union Carbide was obligated to hire local management and employees. A well-known local official in the Congress (I) Party, Indira Gandhi's political vehicle, became the plant's lawyer. The former police chief of Madhya Pradesh got a contract to protect the plant. A nephew of the state's former education minister was hired to handle public relations. And the brother-in-law of the deputy chief secretary of the state of Madhya Pradesh took a high-level job at the factory. Lavish parties for local dignitaries were often thrown at Union Carbide's luxurious guesthouse in the Shyamala Hills. In 1983, when the Congress (I) Party held a regional conference in Bhopal, VIPs were put up at the guesthouse.

Because of these cozy ties, some labour leaders and environmental groups charged last week, numerous early-warning signals at the plant went unheeded. On 24 December 1978, a huge fire started in the plant's naphtha-storage area, sending a cloud of billowing black smoke over the city. 'Nobody in Bhopal slept that night,' one local resident recalled. Then on 26 December 1981, a worker named Ashraf died from a leak of phosgene gas inside the factory. A supervisor said Ashraf had collapsed after he 'removed his gas mask'. But the company gave no explanation for the seepage itself. Fifteen days later, another phosgene leak left as many as twenty-four people severely ill, including a number of local residents.

Mini-Riot

On 5 October 1982, in the middle of the night, a flange joining two pipes broke and gas seeped into the shantytowns. The incident caused a mini-riot which, in retrospect, looked like a preview of last week's stampede. In 1983 there were two minor leaks. And in January 1984, a factory worker named Arun Mathur died of a chemical allergy after working at the plant. According to local union sources, Union Carbide persuaded Mathur's family to move to Rajasthan. Last June, Raj Kumar Keswani, a columnist for the Hindi-language paper *Jansatta*, wrote a lengthy article detailing the record of the Bhopal plant. 'It's not that the government knew nothing of these incidents,' he concluded. 'After every accident the [Madhya Pradesh] administration talked of setting up an inquiry. But no one knows what steps were taken after the inquiries were completed or even if they were held at all.'

Over the years, one local official did draw attention to the potential dangers of the pesticide plant. He was Mahendra Karma, a communist party representative in the state legislature. In 1981 and 1982, Karma waged a one-man campaign on the safety issue, but he was consistently ignored by his fellow politicians. During one state-assembly debate, he had a heated exchange with the state's labour minister, Tarasingh Viyogi, a member of the Congress (I) Party. 'A sum of Rs 250 million has been invested in this unit,' Viyogi argued. 'The factory is not a small stone which can be shifted elsewhere. There is no danger to Bhopal, nor will there be.'

Until 1980, the Union Carbide plant imported methyl isocyanate. Then, in accordance with India's industrial self-sufficiency policy, it started manufacturing the chemical on the premises. The process was highly dangerous. Carbon monoxide, itself highly toxic, was mixed with chlorine to form deadly phosgene gas. Phosgene was then combined with methylamine to produce methyl isocyanate. It was in turn used to make Sevin Carbaryl, a pesticide effective on as many as 100 different crops and some 180 types of insects. At Union Carbide plants in America, Sevin is made with US technology. But the process used in Bhopal was researched and developed by an Indian research team. The Indian product was also known for its extra strength: it could kill insects, mites and nematodes at the same time, and required only twenty-four hours of spraying.

Experts were still unsure what caused the massive gas leak. It happened in one of three storage tanks, each holding some 40 tons of MIC, which were lodged partially underground in the Union Carbide complex. A sharp change in temperature, impurities inside the tank or even a minuscule crack could have caused a rapid buildup in pressure. But the real problem came as the gas began to seep into the air. The MIC should have passed through a 'vent scrubber', a small chimneylike protuberance filled with caustic-soda solution, which renders the gas harmless. But this time the vent scrubber failed to work. Nor did the Bhopal plant have other safety devices, common in many US plants, that would have alerted workers to the pressure buildup sooner.

As it was, the needle on the tank's pressure gauge had inched up well beyond the danger level before the night-shift worker noticed it and notified his supervisor. The chemical has a very low boiling point. So by the time it started leaking out, it had turned from liquid to gas. MIC is so powerful that it must be let into the atmosphere in less than 2 parts per 100 million in order not to cause harm. During the accident, it escaped much faster than that. According to union officials, at least five tons of MIC seeped out in thirty minutes before the tank was sealed. The effects of the chemical on human beings resemble those of nerve gas. When inhaled, it reacts with water in the lungs, often choking the victim to death instantaneously. It can be just as lethal when absorbed through the skin.

After the accident, local authorities immediately shut down the Union Carbide plant. No one expected it to reopen. Given the angry mood of the Indian government, the pressure of public opinion and litigation over compensation, it was also unlikely that India would allow Union Carbide to start up any new operations in the country. Gandhi's chief concern will be to keep the incident from becoming a major issue in the 24 December elections. Opposition parties in Bhopal were already calling on the Congress (I) administration in Madhya Pradesh to resign. But most political analysts didn't think the disaster would hurt Gandhi's chances. Except for the communists, most other politicians in the country have similar records on industrial safety and relations with foreign companies.

Shrouds

For the people of Bhopal, no amount of compensation from New Delhi or Union Carbide could ever make up for what had happened. By the weekend the streets were bustling again with cars, cattle and crowds of people. But reminders of the disaster were everywhere. People were still falling sick from eating fish contaminated by the poison. Hundreds wore dark glasses and covered their faces with shrouds to protect their injured eyes from the sunlight. At the city's main police station, women and children lined up to demand something—anything—to help piece together their shattered lives. And in homes, shops and offices across the city, people brooded over the same questions: How many more of the sick would die? How long would the discomfort of the less severely injured last? How serious and how lasting would side effects be? No one could give them answers. The residents of Bhopal had become the victims of an age when the rush to produce dangerous chemicals has often overstepped concern for human safety.

~

William K. Stevens

Indian Army Goes into Nine Cities as Anti-Sikh Battling Flares
Throngs File by Gandhi's Bier

The New York Times
2 November 1984

New Delhi: ARMY TROOPS MOVED into the capital and eight other Indian cities today to quell a nationwide wave of lynchings and arson that began soon after the assassination of Prime Minister Indira Gandhi on Wednesday.

Soldiers were ordered to shoot rioters on sight in New Delhi and five other cities: Indore, Patna, Rae Bareli, Kanpur and Dehra Dun. Curfews were also imposed in thirty cities, including New Delhi. More than 150 people have been killed and 1,000 hurt since Wednesday, according to unofficial tallies tonight. Earlier in the day the government said it knew of only nine confirmed deaths.

Slaying Laid to Two Sikhs

Most of the deaths and injuries were believed to have resulted from attacks by the majority Hindus on Sikhs in revenge for the slaying of Mrs Gandhi. On Wednesday the police identified her assassins as two Sikh members of her personal bodyguard. The new Prime Minister, Rajiv Gandhi, and fifteen national Opposition party leaders issued a joint appeal tonight for a restoration of 'sanity and harmony'. 'This madness must stop,' the statement said, adding that it was a mockery of tolerance 'to subject Sikhs as a whole to violence and indignity for what a few misguided persons have done, however heinous their crimes'.

Mr Gandhi, the slain leader's forty-year-old son, called on officials from riot-torn states to return home immediately to deal with the situation. The appeal was seen as a preliminary effort by the new Prime Minister to secure his power. Sikhs number 13 million out of India's 750 million people, the majority of whom are Hindu. Many Sikh men are distinguishable by their traditional long hair, beards and turbans.

Before Mrs Gandhi's death, some Sikhs vowed revenge after she ordered the army in early June to storm the Golden Temple, the Sikhs' holiest shrine, which had been occupied by a group of Sikh extremists. At least 600 people died in the battle at the Golden Temple, which is in Amritsar, in the northern state of Punjab. The state, which is where the majority of India's Sikhs live, has been under army control since then. The United News of India, a news agency, said today that sixty people had died in New Delhi alone, with thirty dead in Madhya Pradesh state, twenty-four in Bihar, twenty-two in Uttar Pradesh, five in Tamil Nadu, six in the city of Calcutta and three in Chandigarh, the capital of Punjab.

Twelve Sikhs Reported Hanged

In one case, twelve Sikhs were reported hanged by a mob at a train station in Madhya Pradesh state, and four others were said to have been pulled off a train and beaten to death just outside New Delhi, according to Indian news agency reports. There were also reports of Hindus burning homes, shops and cars of Sikhs. In New Delhi, as hundreds of thousands of people converged on the spot where Mrs Gandhi's body lay in state, columns of smoke from burning buildings and vehicles rose above the city. Mr Gandhi, who was sworn in Wednesday, spent much of the day greeting the thousands of people who filed by his mother's bier in Teen Murti house, a former British imperial palace where Mrs Gandhi once served as unofficial first lady for her widowed father, Prime Minister Jawaharlal Nehru.

Government officials declined today to comment on any aspect of the investigation of the assassination. Many questions have been raised about the identity of the assassins, how they were able to apparently infiltrate the Prime Minister's security force and whether they were, either directly or indirectly, the agents of any foreign government. India has charged angrily in recent months, without offering concrete proof, that Pakistan has equipped, encouraged and trained the Sikh extremists who have been conducting a three-year-old terror campaign in Punjab, on the Pakistani border. Pakistan has denied the charge, but it has been the cause of a major breakdown in relations between the two countries.

Amid the mourning and the violence, questions persisted as to whether Mr Gandhi could effectively establish his claim to the prime ministership and bring stability to the country. Such considerations were regarded as likely to come to the fore after Mrs Gandhi's funeral and cremation, scheduled for Saturday. Many world leaders and dignitaries are expected here for the funeral. But today, as arson and clashes between Sikhs and Hindus increased, heavily armed soldiers in olive-green battle dress moved in to restore order with permission to shoot rioters, arsonists and looters on sight.

'The full power of the state is being brought into action to control the situation,' P.V. Narasimha Rao, the home minister in Mr Gandhi's new cabinet, as in his mother's, said in a statement today. 'Communal harmony is our need number one. We must and shall preserve it with all our might.' Throughout the day, gangs of Hindu youths sought out Sikh homes, businesses, cars and motor scooters and set them on fire. By evening the streets of the city, even in affluent neighbourhoods and areas inhabited by foreign diplomats, were littered with the smoking hulks of vehicles.

Many Sikhs Are Fearful

Many Sikhs stayed behind closed doors, afraid to venture out into the charged climate. Many Hindus took out their anger on Sikhs in general, since two Sikh policemen, Beant Singh and Satwant Singh, were identified by police officials as the assassins. Beant Singh was said to have been killed by other security guards. Satwant Singh, who was also shot, was reported out of danger in the hospital, making him the key to whatever conspiracy led to Mrs Gandhi's death. In the violence today, some Sikhs fought back against the attacks by a minority of Hindus—a 'lunatic fringe', Home Secretary M.M.K. Wali called them—in traditional fashion. This morning, for example, on the principal street of Janpath near Connaught Circus, the centre of downtown, a group of ten to fifteen Sikh taxi drivers held off a much larger mob of attackers by swinging the traditional long, curved swords of the Sikh warriors that are called kirpans. Most of the violence apparently consisted of arson. Compared to past sectarian warfare and rioting in India, personal attacks were few. Mr Wali, in a meeting with news representatives this evening, said this appeared to be the case in other cities today as well. In addition to New Delhi, the army was called out to restore order in Calcutta, Bhopal, Jabalpur, Kanpur, Allahabad, Lucknow, Ranchi and Benares. These are in widely scattered areas of the country, but mostly in the north.

Mr Wali said two people had been confirmed killed in New Delhi. But the Press Trust of India, a news agency, which sent a number of reporters into the street, placed the confirmed number by late afternoon at fifteen, and said more than thirty unconfirmed reports of deaths had been received. Meanwhile, political commentators and politicians talked of the future. There were reports in the press that an early session of Parliament might be called so that Mr Gandhi might receive an expression of confidence. His Congress Party, of which his mother was president, holds a two-thirds majority in the Lok Sabha, or lower house of Parliament. For him to remain Prime Minister, he must retain the support, as leader, of a majority of the body's Congress Party members. Even if he does succeed in holding off any rivals who might seek to thwart his succession, in the view of some commentators who expressed themselves publicly today, his elevation to the prime ministership can be viewed only as temporary.

'Interim in Nature'

'While one must wait on events,' the *Indian Express* said in an editorial, 'it is clear that the present decision can only be interim in nature.' The reason for this, the newspaper argued, is that national elections to Parliament are constitutionally due by next 20 January. Although Mr Gandhi may be paramount for now by virtue of his office, it went on, 'the real leadership contest will ensue after the polls—provided the Congress-I is returned to power'. This was apparently a reference to a possible battle for supremacy between Mr Gandhi and other Congress-I (for Indira) Party leaders whose prospects for supremacy had been dim as long as Mrs Gandhi lived.

Before Mrs Gandhi's assassination, the Congress Party was widely regarded as likely to retain a slim majority in Parliament at best, and to slip below the majority mark at worst, forcing Mrs Gandhi to rule at the head of a coalition government. The funeral for Mrs Gandhi promises to be a solemn and spectacular affair. A military procession is to take her body from Teen Murti house to a place of cremation, called Shantivana, on the Jamuna river. Her father was also cremated there, in 1964, as was her son Sanjay, who died in a crash of his plane in 1980. The spot is near the Raj Ghat, where Mohandas K. Gandhi—the last top-ranking Indian leader to be assassinated, and no relation to Mrs Gandhi—was cremated in 1948.

It was against this background of evocative memories that ordinary Indians began filtering toward Teen Murti house after dawn this morning, just as, a generation ago, they drifted toward the bier of Mohandas Gandhi. Along the streets and through the small ravines, called nullahs, they came, finally to confront a thin line of policemen and young boys in rough white cotton garments and Nehru caps—the Congress uniform of old—with badges reading 'Nehru Brigade' on their chests. These were the only barriers, except for a rope, between the surging throng and the gates of Teen Murti house. At one point, the crowd was estimated at 300,000. More than seventy people were injured and many fainted in the crush.

Eventually an edge of the crowd broke through the thin cordon. Policemen drove it back with tear gas and flailing wooden riot sticks. The area was finally cleared, and the entrance to the Teen Murti reception hall, where Mrs Gandhi's body was displayed, was barred for a time. It reopened in early afternoon, just about the time the first army troops appeared. Knots of young men watched with solemn curiosity as the soldiers marched off to take up their posts. Earlier, groups of youths had dog-trotted in almost military style along the same street, chanting anti-Sikh slogans.

In the same area, a member of Mr Gandhi's cabinet, a turbaned Sikh named Buta Singh, was prevented by the crowd from going to Teen Murti house. He had to turn back. Later in the day, paramilitary forces, with Gurkha troops standing by, entered a Sikh temple near the Parliament house to clear it after gunfire came from inside. No injuries were reported. At another Sikh temple, called Bangla Sahib, the capital's largest, Sikhs with swords and spears broke out and tried to attack a group of Hindus across the street. Policemen drove them back. A resident of a south New Delhi neighbourhood said he stood on the roof of his house and watched while a number of men burned a Sikh temple, seized its priest and stabbed him. Mr Wali said today that he hoped and expected that the violence would be stopped by Friday, adding that Mr Gandhi had given 'very strict instructions' that 'at no cost should we allow these kinds of incidents to continue'.

~

Michael Hamlyn

The Despot Who Rides a Hungry Tiger
The Times Profile—President Zia

The Times
2 January 1986

PITY PRESIDENT MUHAMMAD Zia ul-Haq as he rides the tiger of despotism. The more be indicates that he would like to get off; the more the

*President Zia ul-Haq was killed in a plane crash on 17 August 1988.

possibility grows that he will be eaten alive. So he smiles his famous shark-like grin and stays on top.

Now that martial law has been lifted, the general remains not only President but also chief of staff of the army. Since the chief of staff has invariably been the one to ease out the previous ruler and bring in martial law, this is at least one danger that he does not have to face immediately.

The lifting of marital law has been welcomed as no more than a change of clothing for the military regime which has ruled Pakistan for the past eight and a half years. If he does give too much away and allows the politicians to get out of control, he knows that the lieutenant-generals of the junta surrounding him are likely to be as ruthless in toppling him as he was in toppling the previous Prime Minister, Mr Zulfikar Ali Bhutto.

Yet, at first, Lt. Gen. Zia showed no signs of wanting to hang on to power. When he took over and politely escorted Mr Bhutto and his ministers to Murree, the queen of hill-resorts, and lodged them comfortably in the guest houses of the town, he planned a brief clearing up of the disorders and a speedy return to elected democracy.

People who knew him insist that the intention was real. He had not wanted to seize and hold power at that time, but wanted to avoid a civil war and put democracy back on its tracks. General Zia, who had been appointed chief of staff of the armed forces by Mr Bhutto a year earlier, was anguished by what was happening in the country in mid 1977. Opposition to the increasingly tyrannical and eccentric Prime Minister grew into a mass movement.

Bhutto, unwilling to involve the armed forces, told Zia he had arranged for cadres of PPP—the Pakistani People's Party, the biggest political grouping at that time and the Bhuttos' vehicle to power—to be given arms.

Friends of the general say that when the opposition parties heard this news, they, too, started distributing arms to their supporters, though guns are a commodity rarely in short supply in Pakistan.

The generals gathered in the chief of staff's residence, close to the brewery in the cantonment area of Rawalpindi. There were only eight generals present (and only thirty-five generals) altogether, a situation that has since been remedied: there are now 100). They agreed to take power. General Zia decided, after giving further assurances of support, to the Prime Minister, to move at midnight on 7 July. 'Operation Fair Play' he called the coup.

Having taken control, without a drop of blood being spilt, he announced that new elections would be held in ninety days' time, under strict supervision and so entirely free and fair. Whichever of the warring groups won would be installed in power and the army would return to its barracks.

After supervising the installation of the apparatus of military control, General Zia went to see Mr Bhutto. They negotiated for a while, and eventually Mr Bhutto was freed to gear himself up for the elections.

Once in Karachi, say the general's supporters sadly, the Prime Minister began a campaign against the imposition of martial law, and mayhem again threatened in the streets. Mr Bhutto was locked up and the elections were cancelled.

There was now a bitter judgement to be made, the effects of which still have not been lived down by the martial law regime. A prosecution implicating Mr Bhutto in the murder of a political opponent was brought. Under the prevailing conditions it is scarcely surprising that he was found guilty and sentenced to death. What was astounding, however, is that General Zia, no doubt with the encouragement of his junta, allowed the sentence to stand, and despite world-wide appeals Mr Bhutto was hanged on 4 April 1979.

World opinion was outraged. General Zia was depicted thereafter as a bloodthirsty killer. The clean, straightforward, disciplined image of the martial law regime became tarnished with blood. The martial law courts and their sentences of flogging became the symbol for the regime. Opponents estimate that 11,000 criminals and political dissidents have been flogged by General Zia's executioners.

The growing Islamization of the country was regarded in the same way. Outlandish punishments—amputations, stoning to death, flogging of women caught in adultery—were attributed to the religious courts, even though none was actually carried out. Islamabad, which had been a reasonably cheerful town under the Bhutto regime, became the dour and alcohol-free zone it is now.

General Zia rescheduled elections for November 1979, but found them boycotted by most of the political parties. Only the Tehrik-I-Istiqlal party (solidarity party) of Air Marshal Asghar Khan said that it would participate.

The generals meet once more. 'Why,' they asked themselves, 'should we hold elections just for the benefit of old Asghar Khan?' It would be better, they felt, if they settled down to run the country on a more extended basis themselves and attempted to bring sobriety, cleanliness, good order and military discipline to Pakistan.

Then came General Zia's most dangerous stroke of luck. On 27 December 1979, just a month or two after the junta had decided to stay in power indefinitely, the Soviet Union invaded Afghanistan. Pakistan, which had hitherto been friendly with the United States—it had to be, in deference to India's close ties with the Soviet Union—now became the front-line state on the very border of expansionist international communism.

It could not have come at a better time. Pakistan found itself the special target for favours of finance and aid, particularly of a military kind, and the Zia regime was encouraged to stay in power and promote stability and military strength.

Stabilized in his position with American money and guns, General Zia remained in power, plainly believing that he was the best person to bring order to Pakistan. His moves towards the re-establishment of a carefully controlled democracy have all been devised with the aim of keeping General Zia in power, no matter how much he may publicly disclaim such ambitions.

The future dictator was born in Jullunder, now an important commercial town in the Indian half of Punjab, in August 1924. His father, Mr Akbar Ali was a government clerk. Young Zia went to a local school, but was bright enough to be sent to prestigious St Stephen's College in Delhi for his further education.

It was wartime, and the young Zia was much taken with a recruiting poster showing a daredevil tank commander, wearing the black beret of the Armoured Corps, grinning out of a turret. Second Lieutenant Zia first clipped on his pips and wore his tank commander's beret in May 1945. In the three months before the war ended he saw service in Burma, Malaya and Java.

He must have been a rather difficult colleague. The Indian army of that time, both before and after independence, built the officers' social life around the mess, with uninhibited drinking, highjinks and much social contact between the sexes. Zia was a committed Muslim who would not touch alcohol, shunned open friendship with women and prayed five times a day. On the other hand he was, and always has been, agreeable, polite and considerate in social situations.

When Independence came, he was serving on the north-west frontier, that austere Muslim rock-scape. His family chose to migrate to Pakistan and he settled them in Peshawar, where his mother still lives. His brothers have not done famously: one owns a Karachi shoeshop, the other is a spice merchant.

His frontier posting meant also that he saw no action in the post-Independence Kashmir war and, indeed, has not seen action since. In the 1965 war with India he was a staff officer at the headquarters of an armoured division and at the outbreak of the Bangladesh war of independence in 1971 he was on secondment commanding the Pakistani forces lent to Jordan. However, he has proved himself again and again as a punctilious, highly competent staff officer.

His country's first experience of martial law came in 1958, when the President, Major General Iskander Mirza, abrogated the constitution only to find himself eased out of the job by his chief of army staff, General Ayub Khan, a fortnight later. Major (as he then was) Zia was given charge of bringing calm and cleanliness to the town of Multan. 'He made sure there were no flies or mosquitoes on the tea tables,' said an admirer later.

When Zia, who had been promoted to brigadier two years earlier, returned from Jordan in 1971 for the end of Bangladesh's war of independence, he found the army almost bereft of generals because so many had been disgraced in the war. His promotion was rapid. He was made major general in 1971 and lieutenant general in 1975.

When Mr Bhutto looked for someone to replace Lt. Gen. Tikka Khan, the so-called 'Butcher of Bengal', as chief of army staff, his eye fell on the punctilious, loyal and religious Zia. General Tikka Khan did not recommend him. 'I thought he was dull,' he complained later. 'In any case, he was the most junior of all the eight lieutenant generals.'

General Zia's task since he took over as the country's ruler has been much like his job in Multan in 1958, only with a larger canvas.

When the army decided that holding elections was to be a second priority, he set about instituting cleanliness and order nationwide. Given his background, it was natural that the ascetic virtues of Islam would be his preferred vehicle.

While Pakistan has accordingly become a much duller place, the key to its carefully controlled descent into democracy has been in General Zia's own determination to avoid the over-excitement of popular politics, the untidiness of charisma and the imprecision of mass appeal.

Provided such excesses can still be restrained after the lifting of martial law, he seems likely to be able to remain at the head of affairs for some longer time—a standing tribute to the virtues of good staff work. He need not, however, be pitied too much.

~

Matt Miller
Indian Phones Stuck in Primitive State

The Asian Wall Street Journal
17 September 1986

Calcutta: SINCE HER TELEPHONE was installed eight years ago, Monideepa Banerjie hasn't once been able to contact Calcutta's directory-assistance service. 'Every so often I keep trying,' she says, 'just to stay in practice.'

Others here tell similar stories: Telephones that don't work for months and won't until bribes are paid; perpetual wrong numbers; exchanges knocked out because of rain; huge bills for calls that were never made.

Calcutta residents 'wage a constant war against the telephone', says Sailen Ganguly, who seven years ago formed Calcuttas' Telephone Consumer's Guidance Society to coordinate public pressure for better service.

According to Mr Ganguly, only a fifth of all calls made in Calcutta get through. Of the city's 250,000 connections, at least 60,000 are out of commission at any one time, he says.

Notoriously Bad

Calcutta's telephone system, inaugurated in 1881, is India's oldest. It also is considered the least reliable operation of India's notoriously bad telecommunications systems. Millions of man-hours and dollars are lost to wrong numbers and faulty lines.

Poor telecommunications service is often cited by foreign businessmen as a major impediment to operating in India. A Bangalore executive tells of having to put a clerk on a plane to Calcutta with a message because he couldn't get through on the telephone. Because it's often easier to place an international call than a domestic one, a Bombay businessman says that he is forced to call his Singapore office and ask them to relay a message to his Madras operation. (It can take days to make a call from one Indian city to another.)

New Delhi businessmen routinely travel an hour or so each way to their factories located outside the city to deal with mundane matters because phone links don't work. There is a twenty-year waiting list for telephones in the city.

Last month, former home minister P.C. Sethi, upset at being unable to place a call from New Delhi to Bombay, descended on a telephone exchange in the middle of the night, packing a revolver and accompanied by two armed bodyguards. Heated words, pushing and shoving followed. The next day, telephone operators at the New Delhi exchange retaliated with a two-day strike. Others, however, applauded Mr Sethi. 'I've received fifty telegrams and 100 to 125 letters,' he says. 'All of them support me.'

Emotional outbursts seem to be the only recourse available to frustrated phone users. Despite Prime Minister Rajiv Gandhi's much-vaunted calls to modernize India, the government continues to debate ways to improve telecommunications.

Quick Fix

'While the country is racing toward the twenty-first century, the telephones are backpedalling toward the nineteenth century,' said V. Gopalasamy in a speech last year in Parliament.

Some advocate a quick fix through huge imports, while others believe the country must develop its own industry for making telecommunications products. Then there is the question of whether the industry should remain largely the preserve of the state or be further opened up to the private sector. (India doesn't have a single telephone company. In New Delhi and Bombay, telecommunication is under the Mahanagar Telephone Nigam, a government corporation established in April 1986. Elsewhere, the national department of telecommunications, part of the ministry of communications, takes control.)

A decision on opening a second factory to manufacture electronic switches has been on hold since 1983, when a letter of intent was signed with the French company Alcatel-Thomson SA (The first factory, in Mankapur, Uttar Pradesh, is run by Indian Telephone Industries Ltd. Alcatel-Thomson provided the technology.)

The telecommunications ministry requested Rs 137.7 billion ($11 billion) as its share of India's five year plan, which began last year. The ministry received Rs 40 billion, of which Rs 25 billion is money generated through its own earnings.

Isn't Enough

Telecommunications Department Secretary D.K. Sangal says that isn't enough, and he has asked the government for an additional Rs 20 billion. Mr Sangal says that the extra funds won't necessarily mean a drain on government coffers. 'Commercially we do better than the best private sector company,' he says.

Indian government officials routinely blame a cash crunch for the sorry state of the country's telephone system. But many critics—and there are many—of India's telephones believe that new equipment alone won't solve the problem.

'Technology is just a small piece of the puzzle,' says Sam Pitroda, chairman of the Centre for the Development of Telematics, a government-funded effort to develop an indigenous electronic telephone-switching system. 'How can you implement 1990s technology with a work culture stuck in the 1930s?'

Meanwhile, India's 750 million people make do with 3.2 million telephones. The US, with less than a third of India's population, had 134 million telephones in use in 1984. And in India there are 103 telephone-service employees per 1000 lines, ten times the US figure, Mr Pitroda says.

Mr Sangal, the telecommunications secretary, admits that overstaffing and absenteeism are problems. As for the comparison with the US, however, he points out that India has 500,000 phones that aren't automatic and need operator service. His department also employs 30,000 workers to man the country's telegraph service. And, he says, India has 300,000 kilometres of open wires, while the US uses only microwave relays, satellites and coaxial cables.

Ten employees appeared recently to install this reporter's telex. Six did nothing more than watch. One, who said he was a line inspector, appeared to be concerned primarily with soliciting a tip (he didn't receive one). 'We have to help each other,' he said in Hindi. 'If you look after us, we'll look after you.' The telex went on the blink the day after it was installed.

Telephone cables are still laid by teams of men who drag the huge wire strands along the ground and dump them in trenches, sometimes just a few centimetres deep. The cables, unprotected by ducts, often short when it rains.

Outside the Oberoi

Maintenance is minimal. A telecommunications scientist, who works for Indian Telephone Industries, terms Bombay's major telephone-maintenance centre 'hell on earth'. On the sidewalk outside Calcutta's Oberoi Grand Hotel, Calcutta Telephones' employees dig up the sidewalk and pull out a cable. They attach the cable to a crude generator. One man turns a crank, generating an electric current that is supposed to indicate which line in the cable is faulty. Two hours later, they're still at work.

Efficiency is no better inside than out. Most Indian telephone exchanges aren't much more than masses of wires. Operators sit in front of obsolete consoles, manually plugging in lines. Air-conditioning systems, if there are any, often don't work.

When the power goes, which in many Indian cities is several hours a day, exchanges overheat. Dust gums up the switches. One Calcutta exchange is thirty-three years old and uses technology developed before the turn of the century.

Often a city will have two or three different switching systems, some of them already obsolete when they were sold to India. 'It's patch on top of patch,' says Mr Pitroda, of the telematics centre. 'We lack standardization.'

Calcutta has additional problems. Workers appear to be constantly tearing up the city's narrow roads. A telephone company official says that during the replacement of lights along a half-kilometre stretch, the cable was damaged in twenty places. Theft of cables is rampant, says the official, who asked not to be identified. However, Mr Ganguly, the consumer-group leader, maintains that most of the thieves turn out to be telephone employees.

The telecommunication department's Mr Sangal says that Calcutta's system is 'on the mend'. The situation will be much better by the end of the year, he adds.

There are signs of optimism elsewhere. Private-sector companies can not manufacture telephone instruments, formerly the exclusive domain of the national government's Indian Telephone Instruments. Based in Bangalore, the state company admits it has a hugely bloated and unproductive work force. Asked about productivity at the concern, a spokesman said: 'That's the main problem. The choice has always been for more people when (the money) could have gone for new equipment.'

In addition, the government has approved technology transfers with three foreign companies—Jeumount-Schneider of France, Oki Electric Industry Co. of Japan and Belgium's GTE-Atea NV—for the manufacture of telephone exchanges.

The government has opened the manufacturing of microwave relays to the private sector and is considering a proposal to allow private companies to operate their own microwave systems. 'The public sector is losing out more every day,' says a government official. Foreign companies continue to come to India with numerous proposals to improve the system.

Market Improvement

Indian Telephone Instruments has begun to manufacture electronic switches, with technology from France's Alcatel-Thomson. There's a marked improvement in reaching those Bombay and New Delhi exchanges that have been replaced with electronic switches.

Electronic switching means nothing if the call can't get from one exchange to another. And junctions between exchanges usually can't cope with the number of calls placed. Long-distance lines are minimal.

Mr Sangal says that long-distance transmission is a major problem. He says that the government will within the next two months award contracts for the importation of technology in the manufacture of microwave relays, digital coaxial transmission equipment, and digital multiplex transmission and optical-fibre transmission gear. Several multinational telecommunications companies have bid.

But all this is only a beginning. And the government seems in no hurry. Some of the bid decisions are a year overdue. Mr Sangal admits that it isn't likely the government will make a decision on the second electronic-switches factory until next August, when Mr Pitroda's Centre for the Development of Telematics must submit its design.

Mr Ganguly, who says corruption is the main culprit behind the Indian telephone's sorry state, believes service is getting worse. His consumer group, which has more than 4000 members, has held a mock funeral procession for the telephone and constructed a tomb in Calcutta dedicated 'in memory of dead telephone'.

This was the inscription :

Oh! child of communication
You were born to bridge the gap.
But corruption has caused a mishap.
Inefficiency and procrastination
Caused the telephone lines to go . . .
Snap

~

Matt Miller

Indian Firm's Success Stirs Controversy
Often Aided by State Licences, Reliance May Stumble with Gandhi

The Asian Wall Street Journal
24 June 1987

Bombay: IN INDIA, SOME companies are more equal than others.

On 7 May, the finance ministry lowered the consumption tax on purified terephthalic acid, or PTA, a substance used in making polyester fibre. Only one company in India is a major consumer: Reliance Industries Ltd. It stands to save Rs 225 million ($17.5 million) a year because of the tax change.

Government policies that appear tailor-made to benefit Reliance are nothing new. Now India's third-largest private corporation, Reliance could hardly have risen from its humble beginnings without numerous official favours. And despite several setbacks over the past year, including official investigations of questionable activities and the threat of a devastating customs assessment, Reliance continues to show remarkable powers of survival.

During the past decade, the textile and petrochemical company has been granted industrial licences while others waited in vain for government approval. On several occasions, Reliance, more than any other company, profited when duties were suddenly raised or lowered, or when imports were restricted. Since it went public in 1977, the company's assets have grown by a factor of thirty-three times, now topping Rs 11 billion. A long string of annual profits was broken only last year.

**Dhirubhai Ambani died on 6 July 2002 and two years later his two sons, Mukesh and Anil, split the group after a bitter public battle. They are now two of India's richest men. Mukesh Ambani's group keeps the original Reliance Industries (RIL) name. Anil Ambani's is called the Anil Dhirubhai Ambani Group (ADAG).*

Since the late 1970s, government officials have been accused in the press and by the Opposition in Parliament of bending the rules to suit Reliance. The company and its chairman and founder, Dhirubhai Ambani, have been accused of making secret contributions to the ruling Congress (I) Party as well as widely distributing shares, gifts and loans to reporters, bureaucrats and government officials. The company denies the allegations, as does Congress (I).

In the past few weeks, the controversy swirling around Reliance has assumed another dimension. The company is seen as a root cause of the government's recent leadership and credibility problems. (Mr Gandhi's latest blow was his party's overwhelming loss last week in a state-assembly poll in the northern Indian state of Haryana.)

Forced Resignation

The troubles arose with a finance ministry decision late last year to have American detectives investigate a Reliance purchase from Du Pont Co. of the US and the possibility of secret overseas bank accounts to buy Reliance shares or debentures. That started a chain of events which led to the resignation of Vishwanath Pratap Singh, formerly finance and defence minister.

Real or imagined the perceived link between Reliance and the government has become a symbol of officially condoned corruption.

(Mr Ambani refused to be interviewed for this article, saying a stroke suffered last year has left him in poor health. His company agreed through a spokesman to answer in writing a list of questions.)

Reliance's after-tax profit for the year ended 31 December 1986 dropped 80 per cent from the previous year, to Rs 140 million. During the past twelve months, the company's share price has dropped by more than 60 per cent and has taken the stock market down with it.

Official Harassed

But on 8 May, the day after the decision on PTA was announced, Reliance's share price gained 25 per cent; it has since dropped slightly. The various inquiries concerning the company haven't resulted in prosecution. The two principal finance ministry officials who had been investigating Reliance have been transferred; one is being harassed by authorities for his role in hiring the US detective agency.

The public focus of investigations has shifted from Reliance to the finance ministry and the detective agency. Reliance's proposal to establish a one-billion-rupee finance company, delayed by Mr Singh, is now being reviewed again.

Behind this resilient concern is the fifty-four-years-old Mr Ambani, the son of a rural schoolteacher. He founded Reliance Textiles Pvt. Ltd in 1967, with four knitting machines housed in a small factory in the industrial city of Naroda. His 'Vimal' line remains the most recognized brand in India.

Reliance got its first big break in the emergency period of 1975–77, when democratic rule was suspended. During that time, the company grew to produce 50 per cent of the country's yarn-processing capacity, thanks to a minister's decision that gave Reliance approval for expansion and denied approval to five other manufacturers.

The company also persuaded the government to allow manufacturers to import scarce polyester-filament yarn if they were able to export nylon fabric. This decision helped only Reliance, the sole Indian exporter of the material. In early 1977, the government further favoured Reliance by exempting those yarn imports from a previous duty of 125 per cent.

Reliance gained a virtual monopoly on the imported yarn (none was produced domestically) and could charge exorbitant prices. Customers continue to complain about the company's tactic of raising prices once it controlled a market or of creating artificial shortages by holding back supplies.

'At the Cost of Others'

One customer says that in 1982, on the day import duties were raised for a certain type of yarn that only Reliance produced domestically, the company increased its price by 40 per cent. 'He doesn't want to grow by himself. He wants to grow at the cost of others,' says the customer, a textile manufacturer.

In a reply to a list of specific criticisms that included crowding out competition, Reliance said: 'Any organization which is prospering is bound to be envied.'

Reliance went public in 1977. Over the next several years, the company infuriated competitors and customers alike by acquiring manufacturing licences to produce not only synthetic yarn and fibre, but also more and more of the raw materials used in making those products. Other manufacturers consistently failed to get the required licences.

In 1981, more than 400 companies applied for a license to produce polyester filament yarn; forty-three made the waiting list. Reliance was given the major licence of 10,000 tons annually. Another company obtained the only other licence granted, one for 6000 tons.

Reliance built a fully integrated plant. The other company, Orkay Silk Mills Ltd, decided to begin production by importing polyester chips, the raw material used in making the yarn. But the government twice raised the duty on the imported chips, then banned imports altogether, effectively crippling Orkay's production.

Many government decisions that favoured Reliance were made by ministers over the objections of bureaucrats. And in a country where it takes years to get through the bureaucracy on the simplest of requests, Reliance could obtain action in a matter of weeks. During a three-month period in 1984, the company obtained three major licences.

While Reliance may have been the industry's villain, it soon became the investors' hero. One magazine even referred to Mr Ambani as the investor's 'messiah'. Reliance dividends were very high. The share price kept climbing even as the company distributed bonus scrip. Investors who had never before chanced the country's highly volatile capital market flocked to buy Reliance shares.

The company says 2.8 million shareholders now own its shares and debentures, a considerable portion of the country's estimated ten million stock investors. Says a local merchant banker: 'The whole stock market has become Reliance.'

Reliance also capitalized on the marketing of debentures, a kind of bond, to overseas Indians as a way to minimize the need for commercial borrowing. From 1979 to 1983 the company issued non-convertible debentures totalling Rs 735 million.

In the following year, the company lobbied successfully to have the finance ministry allow conversion of the debentures into shares. This both reduced Reliance's high debt and added to its share premium account, which is separate from share capital and can be used at the company's discretion. Fund investors jumped at the offer since shares were being traded on the stock market at a price far higher than the premium paid for the conversion.

Brokers, merchant bankers and other industry observers have long accused the Ambani family of intervening in the stock market to keep Reliance's share price high, especially before new issues, when the share premium was being determined. The central bank's report on bank loans to Reliance-associated corners, a copy of which was made available to this newspaper, substantiates this charge.

According to the confidential report, eleven Reliance associates bought nearly four million shares—or about 7 per cent of total shares—in the stock market in 1984 alone. This doesn't include substantial purchases by so-called trading associates, many of whom appear linked to Reliance or the Ambani family.

It was the marketing to overseas Indians that first caused public scrutiny of Reliance's methods. In 1983, the *Telegraph*, a Calcutta-based newspaper, revealed that Rs 225 million of Reliance shares supposedly bought by non-resident Indians in 1982 and 1983 were in fact held by nominee companies registered in the tax haven of the Isle of Man.

The *Telegraph* investigation triggered bitter debate in Parliament, with accusations that the Ambanis had salted away money overseas in violation of foreign exchange controls. (It is illegal for Indians to hold foreign exchange, either in India or abroad, without central bank approval.) Critics said the Ambanis also were trying to profit from a recent policy change that raised the ceiling on the amount of shares non-resident Indians could hold.

Members of Parliament speculated that an Ambani-controlled nominee company could invest in Reliance shares and enjoy the security of knowing that the investment and any profit from increase in share price could be repatriated in hard currency. The Ambani family denies any association with the nominee companies.

The finance minister at the time, Pranab Mukerjee, refused to start an investigation, saying he wasn't interested in what he called a 'roving inquiry' into possible foreign-exchange violations. He added that if companies already had succeeded in underinvoicing exports to hide money abroad, 'nothing extra can be done'.

Founder's Bragging

But the minister's performance in Parliament and Reliance's string of successes in getting its way led many to assume that the company had substantial government backing. Mr Ambani did nothing to stop the rumours. When this reporter first met him in early 1985, he bragged of his ability to know of government decisions before they were announced.

Reliance sailed along until Mr Gandhi came to power in 1984, appointed Mr Singh as finance minister and gave the ministry broad directives to weed out corruption and tax evasion. The ministry started several investigations against numerous companies. Reliance wasn't exempt.

Mr Singh also ordered that PTA be taxed to bring its price in line with a more commonly used material. And he thwarted Reliance's efforts to covert some non-convertible debentures, a decision that caused the market price of the debentures to crash by 40 per cent in one day.

In May 1985, the finance ministry restricted the import of PTA. The day before the policy change, Reliance opened letters of credit valued at Rs 1.14 billion to import a supply of the material that would last the company at least five years.

After the government discovered the letters of credit, it ruled that the contracts were good for only ninety days. Reliance went to court to overturn the new ruling. But in submitting evidence, the company gave the impression that its letters of credit were composed in haste. One was handwritten, and one confirmed a letter of credit two days before it ostensibly was issued.

The most damaging documents concerned several letters and telexes between Reliance, its source for the PTA and government-owned Canara Bank, copies of which were made available to this newspaper. The documents refer to a letter of credit issued on 29 May, one day after the policy change, and a subsequent request to the bank to change the date to 28 May.

Both the Central Bureau of Investigation and the central bank investigated the letters of credit to determine how Reliance could have either discovered the rule change before its announcement or instructed the banks to backdate the letters. The central bank suspended three officers from Canara Bank, which had opened a letter of credit for Rs 120 million.

The CBI's investigation into criminal fraud has been completed—for more than a year, according to sources close to the inquiries—but no action has been announced.

Customs Inquiry

The customs department also is checking into Reliance. In February, customs officials accused the company of smuggling, asserting that in 1982 it imported a much larger polyester-filament-yarn plant and more equipment than allowed or declared. Customs demanded an additional duty of Rs 1.2 billion. If the company is assessed penalties, the total amount due could exceed Rs 6 billion. With net assets of Rs 3.12 billion in 1986, Reliance could collapse under such an assessment.

Few believe customs will actually levy the entire fine, however, and Reliance could tie up the matter in the courts for years. In response to queries on this matter, the company would say only that it has replied to the customs charges.

Reliance's financial health is an ongoing preoccupation for the Bombay stock market, where the company's shares have dropped almost 70 per cent from their 1986 peak. Mr Ambani's stroke left much of the company in the hands of his two young sons, thirty-year-old Mukesh and twenty-eight-year-old Anil. Both are graduates of US business schools, but bankers and clients say they lack their father's street smarts.

Nevertheless, Reliance remains the country's biggest textile manufacturer. This year it is scheduled to open both its PTA plant and one to manufacture the ingredient used in synthetic detergent. Holders of the company's most recent issue of convertible debentures—Rs 5 billion—must trade them in for shares next year. That will add Rs 4.3 billion to the share premium account and ease the interest burden on its outstanding debt.

And although many observers believe the company's boom days are numbered, others say its fortunes ultimately hang on the beleaguered Mr Gandhi's assessment of how business should function in India. At the moment, the Prime Minister may be more concerned with his own survival.

~

John Elliott
The Punjab: Gandhi's No-Go Area

Financial Times
23 April 1988

A COUPLE OF hours' drive from the Sikhs' sacred city of Amritsar lies a small dusty village in the rich farmland of India's troubled northern state of Punjab. There is a small, white, flat-roofed *gurdwara*, or Sikh temple, in the village, its doors barred for most of the day. It has none of the style nor charisma of Amritsar's famous Golden Temple, which has become a symbol to the world of extremist Sikh demands for an independent country, Khalistan.

In a way it is more threatening because it is a public and religious memorial to two Sikh extremists, Baba Ranjit Singh and Bhai Jagir Singh, killed nearby by security forces. Prayers are said here morning and night. Above a *palki*, or covered altar, are pictures of militants brandishing weapons, including Jarnail Singh Bhindranwale, the leading extremist killed in 1984 when Prime Minister Indira Gandhi, since assassinated, ordered the Indian army into the Golden Temple. Bhindranwale became a martyr and an inspiration to young extremists.

Surprisingly, the village temple also reflects the cry for peace and the exasperation of ordinary people with both terrorists and the often-corrupt security forces. Nearly 800 people have been killed already this year, about eighty of them—including twenty terrorists—this week. The figure in the previous two years was 1800.

'The gurdwara was built by the militants to keep their sentiments alive, yet they never come here,' said a villager dismissively when asked the significance of the shrine built in 1986. 'We know Khalistan is impossible and we want peace, so the government should accept realistic Sikh demands. We are tired and sick of all the violence and killings.' This attitude is ripe for harnessing in the peace initiative launched last month by Rajiv Gandhi, who succeeded his mother as Prime Minister

**The Punjab violence ended in 1993 after an intensive campaign by security forces, but rumblings of the call for Khalistan are still sometimes heard, especially among some Sikhs living abroad.*

after she was shot dead by her Sikh security guards five months after the army raid on the Golden Temple. The initiative is based on the release of some militant priests from prison—including thirty-four-year-old Jasbir Singh Rode who, the government hopes, will appeal to Sikh youth.

The idea is that during the coming months he should unite sufficient militants who are willing to give up Khalistan and negotiate a settlement for what Rode calls *pran azadi*, or 'complete freedom' within India. It is hoped this would help to defeat the terrorists by cutting their popular appeal and stemming recruitment among the young. Extremists already are undermining the initiative—launched without sufficient political preparation—and Gandhi is under fire for abandoning moderate Sikhs in favour of the militants and for demoralizing security forces who were fighting the extremists on a 'bullet for bullet' policy.

Ironically, Punjab is India's most successful state economically. The Sikhs are not a deprived or persecuted minority; instead, they boast achievements far surpassing their statistical position as 2 per cent of the country's 800 million population. Yet, a movement which started five centuries ago as an assertion of distinctive religious pride, and later of military prowess, has been allowed by successive governments to escalate through India's Machiavellian world of self-seeking power politics into a widespread problem of alienation, especially among youth. A desire for a stronger identity within a united India has developed unnecessarily into a call for complete independence which challenges the stability of the country, its government and police as well as the lives of its top leaders.

The Amritsar temple complex, with its central golden shrine sitting in the middle of a rectangular lake surrounded by white cloisters, is a no-go area for police. Never repaired properly since the 1984 battle, it has lost much of its dramatic impact and is no longer thronged with pilgrims. Instead, it is ruled by extremists who openly carry, and sometimes fire, AK47 assault rifles and other weapons, and who display maps showing almost the whole of north India, not just the Punjab, as the area demanded for an independent Khalistan.

Khalistan literally means 'land of the pure', but the extremists have a potential assassination list of 'culprits' which, they acknowledge, exceeds hundreds of thousands. At the top is Gandhi, who is forced to live with his ministers and senior officials in an unreal world of security cordons, surrounded by aggressive, but often inefficient, gun-toting guards. India's elegant, relaxed capital of New Delhi has been transformed. High fences surround embassies and large house, police posts and road blocks are sandbagged, and armed guards are everywhere—albeit often only with Second World War .303 rifles. The worst fear is that Sikh extremists, helped by neighbouring Pakistan, will assassinate Gandhi and cause a Hindu backlash of riots and bloodshed that would far outstrip the anti-Sikh riots that occurred in Delhi and elsewhere after Indira's death.

India is a diverse country with fifteen main languages and countless dialects, five religions, numerous deeply-felt regional and social rivalries, and widening economic disparities which increase jealousy between communities. In addition to communal riots, there have been many other regional disturbances apart from the Punjab in India's forty years of independence. They have included almost continual insurgencies in the north-east states around Assam, although these are far away from the country's main land mass and are scarcely noticed in the rest of India.

There were demands in the southern state of Tamil Nadu during the 1950s and 1960s for some form of separate identity, and various states were reshaped after Independence along linguistic lines. But divisions along religious lines such as those demanded by the Sikhs are refused by the government, which insists that India is a secular nation. Unity has usually been based on consensus rather than the bullet—apart from the North-East and now the Punjab. There is no real risk of the country breaking up because it is held firmly together by the Hindu ethic of its majority religion, which embraces more than 80 per cent of the population, reinforced by the complex and pervasive caste structure.

However, unity needs constant nurturing and guarding and another Punjab could be created by the recent mishandling of Gurkha demands. The Gurkhas are based around the tea estates and hill country of Darjeeling and want some form of independence from their Calcutta-controlled state of West Bengal. Like the Sikhs, the Gurkhas are a martial race who did well under British rule, especially in the army, and now want a better deal in independent India.

Such disruptions have much more chance of fermenting into crises in states bordering other countries where militants can find safe havens, arms and, perhaps, training. Indian diplomats insist that, since the late 1950s, Pakistan has seen destabilization of the Punjab as a way of winning the adjacent state of Jammu and Kashmir to the north, which is disputed territory. Arms undoubtedly are smuggled from Pakistan but India's claims, all rejected by the Pakistanis, include allegations that the arms now are being supplied free.

The Sikh religion—Sikh means disciple—was founded in the fifteenth century by Guru Nanak, son of an accountant living near Lahore. A mixture of Hindu and Moslem upbringing led Nanak, living in a Hindu area over-run by Moslem Mogul conquerors, to found a distinctive religion which fed on both. Sikhism has the monotheism of Islam—the focus of worship is the Granth, or holy book—and the Hindu belief in reincarnation, but it shuns the worst inequalities of the Hindu caste system. The faith took roots in Punjab; and 400 years ago the fifth guru, Arjun, wrote the *Granth* sitting on the banks of a large, sacred pool called Amritsar—which means the pool of nectar. In the middle of the pool he built the Golden Temple, called *Harimandir* or Temple of God.

At the end of the 1700s the tenth and last guru, Gobind, gave the religion its distinctive martial or warrior style in order to prevent the Sikh identity from being subsumed into Hinduism. The word *Singh*, or lion, was added to all male Sikhs' names. The heyday of Sikhism was the Sikh kingdom of the early 1800s stretching from Peshawar, near Afghanistan, to Kashmir.

Unlike Hindus and Moslems ordinary Hindus and Sikhs always have lived in harmony and still frequently intermarry. Until very recently, Hindus in north India continued a tradition of bringing up one son in the Sikh religion. Such close family ties and other links, based on Hindu businessmen acting for generations as respected moneylenders and grain merchants to Sikh farmers, helped recently to prevent Hindu–Sikh riots in the Punjab where about 60 per cent of the 19 million population are Sikh and 40 per cent Hindu.

Politics and religion became mixed inextricably from the 1920s when the Shiromani Gurdwara Prabandhak Committee (SGPC) was formed. Its job was to take over the Golden Temple, which had just been won over from pro-British priests, and to run other gurdwaras and their vast incomes from the faithful. The *Akali Dal* also was formed as the Sikhs' political party but has always been so riven with political infighting that, even when Gandhi gave it power in 1985 in a major peace initiative, it could not stay united for long as a governing party.

India's independence in 1947 brought something of an identity crisis—partly because Punjab was split between India and Pakistan—and led to a language movement in the 1950s called *Punjabi Suba* which eventually caused the Indian part of Punjab to be split into today's Punjabi speaking state and the Hindi-speaking states of Haryana and Himachal Pradesh.

The Sikh population still had only a small majority over the Hindus in Punjab so their search for power and identity continued. In 1973, they drew up the Anandpur Sahib Resolution of economic and religious demands—such as designating Amritsar an official holy city like the Hindus' Varanasi; giving to Punjab alone the capital Chandigarh, now shared with Haryana; an improved share of river waters; and a radio wavelength from the Golden Temple for Sikh programmes. However, none of this was enough to cause today's terrorism, which stems from three more factors: economic frustration, the rise in the late '70s of the extremist Bhindranwale, and the Congress (I) Party's determination in Indira Gandhi's day to crush all opposition parties, regional as well as national.

The Sikhs, who are the farmers of Punjab, were chosen to spearhead India's green revolution in the 1970s. The green fields, brick dwelling, tractors, and television aerials of Punjab are unsurpassed anywhere else in India and the state has India's highest per capita income, the best diet, and the highest consumption of electricity and clothes. But there has been a lack of industrial development, partly because few companies want to invest in a potential war zone close to the Pakistan border, and partly because of the Sikh unrest. The sons of the new-rich farmers, who belong to the proud Jat caste of Sikhs, are not needed on the mechanized farms; in any case, they regard menial work as beneath them—Punjab recruits people from the poor states of Bihar and Uttar Pradesh to do much of the hard labouring in its fields and factories.

The youth became easy recruits early in the 1980s for Bhindranwale's religious extremism, which was said to be trying to save the Sikh identity from sliding back into the easier doctrine of Hinduism. Bhindranwale emerged late in the 1970s as the creation of Indira Gandhi, her late son Sanjay, and a mischievous and wily old politician called Zail Singh who retired recently as India's controversial President. They wanted Bhindranwale to split the SGPC and so weaken the Akali Dal party to the benefit of Gandhi's Congress (I). But Bhindranwale became a force in his own right, turning the peaceful Anandpur Sahib campaign into a reign of anti-government terror run from the Golden Temple which led to the 1984 army raid.

However, even Bhindranwale was equivocal on the issue of Khalistan. He often made his demand sound like some form of devolution within India. This was far less revolutionary than the full independence call which has developed in the past year from the Panthic Committee, the top extremists' body whose members are said to operate from Pakistan and link with an international council of Khalistan. Almost everyone else agrees Khalistan would not work but no one, including Gandhi, is really sure what is wanted as a settlement. 'I don't know and I don't think the Sikhs know, either,' he has said.

Certainly, the original land and water claims are well down the list, long after others which are crucial, such as releasing hundreds of young Sikh detainees from prison and taking court action against Congress (I) politicians allegedly involved in anti-Sikh riots after Indira Gandhi's assassination. Rajiv Gandhi has an economic package ready but there is great suspicion at government plans—some critics think he expects his initiative to fail and that the army will then crack down on the Sikhs, so winning masses of the Hindu votes Gandhi needs urgently in the general election due by the end of next year.

Many Sikhs want Gandhi, who says he recognizes the need for an emotional gesture, to go to the Golden Temple to make amends. The problem is that the events of the past few years have hurt the pride of almost all Sikhs, from the most rabid extremist to the most placid top businessman. Until that is healed by the government, and until the original centuries-old desire for a proud and permanent identity is satisfied, the demand for Khalistan will become stronger and there will be no peace.

~

Edward W. Desmond

War at the Top of the World

Time

17 July 1989

Siachen Glacier: THE BLAST IS startling, and so is the reverberation that echoes like a landslide. But the sound of artillery fire—the sound of war—fades quickly in the gigantic stillness of mountain and glacier. Soldiers clad in dirty white snowsuits, their faces burned black by the sun, scramble to put another shell in the smoking 105-millimetre howitzer and fire again. They are Pakistanis, serving at an outpost 17,200 feet up on the Baltoro Glacier, just short of a sweeping ridge line called the Conway Saddle. Their fire is aimed over the ridge at similar positions manned by Indian troops 7 miles away on the Siachen Glacier, the longest in the Himalayas. When the weather is clear, the big guns sometimes fire round the clock.

On this day, the other side is not shooting back, so only a handful of Pakistanis man machine guns, to ensure that no Indian reconnaissance helicopter passes unchallenged. Others sort mail and work on a broken-down snowmobile, enjoying the rare few hours when it is actually hot under the summer sun, though fast-moving clouds can bring a blizzard in minutes. The blue skies form a stunning canvas for the cathedrals of snow-laden mountains topping 20,000 feet, including K2, the world's second highest peak. The Pakistani brigadier who commands the northern sector of the Saltoro area looks around and says, 'This place is beautiful. It was not meant for fighting.'

But fighting there is—and has been for more than five years. The Karakoram mountain fastness of northern Kashmir is an area no man had ever inhabited—and only a few had traversed—before Pakistani and Indian troops moved in to wage a bitter conflict, largely out of sight of their own people and the rest of the world. Neither side—Pakistan and India each deploy several thousand troops in the region—release casualty figures, but hundreds of men have died because of combat, weather, altitude and accidents, and thousands have been injured. Says the general commanding the Indian sector:

'This is an actual war in every sense of the word. There is no quarter asked and no quarter given.'

The paradox is that India and Pakistan are supposedly at peace and that Prime Ministers Rajiv Gandhi and Benazir Bhutto are trying to move from a chilly standoff into a friendlier era. Both say they want to erase what Bhutto calls the 'irritant' of the Siachen Glacier problem, and both instructed their negotiators to do so at Indo–Pakistani talks that began last month in Islamabad and are scheduled to continue this week in New Delhi. Though progress in earlier discussions was as thin as the atmosphere in the Karakorams, there is optimism on both sides that some sort of military disengagement may be worked out and possibly approved later this month when Gandhi visits Islamabad. But it will be difficult for the negotiators to divide the disputed mountain area between Pakistan and India.

At stake is national prestige as well as control of Kashmir's northern reaches. Since Independence in 1947, both countries have wanted the 85,805 square miles of Kashmir as their own. Three wars (in 1947, 1965 and 1971) have established a temporary boundary through the predominantly Muslim state, but the accords failed to cover Kashmir's northernmost reaches—and that provided the trigger for a conflict costly enough to hurt but not painful enough to be ended. 'We are here to stay,' says an Indian general, 'and we will stay as long as necessary. It does not trouble the Indian army.' Pakistanis are equally resolute. 'Siachen is no land to shed blood for,' says a corps commander, 'but the motherland is the motherland.'

The rules of engagement are clear-cut on both sides: if there is a target, fire. Artillery observers, posted on peaks and ridgelines, keep watch day and night, with night-vision equipment after dark, for the other side's patrols and resupply columns. Says a Pakistani brigadier: 'Any target is fair game. We wait for them to be well out in the open, where they cannot run for cover.' Where Indian and Pakistani bunkers are only a few hundred yards apart, there are frequent exchanges of machine-gun and rocket fire. Both sides insist that combat casualties are light, since the troops are well dug in and artillery lobbed over sky-high mountains tends to be inaccurate.

Infantry assaults are rare, mainly because it is so hard for men to move, let alone charge, at such heights and over crevasse-riddled glaciers. At 18,000 feet and higher, even a fully acclimatized soldier carrying rifle and combat pack can jog only a few yards without losing his breath. 'The terrain does not allow much movement,' says a Pakistani officer at an outpost on the Baltoro Glacier. 'There is a natural limit to this conflict.' But there is no limit to its fierceness. In an engagement that dragged on from mid-April to mid-May, including about a week at close range, soldiers fought near a glacier called Chumic. The battle cost dozens of lives and produced individual heroism but, like most actions on this hostile battleground, no strategic gain for either side.

The principal causes of casualties are terrain and weather. Never before have men fought for any length of time at such altitudes, breathing air that contains less than half the oxygen at sea level, at temperatures that drop below –43° F, in blinding blizzards that can last days. Both sides admit that eight out of ten casualties are caused by those conditions, including soldiers being swept away in cascades of snow or tumbling into crevasses. Says a Pakistani officer at the northern end of the Saltoro sector; 'We are brave. They are brave. And we both face the same enemies: the weather and the altitude.'

One of the killers is pulmonary edema, brought on by high altitude: the lungs suddenly fill with blood and fluid, leading to slow, gasping suffocation. The Indians, who cling to more high posts than the Pakistanis, say one or two men are stricken every day, though most survive if they can be helicoptered to a hospital in Leh, the capital of Ladakh, at an altitude of 11,555 feet. There they are put in a huge iron pressure chamber that simulates sea-level pressure, the only way to reverse the edema. When inclement weather grounds evacuation helicopters, as it often does, the afflicted soldiers usually die. Less likely to be fatal, but still serious and common, are hypothermia and frostbite, as well as eye and skin damage caused by bright sunlight reflected off the snow.

India was the first to deploy troops on the Siachen Glacier. In April 1984 the Indian army launched 'Operation Meghdoot' (Cloud Messenger), placing a platoon at two key passes of the Saltoro Range, which runs along the Siachen Glacier's western edge towards the Chinese border. India says it was pre-empting a planned Pakistani move, a contention Islamabad denies.

Pakistan responded too late to push out the Indians and lost nearly 1000 square miles of territory it claims was under its control. With the Indian army dominating most of the heights along the Saltoro Range, New Delhi wants that natural boundary to serve as the northern extension of the line that divides most of Kashmir between India and Pakistan.

The conflict escalated slowly as each side deployed more men, established more outposts, introduced more artillery and rockets. In September 1987 the action peaked, but neither side was willing to take the next steps, which might have involved introducing air power or expanding the conflict to the south. Says Lieut. General Imran Ullah Khan, a Pakistani corps commander in Rawalpindi: 'Our aim has been to make it expensive for them, and that has worked.' If that is so, the Indians do not admit it. Says an Indian general: 'This is our territory. We will not give an inch.'

The origins of the Siachen conflict trace to the separation of Pakistan and India in 1947. The dispute over the ownership of Jammu and Kashmir led Pakistan to grab just over a third of the territory before a UN-sponsored cease-fire took hold in 1949. In that year, Pakistan and India signed the so-called Karachi Agreement, which drew a cease-fire line but left off at map coordinate NJ 9842, at the southern foot of the Saltoro Range. The negotiators did not extend the line because there had been no fighting in the region. They merely mentioned that the line should continue 'thence north to the glaciers'. Despite minor adjustments after the 1965 and 1971 wars, the line still ended at NJ 9842, leaving the Siachen ownership question unresolved.

Almost from the beginning, New Delhi has argued that India is entitled to control all of Kashmir. Islamabad's claim is more complex. Besides supporting a 1949 UN call for a plebiscite on Kashmir's future, Pakistan points to evidence establishing that it has all along controlled the area from NJ 9842 to the Karakoram Pass on the Chinese border. Islamabad cites the fact that mountaineering expeditions for years sought Pakistan's permission to enter the region. It also points out that in 1963 Pakistan ceded 1544 square miles north of Siachen to China, an agreement India condemned. Islamabad's arguments found unofficial support in the early 1980s, when atlases published in the US and Britain showed the Siachen area under Pakistan's control.

In the end, none of the arguments matter much. 'The legal technicalities will never be brought before a tribunal,' says Robert Wirsing, a professor of government at the University of South Carolina and an authority on the dispute. 'They may never play any role. It comes down to a raw contest of power.'

Or to who tires first. Both sides contend that they can hold out indefinitely and that troop morale is excellent. Indian officers say in some respects the Siachen experience has been a blessing for the army. Says the Indian general in overall command of the Siachen sector: 'This operation has blooded part of the Indian army in a way no other conflict or terrain could have. The positive effects of that will last a long time. Anyone who has won his Glacier Pin [an award for duty in the Siachen area] does not have to look over his shoulder. He has confidence.'

That India has greatly improved its capacity for high-altitude warfare is evident—and this has a bearing not only vis-à-vis Pakistan but also on a dormant dispute with China. Just east of Siachen lies a mountainous area called Aksai Chin, which India lost in a brief war with China in 1962. If that conflict ever flares up again, India will be vastly better prepared in training, equipment, experience. The Siachen action has also pushed Pakistan back from the Nubra Valley, which leads to Leh, and widened the stretch of Indian territory between Pakistan and Aksai Chin that leads to the Karakoram Pass.

A major Indian base at the foot of the Siachen Galcier shows how far the Indians have come. It is at an altitude of 11,400 feet and is 75 miles from Pratapur, headquarters of the 102nd Brigade. Army engineers have linked it by all-weather road with Pratapur and Leh. One part crosses the 18,382-foot Khardungla Pass making the road the highest in the world. The most treacherous stretch is walled by sheer stone cliffs along the 50-mile Nubra valley, which is subject to springtime flooding. The road and a few small villages are perched on thin bands of slightly higher ground between the walls and the flood plain.

The base camp is a busy depot from which arms, ammunition and other supplies are shipped to forward posts in dozens of daily helicopter sorties, mostly on bulky Mi-17s or, for higher-altitude missions, smaller Cheetah choppers. Dug in nearby are several batteries of medium artillery. Troops are trained in the area: they acclimatize for six weeks while being taught skills like ice climbing and winter survival. Equipment includes Austrian mountain boots and Swiss down clothes. At the centre of the camp is a monument to those who died defending India's claims. Indians troops often refer to their enemy as Ravana, the loathsome demon king in the Hindu epic Ramayana.

According to Indian officers, every army regiment, including units from the deep south, has sent battalions to serve on the glacier; painted on the rocky inclines around the camp are their insignia. Soldiers make offerings and leave battalion flags at a small brick enclosure at the base of the glacier. Inside are images of the Hindu gods Rama, Shiva and Ganesha, as well as a portrait of the Sacred Heart of Jesus for Christian troops. 'The men always stop here before going up the glacier,' explains an officer.

The means a six- to eight-day trek along a blue-ice moraine. The men rest at supply camps like Kumar, named after the Indian-army mountaineer who set it up. The camp has a crazy, skewed look because of pillaring, an effect that leaves any covered area of snow several feet aboveground during the summer. Helicopter pads, gun positions, even tents and fibre-glass huts end up on snowy pedestals and eventually have to be moved. Garbage is another problem. Last winter's neatly dug pits resurface in the summer meltdown, inviting scavenging crows that attract the attention of enemy gunners.

From camps like Kumar, men and supplies fan out to the frontline positions in the Saltoro area, all the way to small posts in the mountains and passes where a few men live in bunkers dug deep in the snow. They take turns watching for movement on the Pakistani side—and the opportunity to call in artillery. The effort necessary to supply more than seventy-five posts and well over a brigade of troops on the glacier and in the Saltoro is nothing short of monumental, 'What it takes ten men to do in ordinary mountains,' says an officer, 'you need at least twenty to do here.'

The main supply effort sustains the five-year-old camps on Bilafond and Sia, the two passes that provide access across the Saltoro and onto the Siachen from the Pakistani side. Pakistani officers admit that India has the higher, more commanding posts on the passes, but then, as Brigadier S.A.R. Bukhari, commander of Pakistan's forces in the area, remarks, 'that only proves they got there first'.

Pakistan launched its only significant attempt to dislodge the Indians in 1987. Indian troops had abandoned a post 20,000 feet up on a shoulder of Bilafond the previous winter; they returned in the spring and found it in Pakistani possession. A furious six-day battle ensued in which both sides hammered away with artillery while Indian soldiers scaled the mountain in a drive on the post. According to a Pakistani officer, bad weather interrupted resupply efforts and the Pakistanis manning the post ran out of ammunition. 'But,' says a Pakistani intelligence officer 'all five men there fought to the death.' Of the sixty Indian attackers, only six made the final assault.

Three months later, Pakistan retaliated with the biggest strike of the war: 100 men—the Indians say several times as many—of the élite special-services group hit Indian positions established on Bilafond's other shoulder. Early on the Pakistanis captured a low post and by the third day were practically on top of a second emplacement. The Indian commanding officer radioed for an artillery barrage on his own position. The exposed Pakistanis suffered severe casualties, perhaps twenty dead and thirty wounded, though India claims higher figures. Some of the dead attackers lay frozen in the snow for nearly a year before Indian troops dug out fourteen bodies and returned them to Pakistan.

The Indians keep a curious memento of that clash at 102nd Brigade headquarters in Pratapur. A twisted chunk of aluminum that looks like a bad piece of modern art, it rests on a pedestal with a plaque reading DEITY OF OP75. The metal came from a pressure cooker. During the battle, a heat-seeking missile cleared the slit of an Indian bunker at Observation Post 75 and homed in on the hottest thing around—the pressure cooker.

Pakistani officers say their side's 1987 offensive was a success because it resulted in the capture of a post, although it failed in the larger objective: to secure a commanding position on one side of the pass. The Pakistanis seem to have settled for containing the Indians on the Saltoro rather than expelling them. Says a Pakistani brigadier: 'We learned the lesson that it is too costly to attack. It is possible to push them off, but it would require a large number of troops and huge logistical preparations.' Other Pakistanis explain that forcing the Indians out would necessitate strikes in other areas of Kashmir that would almost certainly lead to all-out war.

Instead, the Pakistani army has strengthened its positions in the areas where India might try to push even deeper into Pakistani-controlled Baltistan, the region adjoining the conflict area. From Skardu, the administrative capital of Baltistan and the centre of Pakistani military operations, all-weather roads—most built in the past four years—run through a maze of narrow river valleys to the foot of the glaciers leading to the forward lines on the Saltoro. Several poor villages in the valleys have grown richer by hiring their men off as porters and road workers for the Pakistan army. Says Brigadier Bukhari, who often plays polo with villagers: 'It's the one good thing that has come from this war.'

At Ghyari, a base not far from the foot of the Bilafond Glacier, Pakistani soldiers wear mostly American-made down suits and snow boots. They live much as their Indian counterparts do, in stone and fibre-glass huts, with pictures of starlets pasted on walls and a radio or tape player and cards or dice to pass the time. They talk derogatorily of the Indian—calling them *baniyas*, a demeaning term for Hindu merchants. (Troops on both sides frequently listen to music and news from the other country, and Pakistanis slyly admit to admiring Indian film stars like Amitabh Bachchan and Sridevi.)

Ghyari has special significance for Pakistani troops because it is the site of a simple stone mosque said to have been built by Sayyid Ali Hamadani, a Persian born Sufi who brought Shi'ite Islam to Baltistan in the fourteenth century. The Pakistanis maintain that the mosque provides evidence of Islam's—and Pakistan's—place in this region. Someone with a literary turn of mind has left a more modern imprint of Islamic culture by painting inspirational lines by Pakistan's national poet Mohammad Iqbal on a huge rock nearby. Not far away is another painted message: KILL THEM ALL.

On the rare occasions when the antagonists fight at close range, the results can be fearsome. In the month-long clash ending in May, troops battled intensely on a mountain and ridges near the Chumic Glacier. It began, the Indians insist, when the Pakistanis tried to establish a new post from which to direct artillery fire onto Indian positions: the Pakistanis claim that the Indians had merely discovered an old observation post. Both sides dispatched men in a furious race to the high ground, an icy peak 21,300 feet high, an eagle's nest that commanded the area. 'The secret in this terrain,' says an Indian officer, 'is to be the first on top.'

Seeing that the Indians would be the first, the Pakistanis took a huge gamble: in howling winds two soldiers were tied to ropes and suspended from the helicopter runners for a seven-minute ride to the peak, not certain whether wind speed and icy temperatures would cause them to freeze to death before they reached their destination. They survived, landed on the summit and held off about a dozen Indian soldiers climbing toward the same spot.

Bad weather prevented the Pakistanis from sending reinforcements for two days; moreover, the advance team's radio was not functioning. 'We spent sleepless nights wondering what had happened,' recalls an officer. 'The men survived, though they suffered severe frostbite.' Over the next month, the Pakistanis claim six of their men died, while at least thirty-four Indians were killed; India refuses to release its casualty figures. Accounts of the struggle differ, but it appears that the Indians eventually requested a meeting between the two opposing brigade commanders. After three sessions, both sides pledged to pull back their men, and the Indians agreed to accept two enemy posts that the Pakistanis said had been there all along. It was the first time local commanders had met face to face to sort out a disengagement from a battle.

By sitting down with each other, the two commanders were clearly acting in the spirit that their Prime Ministers want to establish. Both Gandhi and Bhutto are pressuring their defence ministries to come up with a solution to the Siachen stalemate, an extremely expensive effort to hold territory of little use except as a prop to national pride and abstract strategic considerations. Despite the Indian army's achievements on the glacier, says a Gandhi adviser, 'it is a very costly and uncomfortable situation for us'. The Pakistani view expressed privately is identical. Says a Pakistani defence ministry official: 'The Indian army is fed up with life there, and our troops are not very happy either. It is purposeless.'

Pakistan's position has been that India should pull back from the glacier, after which the two sides could discuss a new line. The key requirement: it must begin at NJ 9842 and end at the Karakoram Pass. Pakistan would be willing to draw a demarcation between those points, which would involve a compromise between its earlier claims and India's current position on Saltoro Range.

India proposes a cease-fire in place, followed by a thinning out of forces in the Saltoro area. Pakistan has rejected both proposals, fearing they would have the effect of ratifying India's current positions in the Saltoro. In the talks last month, New Delhi broached a new formula slightly closer to Pakistan's: pull back the troops and establish a demilitarized zone, then hold talks on establishing a line from NJ 9842 to the Chinese border.

But there was no agreement on the area of the demilitarized zone within which the line would eventually be drawn. India's proposal placed it too far west, too deep in Pakistani territory, excluding the Karakoram Pass as a possible terminus for a boundary line. Pakistan's countersuggestion shifted the zone east, something the Indians were not prepared to accept. Now both sides are trying to work out a compromise, and they plan to meet again in July.

Who will compromise? After investing heavily in lives and money to take and hold the Saltoro, it would be politically difficult for Gandhi to yield even part of the territory to Pakistan, especially with national elections only months away. Bhutto is in an even more sensitive position. Having once taunted General Zia ul-Haq, the late President, for losing the territory in the first place, she now faces poisonous criticism from opposition leaders who accuse her of 'submission' to India. In the end, both Gandhi and Bhutto will have to face down their political antagonists in order to find a compromise settlement on the line in the north's icy fastness. Otherwise it will continue to be drawn in men's blood.

~

Mark Fineman

Nepal Police Kill Scores of Pro-Democracy Protestors

The Los Angeles Times
7 April 1990

Katmandu, Nepal: POLICE SHOT TO death scores of protestors Friday after the largest pro-democracy demonstration in the history of this remote Himalayan kingdom degenerated into street violence. Hundreds were injured, dozens of shops and offices were damaged, and the capital was littered with broken glass and burning tires.

At the height of the street battles, which erupted after demonstrators started marching toward King Birendra's downtown palace, the Nepalese army was called out in force for the first time since the democracy demonstrations began more than seven weeks ago.

Hundreds of soldiers with machine guns continued to ring the palace throughout the night, although the streets of Katmandu were deserted.

Friday's carnage, which left hospitals overflowing with injured, was the worst in recent memory in Nepal's once-idyllic capital city. Analysts said the violence deepened the crisis facing the nation and its king, who has ruled over one of the world's oldest monarchies with virtually unchallenged power for more than a decade.

The killings came after King Birendra, fourty-four, issued a proclamation early Friday dissolving the government, pledging to embrace democratic reforms and appoint a commission on constitutional change, and promising to investigate earlier police shootings, which resulted from the hard-line cabinet's policy of using armed riot troops to break up demonstrations.

'I am for democracy,' the king declared in his radio appeal for support from his nation of eighteen million.

Instead, virtually every sector of Nepalese society answered with a citywide strike Friday, and within hours of the king's announcement, the streets of Katmandu filled with tens of thousands of protesters shouting slogans against Nepal's rubber-stamp National Assembly and the king himself.

By afternoon, according to several independent witnesses, the crowd had swelled to more than 100,000, by far the largest protest in Katmandu's history. Until late afternoon, though, the mood was peaceful and festive, although most witnesses agreed that there was a strong undercurrent of anger.

Protestors were seen embracing and shaking hands with police, who appeared as relaxed as those in the crowd. At one point, a mass of demonstrators moved from the outdoor arena that was the centre of their protest to a nearby hospital where Ganesh Man Singh, leader of the Nepali Congress Party—which has spearheaded the pro-democracy drive along with an alliance of communist parties—has been since his failing health forced authorities to release him from house arrest.

'They wanted to fetch Ganesh, but the doctors said he was not in good enough health to be moved,' a relative said of the seventy-five-year-old leader.

Singh instead released an angry statement flatly rejecting the king's attempt at reconciliation and sharply criticizing the new government that the king had formed earlier in the day.

Calling the royal proclamation 'vague and hollow promises', the party leader declared, 'The people who have been braving the bullets . . . had definitely not expected to witness the flimsy drama of a Tweedledum being replaced by a Tweedledee.

'What they had aspired for and demanded was a multi-party scheme.'

Singh then warned of violence, adding that the king's announcement 'would only add fuel to the fury of the people' and that the blood would be on the government's hands.

Two hours later, the bloodshed began. Masses began marching down Durbar Marg (Palace Road) toward Birendra's sprawling complex. Just 400 yards from the palace gates, they used stones and sticks and their bare hands to attack a prominent statue of King Mahendra, Birendra's father, who ended Nepal's decade-long experiment with multi-party democracy when he staged a palace coup in 1960.

Police first tried to stop the demonstrators with tear gas, but they continued to surge toward the palace, and the shooting soon started.

Witnesses said they saw dozens of demonstrators falling with bullet wounds in their heads and chests. Police chased them through narrow lanes and alleys, firing at random.

'It was wanton killing,' said a Nepalese professional who is among the many professors, doctors, teachers, engineers, civil servants and even airline pilots who have joined the students and politicians in the weeks since the protest movement began.

No official death count was announced, but doctors, eyewitnesses and other independent sources said that as many as ninety were killed and that hundreds were injured.

Demonstrators clashed with police in three other towns, and at least nine people were reported killed outside the capital.

A British tourist, twenty-six-year-old Richard John Williams, was shot to death in the cross-fire in Katmandu, and two other foreigners were wounded, doctors said.

A doctor at Bir Hospital, near the area where most of the violence occurred, said there were seven dead in the hospital morgue and that ninety-eight others were admitted for gunshot wounds. However, he and other sources quoted witnesses as saying they saw police trucks loaded with bodies being taken for cremation at police morgues.

When the shooting started, the protesters 'became a wild mob', according to one witness. They smashed the windows of most of the shops and offices along Durbar Marg, a boulevard usually teeming with tourists, and began chanting insults at the king.

'Birendra, the thief, leave the country!' they shouted of a king who has long been a symbol of Nepal's nationalism and who many Nepalese believe is an incarnation of Hinduism's greatest god.

'The situation is now very bad,' said one Nepalese businessman who has supported the king and the government throughout the protest movement.

'This began as a movement for a multi-party system—not against the king. The politicians were insisting only on a constitutional monarchy. But now, there is chanting against the king himself.'

~

Barbara Crossette
In Kashmir Valley, Alienation Turns Deadly

The New York Times
15 June 1990

Srinagar, Kashmir: SILENT, BAREFOOT MEN dug a very small grave recently at the Idgar Martyrs' Cemetery, a new landmark on the outskirts of this battered city. The grave was for six-year-old Sajad Ahmad Sofi, shot by Indian troops, his relatives said, as he tried to hide between his father's legs during a search of the family home.

'Put aside the malnutrition, the shortage of vaccines, the gastroenteritis, the trauma, the nightmares of children,' said Altaf Hussain, a pediatrician. 'Here we have three-year-olds, four-year-olds subjected to bullets. And to add insult to injury, we hear them dubbed "terrorists" on the evening news from Delhi.'

Over the least two years, there has been a silent revolution in the Kashmir Valley, the verdant home of poetry and song that Mogul emperors called Paradise on Earth.

Separatists Gain Support

Small groups of armed Muslim separatists, who fifteen months ago were described as a radical fringe attractive mostly to unemployed youths, now apparently have the support of an alienated, influential middle class.

Kashmiris say the introduction late last year of thousands of Indian troops and paramilitary forces, who patrolled deserted streets and searched houses, only speeded up a process of alienation that has been going on for more than forty years.

'They have made every Muslim a suspect,' a businessman said of the Indian armed forces' attempts to subdue a fast-growing independence movement. 'We are all militants now.'

More than 10,000 civil servants are said to have signed an 'open letter to the citizens of the world' cataloguing the human toll of extended curfews, violent searches, the interrogations of young men and women, the gang-rape of a bride and the firing on mourners carrying the body of the assassinated religious leader, Moulvi Mohammad Farooq.

'It was not bullets,' the letter says, 'but something worse than venom being poured out of those guns that has shattered hundreds of families, brought shame to Indian democracy and left a scar on the psyche of Kashmir that would never be removed.' [In New Delhi, Jagmohan, who served twice as Governor of Jammu and Kashmir state, said in an interview that by the beginning of his second term 'all the components of power had been taken over by the terrorists or their supporters'. Mr Jagmohan, who uses only one name, served from April 1984 to July 1989 and from January through May of this year. He was dismissed after troops fired on a funeral procession, killing at least forty-seven. 'By mid-1988,' he said, 'they could call a general strike and the government couldn't do anything. In two years they had the upper hand in every aspect of the establishment—administration, schools, hospitals.'

The former Governor said he had no alternative but to impose long curfews—one lasted sixteen days—and crack down on militancy while trying to rebuild local administration.]

Human Rights Monitors Barred

India bars international human rights organizations from visiting Kashmir, where all foreigners must register with the police on entering the Valley. But several Indian teams of concerned citizens have visited the Valley and written critical reports.

In Srinagar, Mufti Bahauddin Farooqi, a former chief justice of the Jammu and Kashmir High Court, and his son, Shoukat Ahmed Farooqi, a lawyer, have begun documenting allegations of human and civil rights violations against Kashmiris.

Talking about their work in an interview at Justice Farooqi's home, they say they focus on both the state administration and on the array of federal forces deployed here: the Indian army, the paramilitary Central Reserve Police Force, the Border Security Force, the Indo-Tibetan Border Patrol, National Security Guards and various intelligence agencies.

Troops in Srinagar alone have commandeered at least fifteen hotels as well as guest houses and private homes.

Justice Farooqi said the armed forces were sent to Kashmir in contravention of Jammu and Kashmir's special status in the Indian Constitution.

Many Detained Without Trial

Between 11,000 and 15,000 Kashmiris have been detained without trial, according to members of the Kashmir Bar Association, who also say that bodies of some have been dumped along the Pakistan border to be labelled as 'infiltrators'.

Reporters visiting the Kashmir Valley are inevitably introduced to victims of torture. Sometimes these are local policemen, who say they are distrusted by Indian forces, who doubt their loyalty. A state police constable in Baramulla said he was picked up, wearing civilian clothes, at a bus stop by federal troops.

'I showed them my police identity card,' he said. 'The colonel said, "This has no value in my eyes."' Refusing to implicate a Kashmir police officer in the terrorist movement, he said, he was subjected to electric shock.

'They also put hot irons on my back and thighs,' he said. 'When I asked for water, they threw petrol mixed with chillis on my wounds.'

'On the fourth day, they threw me in a truck and told the driver to dump me at the side of the road and back over me,' he said. 'I was saved by a shopkeeper, who pulled me away and took me to the hospital.'

He lifts his shirt, and loosens his hospital trousers to show dozens of branding-iron burns on his body.

Kashmiris also charge Indian forces with theft—an allegation also made in northern Sri Lanka when Indians were stationed there from 1987 until early this year.

A woman in her mid-seventies said thirty-two soldiers of the Border Security Force entered the home where she lives with her son and his family. It was just after midnight. There was no warning.

'They came in here where we were sleeping. I had Rs 33,700 [about $2000]. They took 26,000. After they left, we discovered they had also stolen our radio, a watch, shoes, slippers, water glasses, a flashlight and a nutcracker.'

Accounts of Torture

Surgeons and other medical staff of one of Srinagar's largest hospitals crowded into a consulting room, all offering accounts of torture cases they have seen, including a man whose rectum had been torn by the insertion of a dirty bamboo pole.

'Whenever the medical profession has extended a hand to victims of the violence in our society, there have been problems,' a doctor said. 'The security forces have entered hospitals, beaten patients, hit doctors, entered operating theatres, smashed instruments. Ambulances have been attacked. Curfew passes are confiscated. A number of people have died, unable to reach hospitals.'

Doctors say there are shortages of medicines for diabetics, cardiac patients, ulcer treatments, hypertension and cancer. They charge that Indian Airlines won't accept shipments of drugs from New Delhi, 600 miles away. The airline says it is curtailing cargo shipments for security reasons.

~

James Clad
Towards a Hindu Raj
Religious-Based Party Sets Its Sights on Power

The Far Eastern Economic Review
20 September 1990

New Delhi: THE POSSIBILITY INDIA may soon have its first, self-consciously 'Hindu', government has increased recently. Already the timing and outcome of the next general election depends heavily on the Bharatiya Janta Party (BJP), a cadre-based movement promising a Hindu renaissance, an end to Muslim privileges and the production of nuclear weapons.

Formed only ten years ago, the BJP has risen meteorically since 1985. In the November 1989 election its parliamentary representation shot up from two MPs to eighty-six, making it the third-largest party in India's 525-seat lower house. The BJP now trails only behind Prime

**The BJP headed coalition governments between 1998 and 2004, with Atal Bihari Vajpayee as Prime Minister. Vajpayee withdrew from active politics in 2007 because of ill health, and L.K. Advani was named party leader and prime ministerial candidate.*

Minister V.P. Singh's Janata Dal party's 141 MPs and the Congress party's 195.

BJP president L.K. Advani means business when he say he intends to 'take Delhi'. His party is riding a surge in support that shows no sign of slowing. Last November the BJP polled the third-highest popular vote; in February's state assembly elections it won 497 seats, the largest tally.

The party now runs three states—Rajasthan, Himachal Pradesh and Madhya Pradesh—administering more than 100 million people. It has joined a coalition in another state, Gujarat, while propping up a Janata Dal government in Bihar.

The first taste of direct control gives India a glimpse of the BJP's promised *Hindu Rashtra*, or Hindu Nation. Advani also wields indirect power in New Delhi because Singh's minority government depends on the BJP to survive any no-confidence challenge. While the Janata Dal bickers and the Congress party drifts, the BJP's firmness, lack of public squabbling and incorruptible image steadily add to its appeal.

Most of all, the BJP gives the impression of knowing what if wants and how to get it. This is a powerful asset at a time of domestic crises, of which intensifying separatism, possible war with Pakistan and rapid inflation are but three. Yet its goals remain elusive and, to some, dangerously radical.

The respected commentator N.J. Nanporia recently wrote that the BJP is 'sometimes flirting with or repudiating [Mahatma] Gandhian socialism, and sometimes recoiling from, though never wholly rejecting, the spirit of militant Hinduism'. Nanporia added that 'though the BJP's image is sharper than it has ever been in the past, its edges continue to be blurred'.

Basic policy documents do not add much focus. The BJP's constitution wants India to 'emerge as a great world power'. India should become 'modern, progressive and enlightened in outlook', a country which 'proudly draws inspiration from [its] ancient culture'.

These hardly seem shadowy aims, but the BJP strikes many as a mysterious amalgam of mumbling *sadhus*, or Hindu holy men, and avuncular figures like Advani. Next to such leaders as Atal Behari Vajpayee, a former foreign minister and the party's ex-president, stand members like Vijaya Raje Scindia—a member of the BJP's executive board and a major force behind Hindu revivalism.

The party has also garnered support from militant groups like the Vishwa Hindu Parishad (VHP), now embarked on a plan to start building a Hindu temple on 30 October at Ayodhya on a site occupied by a mosque. For the Maharashtra assembly the BJP forged an election alliance with the anti-Muslim and anti-Dalit, or 'untouchable', Shiv Sena party.

Small wonder, then, that many Western observers often refer to the BJP as 'Hindu fundamentalists'. But though convenient, this tag is misleading. For example, the BJP's legislators include Muslims, Sikhs and 'untouchables'. Madhya Pradesh Chief Minister Sunderlal Patwa told the *Review* of a Sikh colleague elected from a district with only twenty Sikh families. 'Is this fundamentalism?' Patwa asked.

India's communists and the Congress portray the BJP as a group of Hindu hotheads endangering national unity. But in an interview, Advani said he wants only to end special privileges that encourage minorities to regard themselves as outside the Indian mainstream. As for nationalism, he hardly needed to defend himself—nothing in India embraces patriotic sentiment more fiercely than the BJP's brand of revivalist Hinduism.

The BJP's opponents brush these explanations aside. They warn that India's 120 million Muslims and other non-Hindus—who together comprise 17 per cent of India's 830 million people—will become alienated under a BJP-dominated government.

They claim the protection now enjoyed by Christians and Buddhists, as well as by Muslims, will be discarded. The result will be irreparable damage to India's ties with Muslim countries, while relations with Pakistan—already bad—will become worse. Finally, they say BJP plans for a build-up of nuclear weapons will force Pakistan to follow suit, and badly frighten South-East Asian countries and the wider world beyond.

Critics also portray the BJP as a puppet of the Rashtriya Swayamsevak Sangh (RSS), a militant Hindu revivalist group to which Advani, on his own admission, belongs—as do most of the other BJP leaders.

Perhaps the only area where critics and supporters agree lies in the BJP's profoundly different attitude to the Indian polity, a view rooted in the notion of *Hindutva*, or 'Hindu-ness'. Advani says Hindutva is as secular as the Western-style division of powers reflected in India's Constitution. He argues that tolerance and pluralism arise naturally from the Hindu tradition. Both Advani and the VHP contrast Hinduism to genuinely militant religions by claiming Hindus have never forbade peaceful foreign faiths from entering India.

Apart from the existing 27 per cent quotas for 'untouchables' and tribal groups, the BJP wants all Indians subject to the same laws, with no special dispensations for minorities. It rejects the separate Muslim family law reaffirmed by the last Congress government under pressure from Muslim fundamentalists.

On 24 August, Advani for the first time attacked the Singh government's decision to lift the 'reserved' public sector job quota to 49.5 per cent. The BJP also detests the existing legislative autonomy constitutionally granted to Jammu and Kashmir, India's only Muslim-majority state.

Recent party policy also reveals firmly expressed foreign and economic positions. The BJP has criticized India's 'ill-prepared' 1987–90 Sri Lankan intervention and the former government's brusque treatment of Nepal.

In its 1989 manifesto, the BJP promised a total ban on the slaughter of cows, an increase of forest cover from the present 19 per cent of land to 33 per cent and—despite its bias against special privileges—a quota of 'up to 30 per cent of certain categories of jobs for women'. Also pledged were a 'massive campaign to eradicate untouchability' and free vasectomies and tubectomies.

In economic policy the BJP espouses a free market approach, while attacking some foreign multinationals, and the imposition of 'statutory ceilings on budget deficits and government debt'. Its language policy is unclear, though on 13 August all three BJP chief ministers endorsed a 'Throw English Out' campaign. This move worried Advani, who does not want to compromise electoral support from India's English-educated, urban middle classes.

The BJP has taken its toughest stance over Kashmir and the Punjab disturbances. At a 'Save Kashmir' rally on 2 May its leaders called for pre-emptive strikes against what it called 'training camps' in Pakistan. It urges sealing the Indo–Pakistan border and forcing people living adjacent to it to carry identity cards.

A simple head count might suggest the Hindu four-fifths of India would automatically guarantee supremacy of the BJP. There are two reasons why this is wrong. The first centres on the how 'Hindu' is defined. The groups under the BJP umbrella tend to have a wide definition of Hinduism, counting 'untouchables', special sects and Sikhs, Jains and Buddhists. But take away the 30 per cent of Hindus defined as 'untouchable' castes, subtract some go-it-alone sects and the BJP claims of an overwhelming Hindu majority begin to look weak.

The second is based on the political parties caste-based 'vote banks'. The Congress lays special claim to Brahmins and 'untouchables', though its appeal is now more uncertain. The Janata Dal commands a spread of middle and farmer castes, including higher caste groups like the Thakurs and the Rajputs.

Apart from these divisions, a powerful line of argument runs counter to any easy equation of 'Hindu' with 'India'. Fewer than 1200 years have passed since caste-bound Hinduism edged out Buddhism and Jainism, also native to India. As scholar Gail Omvedt cautioned in a recent essay, the ascendant brand of Brahmin-at-the-apex Hinduism seen today 'does not mean that Hinduism alone is "Indian"'.

Regardless of these philosophical questions, the BJP is preparing for a snap election that could come as soon as November. Two decisions last year have given the party an extra edge. In Maharashtra it cast its lot with Shiv Sena leader Bal Thackeray, whose party won control of the Bombay municipal council in 1985. Although Thackeray's boast that a saffron flag would fly over the state assembly hall did not materialize in February, the BJP has become a power in that state.

The party's second major decision was to support the temple groundbreaking ceremony at Ayodhya, said to be the birthplace of Lord Rama, a key figure in the Hindu pantheon. This is an emotionally as well as politically charged issue, as a sixteenth-century mosque already occupies the site and the controversy is communally sensitive.

Last year, truckloads of consecrated bricks arrived at Ayodhya after collection drives by the VHP in thousands of villages. Muslims were enraged by the former Congress government's decision to let the ceremony go ahead. The Ayodhya dispute goes straight to the core of Hindu–Muslim relations. The VHP now has a 30 October start-up date for construction; how the BJP and Singh handle the issue could determine the date of the next election.

Congress president Rajiv Gandhi says the BJP keeps 'postponing the plan to construct the temple to keep the issue alive because there is a weak government'. If a new election is called, he adds, 'they will claim the survival of Hinduism depends on the construction of the temple'.

Rioting between Hindus and Muslims erupted across Madhya Pradesh, Uttar Pradesh and Bihar during last November's Ayodhya ceremony. In one Bihar city, Bhagalpur, over a 1000 people died. Tension next month may well trigger another inter-communal slaughter.

Advani has played an adroit game in New Delhi. He holds talks with Singh several times a week and manages his twin aims of improving his pre-election position while reducing the damage from rows within the Janata Dal-led National Front government. Advani's hand is firmly on the tiller. For example, he described to the *Review* how BJP misgivings prevented assembly elections in the Punjab last December. Indirect BJP influence like this is already so strong, Congress claims, that Singh's government has become virtually a BJP proxy.

The BJP is a coming power in India, a beneficiary of vacuum at the broad centre of north Indian politics. But beyond immediate issues, the BJP also has a wider world view and contrasting vision to the increasingly bogus socialist and secular rhetoric of the other two main parties.

~

Arthur Max
Calcutta Today

Associated Press
11 November 1990

Calcutta: IT'S ALREADY HOT and steamy at 6 a.m. as Calcutta goes through its morning rituals.

Joggers trot past the marble Victoria Monument and the members-only Mohammadan Sports Club. The trimmed grass of the nearby Calcutta Race Course is wet from the overnight monsoon rains.

Sheltered under the Hooghly Bridge a mile away, women cook a meagre breakfast over a fire of dried cow dung for a gaggle of children, some naked, some in rags.

Hundreds of people bathe in the sluggish brown water of the Hooghly river. Devout Hindus, blessed by a nearly naked priest, stand waist-deep in the river dipping copper bowls of spices and flower petals into the water. Later their women will return to the river steps with the laundry to slap the clothes clean on the stone.

Fifty yards upriver, near the flower market where servants of the rich buy garlands of fresh marigolds and hibiscus, street dwellers defecate into the water. But the river is holy, an arm of the Mother Ganges and, therefore, cannot be unclean.

Across the river, in a sprawling conglomerate of slums called Howrah City, children splash under the hand pumps which supply water for drinking and washing. People politely avert their eyes from others using the open sewage canals between the shacks.

In an hour the roads will be choked with traffic, and the air will begin to thicken with a blue haze of exhaust fumes.

For a few Calcutta residents, today may be a relaxed day at the club. For millions of others, the day will bring another test of survival.

Everyone in the city will go without city-supplied electricity for at least two hours. The hit-and-miss telephones will create hours of frustration. Roads, pitted and impassable after a heavy monsoon, will trap tens of thousands of cars like flies in a spider web.

Calcutta is 300 years old this year. Job Charnock, an agent of the East India Company, founded the trading post on the Hooghly on 24 August 1690 near the village of Kalikata, named for Kali, the feared goddess of power and destruction.

It was, until 1912, the capital of British India, the second city of the British Empire after London, a city that pandered to the pleasures of the great men of the Anglo-Saxon world.

Today Calcutta is in decay. Its Gothic Victorian-age buildings are crumbling and blackened with grime and mould. Shanties sprout like weeds in the sidewalk cracks.

Even Calcutta's stately clubs look shabby. Walls are peeling at the Saturday Club, where wealthy Indians sip gin and tonic on the veranda overlooking grass tennis courts. The once-white uniforms of the bearers, as the waiters are called, are stained and grey with age.

Decades of migration from impoverished villages and from neighbouring Bangladesh have swollen Calcutta's population to twelve million.

City services are collapsing, concedes Hassia Abdul Habib, the speaker of the West Bengal state legislature.

'The roads are mind-boggling. Communications are horrible. You can phone London directly, but you can't phone your next-door neighbour,' he says.

Calcutta, he adds, 'is coming to a boiling point'.

At the same time, Calcutta throbs with life. It is the home of a vibrant Bengal culture, poetry and experimental theatre.

'Bengalis are not business people,' says Ajay Chatterjee of the Calcutta Municipal Development Authority. 'They love literature, songs, drama. They are not pragmatic or practical.'

Calcutta fostered all three of India's Nobel Prize laureates: poet Rabindranath Tagore in 1913, physics researcher Chandrasekhara V. Raman in 1930 and Mother Teresa, a naturalized Indian citizen who won the 1979 Peace Prize for her work with the destitute.

Perhaps only Calcutta, with its appalling poverty and capacity for survival, could have given rise to the phenomenon of Mother Teresa.

Forty years ago the Yugoslav-born Catholic nun began to scoop up the dying homeless from the gutters and rescue them from an anonymous death. Her mission for the poor has spread to ninety-two countries.

From the start, wealth and deprivation have coexisted in these inhospitable surroundings.

Built on mosquito-infested delta land 80 miles above the Bay of Bengal, Calcutta suffers temperatures above 100 day after day in summer. The drenching rains of the monsoon season, from July to September, bring only humidity, not relief.

British author Geoffrey Moorhouse called it an act of lunacy to build a city here. 'Everything in Nature was against it.'

Robert Clive, who turned the East India Company into an empire for England in the 1750s, called Calcutta 'the most wicked place in the Universe'.

Mark Twain, who visited in 1896, said the weather was 'enough to make a brass doorknob mushy'.

Calcutta's reputation also is stained by corruption and unending political intrigue. That, too, is nothing new.

Lord Cornwallis, who was made Governor of India after his surrender at Yorktown in the American War of Independence, wrote from his headquarters in Calcutta: 'Every native of India, I verily believe, is corrupt.'

With all its faults, most Calcuttans are intensely loyal.

'Bengalis love their wretched city with the same passion as a mother loves her sick child,' wrote Khushwant Singh, a leading Indian author and journalist.

'We know all about our problems, but I love Calcutta,' said Yvonne de Silva, who runs a private bus service. 'It bugs me that people come to Calcutta and take pictures of our garbage and our streets. Why don't they take pictures of their own garbage?'

Thousands of people live from the refuse which the city can't collect fast enough. Some sift through it for peelings or chicken skins for soup, competing with crows, cattle and pariah dogs. Ragpickers search it for anything to sell.

Women collect, dry and shape the droppings from the brahman cattle, which roam freely. Others sweep up coal dust, wet it and roll it into balls of black mud called gril that also can fuel a cooking fire.

Looking down from her second-story veranda, Sheila Lahiri pointed to a shantytown that had sprung up opposite her apartment on Ballygunge Road, a street of elegant residences.

'Could you believe this was possible fifteen or even ten years ago?' said Mrs Lahiri, whose father, Lord Sinha, was given a hereditary seat in the British House of Lords.

Authorities long ago gave up the idea of tearing down the slums and focussed instead on alleviating the misery.

Calcutta used to have 1000 deaths a year from cholera, but the disease was brought under control by water filtering and installing 20,000 public hand pumps in the slums.

Calcutta has always been the refuge for the poor and displaced of eastern India. Waves of immigrants came with every ethnic upheaval, famine or war.

The population more than doubled from 4.4 million in 1950, to 9.2 million in 1975.

While the city grew, its resources shrank. A silting of the Hooghly virtually killed the port, which just forty years ago received nearly half of India's imports.

Recession, labour strife and political terrorism in the 1960s persuaded many businesses to leave. Fifty years after the government shifted to New Delhi, the economic centre of India has gravitated to Bombay.

The communists, now thirteen years in power, blame the policies of the federal government in New Delhi for giving the state less than what they say is its share of national funds.

About 300,000 people have no home other than the pavement, according to some estimates. Stretched out on dirty rags or on the hard stone, they sleep undisturbed by the trucks and cars roaring past.

They have an average weekly income of less than $5.55, said a study by the Institute of Local Government and Urban Studies.

Thirteen per cent of the street dwellers work as rickshaw pullers, earning an average 66 cents a day. It's the last major city on earth where men pull passenger carriages like human horses.

The study estimated that 43 per cent of the city's residents live in huts in squatter settlements, refugee colonies or slum neighbourhoods, known here as a bustees.

But an outsider walking through even the deepest slums of Howrah senses no anger, nor danger.

'Life is hard here. These people have nothing to look forward to,' said Bettina Borgmann, a German doctor who volunteered to spend her summer vacation in a slum clinic.

'But the people surprise me. Most seem quite happy. They are content with what they have. Just look at the children playing outside with whatever they can find. I have never felt uncomfortable here.'

~

Mark Fineman
Lynchings over Caste Stir India

The Los Angeles Times
12 April 1991

IT WAS AT the entrance to this little village of mud and brick, beside an ancient shrine to Lord Shiva the destroyer, that Mehrana's star-crossed young lovers recently ended their lives side by side.

From a sturdy limb of Mehrana's holy banyan tree, Roshni, sixteen, and Bijendra, twenty, were hanged just after 8 a.m. for all the village to see, a symbol of order, the elders had said, of tradition and of the village's izzat—chastity and honour.

The young woman, Roshni, was a high-caste Hindu, after all, one of the Jats who own the land, the village and power over the likes of Bijendra and his fellow Jatavs. Bijendra, with whom Roshni had eloped three days before, was from a 'backward' caste, traditionally so impure and inferior that they became known as Hinduism's Untouchables.

So separate are the Jats and Jatavs—not unlike Shakespeare's Montagues and Capulets, only centuries older and with a feud far more stubborn—that each has its own well in Mehrana. The Jats live on one side in houses of stone and tile, the Jatavs on the other in huts of mud and straw. Their separate realities intersect only when the Jats need a Jatav to pick a crop, build a house or mend a shoe.

For both sides, Roshni's and Bijendra's was a love impure.

They had to die. With that, even Roshni's father, Ganga Ram, agreed. 'For me,' the Jat elder had said at the nightlong meeting in the village square that condemned the couple to hang 27 March, 'the girl is dead already.'

And so he helped string up his daughter, her lover and the couple's best friend from the centuries-old banyan tree. But even after three strong tugs on the rope, Roshni and Bijendra refused to die. So the Jats gathered a heap of dry wood, then dragged the young couple, writhing in pain, to the makeshift funeral pyre they had built nearby. And in a final ritual of ancient village justice, the elders burned them to death, Jat and Jatav together, so that none would forget this day.

A single Jatav escaped the village, dodging armed Jat sentries posted all around Mehrana. It was Amichand, the uncle of Bijendra's best friend, who reported every detail to the nearest police station, 10 miles away.

Now Mehrana's modern-day Romeo and Juliet have become a symbol of a far different sort for India, a grisly illustration of the magnitude of the forces defying its march into the modern age—forces increasingly outstripping logic and the rule of law as the divisions in its society grow ever deeper.

Decades after India's caste system was constitutionally banned, the lynching of the lovers in Mehrana triggered an outcry from Indian liberals and intellectuals in the nation's capital. The newspaper *Indian Express* condemned it as 'savagery at its appalling worst' in an editorial headlined 'Monstrous!'

'What has the modern Indian state done to prevent these monstrous triumphs of kangaroo justice?' the newspaper asked, concluding, 'What is necessary is not more speeches and promises, but arrest and punishment of the guilty.'

Under unprecedented popular pressure, the politicians and police ordered the arrest of thirty-seven Jat elders who approved and carried out the lynching; twenty-one of them are now in jail.

But in deeply polarized India—poised on the brink of yet another bloody national election, in which the ancient caste system already is a prominent issue—the Mehrana village elders who ordered the hangings have drawn an unprecedented number of defenders, as well.

One state government minister paying a condolence visit to the village, for example, lavished his greatest gift not on the Jatavs, but on the Jat mother of Roshni—a pledge to free her husband from jail within days so he can supervise the spring harvest.

And in a politically paralysed country where three national governments have come and gone in eighteen months and where the institutions of government and its bureaucracy have all but ceased to function at the grass-roots in many regions, defenders of the elders of Mehrana say they are to be commended for keeping a semblance of order in a village that seems centuries removed from the ideal of a modern Indian state.

In reality, Mehrana is just 70 miles south of the capital, New Delhi. It is three hours away, a drive that peels back time and ends in a bumpy ride through rocks, dust and wheat fields.

The Jatavs were out for the harvest this week, plucking the golden sheaves by hand for their Jat masters, even after most had been jailed or had fled to distant villages to escape arrest.

Inside the divided village of 3000 or so, accounts of the tragic saga of Roshni and Bijendra varied wildly. (Most villagers denied having watched the lynching, although police say nearly everyone did.)

Detectives say that behind the ritual killings was a disbelief in both communities that what occurred between Roshni and her lover could ever have happened between members of two groups who refuse to even touch each other.

'My girl was kidnapped by these Jatavs,' Bishan Devi, the mother, shouted angrily to visitors. 'Everything was forced. First, the Jatavs took away my daughter, fed her liquor and took her in a hayloft. And then the Jats found her there, locked her in our house, threatening to break our bones if we let her out and finally took her away and killed her.

'I would never have married her to the Jatav boy,' she said. 'She was a good girl. Four months ago, she was engaged to Ramesh, a boy from another village. On 8 April, she was to marry.'

Asked whether Ramesh is a Jat or a Jatav, a look of horror washed over her face. She was furious. 'What are you saying?' she screamed. 'Of course he is a Jat. How could you even ask such a thing of me. Now leave this house!'

On the Jatav side of the village, a similar wave of shock swept across the face of Sarawati, the mother of Bijendra. After several minutes of wailing, 'My son! My child! My little boy!' she wiped her tears. And as she sat cross-legged in the mud wearing shreds of a shirt held together by a single safety pin and loose stitches, she explained that a love affair between her boy and the Jat girl was, well, simply impossible.

It was another boy, a Jat boy named Shyam, who had eloped with Roshni, she explained. Indeed, the police confirmed that Roshni had eloped with a Jat boy named Shyam but that it took place nearly two years ago.

'She was a whore,' Sarawati said of her son's lover. 'Never could this have happened.'

But several yards away, at the house of Bijendra's best friend, Ram Kishan, relatives told another story. Ram Kishan's mother confirmed that 'Bijendra and Roshni were lovers', who were aided in their elopement by her son.

It was the village's most powerful elder, a wealthy Jat named Mangtu, who convened the village panchayat (traditional council) at the request of Roshni's family. 'Papu, a brother of Roshni, insisted that these people should be hanged, otherwise he was going to hang himself,' the mother said.

It is from the official statement of Amichand, Ram Kishan's uncle who escaped within minutes of the hanging, that police say they have gotten the most detailed account of what happened after the young couple returned from a three-day absence from the village and announced their desire to marry.

At the insistence of village elder Mangtu, the panchayat convened in a 25-foot-square dirt meeting place in the village at 9 p.m. on 26 March. There were thirty-seven of them, all Jats.

'The whole night, the panchayat was on,' he recalled. 'And throughout the night, Mangtu and the others beat Bijendra and Ram Kishan by turns. Then, they were hanged upside down by their feet. They soaked their private parts in kerosene and burned them. . . .

'At 5 a.m., the Jatavs were called to the panchayat, and they were asked about their opinion (of hanging the accused). They were all scared, so they accepted the decision by consensus. At that time, Mangtu and the others formally accused Ram Kishan and Bijendra of eloping with this girl, and they decided to hang the two boys and the girl.

'They were brought to the banyan tree, and then the fathers were summoned, and the Jats demanded that the fathers hang their own children. When they protested, they beat them up. At that point, the mothers were summoned, and they also were beaten.

'After that, the fathers of the children were forced to hang them. Then, they were taken down. They only appeared to be dead. They were dragged to the cremation ground, where . . . they were forcibly cremated.'

To stop the Jatavs from leaving to report the crime, the Jats surrounded the village. But Amichand told police: 'I sneaked out to give you this report. Please take action on it.'

The police did act swiftly. Vijay Kumar Gupta, the police superintendent for the district who is based in Mathura, 40 miles away, boasted that he personally arrived on the scene at 12.30 p.m., just four hours after the lynchings.

Although Gupta now insists that the crime was not committed purely because of caste, calling it 'a multi-causal phenomenon', his own police report blames caste for the killings. Most analysts insist that the police were aggressive in publicizing the case and acting on it because of the Indian national elections, now scheduled for late May.

Among the key issues in the campaign is a controversial quota system, which reserves university slots and government jobs for low-caste Hindus like the Jatavs. High-caste leaders such as the Jats have condemned the new system as reverse discrimination.

When the new law was first proposed eight months ago, it triggered a nationwide wave of teenage suicides by protesting high-caste youths.

Ever since, Mehrana's state of Uttar Pradesh, a populous and vote-rich area where most of the villages remain physically and socially divided along caste lines, has become a flash point for the caste dispute. So it was little wonder that the state's powerful chief minister, Mulayam Singh Yadav, dispatched his minister of religion and sports to Mehrana recently as a gesture to maintain support of both Jats and Jatavs.

But as the minister, Sardar Singh, worked his way through the village's narrow lanes, it was clear that he was more attentive to Jats than to Jatavs. Although Singh is a high-caste Hindu, it was only in the Jatavs' mud enclave that a deeper reason became clear.

When asked how their village's love-and-murder drama is likely to affect their vote next month, Jatavs gathered outside Bijendra's tiny hovel fell silent and looked blankly at one another.

Finally, Bijendra's sister, Kesar, spoke. Shaking her head beneath a soiled green scarf, she said quietly: 'The vote? Well, we are always forced to vote. Whoever forces us, that is who we vote for. And it has always been the Jats who force us. So that is how we will vote.'

~

Barbara Crossette

Assassination in India
A Blast, and Then the Wailing Started

The New York Times
22 May 1991

Sriperumbudur: ON THE WAY to the rally 25 miles south-west of Madras, Rajiv Gandhi had been riding in the front seat, window open. A special fluorescent light mounted on the dashboard of the small Indian-made Ambassador car played on his face so that people could see him in the evening darkness.

They threw in flowers as the car moved slowly by, their faces frenzied with happiness. The biggest smiles in India live in the gentle south. He tossed the garlands back to others, along with scarves and shawls presented to him at stops along the way.

At one point, he stopped to greet a shy woman being jostled by the crowd. He placed a scarf around her neck and spoke to her. She covered her face with her hands and then clutched the cloth and held it close to her.

Visit to Friendly Territory

Just five minutes before arriving here, Mr Gandhi had been talking to this correspondent and Neena Gopal of the *Gulf News* of Dubai. We were riding in the back seat of his car with Maradadam Chandrashekhar, the local Congress candidate, and a local party official as the former Prime Minister began one of his final campaign trips. The south was friendly territory, and he expected the Congress party to do well here.

In the last national election campaign, Mr Gandhi had been criticized for being too aloof, too insulated from the people he hoped to lead. This time around, determined to carry his message directly to the people, he went on punishing road journeys, stopping at hamlets to shake hands and ask for votes as if he were a town council candidate.

'What else can I do?' he said in the last interview of his life, as the car in which we were riding pulled away from Poonamallee, a town along the route. He had been asked dozens of times a day whether he was afraid of this new style of campaigning. He was asked again tonight, as he arrived at Madras airport for his campaign trip.

'I campaigned this way before I was Prime Minister,' he said. 'I'm not Prime Minister now so I'm campaigning this way again.'

As his caravan pulled into this small town, he asked Mrs Chandrashekhar, whose campaign he had come to boost, 'What shall I tell them here?'

'Talk about village development,' she said as they stepped out of the bullet-proof car into the balmy tropical night.

A minute or two later, Rajiv Gandhi was dead, killed by a bomb explosion only about 10 yards from this reporter. Mrs Chandrashekhar survived and was taken to a hospital.

Where have they taken the body? reporters asked police. His driver, who was the first to the scene, said that all that was left were his head and his feet, which were still wearing a pair of expensive running shoes that he had recently taken to wearing for long days on the hustings.

Bystanders began to wail. The carnival lights of a South Indian political rally went on twinkling grotesquely all around the field of death. Bodies were strewn in a circle at least 20 feet wide.

Few Security Precautions

His security had been almost nonexistent tonight. A hundred times one of those hands that reached into the car to grab his arm or stroke his hand could have stabbed or shot him.

At campaign rallies in cities and in rural areas of unfriendly states that are assumed to harbour candidates' political enemies, metal detectors have been installed through which the crowds have to pass. Here, however, no such precaution was taken, and people were milling around the platform. In southern India, political violence is rare, and elections feel and look more like festivals than serious political events.

'I have been on the road twenty-three and a half hours a day almost every day since the first of May,' he said during the ride. 'At the end, I am swollen and bleeding or have a cut arm. Here and in Kerala there is this cheek-pinching. And sometimes in Muslim neighbourhoods they kiss me—you know: one, two, three times, that special hug.'

For this rally, Mr Gandhi's car stopped about 25 yards short of the platform erected on an open meadow. As Mrs Gopal and I paused to talk to Suman Dubey, Mr Gandhi's campaign press adviser, about whether we had had enough time with the former Prime Minister, and would make way for other reporters, Mr Gandhi went on ahead toward the stairs to the platform. As Mrs Gopal and I followed there was a sudden burst of what sounded like firecrackers and then a large boom, an explosion and a cloud of smoke that scattered people all around. It was over in a matter of seconds. The crowd at first froze and then began to stampede.

A Stop at a Hospital

A few minutes later, Mr Gandhi's driver pushed me and Mrs Gopal and another reporter into the car and started driving quickly toward Madras. It was only when we were out of town that he said he had feared that someone might try to attack the car, recognizing the licence plate. Along the way, we stopped at the Tanarai Institute of Medical Sciences near Madras, where Mr Gandhi's remains and the wounded had been taken. All along the route, however, it was clear that no one had heard of the assassination. It took the news agencies nearly an hour to begin telling the people of India that Mr Gandhi was dead.

There were probably several thousand people in front of the platform waiting for Mr Gandhi when he arrived in Sriperumbudur, an agricultural town that local reporters described as 'nothing special'. He was about two hours late, not long by the standards of South Asian political campaigns. The friendly crowd was made up mostly of men, wearing sarongs called lungis and sport shirts or collarless kurtas, long, shirtlike Indian garments.

Stops along the Way

Coloured lights were strung in many places along Mr Gandhi's route from Madras tonight. From time to time, he would signal the driver to slow down or stop the car, so he could get out and shake a few more hands and ask the crowd, in English, to 'vote for Congress'. Longer remarks were translated into Tamil to the cheers of the crowd.

He carried with him a small grey airline-style bag, into which he put notes and letters thrust upon him by people along the way.

In his last interview, I had asked if he had any special regime, any vitamin supplements or diet designed to sustain his energy, particularly in the intense heat, with temperatures reaching 110 degrees or higher. He laughed.

'Most of the time I get nothing to eat at all,' he said. In the car, there were a few bottles of water and a thermos of tea or coffee—we never found out which.

In the interview, Mr Gandhi was able to speak philosophically about India and where its political turmoil was leading it—in between impromptu whistle stops. He remembered the last unanswered question as the car hit a stretch of empty road again.

'Now, where were we?' he would say. 'Oh, yes, it was . . .'

He admitted that for him this was a 'tough' election in every way. But he agreed that the growth of strong new political parties was an indication of a democratic coming-of-age in India, where one party could no longer expect to have a monopoly.

'But I feel that these are the wrong kind of parties,' he said, referring specifically to the Bharatiya Janata Party, a right-wing pro-Hindu group that has aroused religious passion among Hindus, who form 80 per cent of India's population. The rise of the Bharatiya Janata Party has had a lot to do with increased tensions during the recent election campaign and in the voting that began Monday.

'A tremendous frustration is building up in the people, which is causing these swings from one party to another,' he said. 'They are frustrated that the system is not delivering, not meeting their aspirations.' He added that he thought the problem went back into the late 1960s, after the death of his grandfather, Jawaharlal Nehru. In the early years after independence from Britain, expectations in India were very high that the country would grow and prosper quickly.

Mr Gandhi said the Congress party had tried 'to bring those aspirations down to a kind of realistic level'.

'So Much More to Do'

'But we do have so much more to do,' he said. 'We have to make the system more efficient.'

Mr Gandhi mused about some of the plans he had for the next administration he hoped to form after the elections. Commenting on popular criticism of the government-controlled television services in India, he talked about opening up broadcasting to private corporations, but under 'some sort' of government oversight.

He returned again and again to his fears of more separatism in India, more regional violence, which has disrupted life in three states—Assam, Punjab and Jammu and Kashmir.

At Madras airport earlier in the evening, he explained why he was against allowing Punjab to hold state elections, saying it was very likely that they would elect an administration that would pass a resolution in favour of autonomy or independence.

Above all, Mr Gandhi said, he was determined 'to kill all controversies over religion'. He said that he was not worried that Hindu fundamentalists, and the Bharatiya Janata Party in particular, would go to the holy city of Ayodhya and tear down the Babri Masjid, a sixteenth-century mosque, to build a temple to the Hindu god-king Rama. He said he thinks Hindu extremists were jolted out of their crusade by the violence they provoked last year when zealots tried to storm the mosque.

'The BJP doesn't have the guts to do that again,' he said.

Asked about how he thought he would get along with Pakistan's new Prime Minister, Nawaz Sharif, who is pushing through economic liberalization policies that Indian politicians including the Congress party talk about but never put into practice, Mr Gandhi said he had never met Mr Sharif and could not judge what kind of relationship they would have.

'But I know who could have solved these problems with us,' he said. 'General Zia. We were close to finishing agreement on Kashmir, we had the maps and everything ready to sign. And then he was killed.' As Prime Minister from 1984 to 1989, Mr Gandhi had a good working relationship with President Muhammed Zia ul-Haq, who died in an unexplained plane crash in August 1988.

Assassination Suspected

Mr Gandhi said there was evidence that General Zia had been murdered, but he wouldn't say more. Mrs Gopal asked him if he didn't think that some outside power had decided to upset the development of better relations with Pakistan. He said he thought that was likely. She asked whether India and Indian leaders might not be targets as India took on a larger role in the region. He agreed. He said that the danger would not come from the Soviet Union, however, which was too busy with its own problems.

'Are you talking about the CIA again?' I asked him. Prime Minister Indira Gandhi, his mother, used to say that she feared the American intelligence agency would kill her one day, an apprehension dismissed as paranoia by all but some Soviet diplomats in New Delhi.

Mr Gandhi smirked.

In the end, Mrs Gandhi was shot in 1984 by Sikh bodyguards, four months after she sent troops into the Sikhs' holiest shrine, the Golden Temple in Amritsar.

Now her son, who had many enemies among disaffected Indians, not the least the separatist groups, has followed her into martyrdom, and no one may ever know who was to blame for the crime. In that blinding second of his death, he was walking toward a sea of people, a picture uncannily reminiscent of Mohandas K. Gandhi's last stroll in the garden in New Delhi moments before he was struck down by a Hindu fanatic.

~

Mark Tully
Nehru Dynasty

BBC
25 May 1991

Election campaigning in India was brought to an abrupt halt when the leader of the Congress (I) party, Rajiv Gandhi, was assassinated. Rajiv was the grandson of India's first Prime Minister, Jawaharlal Nehru. His mother, Indira Gandhi, was killed by her own bodyguards six years before, and Rajiv was immediately chosen to succeed her. Anxious to continue the Nehru dynasty, the Congress party immediately elected his Italian-born wife, Sonia, as the party's president, an offer she declined.

THE KING IS dead. Long live the Queen. Thus spoke the frightened men and women who had made their political careers out of being courtiers of Indira and Rajiv Gandhi. They had, as one friend of mine put it, become political. That was why they attempted a coup in the Congress party by starting an immediate move to make Rajiv's widow, Sonia Gandhi, the party's president. It was all too easy because once her name was proposed, even those congressmen who did have political stature of their own were reluctant to oppose her, for fear of being accused of disloyalty to the Nehru family.

Nevertheless, it was quite extraordinary for a party in the middle of a general election, and facing a determined onslaught from a Hindu nationalist party, to choose a woman who was Italian by birth and a Roman Catholic by baptism as their new leader. Sonia issued a dignified statement rejecting the offer. But the efforts to persuade her continue. It all just goes to show the extent to which India's only national party has become the fief of the Nehru family.

How have the Nehrus developed into a dynasty? When Nehru became Prime Minister, he was a stickler for democratic nicety, but leadership is lonely and he was a widower, and so he fell back more and more on the company of his only child, Indira. It would be wrong to say that Nehru deliberately groomed Indira as his successor. After all, there was a brief interregnum when he died. But he certainly pushed her into prominence in the Congress party. After the death of Nehru's successor, Lal Bahadur Shastri, there was an unseemly scramble for power and Indira was chosen by a group of senior politicians who wanted to keep out their rivals and thought she would be like clay in their hands.

That was where the transformation into a dynasty started. Indira Gandhi never forgot the humiliations heaped on her during the early years of her prime ministership and was determined she should never again be *prima inter pares*, or first among equals. But, like her father, Indira found her pre-eminence lonely. And like him, too, she fell back

**Sonia Gandhi became the president of the Congress party in 1998. She headed a Congress-led coalition that formed a government in 2004 with Manmohan Singh as Prime Minister.*

on her family. First on her son, Sanjay, and then, when he was killed doing aeronautical stunts over the centre of Delhi, on Rajiv.

Indira's refusal to tolerate rivals led to a cult of sycophancy in the Congress party. When she was returned to power, after being punished by the electorate for her Emergency, I asked a senior member of the party what role he would play. He replied: 'Oh Mr Tully, don't ask me that, I'm just a sepoy of Madam.'

It was almost inevitable, therefore, that when Indira Gandhi was shot the party should automatically turn to Rajiv. Although one of Rajiv's most outstanding qualities was his charm, within the Congress party he was even more regal than his mother. A few days before his death, I was discussing the election campaign with a member of the committee running it and I noticed that he never referred to Rajiv by name but spoke only of the Congress president.

Towards the end of his life Rajiv himself realized that the awe in which he was held within the party was cutting him off from the people. That was why he changed his whole style of campaigning in this election, brushing aside the security and the sycophants who surrounded him last time round and allowing himself to be mobbed wherever he went. A close friend of his who travelled with him throughout the campaign told me that his last day had been a particularly happy one because the reaction of the crowds, wherever he went, had been so warm.

Rajiv Gandhi paid for that democratic decision with his life.

Obviously the Nehrus could not have been so successful if the Indian people regarded dynasticism with distaste. Perhaps one reason why they don't is that India has an old tradition of dynasticism which is different from the West. It's the tradition of the king as a servant of the people. The god Rama is regarded as the model of the perfect king and he and his faithful lieutenant, Hanuman, are the two most popular gods in India now, at least in the politically crucial north.

And that must be reinforcing fanaticism. It would therefore be very dangerous to write off the Nehru dynasty, whatever the outcome of the present power struggle in the Congress party; a struggle I foresee not being finally resolved, at least not until the results of the general election are known next month.

~

K.K. Sharma
Promising Start Down a Rocky Road

Financial Times
9 August 1991

ONE OF THE most fragile governments in India's history has, paradoxically, started to make the bold economic policy changes that not even Mr Rajiv Gandhi's ostensibly more stable administration of the mid-1980s could risk.

The minority government of Prime Minister P.V. Narasimha Rao has realized that the widespread unwillingness to contemplate another general election campaign has given it an opportunity for decisive action, while the danger of a default on India's $70 billion external debt has provided an incontestable case for it.

Yet, even though the proposed reforms are a response to a balance of payments crisis, their content is far wider than stabilization and export promotion. They introduce a long-discussed and widely-desired, if still limited, liberalization and deregulation of India's sclerotic economy.

The liberalization appears decisive, at least by Indian standards, and the International Monetary Fund is likely soon to announce a loan to ease India's current balance of payments crisis. The IMF's response reflects India's importance and an appreciation of its changed policy stance at least as much as the stringency of the proposed stabilization.

Mr Michel Camdessus, the IMF managing director, has welcomed the reforms, 'including the initial stabilization measures and the initiation of a more liberal trading system. We want to continue supporting India's efforts to strengthen its balance of payments and build the foundations for strong and sustained growth.'

But is what the government intends to do enough? Will it even be allowed to do what it intends? These questions retain their force.

**Facing a dire fiscal crisis, the government launched economic reforms with an industrial policy statement on 24 July 1991.*

Nevertheless, what has been done is significant. For that two pivotal figures must take the credit: Mr Rao and Dr Manmohan Singh, the new finance minister.

Of the two, Mr Rao has perhaps proved the more surprising. By giving Dr Singh the go-ahead, he has shown himself to be a far more astute political strategist than thought when he became the consensus Prime Minister of a minority Congress government nearly two months ago. Opposition parties can throw out the reforms only at the risk of toppling the government, which would entail yet another election only two and a half months after the assassination of Mr Gandhi during the last.

The result is that the Indian government has moved at an unexpectedly rapid pace. If the reforms go through—and they could still founder if Mr Rao permits the factional quarrels within Congress and rumblings from the opposition to get out of hand—India will finally have moved to end its fifty-year isolation.

'The government is committed to macroeconomic stabilization and structural reforms which will unleash the nation's latent energy to bring about accelerated development,' said Mr Singh. 'The country has been living beyond its means and adopting soft options. It must prepare itself to take hard and unpleasant decisions.'

The need to secure a further IMF loan to shore up India's foreign exchange reserves, on top of the $1.9 billion already in hand, has undoubtedly spurred the government into speedy action. But Dr Singh—a technocrat who has held almost every important official position in Indian economic policy-making—is not being disingenuous when stating that the reforms are in India's own interest. He has conviction inside him and the crisis behind him when acting to:

- Sweep aside the complicated regulations governing foreign trade, following a decisive two-phase devaluation of the grossly-overvalued rupee early in July;
- Welcome direct investment by multinationals;
- Dismantle the 'licence raj' (reign by licences) on Indian industry—84 per cent of industry has now been freed from licencing requirements;
- Partially free the financial system from controls on interest rates, and;
- Propose a more limited role for the public sector.

In addition, by reducing the fiscal deficit from 8.5 per cent of gross domestic product to 6.5 per cent, the government has made at least an initial step towards returning India to its historic fiscal conservatism.

None of this has been easy. Critics have lamented what they consider the shedding of Nehru's socialist model, based on self-reliance and a public sector that holds the commanding heights of the economy.

The reforms were also frowned upon by many bureaucrats who fought a brief but bitter battle against them, partly because of their vested interests in a government-regulated economy and partly because of conviction. Mr B.K. Modi, a leading industrialist, said: 'I don't think the bureaucrats are going to change overnight. You can feel the resistance already.'

But Dr Singh acted decisively, by telling senior officials that those who could not support the programme would be transferred. He was helped by the fact that many senior officials, particularly in the ministries of commerce and industry, have been unsuccessfully clamouring for deregulation for years. They feel the finance ministry has obstructed the process of liberalization by exerting too great a control over economic life.

While the reforms have begun to have an impact, many are only statements of intent. Much has still to be done, including the implementation of what has now been decided. And although Dr Singh has cut subsidies and government expenditure, for example, and reduced the fiscal deficit, he has failed to introduce long overdue tax reform.

The minister has declared a virtual open-door policy for foreign investment by increasing the limit on foreign ownership of the equity in Indian joint ventures from 40 to 51 per cent, thereby assuring them of control. He has also suggested that they could be allowed 100 per cent ownership if high technology and an export commitment are involved. Yet foreign investment is still not permitted in key areas such as energy or oil and mineral exploration.

The Monopolies and Restrictive Trade Practices Act has been considerably liberalized and there are now no restrictions on fresh investments by the so-called 'large monopoly houses'—companies with assets of Rs 1 billion. Nevertheless, industrial licences are still needed for some products including coal and cars.

Mr Rahul Bajaj, chairman and managing director of Bajaj Auto, a scooter maker, praised the lifting of most licencing requirements: 'I know how difficult it can get to chase someone in New Delhi for a licence. Then some fool delays the whole project by procrastinating, because he wants something for himself, or a thousand other things. But now I think things will change.'

Industrialists say the reforms have not gone far enough and they urge the ministry of industry to play a role that would help in the restructuring of industry by encouraging expansion, amalgamations and mergers while keeping a careful watch for the emergence of cartels.

In spite of the many gaps in the reforms, it is difficult to deny that the present liberalization has finally given market forces a chance to operate more freely. This has presented Indian entrepreneurs with a challenge for which they have long been clamouring.

Mr S.K. Birla, president of the Federation of Indian Chambers of Commerce and Industry, said: 'The industrial policy is the first major step in what is necessarily a continuous process of deregulating the economy. Many retrograde restrictions have been either removed or amended, and the conditions created for a market-friendly system.'

Industry has at last been given an opportunity to prove its claim that the country nurtures entrepreneurs of high quality, ingenuity and flexibility. However, many Indian industrialists still lack the confidence to face competition, both internal and from foreign companies, and they are already pressing the government to go slow, at least on changes in foreign investment policy.

But most observers think this response reflects fear of change stemming from years of living within a system of harsh regulations, however frustrating. Painful adjustments are inevitable now that the government has begun the process of reform. Dr Singh says that while the government plans to go further along the same road, the pace will be slower, and that it will take three years for results to show up in the economy.

The question is whether he will have the time he needs. Both Dr Singh and the Prime Minister will have to show skilful management of the Congress and the Opposition. The government may also find that it faces a far from unprecedented policy dilemma: without successful stabilization, liberalization usually founders; but the pain imposed by stabilization can make the government founder, instead. The government has made an excellent start. But both luck and much determination are needed for ultimate success.

~

David Housego
India's Financial Architect

Financial Times
2 September 1991

IF THE LONG-OVERDUE reforms on which India has embarked do succeed in turning around the parlous state of the economy, much of the credit will go to Dr Manmohan Singh, the minister of finance.

India faces a $6 billion current account deficit this financial year (after a $10 billion deficit last year) at a time when its foreign exchange reserves are virtually exhausted and when it is having acute difficulty in borrowing on the international commercial market. The new government has cut the fiscal deficit and has embarked on a policy of industrial and trade deregulation designed to improve competitiveness.

The task ahead is indeed enormous. Dr Singh, a cautious bureaucrat who has held most of the senior economic posts in the Indian administration before being unexpectedly pitchforked into his current job, is only too aware of the many pitfalls that lie ahead and of the risks of stumbling.

'There is no doubt in my mind that the reform process has acquired a momentum of its own. It will be difficult to reverse,' he says. 'This is not to say it is going to be smooth. There are many risks and dangers. I hope the international community will recognize that changing direction in an open society like ours is not a risk-free enterprise.'

A softly spoken Sikh, Dr Singh has served as governor of the Reserve Bank of India (central bank), chief economic adviser in the ministry of finance, and most recently as a special adviser to the former Prime Minister, Mr Chandra Shekhar.

In the 1970s he was thus associated with implementing the type of socialist policies he is now seeking to reverse. At the time, he told friends that in a country with widespread poverty such as India governments were inevitably leftist.

**Manmohan Singh became Prime Minister of a Congress party-led coalition government in 2004.*

By the mid-1980s he was already pressing for an opening-up of the economy. What really seems to have changed his outlook, however, was his becoming secretary general of the South Commission in 1987, when he visited South Korea and Taiwan. He was much struck by the pace of economic growth under export-orientated policies. Though he now has a clear vision himself of where he wants India to go, he is also a pragmatist in adapting to the political pressures of the moment.

In one of his first press conferences as finance minister, he cited the example of South Korea's internationally competitive industry—a reference that had until then been taboo in the mouths of government ministers.

His change of heart was reflected in a speech earlier this year before taking office, when he said on returning from his Geneva-based post in November 1990, that he found 'a growing feeling of scepticism, self-doubt and even of despondency' in the national mood. He told a university audience in Bangalore, in southern India, that 'the laxity in recent years in dealing with India's fiscal and balance of payments problems and a failure to press ahead with long-overdue structural reforms' had also contributed to the mood of despondency.

But the speech equally showed that he was no radical reformer storming the barricades. 'A well thought-out plan has to be devised to make the rupee a convertible currency in a reasonable period of time, in any case before the end of the decade,' he said.

Dr Singh had retired to the backwaters of the University Grants Commission when Prime Minister P.V. Narasimha Rao unexpectedly plucked him out—to his obvious delight—to become finance minister after the Congress party won the general election in June. Once in office, he acted rapidly to devalue the rupee by 18 per cent to halt speculation against the currency, which had been hit by capital flight. The government's sales of gold stocks were an admission that the foreign exchange reserves were nearly exhausted.

In mid-July he unveiled a budget that cut the fiscal deficit from 9 per cent of gross domestic product the previous year to 6.5 per cent. Parallel with this, the government embarked on a programme of industrial and trade deregulation.

Quiet and self-deprecating, Dr Singh has an unquestioned reputation for honesty. He finds it difficult to dodge a direct question. When pushed to be specific on something he is reluctant to disclose, he falls back on the implausible 'I have no head for figures.' Friends say his responsibility in navigating the reform package through cabinet and parliament imposes on him a huge load. 'It is not a job I would wish on a friend,' says one.

His enthusiasm for reform does not mean that he thinks that the market alone is the answer to India's problems.

'We can't assume that the market will take care of all our problems. There are millions outside the market who live on the edge of subsistence. They cannot be dealt with through the market mechanism.'

The strength of the appointment is that Dr Singh is a respected figure among international bankers and financial institutions on whom India depends to stave off default. He also knows that what India has embarked on is a readjustment programme that will last from three to five years and that the hardest part in many ways is yet to come—deeper cuts in public expenditure, opening industry up to competition through steep tariff reductions, reducing the labour force in public-sector industries and the banks, and allowing multinationals a freedom to operate in India that has so far been denied them.

So daunting are the tasks ahead that many colleagues in cabinet and Congress have no idea of where the road of reform will take them and little stomach for the flight.

Dr Singh's weakness as finance minister is that he has a tendency to succumb to pressure and has no experience of the bear-pit of Indian politics. He partially gave way to farmers' lobbying against the cut in fertilizer subsidies announced in his budget. Will he 'cave in' as well to lobbying by industrialists against the wealth tax also imposed in the budget? 'No comment,' he says. But he adds—suggesting that he might lend an ear to their grievances—that 'I am sympathetic to all segments of the economy who actively participate in the creation of national wealth.'

His other problem is that he is part of a government that is itself a minority administration and is riddled with dissension. It is to offset these factors and to provide a guarantee of the continuity of reform that he is keen that India should seek a further loan from the International Monetary Fund under its Extended Fund Facility—which could provide India with $5 billion to $7 billion over three years. 'There is no doubt in our mind that we shall have to go for this [EFF loan],' he says. 'But asking for it is one thing. The Fund accepting it is a different. So I am not in a position to say there will be an agreement.'

Dr Singh is aware of apprehensions that the greatest threat to his policies comes from the risk of devaluation and import shortages precipitating an inflationary spiral that could be tough to control.

Elsewhere, he is under pressure from the World Bank and the IMF to hasten tariff cuts. India has one of the highest tariff barriers in the world, with an average weighted tariff of 112 per cent. Industrialists are also holding off investments until they know the extent of the tariff cuts.

The finance minister says he will reveal his medium term target for tariff cuts in the next budget due in March next year. Then, he will also need to start offsetting the loss of customs revenues by increasing direct taxes or excise duties.

'I know what I want to do. At the end, we will have tariff rates providing a reasonable level of protection which do not constitute an unreasonable barrier to foreign competition.'

He said he would like to shift the loss of customs duties to direct taxes, but says there are 'obvious administrative problems'. Broadening the income tax base to include farmers would, for instance, provoke a political outcry.

Politicians in Delhi feel that, as a technocrat with no party base, he will be sacrificed if the reforms run into trouble, or inflation—currently exceeding 13 per cent on the consumer price index—rose much higher. He says himself that being a technocrat, rather than a politician, has had some 'short-term advantages'. As to the possibility of his being made a scapegoat for the unpopularity of the measures and high inflation, Dr Singh shrugs his shoulders and smiles—adding that in a democracy nobody is indispensable.

~

Edward A. Gargan

Satyajit Ray Honoured Without Profit in His Land

The New York Times
16 February 1992

SLOUCHED IN HIS favourite leather armchair, a fine wool shawl pulled around his cloud-white cotton pajama-style kurta, Satyajit Ray peers around his familiar study, books and manuscripts stacked and crammed into sagging wooden shelves, a desk smothered with letters—many congratulatory epistles for winning an Oscar for his life's work—while an overhead lamp flickers momentarily as Calcutta's persnickety power supply seems to dither over what to do. As he often does, he lets his fingertips play along the edge of his lips, almost as if he wants to sculpt each word, each thought.

In the streets beneath his genteelly shabby and rambling apartment on the third floor of what Indians call a 'mansion', horns blat and trucks grind their gears as they attempt to navigate a maelstrom of vehicles, people and ideas. At each sunrise, there seem to be more people, more slums, more garbage, more political rallies, all compressed into a metropolis of blackening buildings, moonscaped roadways and thick swaddlings of air pollution. Visitors shake their heads here, wondering what can become of this city, once so grand and now often politely referred to as a hellhole.

'Calcutta? Where is it going?' the seventy-year-old Mr Ray asks with mock weariness. 'The same question has been asked for the last fifty years.' He laughs loudly, a deep, euphonious rumble that almost jiggles his china teacup. 'It's heading. It's heading. Nobody knows where. But it's heading. Things are happening. People are buying tickets to see theatre or cinema, going to concerts, buying books, going to the book fair—it takes place in all the big cities of India, but it is only in Calcutta that it is a total success.'

It is always said that Calcutta is a place of poets and singers, novelists and dreamers. Taxi drivers and postmen, hotel maids and office workers all take up pens and compose and publish. Bengalis here think of themselves as better than other Indians, more intellectual, more thoughtful, less superstitious, less materialistic. Their intellectual saint, Rabindranath Tagore, won the Nobel Prize in Literature. Now, their patron of the screen, Satyajit Ray, has won Hollywood's highest accolade for his moving pictures.

The honorary Academy Award, announced prior to this week's revelation of the traditional nominees in various categories, will be presented 30 March during the annual ceremonies. The citation recognizes Mr Ray's 'rare mastery of the art of motion pictures, and of his profound humanitarian outlook, which has had an indelible influence on film makers and audiences throughout the world'. Among directors who have been similarly honoured are Akira Kurosawa, Hal Roach, Jean Renoir, Howard Hawks, King Vidor, Charles Chaplin and Orson Welles.

'I'm surprised,' admitted Mr Ray, a tall, lanky man who looks a bit like the silent, gaunt statues on Easter Island. 'I'm surprised particularly because my films are not that well known in the States. They are much better known in Britain, Paris certainly now, and even Japan. But obviously there is a certain section, in any case, who like my films. Anyway, it means a lot to me. It means a lot to me because I've learned my craft of making films by watching Hollywood films of the '30s, '40s and '50s. And I never went to a school. That was my school.'

It is not only in the United States that Mr Ray's work is scantily known. Here, few Indians will admit to having seen one of his films. No theatre in India is currently showing a movie by him, and it is unlikely, despite the Oscar, that they will. Like that of Bunuel or Renoir or De Sica, or Federico Fellini or even Mr Kurosawa, Mr Ray's work is thoughtful, wrenching, uncomfortable, often distressingly quotidian in its explorations. Instead, India's theatres are filled with the commercial froth of Bombay's huge movie studios, what they call Bollywood, which churn out saccharine and predictable stories of love and violence, all liberally lathered with song and dance.

Even in his beloved Calcutta, it is virtually impossible to find a showing of a movie by Mr Ray. Every few years, for a week or so, a theatre will run his latest endeavour, but despite this city's intellectual pretensions, his films rarely run longer. Partly, Mr Ray says, this is because of the changes sweeping across India, the pressures of work and, perhaps ultimately, television.

'There are still poets and novelists and film makers and whatnot, but not as many as there used to be,' he said, his long fingers toying with his pipe. 'And the novelists and the poets all have very good jobs with good salaries, and the writing has fallen down. They have no new experience to write from. It's very disappointing. Films, of course, are not doing very well at all because of video partly, partly because the theatres are so badly maintained. In summer, there's no air conditioning. They won't run the air conditioning. They use the fans, the electric fans. The projection is bad. The sound is bad. The seats are bad. I mean, we had some of the finest cinemas in India. But no longer. I have stopped going to the cinema. I watch films on video.

'Video is not the same as films,' he continued. 'Certain films work all right, like a film like *Scenes From a Marriage* by Bergman. That sort of thing works all right because that's made with the television in mind, because it's two people talking most of the time in close-up, fighting and quarrelling and loving and whatnot. But, for instance, my first film, *Pather Panchali* : there's a lot of pictorial quality about it. All that is lost. You can hardly see them on the screen. There is such a thing as a special subject for the cinema. One of the reasons why I enjoy making films is that I enjoy also eventually watching the films with the audience. Otherwise, there's no feedback.'

Once, in one of his rare lectures about his work, Mr Ray described what he was trying to do in his early films, and unconsciously explained perhaps, why his work seems so shrivelled on television.

'You had to find out yourself how to catch the hushed stillness of dusk in a Bengali village,' he said, 'when the wind drops and turns the ponds into sheets of glass dappled by the leaves of the trees, and the smoke from ovens settles in wispy trails over the landscape, and the plaintive blows on conch shells from homes far and wide are joined by the chorus of crickets, which rises as the light falls, until all one sees are the stars in the sky, and the stars blink and swirl in the thickets.'

It was in 1955 that Mr Ray filmed *Pather Panchali*, the first realistic look at life in the Bengal countryside and the problems individuals and families wrestle with, a picture far from the idealized notions of rural life portrayed in the commercial song-and-dance films beginning to take hold in India. He went on to complete two other films—*Aparajito*

(1956) and *The World of Apu* (1959)—following the protagonist in *Pather Panchali* from adolescence to adulthood, through tragedy to a sort of spiritual renewal, from rural naivete to glossy urbanism. Together the three films became known as the *Apu Trilogy*, and they established Mr Ray as one of the world's finest directors.

In 1955, the Museum of Modern Art in New York gave *Pather Panchali* its United States premiere; and in 1981, it gave Mr Ray a retrospective. 'We consider Satyajit Ray one of the great film makers of all time,' said Mary Lea Bandy, the director of the museum's department of film. 'I think he ranks as one of the great humanists in cinema, and he has done a great deal to influence film making and to demystify India.'

But film is not Mr Ray's only pursuit. Like all Bengalis, he has been propelled into other realms by his catholic curiosities. Indeed, the reluctance of India movie houses to show his films means that many Indians know him better as an author of a detective series and several works of science fiction dealing with the derring-do of the mysterious Professor Shonku, inventor of the micromagnascope. He has also written a popular children's book, *The Golden Fortress*, which later was made into a thriller, and he edits *Sandesh*, a children's magazine. 'Some of the stories I have written,' he wrote in an introduction to one of his collections, 'reflect my love of Verne and Wells and Conan Doyle, whose works I read as a schoolboy'.

Despite his own health problems—two heart attacks and bypass surgery—Mr Ray has plunged on. 'I will tell you what happened,' he said, his storytelling impulse bubbling to the surface. 'After my bypass surgery, for four years I did nothing. I was not allowed to do anything. Finally the doctor said, "You can make a film, but you have to make it entirely in the studio. I won't let you work on location." So for the first time in my life I adapted a play, Ibsen's *Enemy of the People*. I shot it entirely in the studio. But I Indianized it. Well, in his play, the spa water is polluted. But there is no such thing as a spa in India, so I converted it into a temple tank that people drank from. That was polluted. That caused all the drama.' This film, released under the title *Ganashatru* was received unkindly by many of India's critics, critics who have traditionally been admiring of his work despite its lack of commercial appeal.

Undeterred, Mr Ray went back to his camera and returned with a film that has unsettled many of his Indian viewers. The film, *Shakha Proshakha*, or *Branches and Trees*, examines a father's awakening to his sons' moral corruption despite his own determined, almost Gandhian, rectitude. In Mr Ray's characteristic fashion, the themes of family transition, betrayal and tragedy are superimposed upon India's changing face, the contrast between small-town life and the virtues inherent in family life there, and the veneer and sophisticated alienations of urban existence. His film portrays not only a father's disillusionment but hints at the fragility of Indian moral values as an invading modernity rearranges the priorities of the new generation. 'You can see corruption in India, can't you,' sighed Mr Ray. 'At every level. At every level. I don't know what it means for India.'

The idea for his most recent film, unreleased yet and for which he has not settled on a title, came to him after delving into the work of the French anthropologist Claude Levi-Strauss. As in *Shakha Proshakha*, Mr Ray again looks for the inner soul of man, this time asking whether truth and wisdom inhere in the simplicity of primitive peoples. 'This film,' Mr Ray said, 'questions urban civilization. The idea came to me of civilization itself.'

These films, like his others, are unlikely to find a wide audience in India, yet Mr Ray continues to believe that his work is meant first and foremost for the eyes of his countrymen, for average Indians, if only they would take time to watch. This, he laments, is not true for the crop of new young directors in Calcutta who aspire to follow in his footsteps.

'In Calcutta,' he said, 'what happens is that the young film makers make films which are shown privately to friends and small cinemas. They slap each others' backs and say, "How wonderful." Then the films are sent immediately to the festival, get some good reviews from English critics, maybe even win a prize. But they are never released in Calcutta.

'I think that's a horrible situation because I never made films without my own audience in mind. I never made films for England or America. I make films for Bengalis to watch.'

India's critics puzzle over Hollywood's recognition of his work. 'Belated,' is an adjective that has seen prominence in newspapers in recent weeks. In fact, there is a touch of irony to Mr Ray's Oscar, for it contrasts with his own rather difficult association with America's movie capital. Once, in 1968, he attempted to have a screenplay of his produced there. It was called *The Alien* and recounted the tale of a young Indian village boy who encounters an extraterrestrial, a script illustrated with Mr Ray's own drawings of space creatures with large heads and wispy bodies. Despite the widespread continuation of Mr Ray's script, it was never produced.

Now, though, it does not seem to matter much to Mr Ray. He has plans to return to his camera before travelling to Hollywood for the Oscar ceremony, a trip he will combine with a visit to his cardiologists in Texas. 'I could kill two birds with one stone,' he said.

In the meantime, Mr Ray responds to his well-wishers' letters, frets over where to put the bounty of flowers that arrives daily and watches movies on his television.

'I started as a film fan, writing letters to Deanna Durbin and Ginger Rogers,' he admits. 'I look at Ginger Rogers and Fred Astaire quite often. Astaire is incredible. There's no one like Fred Astaire, even the early comics like Buster Keaton and Chaplin and all the rest. I've been watching them again and they haven't faded, you see.'

~

Bernard Imhasly

Destruction of the Mosque in Ayodhya Violent Resolution of the Indian Temple Dispute

Neue Zuercher Zeitung (Switzerland)
7 December 1992

Ayodhya: ON SUNDAY AFTERNOON militant Hindu activists stormed the Babri mosque in Ayodhya, a town a hundred kilometres from Lucknow, the capital of Uttar Pradesh. Shortly after five in the evening the central dome collapsed while the police stood by. Almost at the same moment, numerous houses and huts around the city belonging to Muslims went up in flames, while religious slogans rent the air. Two hours later the Central government dismissed the Uttar Pradesh government. Prime Minister Rao called on the people to remain calm and not to indulge in violence.

A symbolic ceremony was to take place in front of the controversial mosque, signalling the start of the construction of a Ram temple at that very spot. Protected by barbed wire, steel fences and several hundred policemen the mosque was to be left untouched till the Muslims could be persuaded to shift it to another place. Shortly before noon, however, young activists easily broke through the security perimeter set up by Hindu organizations and began to climb over the fences and scaffolding around the Babri mosque. Without offering any resistance the police inside the area marched away in orderly fashion, while the young fanatics climbed to the top of the building, with the help of ropes and pickaxes.

Charged 'Temple Builders'

The hoisting of the saffron flags was greeted by a gale-force call of 'Jai Shri Ram' from the roofs of the surrounding building, where thousands of enthusiastic pilgrims had gathered to watch the event. Those milling around the compound took it as a signal to then pull down the fences on all sides and to attack the walls of the mosque, using the iron rods from the fences. After several hours of uninterrupted hacking, one after the other of the three domes crashed down. Shortly after five o' clock the largest came down in a burst of dust. The accompanying noise was drowned by the roar of thousands of 'pilgrims' who had fired on the young men for five hours with their shouts of encouragement. The police didn't step in even once during the entire afternoon.

On the previous day the Hindu BJP-government of Uttar Pradesh had come to an agreement with the Hindu organizers that the latter would protect the mosque in order to prevent any clashes between the police and the 'pilgrims'. H.P. Seshadri, the general-secretary of the cadre organization RSS, had appeared confident while talking to journalists, ensuring them that the commitment would be kept.

A walk through the town in which 3,00,000 of the faithful had gathered, had seemed to justify this assessment on Saturday. Everywhere, RSS security-men, noticeable with their yellow sashes and headbands, were busy directing the flow of people.

However on Sunday the 'Kar Sevaks' ('the religious workers') among them made it clear that they were not willing to be content

with a mere religious ceremony. For weeks they had be
radical Hindu politicians, with the aim of forcin
government to hand over the mosque to the Hindus.
of religious propaganda in July had left them feeling du
it seems, they were not going to be satisfied with a mer

In the course of the afternoon it became clear t
VHP, the 'World Hindu Organization', disagreed wit
moderate politics of the BJP and the RSS. They pla
the ceremony with a 'spontaneous act', and to pres
with a *fait accompli*. Curiously, already on Sunday mor
of Ram, worshipped within the mosque since 1
removed. The media too were to be prevented from r
incidents. On Saturday some reporters were tempo
And on Sunday, others were systematically attacked by
suffered minor injuries, and the camera and tape-
correspondent were thrown to the ground.

Beginning of a Conflagration?

The fall of the mosque in Ayodhya has pushed the
new crisis. On Sunday evening itself, the Uttar Prad
which was responsible for the protection of the mosq
The BJP thus lost the most populous state, and it is n
of having allowed the destruction of the mosque by i

But the Congress government of Narasimha Rao
too. Rao had given firm assurances to the Muslims th
allow the destruction of the mosque. But he had tri
by a police of stalling and appeasement. In the de
could not fulfil his promise. He thus betrayed the tr
minority which has, so far, conducted itself with rem

Sunday's event will heighten their feeling of inse
of an increasingly strident Hindu chauvinism. On
first indications of new troubles appeared in the
Ayodhya, only minutes after the collapse of the mo
smoke rose from the homes of Muslims, burnt b
euphoric frenzy. There is now a clear risk that the
mosque and the subsequent arson will spread throu

~

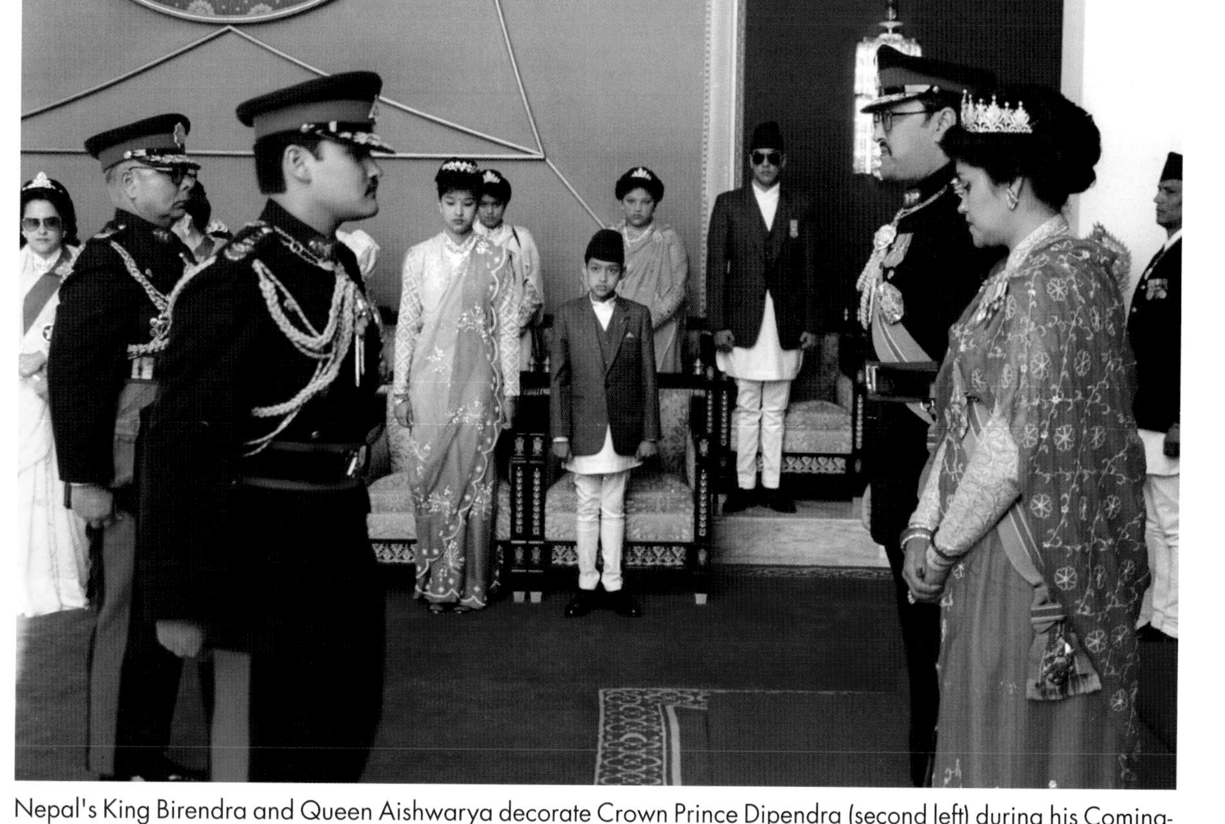

Nepal's King Birendra and Queen Aishwarya decorate Crown Prince Dipendra (second left) during his Coming-of-Age ceremony at the Narayan Hity Palace in Kathmandu in 1990. On 1 June 2001, a drunken Crown Prince killed his parents and seven other royals before turning his gun on himself. Photograph by Gopal Chitrakar/Reuters.

Foreign correspondents pushing luggage trolleys on the road to Kathmandu. A general strike was in force in the Nepalese capital on the day of their arrival in 1991, forcing them to walk to their hotels. Left to right: Mark Fineman, *Los Angeles Times;* Anita Pratap, *Time* magazine; Steve Coll, *Washington Post*; Peter Heinlein, *VOA*; Mark Tully, *BBC*; and Tim Hanson, *UPI*. Photograph by Robert Nickelsberg/Getty Images.

'Paradise on earth': a view of Dal Lake, Srinagar, from the deck of one of Butt's Clermont Houseboats. The guest books contain entries by hundreds of foreign correspondents who have covered the insurgency in Kashmir down the decades. Photograph by David Orr.

Hindu militants raze the Babri Masjid in the north Indian town of Ayodhya in 1992. The site has long been contested by Muslims and Hindus with the latter claiming the mosque was built on an ancient Hindu temple to Lord Rama. The destruction of the mosque prompted nationwide religious riots that left 2,000 dead. Photograph by Pablo Bartholomew.

The Ali Kadal Bridge over the Jhelum River in Srinagar, Kashmir, in 1991. Militants set fire to the structure in response to a police paramilitary action. Photograph by Robert Nickelsberg/Getty Images.

Taliban soldiers fire rockets from a BM -12 launcher at retreating Northern Alliance troops loyal to Ahmed Shah Masood, north of Kabul, Afghanistan, in October 1996. The Taliban were ousted by US and mujahideen forces in late 2001. Photograph by Robert Nickelsberg/Getty Images.

Women from the Dalit community at an election rally by Mayawati near Lucknow, northern India, in 1999. In her fourth term as chief minister of Uttar Pradesh state in 2008, Mayawati said she wanted to be the first prime minister of India from her oppressed class. Photograph by David Orr.

The state funeral of Mother Teresa in Calcutta in 1997. A Roman Catholic nun of Albanian origin, Mother Teresa ministered to the poor, sick, orphaned and dying for more than forty years while guiding the expansion of the Missionaries of Charity throughout India and the world. Photograph by Raghu Rai.

Stephan Wagstyl
The Child Victims of India's Slave Trade

Financial Times
19 December 1992

THE DUSTY CARE-WORN villagers wait expectantly. They have travelled to Mirzapur, the sprawling north Indian city which is the centre of the country's carpet industry, hoping for a miracle. The man they have come so far to see smiles reassuringly and says: 'We'll get your children back.' He picks up the telephone and so begins a desperate effort to rescue the men's sons from illegal bonded labour.

The villagers have travelled by bus for days from their poverty-stricken farms.

All are illiterate Untouchables, members of India's lowest caste and an easy target for exploitation. To ease their lives of abject poverty, they have sold their sons to carpet loom owners in return for Rs 500 each and promises of well-paid work for the boys. Now, they want them back.

This tall man with the black beard is their last hope. He is Kailaish Satyarthi, a thirty-seven-year-old former electrical engineer, who has given up his career to become a social activist. To the horror of his family, he has also abandoned his own caste, the priestly Brahmins, to fight for the rights of Untouchables.

Satyarthi telephones Suresh Kumar Singh, the local magistrate, who is required by law to investigate violations of India's child labour legislation. But he is unobtainable, said by officials to be 'too busy' to answer the call. After a fruitless six-hour wait, Satyarthi, accompanied by fellow campaigners against child servitude and a number of journalists, storms Singh's office—only to find it empty.

They wait in vain for a further hour, sitting on chairs before a large desk on which is written the motto: 'Good public relations is the best policy.'

Eventually, a message comes, proposing a 7 p.m. meeting at Singh's house.

Armed guards meet the group at the magistrate's colonial-style mansion. They lead the way inside where a smiling Singh apologizes to Satyarthi for the delay—and promptly suggests postponing the meeting to the next day. Barely able to control himself, Satyarthi refuses. He insists that Singh or one his subordinates accompanies the group to rescue the children. 'It's your duty,' he argues.

Singh asks for the location of the two villages where the children are believed to be held and promises, in the best bureaucratic tradition, to see what he can do.

Child labour is banned in India in many industries, including carpet weaving.

Bonded labour, where the workers' freedom of movement is restricted, is illegal for employees of any age.

But India lacks the resources to properly police laws on child labour, as on many other social evils. The authorities are often loathe to upset businessmen such as the loom owners of Mirzapur who make a profitable living employing children to produce hand-knotted carpets for the showrooms of London, Berlin and New York.

Still less does the country have the means to quickly eradicate the economic pressures which force parents to sell their children into bondage, not just in the carpet industry but also in metalwork, quarrying and the manufacture of fireworks.

Moreover, even though caste equality is enshrined in the Indian constitution, caste consciousness makes many Indians insensitive to exploitation of Untouchables.

Slavery is an emotive term, child slavery particularly so. But it is difficult to see the bonded child labourers of Mirzapur as anything other than child slaves. The words are repugnant to carpet manufacturers and to officials of the textiles ministry.

However, as early as 1984, a local government official in Uttar Pradesh province, which includes Mirzapur, admitted the truth in a note for a visiting labour ministry delegation. He wrote: 'The apprentices and wage earners . . . often work in conditions of semi-slavery.'

Ignorance, greed and corruption ensure that the law is widely flouted in rural India. A Supreme Court Commission estimates that 75,000 children work in the carpet industry alone—most of them bonded workers. Anti-child labour campaigners put the figure at 300,000. Carpet industry employers maintain such figures are 'lies' and insist there is no bonded child labour in the industry.

The events of Satyarthi's rescue raid, which I witnessed, suggest otherwise.

The mission begins the morning after our tense meeting with the magistrate.

Somewhat to our surprise, Singh has been as good as his word and arranged for a junior magistrate and four policemen armed with ancient ex-army rifles to travel with us. (It later emerges that Singh also found time to warn carpet industry bosses about the raids, as Satyarthi had feared.)

One father, Paltan Ram, said he sold his eight-year-old son Madan Lal to a loom owner for Rs 500. Only later did he realize he, along with other parents, were losing their children for good.

To their horror, they discovered loom owners banned home visits and, sometimes, contact of any kind. Paltan Ram says when he tried to visit his son, he was driven away by a man armed with a shotgun. He and the others arrived in Mirzapur after hearing about Satyarthi's campaign from his co-workers, volunteers who travel to remote villages to collect information and contact parents who want to recover their children. (Although the families did not say, another spur may be the government grants of Rs 6250 for the families of rescued bonded labourers.)

Satyarthi tries to reassure the fathers as they stand in silence waiting for the rescue to begin. The junior magistrate seems distinctly unhappy about his assignment. Perhaps he is afraid there might be violence—as there was on previous rescue raids. Perhaps he does not relish the idea of challenging the carpet industry bosses, a power in the land in Mirzapur.

We drive out of the city in a dusty convoy of battered vehicles. Along the roadside stand the weavers' workshops, mostly huts housing a weaver and his family and one or two wooden looms. Every so often, there are large factories and warehouses—the premises of exporters who dominate the industry. They take orders from overseas buyers and then parcel out work to the loom owners, who in turn employ the weavers.

As we reach deeper into the countryside, the road deteriorates into a sandy track. The cars swerve constantly to avoid children, animals and the occasional bullock cart. The boys' fathers sit in silence, their faces drawn and fingers clenched. Satyarthi says he is worried that the delays may have given the loom owners a chance to learn about the planned raids.

As we near the first of the two chosen villages, the vehicles slow down and stop. We jump out and run through a maize field to some mud-brick huts surrounded by trees. Satyarthi heads straight for a large hut with a loom outside it, and discovers three boys cowering inside.

Satyarthi rushes outside. 'There must be more. Search everywhere,' he shouts to his fellow campaigners. The activists fan out across the village and into the surrounding fields. They find three more boys. Six altogether. Satyarthi is disappointed—he had expected eight. The loom owner is also missing.

Satyarthi urges the group back into the cars—it is essential to reach the second village before word about the first raid spreads. Already about fifty villagers are milling around us. As before, we drive as close as possible to the village, and then rush in on foot. Satyarthi sprints into a courtyard where the looms are housed behind walls studded with broken glass. But it is too late. The boys he expected to find are gone.

Paltan Ram, Madan Lal's father, is distraught. 'I want to die,' he says, tears welling up in his tired, blood-shot eyes.

But all is not lost. Searching through one of the village huts, Satyarthi's co-workers find the loom owner, Govind Singh. They drag him before the junior magistrate, demanding action. 'What are you waiting for? The parents are here. The loom owner is here. You have the power to hold a summary trial,' shouts Satyarthi. He pulls out a file containing the details of child labour legislation. 'The maximum penalty is three years' jail,' he says, glaring at the loom owner.

The junior magistrate now seems more uncomfortable than ever. As he sits wondering what to do, the loom owner's servants come out with water and biscuits and beds for the visitors to sit on. Satyarthi takes written statements from the fathers, including lines expressing their fears that the loom owner might kill their children. He threatens the loom owner, saying he would be charged with kidnapping unless he produced the boys.

For more than an hour, we sit in the sun as the junior magistrate, the loom owner and Satyarthi talk and shout at each other. Eventually, the loom owner caves in and promises to surrender the children. He leaves, accompanied by the junior magistrate. Another thirty minutes' wait. Finally, the junior magistrate and the loom owner return, bringing with them three boys. Shyly, they take their fathers' hands, barely understanding what is going on. Among them is Madan Lal.

Paltan Ram hugs his son saying: 'I feel so good.' Madan Lal allows Satyarthi to examine him. His arms are covered with scars from scabies, caused by a common allergy to wool. On one finger he has a cut, black with diesel oil, which the loom owner applied to the wound to stop the blood from staining the carpets.

The junior magistrate reluctantly arrests Govind Singh, the loom owner.

Satyarthi is triumphant. The rescued boys and their fathers walk quietly back to the cars, overwhelmed by what has happened.

Back in Mirzapur, the boys are registered by clerks at the district magistrate's office. Madan Lal is the youngest. The oldest is fifteen and has spent five years at the loom. All look thin, and several have signs of scabies.

For the most part, the boys have few complaints about their food, which consisted of thin soups, vegetables and bread. But in almost every other way they were abused. They worked twelve hours a day from 6 a.m. to 6 p.m., with three half-hour breaks for meals—seven days a week, every week of the year.

They were rarely allowed out of the huts in which they worked and slept. One says: 'Even when I went to relieve myself (in the fields), someone went with me.'

They were never paid. If they worked slowly, they were beaten, sometimes with a wooden stick. Worst of all was the common treatment for cuts to the fingers suffered during weaving. The loom owners would scrape the powder off a match on to the wound and then set fire to it to staunch the bleeding. 'It hurt very much,' says twelve-year-old Chilatra Choudhray.

Above all, the children suffered acute psychological distress. Madan Lal's only thought was for his mother. 'I always missed my mother. I always cried for my mother but there was nobody there to listen.'

Satyarthi says that since the early 1980s, he has helped in the release of 5000 children, almost all of them untouchables. He has won financial support from western charities such as Britain's Christian Aid and Bread for the World, a German group.

The employers, he says, only started to take notice when he began publicizing the raids—which is why he invites journalists along.

Now he is trying to generate interest in the plight of Indian child labourers in Europe and the US—where the bulk of Mirzapur's carpets are sold. He believes that if Western consumers can be taught to take notice of the fate of whales, they can also be made aware of the sufferings of child labourers.

Carpet industry leaders loathe Satyarthi. Despite the evidence, including the Supreme Court Commission's survey, they flatly deny the existence of large-scale bonded labour. 'There may be isolated cases in remote villages, but no more,' says Mr Prakash Chandra Jaiswal, president of the All India Carpet Manufacturers Association, and a prominent exporter.

Jaiswal claims that allegations of parents selling children to loom owners stem from a misunderstanding. In such transactions, loom owners have merely made loans to the parents—advances on the wages the children will earn. Moreover, such cases concern a small minority of children. Most child labourers work in the homes of their parents or relatives where they learn a valuable trade.

Nevertheless, Jaiswal and his fellow employers are worried enough to have planned counter-measures. With the support of the textiles ministry, they intend to begin to inspect looms. Any weaver found employing non-family children will be blacklisted.

A breakaway group of carpet manufacturers is even introducing early next year a special trademark certifying carpets as 'made with child-free labour'. However, Satyarthi does not trust the employers. He argues checks will be worthless unless they are carried out with the cooperation of campaign groups.

India has been particularly slow in ensuring that children attend school.

Elsewhere, education has proved a valuable way of teaching parents that their children are worth nurturing, if for no other reason that their ultimate earnings will be higher with education than without.

Myron Wiener, an American social scientist and author of *The Child and the State in India*, says just 38 per cent of Indian children complete five years of education, compared with 70 per cent in China. Wiener argues that it is not poverty which prevents India investing more in its children but caste prejudices.

Upper caste Indians, who dominate central and local administration, simply do not care enough about the children of the lower castes.

Satyarthi agrees: 'I hate caste. After I started eating with untouchables, my own family refused to eat with me. But I chose what I wanted to do. It is the untouchables who suffer the most.'

~

Edward A. Gargan

Hindu Storm, Trust Is Torn Police Role in Bombay Riots

The New York Times
4 February 1993

NAZIRA KHATOON ROCKED slowly back and forth on a dirty mat, a bundle of quilts, a few plastic bags pulled close around her. A stream of tears glistened on her face as she recounted how a mob broke into her house in a Bombay shantytown and seized her son as the police looked on and did nothing.

'I said, "Don't do anything to my son,"' she recalled. 'He was married just two days before. The mob of 250 came. They were with swords and stones, and they pushed me into the bathroom. They took all my property and killed my son in front of me. The police just stood there watching.'

Day after day after day, for nine days and nights beginning 6 January, mobs of Hindus rampaged through this city, killing and burning people only because they were Muslims. No Muslim was safe—not in the slums, not in high-rise apartments, not in the city's bustling offices—in an orgy of violence that left 600 people dead and 2000 injured.

Many Details Unreported

Now, as quiet settles in the city, the full dimensions of the violence are becoming increasingly clear, although many details—including transcripts of police radio transmissions and other evidence showing that the police took part in the anti-Muslim violence—have not been printed in Indian newspapers or magazines.

'It is cold-blooded,' Alyque Padamsee, the chief executive of Lintas, India's largest advertising company, said of the killings. 'This is a very cold-blooded pogrom. There are no concentration camps, though. They just kill people.'

Interviews with victims, relief workers, politicians, civic leaders, police officers and journalists have suggested, moreover, that the killing, arson and looting were far from random.

In fact, they were organized by Hindu gangs, abetted by the Bombay police and directed at Muslim families and businesses. The extent of police cooperation with the Hindu mobs appears to have spread through the entire police force, excluding only the most senior officers.

Transcripts of conversations between the police control room and officers on the streets, taken from the regular police radio band and made available to the *New York Times* by an Indian reporter, show that the officers at police headquarters repeatedly told constables in the field to allow Muslim homes to burn and to prevent aid from reaching victims.

According to one transcript, for instance, the control room referred to the site of a fire by saying it must be a garage owned by a Muslim man, with the speaker using a vulgar term for a circumcized man in the language of Maharashtra state.

'Let it burn,' he added, according to the transcript. 'If it belongs to a Maharashtrian, don't burn anything that belongs to a Maharashtrian.' The voice added that the police should 'burn everything' belonging to a Muslim, this time using another obscene reference to Muslims.

Throughout the nine days of rioting, witnesses said that neither the Maharashtra authorities nor the Central government in New Delhi made any effort to stanch the flow of blood.

According to witnesses, Muslim mothers watched as their sons were pulled from their homes, slain or burned alive while mobs of chanting, cheering Hindus danced around the blazing bodies. Mosques and Muslim stores were firebombed. Men on the street were made to drop their trousers so Hindu mobs could see if they were circumcized, as all Muslim men are.

In the aftermath of the violence, hundreds of thousands of Muslims have fled the city, many of them unlikely ever to return.

The Background Violence Becomes More Systematic

Since its independence from Britain and partition with the Muslim nation of Pakistan in 1947, India has been regularly torn by sectarian violence and bloodshed, especially between Hindus and Muslims.

There have also been cases when the violence seemed organized. In 1984, after Prime Minister Indira Gandhi was gunned down by her Sikh bodyguards, a campaign of murderous retribution that many charged was abetted or instigated by governing Congress party politicians left thousands of Sikhs dead in New Delhi.

But after the riots in Bombay, India's mightiest economic centre, many people say the violence has never before been so systematic, concentrated and foreboding.

The bloodshed has stunned Bombay and raised doubts about whether the city will ever recover. Before the riots, many Bombayites had let themselves think that their city had triumphed over caste and religious conflicts and that nothing like this could happen here.

'Some of the happenings in Bombay do bear a resemblance to Germany in the 1930s,' said Nani Palkhivala, a constitutional lawyer and former Indian Ambassador to the United States. 'These are things we have never seen in 300 years of Bombay. People were literally burnt alive. Is this civilization? Is this humanity?'

Much of Bombay's gloom comes from the inaction of the government. Neither the Chief Minister of Maharashtra state, Sudhakarrao Naik, nor the Indian Prime Minister, P.V. Narasimha Rao, reacted to the violence as it consumed the city.

In the eyes of many people in Bombay, Mr Rao has been indifferent to the problem. Delegations of this city's leading citizens, its business leaders, movie stars and even the Roman Catholic cardinal met with him in New Delhi to urge some action.

'He just sat there,' a participant said. 'He just said, "Yes, yes," and then we were led out.'

The physical scars of the violence can be seen everywhere. Bombay is a megalopolis of 12.5 million people with luxury high-rise buildings, great swathes of shantytowns, avenues of glittering jewellery and fashion shops and pavements carpeted by street dwellers.

But now the hulks of charred cars, trucks and buses, like the carapaces of desiccated beetles, litter the gutters. Rows of storefronts are interspersed by the firebombed shells of Muslim-owned shops, like missing teeth. Bombay's bread shops, almost exclusively owned by Muslims, have been gutted. Lumber yards were torched, as were much of the city's leather workshops, all Muslim-owned.

For much of the last six months, India has been wrapped in a tightening web of tension as Hindu religious and political organizations have called for tougher treatment of India's 110 million Muslims.

The first overt violence supported by this broad coalition was the demolition of a sixteenth-century mosque in December in the northern religious town of Ayodhya that Hindus said had been constructed on the site that they revere as the birthplace of the god Ram.

The destruction of the mosque led to widespread Muslim protests and clashes with the police and security forces in which more than 2000 people were officially reported to have died all across India, including 200 in Bombay.

After the destruction of the mosque, the Rao government did order a ban on some militant Hindu and Muslim organizations and arrested several leaders. But here in Bombay, the authorities did not ban a virulently anti-Muslim organization called Shiv Sena or arrest any of its members.

The Beginning Two Sparks Ignite Waves of Rioting

As the first wave of violence over the mosque subsided, Shiv Sena was apparently preparing a systematic campaign against the city's one million Muslims. What it needed was an incident, real or fabricated, that might call forth mobs of Hindu street thugs to carry out the attacks.

The moment came 6 January, with the stabbing of two Hindu dock workers, and on 7 January, when a Hindu family of four was burned to death in its hut in the slums of Jogeshwari in north Bombay.

Soon after the first incident, the wave of arson and attacks began.

The violence was recounted by Shamim Mohammed Khan as she stood in a silent line of other women waiting for relief workers to distribute grain from a small sack. Although nineteen, she looked older, having lost her home and her belongings in the attacks. The violence, she said, did not seem spontaneous.

'After the first wave of riots in December, some people came and asked what I had in my house,' she said. 'They were very friendly in manner. When the second wave came, they came and killed my husband. The Shiv Sena, they came. Fifty people came, armed with sticks, chains, pipes, axes.'

'I think my neighbours came only because they were forced,' she said. 'They were told, "If you don't help, we will get you." So my neighbours took my utensils, my pots and dishes, and sold them.'

She added that afterward they burned down the entire slum area, leaving 500 people homeless.

As the violence and the death toll climbed, *Saamna*, the daily newspaper published by Shiv Sena, urged its followers on. The paper is read by hundreds of thousands of lower-middle-class and lower-class people of Maharashtra, whose capital is Bombay.

'They have taken advantage of our helplessness and timidity,' the paper wrote on 9 January, referring to the city's Muslims. Charging that Hindus had been 'massacred' in the two incidents in Bombay, it said, 'If the law cannot protect us, then the hell with the law.'

The Authorities, Police Complicity Is Documented

Along the corridors of retail commerce in Bombay, the once seamless face of shop fronts is punctuated by the blackened cavities of Muslim businesses—a cloth store, a baker, a hardware shop. Along the same street, Hindu shops were left undamaged.

'They had the business licence registers from the city,' a reporter here said of the rioters, asking that his name not be used. 'With the registers, they could find the Muslims, even those which were owned by Hindus but rented to Muslim businesses.'

And nowhere during the attacks on Muslim shops did Bombay's police impede the attacks. Indeed, there is widespread evidence that they ignored the looting and firebombing and even encouraged it or took part.

A Hindu merchant shopkeeper, speaking on the condition that his name not be used, described how a police truck pulled up in front of a neighbouring shop. 'A police inspector, I saw his rank on his uniform, came out with some constables,' he said. 'They broke the lock on the shop and went inside. They came out with all the shoes and put them in the truck. Then they burned the shop.'

'I know many of these Shiv Sena boys,' he said. 'I grew up with them. And I'm scared.'

Even in Bombay's wealthiest residential areas, neighbourhoods filled with the corporate barons of India, the violence penetrated. Shoba De, the author of several popular novels and the wife of a leading businessman, said Shiv Sena mobs had searched apartment buildings for Muslims.

'They went door to door asking who is Muslim,' she said. 'They would look on the name boards in the lobby and then go upstairs and throw the Muslim families out of their apartments and put padlocks on them.'

The most startling evidence of police complicity has been in the transcripts of conversations picked up off the police radio band. These have been obtained by some reporters in India and translated into English, although they have not been printed in Indian newspapers or magazines, apparently because they are too inflammatory.

In one conversation, for instance, the police in a district called Dongri asked the control room what to do about two army trucks filled with milk sent as relief to a slum area where Muslims had been burned out of their huts.

'Why are you distributing milk to them?' the control room asked. 'Do not distribute milk to the laandyas. Have you understood?' Then the control room ordered, 'Seize that vehicle.'

'The police have been playing a very negative role,' said Farida Lambay, a social worker who was trying to resettle Muslim families who had been burned out of their homes. She said the police had become 'very, very communalized', a term referring to virulent sectarian prejudice, and added: 'People have lost faith in the police.'

Confronted with reports of police complicity, Babanrao Pachpute, the Maharashtra Home Minister, at first denied that the police had been involved in attacks on Muslims. But when it was pointed out that there were tapes of police radio conversations and accounts by witnesses, he said: 'It was so difficult for the police. There were so many people in the mobs, it was difficult for them.'

Pressed further, the minister said: 'All these things will be revealed in the judicial inquiry. We are taking actions and putting people behind bars.'

The state government has appointed a Bombay High Court judge to investigate the riots, although many doubt that it will lead to any firm conclusions or to prosecution of individuals.

The inquiry was established after at least three private groups in Bombay called for an investigation. The groups are the Committee to Protect Human Rights, a small group; the Bombay chapter of the People's Union of Civil Liberties, a legal rights agency, and an ad hoc group of senior industrialists led by J.R.D. Tata, who heads India's largest industrial house.

The Militant Group's Leader Defends Attacks

The man driving the Shiv Sena forward, and the voice behind its newspaper *Saamna*, is Bal Thackeray, who rose to visibility a decade ago by leading a violent campaign against southern Indians who had settled in Bombay.

In an interview at his home, Mr Thackeray refused repeatedly to respond to charges that his followers had engaged in killing and destruction throughout the city.

'Those who started the riots,' he said, referring to Muslims, 'have learned their lessons well.'

In an interview with the *Economic Times*, a leading financial journal, he said his followers were only responding to violence committed against them. 'They participated only to the extent of retaliating to the attacks,' he said.

Mr Thackeray's political activities started in the 1980s, when he demanded that Bombay be kept for the citizens of Maharashtra state, who speak a language and have an ethnic identity distinct from those of neighbouring states. Immigration from other parts of India has continued unabated, and now Mr Thackeray has turned to his anti-Muslim credo.

During the interview, Mr Thackeray allowed only a few notes to be taken, and he was guarded by Bombay policemen with submachine guns. He insisted that he wanted only to evict Muslims who were from Pakistan or Bangladesh, not all Muslims.

'All Muslims from Bangladesh and from Pakistan, those elements come to my country to create trouble to see we would never live in peace,' he said. 'Those Muslims who might have given them shelter must be kicked out.'

When it was suggested that many Bombay residents were comparing his group's actions to the Nazi attacks on Jews, he reacted angrily. 'I have no respect for intellectuals,' he said. 'They create problems by giving dirty opinions. I am a man of the masses.'

The Reaction: Bombay Ponders Legacy of Hatred

Like much of India, Bombay has a prosperous intelligentsia proud of its commitment to the principles of secularism and sectarian harmony enshrined in India's constitution, but often ignored in the nation's impoverished slums and villages. The Bombay events have left this elite group shaken.

'This will change the face of Bombay forever,' said Shabana Azmi, a leading movie actress in this film capital of India. 'In January, what happened is that the elite and the middle class were exposed for the first time to the kind of violence the poor are exposed to.'

Others say that the riots exposed how the elite has been complacent and distant from India's real problems.

'I think we are guilty of being out of touch,' said Tariq Ansari, the managing director of Midday Publications. 'The Shiv Sena evolved from a very violent genesis to become part of us. We would do business with them. We've told ourselves, "They don't do anything major; they do their little violence."'

'It was interesting that the mobs came out of the slums,' Mr Ansari added. 'This was really an upper-class nightmare, the monster coming out of the slums. And I'm convinced it's not over.'

Now, although the worst of the violence has passed, at least for the moment, the signs of hatred continue. Labour unions run by Shiv Sena are intimidating Muslim workers, preventing them from returning to their jobs in some of the city's largest industries, including Otis Elevator, the Mahindra jeep and tractor plants and companies on the docks.

Meanwhile, the 'ethnic cleansing' of the city's Muslim population proceeds, perhaps not so violently, but still methodically. Railway officials report that 215,000 people, virtually all Muslims, fled the city on special trains. A Hindu Brahmin business woman who employed fifteen Bengali Muslims in a fabric business reported that her workers had returned to Calcutta and had said they would never come back to Bombay. 'They said if I moved my workshops out of the city, they might come back,' she said.

Every night, rumours swirl through the shantytowns, bringing fear and desperation. And every night as well, one or two people die in flare-ups of violence, even though the city government insists that Bombay is recovering.

'At the end of the tunnel we are in, there is no light,' the editor of the *Illustrated Weekly* wrote in a recent edition. 'There are only the gas chambers. We have to decide whether we want to do something about it, or head straight into the blinding darkness.'

~

Olaf Ihlau
Sai Baba: 'Miracles Are Part of My Being'

Der Spiegel
September 1993

THE MAN OF god makes an appearance twice a day and thousands of people are transported into a rapturous ecstasy. Cymbals ring out, drums boom and Hindu prayers resound when the slender form appears in a vermilion robe and moves slowly between the rows of disciples sitting in lotus posture.

'O Baba, your god is love', the pubertal Praetorians rejoice, two hundred college boys dressed in white. Sai Baba, India's most popular and most controversial miracle-man is celebrating 'darshan', a mass audience.

The temperature soars under the plexi-glass dome of the large audience hall in the Trayee Brindaban Ashram at Whitefield, a suburb of the south Indian high-tech metropolis Bangalore. Even the man of god is sweating profusely. He uses a white silk handkerchief to wipe a face characterized by burlesque ugliness. It is dominated by a heavy nose above thick lips and framed by a curly Afro-mane.

Hundreds of hands bearing petitions reach out to Sai Baba accompanied by pleading looks. Although he doesn't take all the envelopes, he does accept many of them. Only a few chosen ones receive a special mark of favour: the saviour stops in front of them and smiles pensively. He then circles his right hand three times in the air and drops 'vibhuti' into the hand of the blessed—white ash as a symbol of divine mercy and also as a kind of talisman.

Millions on the subcontinent believe that Sai Baba is an incarnation of god, an embodiment of the omnipresent divine principle among humankind and that he can make objects materialize from thin air. His opponents accuse him of homoerotic tendencies and shady magician's tricks. Sai Baba has a more worldly word for his 'ash-magic' and calls it his 'visiting card'.

The card is not distributed too often on this humid morning although many disciples kiss the bare feet of their chosen one who they call Swami. He, however, does not particularly like this. In public physical contact is kept to the minimum: a pat on the shoulder here, a caress on the head there.

After ten minutes Sai Baba has had enough of mingling with the crowd. Waving graciously he sits down on a throne-like chair with a bronze statue of the preserver of the world, Vishnu, behind him and the elephant-headed god Ganesha at his feet. Above him a pastel-coloured canopy made of plaster is resplendent with the symbols of the great religions in a wreath around the torch of enlightenment.

'O Baba,' the hymns of the devotees proclaim, 'truth is your bread, and you are our life.' The man being praised nods complacently and remains silent. However, this adoration soon begins to annoy him and he disappears with a feeble gesture of blessing. His followers reel in a trance.

'Baba wants to make god a reality for everyone,' gushes V.K. Narasimhan, eighty-two. The former chief-editor of the *Deccan* newspaper has been living in the ashram for thirteen years. He considers his swami to be the 'greatest spiritual master of the universe, the consolidated form of the longing expressed by seekers'.

Even die-hard agnostics like the highly-decorated retired Rear Admiral, J.J. Baxi, fifty-seven, lose their power of rational observation on meeting the miracle-man. Baxi, now the director of an electronics company, is convinced 'that Sai Baba possesses superhuman powers which he uses for the benefit of the people'.

Sai Baba is the most bizarre presence among the saints, gurus, yogis and false prophets in India's spiritual supermarket. His message is simple, sometimes at the level of edifying sayings, and enriched with pieces from the store of world religions.

Be happy and selfless, the Baba preaches, do good and be of service to your neighbour! Or: 'There is only one religion, that of love, and only one caste, that of humankind.' Who would want to disagree with that? What is debatable, however, is that this messiah sees India as the 'teacher of the world'. He considers the vast Hindu pantheon to be of special advantage: 'Many gods means that everyone can get something: after all there are also many kinds of shirts.'

His devotees, however, have to wear white cotton shirts. This is the dress code for visitors to the ashram complex at the centre of which Sai Baba's stone cosmodrome towers up. The use of tobacco and alcohol is frowned upon as is that of meat and eggs.

Sai Baba doesn't give any interviews. He doesn't demand payment for his spiritual services and finances hospitals and colleges from donations received. In this he differs vastly from those mystics in the Hindu ensemble of saints who market their soul-searching techniques in a brutally calculating business-like manner: the dream-merchant Bhagwan Shree Rajneesh, for example, who ripped off sex-hungry yuppies from the West; the brawny jet-set guru Chandra Swami or the pope of the transcendental sect, Maharishi Mahesh Yogi, once the guru of the Beatles.

One of them, George Harrison, was later drawn to the Sai Baba. This preacher of salvation has also helped many enlightened bosses of industry, scientists, publishers, diplomats or music-conductors like the maestro Sergiu Celibidache to achieve an exotic self-cleansing and albeit only in an existential crisis.

The number of global followers of this guru is estimated to be a good hundred million. Almost the entire political establishment of India is part of this. When Prime Minister Rao miraculously survived a no-confidence vote in the present monsoon session of Parliament he lost no time in hurrying to a temple to make an offering of milk to the silver statue of Sai Baba.

No one has seen Sai Baba bringing back people from the dead. But, just as Søren Kierkegaard locates Jesus' greatness in his miracles, it is Sai Baba's performances and acts, which appear to contradict the laws of logic, physics and medicine, that have made the guru a spiritual superstar.

In a private audience the man of god confronts any doubts about his supernatural powers with mild astonishment. He denies putting on an act and says: 'Miracles are part of my being, my life is my message.'

Legend has it that even as a young boy he made his school-mates very happy by reaching into the air and producing colour-pencils and sweets. Two agony-filled days after the sting of a poisonous scorpion this farmer's son from Puttaparthi in south India was catapulted into a mystical twilight zone much to the horror of his parents who even took him to an exorcist. From then on Sai Baba performed miracles—small ones at first and later more astonishing ones: Gold chains and Rolex watches materialized out of thin air, the paralysed stood up at his sight, the mentally weak were restored to reason. In front of a large audience he dragged a heavy truck from a sand-bank with the help of a rope tied to his hair. The scene was recorded with a camera. Unfortunately, when the film was developed the crucial scene came out black.

Is he then just a charlatan? 'Insignificant worms' is what the man of god calls those who doubt him. Such people are to be found mainly among the Indian rationalists and they accuse the swami of jugglery. They state that during an alleged murder attempt recently the man of god revealed himself to be a normal human being with very human fears.

The reference here is to the bloody incident in June in one of his other ashrams in Puttaparthi, when the incarnation of god behaved like a frightened mortal: Sai Baba locked the door and escaped via the back stairs while four of his followers who had been banished from the inner circle were trying to force their way in. Six people died.

'Why didn't the Almighty turn the intruders into pillars of salt?' the rationalists ask scornfully. Ugly rumours then began to circulate about factional fights in Sai Baba's multi-million empire—about feuds among the young masseurs.

Naturally, the Indian press also remembered the story of the young American admirer whose book about the Baba (*Lord of the Air*) was the outcome of his shattered illusions, since the Baba had allegedly gone for his genitals: 'I was horrified. I had sworn to search for the truth, but why did the way there lead me through such a labyrinth?'

According to the man of god pleasure is 'an interval between two bouts of pain'. Jealousy and an obsessive ego are 'the roots of evil', said Sai Baba after the blood-bath at Puttaparthi. The incident will, however, only ensure that more people throng to him, he summed up in an altogether worldly manner.

The hall in front of Sai Baba's audience chamber is filled with his college boys. In anticipation of their master they move across the floor in a servile fashion like the Nibelungs before the Balck Alvan Alberich in Nibelheim's Night.

'My divine power knows no boundaries,' says Sai Baba. He claims to be able to transform earth into heaven and heaven into earth. 'But there is no reason to do it.'

~

Stephan Wagstyl
PSUs: Reluctant to Give Up Its Grip

Financial Times
6 June 1994

IN THE CONTROL room of the Hindustan Fertilizer plant at Haldia near Calcutta three men watch dials for eight hours a day. When they are finished, another shift of men in grey uniforms takes over, and then another, keeping watch twenty-four hours a day—just as they might in any other modern chemicals plant.

Except that at Haldia the plant produces nothing. It has produced nothing since attempts to commission the state-owned complex failed in 1986 because of fundamental design flaws. Needles on control room dials never move.

Some 1550 people report for work at Haldia. There is a canteen, a personnel department, and an accounts department. There are promotions, job changes, pay rises, audits and in-house trade unions. Engineers, electricians, plumbers and painters maintain the equipment with a care that is almost surreal. Signs are freshly painted, the roads swept and the grass verges cut.

The absurdity of their position has driven some workers to mental illness. Many workers have been idle so long they have become unemployable.

The origins of Haldia's failure lie mainly with Mrs Indira Gandhi's ill-conceived pursuit of economic self-sufficiency in the 1970s: the complex was built by inexperienced Indian engineers with an inadequate budget and with insufficient expert foreign supervision.

But the fact that Haldia, which loses about Rs 150 million (£3.2 million) a year, has been allowed to survive until the mid-1990s is also a telling criticism of the present government's reluctance to deal with the legacy of the past. With Prime Minister Mr P.V. Narasimha Rao's economic liberalization programme now in its third year, there is still little sign that he will drastically overhaul the country's bloated publicly owned industries through rationalization, privatization or the rapid introduction of competition into state-run monopolies.

The main reason the government fears to act is that serious reform would mean deep job cuts. India's labour laws give workers an almost impregnable defence against compulsory dismissal. The insolvency laws are so restrictive that it takes an average of over ten years to liquidate a company. A serious attempt to tackle the labour or insolvency laws would be seen as an attack on jobs—so Mr Narasimha Rao is understandably reluctant to act, particularly with the 1996 general election on the political horizon.

Moreover, full-scale privatization would destroy the network of patronage which politicians have built throughout the public sector. While the government is selling shares in thirty-one state companies, it is committed to retaining 51 per cent and managerial control. Similarly, where private companies are being permitted to enter markets dominated by state monopolies, there is much foot-dragging and back-sliding. Mr Manmohan Singh, the reform-minded finance minister and his supporters in the government, know what needs to be done—but the Prime Minister will not let them act for fear of political turmoil.

To be fair, the Prime Minister's quiet approach has yielded some results. The government has introduced voluntary retirement schemes which are slowly reducing employment. Total employment in the 237 centrally controlled industrial enterprises (excluding state-owned banks and services such as telecommunications) has dropped from 2.23 million in the late 1980s to under 2 million.

Government subsidies are also falling, though more slowly than planned. Mr Manmohan Singh intended to eliminate public financial support for loss-makers from April 1994. But when the 1994–95 budget was published it contained another cash injection: Rs 6.3 billion altogether.

Privatization may be half-hearted but the entry of strong state-run companies into the stock market has encouraged investment, including foreign portfolio investment. It was not a private company but the government's Videsh Sanchar Nigam, India's international telecommunications monopoly, which attempted the country's largest Euroissue—$1 billion. The offer had to be postponed because of the turmoil in world stock markets earlier this year—but the group is considering a second bid later this year.

Perhaps the government's biggest success in public sector reform has been in shaking up domestic air travel by permitting the entry of private operators in late 1992. Their competition has forced great improvements in time-keeping and quality from Indian Airlines, the state-owned carrier.

But when it comes to other industries, the interests of consumers seem to be of little account. Indeed, for some government ministers, the fact that the launch of private air lines has been accompanied by some teething troubles, including strikes, poaching of staff and arguments over routes, is taken as a reason for treading carefully in other markets.

Private investment is being allowed in power generation but competition from private stations will have little effect on existing state-run plants. Moreover, private companies are mostly being kept out of electricity distribution, where political patronage is pervasive. Dispensing cheap power to privileged groups such as farmers is a right few politicians will abandon lightly.

Mr Rao argues that by deregulating the economy, including liberalizing foreign trade and investment, he has created more than enough opportunities for private companies without the need for upheavals in the public sector. But poorly performing public enterprises impose a heavy burden on the rest of the economy, not only by siphoning public funds but also by often providing high-cost, low-quality goods and services. As Mr Aditya Birla, head of a leading business grouping, says: 'If the public sector is not competitive, then we can't be either.'

People suffer as well as companies. Legal job protection extends only to workers in the public sector and in large privately-owned enterprises—about thirty million people, or 150 million with their families out of a total population of 890 million. The economic cost of providing the safeguards falls on other Indians, many of them very poor and permanently jobless.

State-owned units still dominate transport, telecommunications, banking, oil, electric power and other basic services. They are also important producers of raw materials. Of the Central government's 237 active industrial enterprises, 104 lost a total of Rs 39.5 billion in the year to March 1993. The profits of most of the rest were inadequate—the total return on capital was just 2.4 per cent.

Hand-outs for loss-making public enterprises contribute to government borrowing helping to raise the fiscal deficit last year to 7.3 per cent of GDP. Further support comes from state-controlled financial institutions in low-cost loans. Also, even though the government has cut import duties and relaxed internal price controls, the remaining protection is biased towards protecting public enterprises.

Some state concerns perform well, despite the uncompetitive environment. Bharat Heavy Electrical, India's dominant maker of generating equipment, has won export orders, so has the Steel Authority of India, the steelmaker. Others could join them if they were free to compete, cut costs and run themselves independently.

But Delhi's influence over senior appointments is stifling—Air India, the international carrier, is one of about ten big enterprises currently without a chairman because politicians and bureaucrats cannot agree on a candidate.

Nevertheless, some enterprises are beyond redemption: obsolete textile mills, steelworks and bicycle factories as well as fertilizer plants, including Haldia.

The latter is a unit of Hindustan Fertilizer Corporation, which is one of forty-nine centrally-run public enterprises referred to the government's Board for Financial and Industrial Reconstruction, the agency established to expedite restructuring or liquidation. But only one public, centrally-run enterprise has ever been recommended for liquidation.

The government hopes that it will avoid big closures until the newly-liberalized economy grows fast enough to absorb the unemployed—perhaps in the late 1990s.

Even then, ministers will bite the bullet only under pressure. As Mr P.B. Krishnaswamy, secretary of the fertilizers ministry whose responsibilities include Haldia, says: 'This kind of picnic should not be allowed to go on for ever. But things won't change in this country unless it's the hard way, through sheer economic compulsion. Until then, politicians will keep making statements and keep alive the hopes of the dead.'

~

Trevor Fishlock

Rebels Show Father New Pictures of Kidnapped Son

The Daily Telegraph
18 June 1994

Three days into a family trek in Kashmir during the summer of 1994, Kim Housego, a son of the Financial Times' *former South Asia correspondent David Housego, was kidnapped by Islamic militants, along with David Mackie, a tourist from London. Instead of allowing government diplomats to take charge of rescue efforts, David Housego led an intensive lobbying and publicity campaign that secured their release after seventeen days. He was helped by journalists, one of whom wrote these two articles.*

*Kim Housego later said: 'The wider political issues at stake, such as curbing international terrorism or strengthening US–Pakistan relations, overshadow governments' preoccupation with the life of any one hostage. As my father says: "In the end it's only the relatives who really care about the lives of those held."' (*The Independent, 4 *February 1997)*

The kidnappers wanted militant leaders released from prison in India. A year later, five more hostages were taken—one of them was beheaded and the others were never found.

A CRUMPLED NOTE was pushed into Mr David Housego's hand yesterday.

It led the anxious father to a cloak-and-dagger rendezvous in a Himalayan town with four masked men from the Kashmiri rebel group that kidnapped his sixteen-year-old son and another Englishman twelve days ago. The rebels assured him that the two captives were safe.

They gave him colour photographs taken three days after the kidnapping, which show Kim Housego and Mr David Mackie, thirty-six, resting on a hill slope.

They are dressed in baggy blue Kashmiri clothes and sit under the eye of a masked and armed guerrilla.

Mr Mackie's wife Cathy, thirty-three, wept when she saw the photographs last night.

'It is like looking at him as if he were dead. I haven't seen him for so long, it doesn't seem real. He has a cynical sort of stare, as if the photo were taken under duress.'

Mr Housego, fifty-three, said: 'It was a shock to see the picture. Kim is my son, but at the same time I did not recognize him at first. He looked very pale.'

The leader of the four rebels, who met Mr Housego in secret, promised to free the captives soon.

But, with some emotion, the spokesman said that the activities of Indian security forces fighting insurgency in the region were a serious obstacle to a hand-over. It was reported last night that Indian security forces had killed twenty rebels, including a leader of the Harkat-ul-Ansar group, in a series of gun battles in the region.

Mr Housego was told by the rebels to leave Pahlgam, where he has been searching for news of his son. They told him to return to the Kashmiri capital of Srinagar and await developments.

He agreed to do so.

The day had started when Mr Housego was sought out in Pahlgam by a man who pushed the note into his hand and then melted away.

The note began: 'Respected Mr David', and urged him to go at once to an address in another town.

I accompanied him on the long bumpy drive through spectacular mountain scenery. From the address given in the note another contact took us through crowded, narrow lanes to a house.

We waited for an hour. The door was opened and four men came in, two of them with AK47 rifles. They wore masks of black, red, yellow and blue. They shook hands with us.

The man in the black mask, speaking good English, did all the talking.

He said he brought a message from the high command of the Harkat-ul-Ansar Islamic fundamentalist group.

He complained about the bombardment of a village and of other army activity in the region. Leaning forward on a couch, dark eyes luminous over the mask, he insisted that the two captives, seized on 6 June while on family holidays near Pahlgam, had been 'detained and not kidnapped'.

He said their safety was a priority and, as soon as a safe passage could be found, they would be freed.

'But the army,' he said, with an angry note in his voice, 'are putting hurdles in the way of the release of these detained persons.' It seemed clear that Mr Housego's initiative in setting up a base in Pahlgam, and running a leaflet appeal for the captives' release has had its effect.

The militants' spokesman said that reports of Mr Housego's campaign in the newspapers had irritated and confused the 'freedom fighters'.

'Our request is that you will confine yourself to Srinagar and relax there,' he told Mr Housego. 'We will contact you only in Srinagar. As soon as we find the passage we will hand them over safely.'

The atmosphere in the room was tense. 'We give you a surety that they will be released soon,' the man said.

'God forbid that any harm is done to them.'

Mr Housego, a former *Financial Times* correspondent in India and now a businessman in New Delhi, said: 'This is an unfortunate incident and the quicker we end it the better.'

The masked man said: 'That is what we want.' He began to talk in a rather more agitated way.

'We wanted to take them to Srinagar yesterday, but there were army crackdowns. We are trying right now to release them.

'But we had to shift them to another place.'

He rose to his feet and made clear that he wanted to leave. 'We took risks coming here, we are risking martyrdom. While we would accept that, we do not want it at the cost of the lives of the detained two.' The four men shook hands with us again and quickly left the room.

Mr Housego, who had been cool and controlled throughout, said: 'I must go to Srinagar. We must hope we are in the last phase. I had to hide my feelings during the discussion.

'The rebels do have problems in effecting the release and I will do all I can.'

II

How an Assassin's Bullets Almost Ended Hostages' Hopes of Freedom

The Daily Telegraph
24 June 1995

THE TWO BRITONS kidnapped in Kashmir had a joyful reunion with their families last night. But the emotional roller-coaster week had begun with a horrific blow.

A leading Muslim cleric was found murdered on Monday. He was a preacher who in the past had been a considerable figure in Kashmir politics. The state was shocked by his death and tens of thousands of people went to his funeral.

Only a handful of people knew that the cleric, Dr Qazi Nisar, had been acting as an intermediary between the families of the captives and the pro-Pakistan militant group which had abducted them in the mountains.

News of his murder was a cruel setback for Mr David Housego, and his wife Jenny, and for Mrs Cathy Mackie. It seemed that the best hope for securing the release of sixteen-year-old Kim Housego and Mr David Mackie, thirty-six, had been destroyed by an assassin.

Rumours flew. But no organization working in the political whirl of Kashmir admitted the killing and no one knew whether Dr Nisar's death was related to his secret role as a go-between.

Last Friday Mr Housego and I drove from the Himalayan town of Pahlgam to Anantnag, 30 miles south, in response to a note written by Dr Nisar and delivered by a messenger.

We waited for an hour at an address to which he had directed us. Then he arrived—a large and genial man of forty-two with a broad smile and fastidiously groomed beard. 'Come with me,' he said. The three of us squeezed into an auto-rickshaw and buzzed through narrow streets to his home.

He showed us into a room. 'They will come soon,' he murmured. We waited an hour and the door flew open. Dr Nisar entered, leading four masked men, members of the Harkat-ul-Ansar group which had seized Kim and Mr Mackie on 6 June.

Their spokesman, a tall young man wearing a black mask and speaking good English, assured Mr Housego that the captives were safe. He complained that the presence of the army, fighting militant groups in the mountains, made it difficult for the group to find a safe way through.

He said the four of them had taken risks to get to Dr Nisar's house. They had risked death, he said, and would do so again but not at the risk of the captives' lives. The militants were anxious to go. They shook hands and left the room.

Dr Nisar—widely known as a peace-maker, often consulted in disputes and locally revered as a saint—brought us soft drinks and said: 'The boy and the man will be safe with them.'

As we left he said to me: 'I think it will be about four days.' He added that until there was a release his role should be kept secret. He bade a smiling farewell.

The next time I saw him, three days later, he was lying on a lorry in Anantnag, two bullet wounds in his head, a grieving crowd around him. On Sunday afternoon a man had called at his home and summoned him to a meeting a few miles off. There was no meeting—only a killer.

Only a few of us had known about the part he played in contacting the guerrillas. The Housegos and a senior police officer asked us not to make public the fact that the murdered man was the intermediary: it might frighten off other contacts and imperil the chances of a release.

Dr Nisar's death hung like a pall over the Housegos and Mrs Mackie. There was no word from the guerrillas. There was no news on Tuesday, only a rumour that the hostages were being moved southwards, changing their sleeping place every night.

The Housegos and thirty-three-year-old Mrs Mackie began to resign themselves to the idea that the captives might be held for months. 'It's torture,' Mrs Housego said. She and her husband and son had travelled to Kashmir partly to celebrate her fiftieth birthday on 1 June. They were assured by the authorities they would be safe. They stayed on a houseboat on Dal Lake before setting off for a three-day trek in the mountains with a guide and a cook, their baggage carried by ponies.

They descended to the tiny village of Aru after three days in the mountains. On the way down they were held up by gunmen and robbed of money, watches and clothing. Mr Housego, fifty-three, knew at once they were more than mere robbers. He was the *Financial Times*' correspondent in India until two years ago and had written often about the insurgency in Kashmir.

The gunmen ordered the Housego party to the Milky Way Hotel. There they met Mr and Mrs Mackie, who were already being kept at gunpoint.

Mr Mackie, formerly a director of a design video company in Camden, had been travelling around the world for two years with his wife, a graphic designer. They arrived in Kashmir and went trekking. On the night of 5 June gunmen kicked down the door of their room, stuck a gun in Mr Mackie's chest and began ransacking the couple's luggage.

'Two came back and I thought they were going to rape me,' Mrs Mackie said. 'One groped me and I shouted "Dave!" and they left. It was 1.30 a.m. They bolted the door from the outside but at first light we got out through the window. There were about twenty gunmen in the village. Three of them came to the hotel and told Dave we were safe. The Housego party came down the hill at about noon and we were all put together on the balcony with gunmen watching us.

'That evening about 10.30 we were separated. David and Jenny and I were put into a room. David said: "Where's Kim?" We were locked in but got out at about 4.30 in the morning. David said: "They've taken them."'

The shaken party walked for two hours to Pahlgam and told police what had happened. Mrs Mackie said: 'A police officer had horror in his face and I realized then that it was really serious.'

The Housegos and Mrs Mackie, who never met before but were now bound together by their common fears, returned to Srinagar. In a daring initiative Mr Housego and Mrs Mackie went to Pahlgam to distribute leaflets in Urdu appealing for news.

The idea worked. It was in Pahlgam that Mr Housego received the letter from Dr Nisar—and went to his rendezvous with the militants.

He later saw police and army chiefs and was assured that army operations in the Pahlgam area would be suspended to enable militants a clear run to drop off the captives. After almost three days without news the pace quickened yesterday. The Housegos were told during the afternoon that something was afoot, that they should stay in Srinagar. There was a report that the captives had been removed from the mountains.

A telephone call on Wednesday night, apparently from the militants, summoned six Indian journalists to an unknown destination.

The Housegos and Mrs Mackie had had their hopes raised before. Anxious and weary, they had their fingers crossed. 'We prayed that this was it,' Mr Housego said.

~

John Stackhouse
A Lesson in Village Democracy

The Globe and Mail
27 December 1995

Biharipur: HE WAS KNOWN simply as pradhanji—'respected village chief', purveyor of justice, broker of development, the man who got the broken bridge repaired. For five years, pradhanji lorded over almost every aspect of public life in Biharipur, from the laying of a brick lane to the assembling of a voters list for state elections. At the pinnacle of his power, Ahivaran Singh Yadev—called pradhanji by everyone—would sit on his charpoy cot, puff on a hand-rolled bedi, flash his gummy grin and speak of 'my village'.

But in recent years the people of Biharipur noticed a change in their pradhanji. It was not only the fact that the village's first water pump was installed in front of his house, or that the voters' list contained the names of several deceased farmers. What rankled Biharipur, from the mud floor of the Harijan compound to the concrete roof of the landlord's house, was that pradhanji no longer had time for his people.

'He became a dictator,' said his brother-in-law, Rajinder Singh Yadev. 'He never consulted us. He had to go.'

With that edict, the people of Biharipur decided to launch a village-style putsch. They would band together against pradhanji. They would find a willing opponent. They would embrace India's grand tradition of democracy.

Or so they thought.

What followed in Biharipur was a democratic debacle, a campaign that left a community riven by caste and divided by wealth, and in the end a village without a pradhanji.

When the Uttar Pradesh government announced this year that village elections in the vast state would be held under a new amendment of the Indian Constitution, the people of Biharipur began to plot.

Unlike previous village elections, which were rigged by the landlords, the new round for pradhan (the suffix ji is added for respect) was guaranteed to be free and fair. Polling booths would be set up in villages, and the state would assign outside election monitors.

For Biharipur, with its mud lanes and open drains, and empty dreams of a school, the election seemed a fresh start, as if a new nation were to be born.

When the writ came down, Ahivaran Singh Yadev quickly announced his candidacy. Because of its small size, Biharipur would be lumped in with its rival village of Kuvandanda, which is known to everyone as 'the place over there, by the railway tracks'.

Since the pradhan controls all development funds entering the village, now equal to $1000 a year, Ahivaran Singh expected someone to contest his post. He did not expect Radhay Shyam.

A quiet farmer, barely thirty-five, the only person in Biharipur with a college education, Radhay Shyam is from Biharipur's lowly dheever caste, a people born to be fishermen in a village with no open water.

Although they form the biggest caste in Biharipur, the dheevers could never control the village, for all power rested with the landowning, middle-caste yadevs, who had held the post of pradhan for as long as anyone could remember.

'We wanted to change that,' said Radhay Shyam. 'We wanted our own person as pradhan.'

Such intellectual insurgency sent the yadevs reeling. There was no way on Ram's green Earth that any cow-herding yadev would vote for a fisherman. But the minority yadevs suddenly found themselves divided and vulnerable, while the dheevers, for the first time in living memory, stood united.

Several yadevs wanted to stick with pradhanji; after all, they had put him there. Others, led by the powerful landlord and school teacher Rajinder Singh Yadev, wanted him to go.

Rajinder Singh would have run, but as a government employee he was barred from seeking village office. He would have put his illiterate wife on the ballot, but she already was nominated for another village post.

There was no other obvious contender; that is, until Vaidh Khan, a Muslim trader from the local town of Tilhar, declared his candidacy. Biharipur was Vaidh Khan's birthplace and he still owned land there. He also returned to the village for the fifteen-day campaign with lots of money and whisky.

Vaidh Khan was not Hindu, but he was not a dheever, either. 'He is a rich man,' added Kartar Singh, Biharipur's Sikh patriarch, who was concerned with the dheevers' poor farming skills. 'Maybe he can help us. These other candidates are all poor. What can they do for us?'

By the time the two ballot boxes were brought from town, Biharipur and Kavandanda was an electorate divided. From Kavandanda, no fewer than nine candidates were listed on the ballot with a colourful array of symbols, from the wishful tractor to the pragmatic padlock. From Biharipur, pradhanji and Vaidh Khan fiercely contested the middle-caste vote bank, while Radhay Shyam appeared to have a lock on the lower castes.

That night, after the ballots were counted at the local administrator's office, the two villages fell silent at the reading of the final result.

In sixth place, with only sixty-six votes, was Ahivaran Singh Yadev—pradhanji no more. Two unknown farmers from Kavandanda won more votes than the disgraced Ahivaran Singh. In third place was Vaidh Khan, who collected a respectable 140 votes.

As the results were released, the only hope left for the yadevs was Arun Singh Yadev, a popular farmer from Kavandanda, but when his total was announced it amounted to only 185. The dheevers shouted with glee. After marshalling more than 200 dheevers to the polling booth, Radhay Shyam could almost see caste justice dancing in the air.

But before declaring a winner, the administrator announced that 42 ballots had been rejected. It seemed in each case voters had marked two names: Radhay Shyam's and one other.

The final result: Arun Singh Yadev, 185; Radhay Shyam, 165.

Many days later, in the cool morning light of a north Indian winter, Radhay Shyam milked his only buffalo so that he could serve a visitor chai, and reflect on his valiant campaign and brave defeat. 'Arun Singh is a good man,' he said. 'He will make a good pradhan.'

Warming her hands over the embers of burnt rice stalks, Ram Siri, Radhay Shyam's mother, did not want to be so conciliatory. 'Those other people cheated,' she muttered. 'They stole the election from us.'

But what could the dheevers do? The results, like so many aspects of village life, were final.

Since that fateful voting day, Radhay Shyam has returned to his fields. Ahivaran Singh has fled to another village. Vaidh Khan has moved back to Tilhar with his whisky supply.

Not much else has changed in Biharipur, except that for the first time in anyone's memory the village does not have a pradhan to call its own. Electricity, a paved road, a school: When the farmers want to ask for their dreams, they must now walk to the place by the railway tracks.

It is a long walk.

'You look to be British,' one elderly woman sighed after discussing the results of village democracy. 'Your people were good rulers.'

She paused for a few seconds, and then asked with a hint of a smile: 'Would you like to be our pradhan?'

~

John F. Burns

The Fiercely Faithful

From Cold Wars, Afghans Inherit Brutal New Age

The New York Times
14 February 1996

WHEN THE CROWDS were summoned to the main stadium in Herat earlier this month, they went as Romans did to the Coliseum, to watch the grim ritual of death. First, the crowd sat through a harangue by a Muslim cleric from the Taliban, the Islamic fundamentalist force that emerged from the chaos of civil war in Afghanistan to take control of more than half the country in the last eighteen months.

Then Taliban officials turned their attention to an Afghan man who was said to have been convicted by a Taliban court of a triple murder. After his hands and feet were tied, and a noose put around his neck, he was hoisted slowly by a crane.

Afghans who saw the execution said the man died slowly, jerking spasmodically before finally going limp. From the crowd, there were shouts of 'Allah be praised!' Outside the stadium, slumped against a wall and wailing, were several women, relatives of the condemned man, covered head to foot in the manner the Taliban prescribes.

The new Afghanistan is a world where murderers and 'enemies' of the Taliban are hanged from cranes and the barrels of tank cannon, where the execution of others found guilty of killing consists of being shot in the back with rifles by their victims' fathers, and where convicted thieves are subjected to surgical amputations of their hands and arms.

Not since 1979, when Ayatollah Ruhollah Khomeini led an Islamic revolution in Iran, which borders on Afghanistan only 75 miles west of here, has this region been wrenched so abruptly towards the past. Nor, since the Soviet invasion of Afghanistan the same year, has there been anything to match the Taliban's potential threat of completing a 2000-mile chain of animosity towards the West—through Iraq, Iran and Afghanistan.

The other macabre twist is that in Afghanistan this hostile force is a mutation of American cold war politics. For the Taliban emerged from the chaos of a war between American proxy warriors and Soviet troops, and is still supported by the arms network of American allies created to challenge Soviet power.

Only a year ago, the rise of the Taliban was greeted with widespread enthusiasm in areas of the country that they now control. Their sudden emergence as a political and military force, from a base in the southern city of Kandahar, was propelled by their pledge to 'cleanse' Afghanistan of the killing, rape and pillage that became endemic under the cover of the civil war that ensued after Soviet troops were withdrawn in 1989.

But instead of the relief they promised, the Taliban have plunged millions of Afghans into a new chapter of brutality that echoes the harshness of Afghanistan's distant past.

It is a world where there has been a systematic drive to push women back into purdah, the traditional Muslim arrangement that prevents them from seeing any men outside their immediate families. In Herat, like other places the Taliban rule, this practice has meant a loss of rights most Afghan women had enjoyed for decades.

Education and Work Are Denied to Women

Under Taliban decrees, women have been forbidden to work outside their homes, except in hospitals and clinics, and then only if they work exclusively with women and girls. Girls have been expelled from schools and colleges, and told that, for now at least, education is for boys only. Girls who were only months from finishing high school, or young women graduating from college, have been told their career dreams are over.

Women wishing to go shopping in the bazaars, or to move anywhere outside their homes, must be accompanied by male kinfolk and wear the traditional burqa, a head-to-toe shroud with a netted slot over the eyes.

The regime imposed by the Taliban, across a 600-mile stretch of territory from Herat in the west to the Pakistan border in the east, is one of such hostility to 'modern' influences that the secretive Muslim clerics who lead the movement have ordered public 'hangings' of television sets, video-cassette players and stereo systems.

In Herat, Taliban fighters have gone from house to house pulling down satellite dishes and antennas, and confiscating books judged to be tainted by Western influence.

After the anarchy of recent years, many Afghans have welcomed the harsh punishments meted out by the Taliban to some violent criminals, while others have been horrified.

According to reports published in Pakistan, there were public executions carried out in the eastern Afghanistan city of Khost a few days ago.

A large crowd that had gathered on the grounds of a local hotel cheered when a retired Pakistani soldier named Faizullah Khattak fired a burst from a Kalashnikov rifle into the back of an Afghan named Mohammedullah, who was convicted by an Islamic court of killing Mr Khattak's son. Mohammedullah was the passenger of Mr Khattak's son, a taxi driver, when he crossed into Afghanistan last year.

In another execution that day, the condemned man, Dur Mohammad, an Afghan in his early twenties, was said to have begged forgiveness for killing his cousin, only to be cut down by two bursts of automatic rifle fire by his uncle Shirin Khan.

Modern Enforcement of Some Harsh Rules

As in the Iran of the ayatollahs, the Taliban's rule joins a harsh interpretation of the Muslim holy book, the Koran, with modern forms of enforcement.

Herat bristles with Taliban 'warriors' in long-tailed turbans carrying Kalashnikov rifles. Some watch suspiciously from rooftops, while others thunder through the narrow, crowded streets of the bazaars in Japanese pickup trucks that were bought for them by sympathetic Arab countries, Saudi Arabia among them.

Along with their puritanical beliefs, the Taliban, since winning control of Herat in September, have loosed a wave of banditry. In the privacy of their mud-walled courtyards, Herat's frightened townsfolk tell of Taliban men bursting in at night, stealing money and gold and cars, and press-ganging men, some as young as fifteen, for service in Taliban ranks. So far, the townsfolk say, there has been no known case of the Taliban punishing any intruder.

'For eighteen years, we lived in hope that things would get better,' said an elderly Afghan scholar, one of a minority of professional people who did not flee Herat in the exodus that followed the Soviet invasion.

In a home redolent of a richer past—a glassed-in orangery looking onto a garden flanked by apricot trees—the scholar added: 'We are ruled now by men who offer us nothing but the Koran, even though many of them cannot read; who call themselves Muslims, and know nothing of the true greatness of our faith. There are no words for such people. We are in despair.'

For some Afghans, the Taliban represent the end-product of a war that has worn away what little progress this intensely conservative country made before a communist coup in 1978 led to the Soviet intervention, a decade of guerrilla conflict, and now, seven years after the Soviet forces left, a seemingly endless civil war.

With its cities, towns and villages in rubble, and little left to destroy, these Afghans say, the country has finally reached, in the ascendancy of the Taliban, something close to a primal state.

Apart from their social and religious rigours, the Taliban, who mainly belong to the ethnic Pashtun group that accounts for nearly half the population of Afghanistan, are obtrusive outsiders in Herat.

By their customs and by their language, Pashto, as well as by their appearance, the Taliban are set apart from the majority in Herat, where the population of 200,000 is mostly ethnic Tajik, with its own language, Dari, which is a dialect of Persian. In the nation as a whole, the Tajiks are a minority.

City with Persian Ties Reveals Ethnic Strains

The differences are deeply resented in Herat, a city that was once a major centre for the arts and learning, with close ties to the Persian dynasties that were a fountainhead of culture and military skill.

In the disdain many people in Herat show for the Taliban there is an element of the superiority people here have always felt towards those outside the Persian cultural tradition, particularly Pashto-speakers from Kandahar. In the bazaars of Herat, Taliban are frequently referred to as 'donkey boys', a term commonly used to describe people who are considered crude and uncivilized.

But long before the Taliban seized control here, ethnic and linguistic strains had been sharpened by the war. For 250 years, since Afghanistan came together as a nation, Afghans have had a fierce sense of national pride that has overridden regional attachments. But since the war against the Soviet forces began in 1979, empowering local warlords who made strongholds of every plain and valley, the country has disintegrated into a mosaic of ethnic fiefs.

An Uzbek group, led by Abdul-Rashid Doestam, a former leader of a communist militia, controls much of the north around Mazar-i-Sharif. A predominantly Tajik group led by Ahmad Shah Massoud, a former Muslim guerrilla leader, controls the north-east and the capital, Kabul. A group of ethnic Hazaras, Shiite Muslims with strong links to Iran, dominate in the mountains northwest of Kabul. Ethnic Pashtun groups prevail almost everywhere else.

Of the Pashtun groups, the most powerful is the Taliban. Virtually unknown until September 1994, they gained power first in Kandahar, historically a centre of Islamic conservatism.

The name Taliban was taken from the Arabic word for students, a reference to the fact that the core group of Taliban came together at Muslim religious schools known as madrassahs in Kandahar and, before that, during the Soviet occupation, at similar institutions across the border in Pakistan.

Reinforced by defectors from the communist government's armed forces, and backed by Saudi Arabia and Pakistan—American allies—the Taliban thrived on popular disillusionment with the war.

The Guerrillas' Drive Met Resistance at Kabul

After Kandahar, they drove rapidly east and west, meeting little resistance. Mostly, rival armed groups either handed over their weapons, or joined the Taliban. Within six months of taking Kandahar, the Taliban were at the gates of Kabul. Within a year, they had taken Herat.

The drive on Kabul went into reverse when it met with a stiff rebuff from Mr Massoud. But since September, Taliban forces have once again threatened the capital, maintaining a tight siege in a loose alliance with General Doestam, whose forces are pressing on Kabul from the north.

To the east of the capital, a Muslim guerrilla group led by Gulbuddin Hekmatyar, a Pashtun leader who was a favoured recipient of American money and arms during the war against the Russians, has recovered from his own defeat by the Taliban a year ago to participate in the siege.

Mr Massoud has predicted a major Taliban offensive, probably about 20 February after the Muslim holy month of Ramadan ends, and has implied that he is planning his own pre-emptive strike against the fundamentalists. Many in Afghanistan say that the outcome of the next round of fighting between the two groups could be the decisive event in the civil war.

If the Taliban take the capital—unlikely, but not impossible, in the view of Western diplomats in Islamabad—the prospect would be for a Taliban government much like the administrations they have installed in twelve of Afghanistan's thirty-one provinces. In Kandahar, Herat and other places they have taken power, the Taliban rule through a shura, or council, composed of Muslim clerics known as mullahs. Decisions are reached in secret, and announced as decrees. Resistance is punishable by death.

For the moment, Taliban leaders in Herat appear keen to accentuate their reasonableness, at least to outsiders. This reporter, who spent five days here, and an accompanying photographer moved freely about the city, something that is said to be almost impossible for foreigners in Kandahar.

'We see no country in the world as our enemy, even if they want to consider us as their enemies,' said Noor Mohammed Akhund, a thirty-two-year-old mullah who is the third-ranking Taliban leader in Herat.

Hostility Towards Iran Eases the Rebels' Stance

One reason for the less stringent attitude towards Westerners in Herat could be the growing hostility towards the Taliban in Iran, which has joined India and Russia in an airlift of arms, ammunition and other supplies to the Massoud forces in Kabul.

The Taliban's brand of militant Islam, despite its superficial similarities with Iran, has done nothing to alleviate estrangements that grow from the 1300-year-old schism in the Muslim world between Shiites, the majority in Iran, and Sunnis, who make up the overwhelming majority of the Afghan population.

But politics, more than religion, appear to underpin the Taliban's distrust of Iran.

From the outset, the Taliban have been strongly backed by Pakistan, a fact that has prompted Iranian religious leaders to denounce the Taliban as part of an American plot to encircle Iran.

Recent military preparations by the Taliban suggest that Taliban leaders fear an attempt by the Kabul Government, with Iran's backing, to try to recapture Herat. The Massoud ally who ruled here until September, Ismail Khan, who fled to the eastern Iranian city of Meshed with thousands of supporters, is said to have regained control of several strategic towns south and west of Herat, perhaps in preparation for a possible strike against Herat.

That the Taliban have reason to fear challenges seems clear. Herat residents, anxious to demonstrate the city's capacity to resist outsiders, take visitors on a journey into hills north of the city, where a shrine has been built at the site of one of the worst atrocities of the war against the Soviet occupation.

New Memorials Echo Heroism from the Past

On a saddle in the hills overlooking Herat, glass canopies have been erected over pits where Afghan communists massacred hundreds of Herat residents after an anti-communist uprising in September 1979.

In local lore, the uprising has joined the challenges Herat offered to past conquerors, including Alexander the Great, Genghis Khan and Tamerlane.

But if Taliban fighters visiting the shrine absorbed the message, they did not show it. As they peered into the pits where the victims were buried, taking in the bullet-fractured skulls and bones, the rotting clothing and shoes, the scattered Afghan currency, they seemed unimpressed. 'So? They died,' one Taliban warrior said.

Some of the Taliban troops seemed to be as much victims of the situation as perpetrators.

In a wrecked school that was rebuilt last year by the United Nations, a group of Taliban warriors huddled together in the cold, the bare concrete floor around them littered with vegetable peels. Among the men, all in their early twenties, there was not one who had ever been to school. 'I've been a fighter ever since I started to grow a beard,' said Sher Ali, twenty. 'Since fourteen, I have been fighting. It's all I have ever known.'

Although he has never read the Koran, Mr Ali said he believed that the Taliban, by following its teachings, would be the salvation of Afghanistan.

'Everything we do will be according to the Holy Koran,' he said. 'No negative actions will be allowed. Whatever Allah has commanded, as far as possible, we will do.'

As for those who defied the Koran, Mr Ali said, tracing a finger first across his neck, then across his forearm, 'We will cut!'

A short distance away another group, this time women and babies, sat shivering in another bare concrete room, the malnutrition ward of the main Herat hospital.

In a city where one in every five babies dies before reaching its first birthday, professional care in the ward relied until recently on a French doctor assigned to Herat by a Paris-based medical charity, Medicins du Monde. But in January the doctor, after a shoving match with armed Taliban, was ordered to leave the ward under Taliban strictures on the separation of men and women.

The doctor has kept busy working among refugees in a tented camp on the city's outskirts. But the memory of his banishment rankles the Afghan women staff members, many of them barely trained, who are left to cope with the patients.

One woman with a small baby had her own concise opinion on the Taliban.

'I'd like to kill them,' she said.

~

Suzanne Goldenberg
Riding the Storm with the Wizard of Bihar

The Guardian
2 May 1996

THE COWS AND goats galloped off to the right, and an army of children swarmed in from the left, led by a little girl in a ragged blue dress.

Laloo's helicopter had arrived.

Triveniganj, a hamlet of thatched huts close to the Nepal border, rarely sees a politician, and never one so beloved as Laloo Prasad Yadav, aged forty-eight, the champion of the poor in one of India's poorest states, Bihar.

When Laloo, as he is universally known, stepped up to the wooden stage and faced a sea of expectant faces, it was as a man giving the downtrodden the dignity they have for centuries been denied.

'Brothers and sisters,' he said, 'I am with you. Fifty years of Congress government have left your children poor. All over Bihar, your children cannot read, they do not have enough to eat, they have no roof above their heads.' Their lives, he added, were being squandered in senseless violence between Hindus and Muslims.

'I will give you a better future,' Laloo promised. 'Indian people know that when Bihar awakens, Bihar will lead the nation. Let's take Bihar to Delhi.

'Your vote is the magical key.'

In a state where literacy and per capita income levels fall woefully short of India's average and where violence is commonplace, it is a potent message. And nobody is capable of delivering it as eloquently as Laloo.

The youngest son of an illiterate farmer, Laloo spent his childhood looking after the family herd: two goats, a buffalo and a cow. But he was luckier than his five brothers: he was sent to the state capital, Patna, for an education.

**Laloo Yadav was the Rashtriya Janata Dal (RJD) chief minister of Bihar from 1990 to 1997 when he was forced to resign because of corruption charges. He handed the job to his wife, who remained in office till the RJD lost power in 2005. Laloo Yadav became railways minister in the 2004 Congress party-led coalition government.*

'Even if you have to go hungry, send your children to school,' he said yesterday. And he pleaded with his audience to vote in the next stage of the elections today and on 7 May. He pressed his thumb against a giant green wheel, the election symbol of his Janata Dal Party, to show the people how.

Already a hero as chief minister of Bihar, with a population of ninety-five million and a land mass larger than Germany, Laloo has become a leader of national importance. As president of the Janata Dal, the core of the National Front-Left Front pact, he is a potential Prime Minister should the alliance of regional parties perform strongly in the elections.

India's elite reviles him, because he flaunts low caste peasant roots and refuses to be intimidated by the West.

But the people who heard him yesterday, low caste Hindus like himself or Muslims, wore a look of enchantment. They were transfixed by his rollicking rhyming Hindi, his impromptu snatches of song, his imitations of Bombay movie heroes.

They roared with laughter when Laloo mocked the rich, they nodded in recognition when he lamented the misery of the poor, they beamed with pride when he told them about his visit to Britain and they yelled zindabad—long life—when he got ready to depart.

It was the same at each of his eight stops in the northern and eastern border areas of Bihar—including an unscheduled visit to Rota, a village of 5000 with a stage 6 feet by 10. Only a few hundred people had gathered, and there was no policeman in sight. 'We got the information only half an hour ago,' a party worker apologized. 'Only ten minutes ago,' amended another.

Laloo said: 'Nothing's ready? Don't worry, brothers, it doesn't matter.'

By the time the helicopter whirred again, the people were coming, running across the fields from every direction.

On board, Laloo kept his strength up with tobacco, which he rubbed into a paste on his palm, and paan, or betel nut. He spoke about his dreams for Bihar, punctuating the conversation by sending great red jets of saliva into the stainless steel spittoon at his feet.

He pointed to the changing terrain beneath us: lumps of black basalt bubbling out of the plains; the holy Ganges and the treacherous Kosi, whose floods rob thousands of people of their homes every rainy season; sunflowers, bananas and sun-baked fields awaiting the next crop of wheat; fields of dhal (lentils) and rice, the staple diet of the ordinary Indian.

But amid the beauty, the inescapable poverty of one of India's least developed states: roads bare of cars or even tractors; villages where only Hindu temples and Christian churches dare to rise above the thatched roofs.

As the daytime heat descended, Laloo took advantage of the relative privacy—there were only the two pilots and me—to cool off by sticking one foot and then the other out the window of the airborne helicopter.

By lunchtime we were at Salmari, a village of 10,000 cut off from civilization by a river. The helicopter flew away for refuelling.

Laloo spoke, and went on speaking. By the time the helicopter reappeared more than two hours later, he had invited a barefoot man with his son dangling from his hip up to the stage for a sing-along and listened patiently to harangues from several old women in tattered saris.

We got on board, but it was getting late, and a summer storm was brewing.

Daylight fled. We flew through the rain over high red mountains covered with trees, the helicopter buffeted by strong winds. Laloo flicked his hands palm-side up.

'The weather is very bad,' he said. 'The helicopter may overturn.'

And then at last, Patna appeared and the welcoming lights of the airport runway. The helicopter fluttered down to a landing.

Laloo got out. The airfield was deserted. The fleet of cars carrying his entourage was waiting at another airfield 25 miles away. Laloo telephoned for transport, then changed his mind.

'Let's walk,' he said. We had just left the airfield gates when a single white car came to the rescue.

'We've had worse days,' the pilot said.

~

Tim McGirk
Island Tribe Fights to Stay Alone in Dwindling Forest

The Independent
31 May 1996

Port Blair: AN INDIAN ANTHROPOLOGIST was recently approached by some woodcutters in the Andaman Islands who make amulets from the bones of tiger and deer for witchcraft. This time, they asked the anthropologist for a human bone.

Not any human bone would do. The woodsmen wanted a Jarawa bone. Smeared with mud and armed with bows and arrows, the Jarawa are fierce and almost invisible Stone Age tribesmen who stalk the Andaman rain forests. 'The woodsmen think the Jarawa are powerful and strong people, and they wanted to use their bones for rituals,' said Triloki Pandit, a retired director at the Anthropological Survey of India who has stripped himself naked and gone into the jungle to befriend the Jarawa.

These days, it is more likely a Jarawa would end up with a trophy bone taken from a woodcutter, if the Jarawa so desired.

Loggers who went into the Jarawa's leafy domain recently with armed forest wardens strayed into an ambush. They found themselves under attack by a war party of 100 Jarawa slinging arrows. Camouflaged, the Jarawa were practically invisible in the dense foliage. Forest wardens tried to drive them off with gunfire, but the Jarawa were undeterred. Two loggers were killed and three wardens captured. Grabbing the same axes that the loggers had intended to use to fell the Jarawas' trees, the tribesmen then hacked off their captives' hands before vanishing into the jungle.

'The Jarawa are like cobras,' explained Mr Pandit. 'They'll only attack when threatened. It's not in their ethos to destroy. The Jarawa will only kill habitual intruders.'

Samir Acharya of the Society for Andaman and Nicobar Ecology in Port Blair recalled an incident in which the Jarawa tracked an enemy to his village. 'This was a notorious fellow who had gone and burnt down some Jarawa huts. The Jarawa went to his village, dragged him out and killed him. They could easily have murdered everyone in the village, but they didn't. They only wanted the man who'd done them harm,' he said.

For more than 1000 years, sea voyagers have given this island chain in the Bay of Bengal a wide berth because the Jarawa and the other Andaman tribesmen were thought to be cannibals. A ninth century Muslim wrote of the Andamanese: 'Their feet are a cubit in length and they delighted in human flesh which they tore up almost like wild beasts and devoured raw.'

The British were the first outsiders to settle in the Andaman Islands, arriving in the mid nineteenth century. They turned it into a penal colony for Indian mutineers. Over the years, three of the Andaman tribes have become subdued, but the Jarawa and the Sentinelese have violently resisted attempts to colonize them.

Even though the Jarawa have not learned how to make fire (each family keeps their own coals smouldering in a hollow tree, safe from the tropical rains), they are not, as Mr Pandit says, 'under the spell of our superior culture'. He added, 'They're not over-awed by our boats and gadgets. If they got hold of a gun, they'd probably break it up and make a knife out of the metal.'

Stories of the tribesmen having a taste for human flesh are false, according to Mr Pandit who says there is no evidence of cannibalism.

Mr Pandit and other anthropologists took more than a decade to make friends with the Jarawa, first by leaving gifts of coconuts, then by removing their clothes. 'They're intrigued by our obsession with covering our middles,' Mr Pandit explained. 'They'll pin you down, take off your clothes, and then they'll have a good look and laugh at you.'

The Jarawa are thought to have reached the Andamans more than 2000 years ago, possibly from Burma. They have evolved a complex social system without specialization: there are no chiefs and no witchdoctors. Yet, as Mr Pandit explained, 'The awareness of social duty is so deep among the Jarawa that anyone who violates it must leave the group.'

Their hostility is directed against outsiders, and every tree that is felled in their forest is a threat to the Jarawa.

Although the Indian government has theoretically given the Jarawa 50 square miles of jungle on the south and middle Andaman islands, ecologist Mr Acharya said loggers are destroying the Jarawa forests.

Some hardwoods found in the Andaman forests are rare and exquisite; they adorn Buckingham Palace. Although authorities put a limit of 100,000 cubic metres on timber that can be cut from the islands, nearly twice that amount is being logged, often illegally. The authorities also gouged a road through the Jarawa forest, which some officials later admitted was 'a cardinal folly'. Mr Acharya said, 'Instead of undoing their mistake, the authorities are enlarging the road, and repairing it.'

Only a few hundred Jarawa are left, and the tribe is dwindling. 'These woodsmen, they must be killing the Jarawa sometimes in revenge, but we never hear of it,' said Mr Pandit. A Jarawa boy was recently caught in a saw-toothed, steel trap hidden by poachers, and his foot was crushed.

'We know so little about the Jarawa. They laugh, they cry easily. They love their children. They share everything. But we don't even know what gods they worship or what they call themselves,' Mr Pandit said. 'And the Jarawa know so little about us. They don't know that they're at our mercy, that any mistake we make in protecting them could lead to their destruction.'

~

Tiziano Terzani
Mother Teresa

Corriere della Sera (Italy)
30 August 1996

Calcutta: I WAS TURNING off the recorder and thanking her for the time she'd spared for me, when she fixed her penetrating blue eyes, gone darker with age, on mine, and asked—'But why so many questions?'

'Because I want to write about you, Mother.'

'Don't write about me, write about Him,' she responded, raising her eyes to the sky. Then she stopped, took my hands into her own square, slightly deformed hands, as if she wanted to tell me an important secret, and continued, 'In fact, you should (must) stop writing and go and work in one of our centres. Go and work for a while in the house of the dying.'

That was Mother Teresa.

Shortly after the interview, she had a cardiac arrest and was taken to the Woodland's clinic. I remained with those words echoing in my head. In the end it seemed as if they spoke more about her than anything I was able to garner until then. For two whole weeks I had followed her around. I'd spent hours and hours in Mother's House on Circular Road. I had visited the leprosy centre, the orphanage, the centre for the dying, the house for the mentally retarded and another one for young girls who had gone half-mad while in prison. I had accompanied her to Guwahati, in Assam, where Mother Teresa was to inaugurate the first shelter for AIDS victims, another category of people who were desperately in need of help. Ironically in a country known for its tolerance, HIV positive patients are thrown out of hospitals, ostracized in the villages, and once dead, are not even allowed to be burnt in the community crematoriums, but thrown away along with the rubbish.

I came to Calcutta because of Mother Teresa, driven by an old curiosity—human kindness. Does it still exist? And how does it express itself?

**Mother Teresa died in Calcutta on 5 September 1997. This article was translated from the Italian original by Charu Gupta.*

When I was young, the world seemed full of 'great' people. Now, a young person looking around would be able to identify very few, and even those would not stand much scrutiny. Myths are created and destroyed, and those who seem promising in the beginning, end up being victimized by a new iconoclast, determined to reduce everything and everybody to mediocrity. Even Mother Teresa.

After having enjoyed the admiration and respect of the world for decades, this eighty-six year old Albanian turned Indian nun, founder of a new monastic order 'Missionaries of Charity', who has dedicated her entire life to helping the poorest of the poor, is being questioned. First, an English TV programme, then a book, both with purposefully provocative and obscene titles *The Angel of Hell* and *The Missionary Position*, have presented this saint-like lady as an egoist who has taken advantage of other's miseries to save her own soul and for personal fame. They imply that she has used public funds donated by generous people all over the world, to found her own multi-national enterprise which is run in a dictatorial manner, in the hands of a few dominating nuns.

'Mother Teresa is a demagogue, an obscurantist, a slave of power,' wrote the English journalist Christopher Hitchens, who accuses her of having kept contacts with all sorts of tyrants and thieves, from Ceaucescu to Duvalier, from Maxwell to Hoxha to Keatings, in order to receive their favours and money. Close on the heels of these reproaches, there were others, accusing her of denying medical assistance to sick people at her centres, embezzling funds and forcing Hindus and Muslims to convert to Christianity at gun-point.

The accusations did not particularly hurt Mother Teresa, 'Lord, forgive them because they know not what they do. I shall pray for them,' was how she responded to her critics. But many of those who had been close to the Missionaries of Charity were shocked, and the seeds of doubt had been sown in their minds.

To understand Mother Teresa, one must understand Kalighat. And this was exactly where I set off, to try and understand her path and get a closer idea of her operations. A disquieting signboard greets visitors as they approach the main entrance. 'House for the derelict and dying', the faded lettering on the door proclaims. Another step, and one is accosted by yet another sign, 'The highest point in human life is to die at peace with God.' You could of course disagree with this interpretation of existence and turn your back to it, but then you might notice a bundle of skin and bones on a cot, an agelessly old man, with bright bulging eyes, struggling to take his last breath and a nun sitting beside him, stroking his hand. 'We found him yesterday on a mound of rubbish. He will soon be in Paradise.'

Maybe the signpost about the 'highest point' at the end of life is not wrong after all.

Kalighat is in the periphery of south Calcutta, a desperate and tragic city which has been put on the face of the earth by God as if to prove that He does not exist. Reaching there by foot, passing the crematorium where hundreds of bodies are burnt everyday, stopping in front of the various temples, whorehouses and shops—is a perfect spiritual exercise to strip oneself of prejudices and leave behind lessons in reason and logic, on which we Westerners tend to count so much for explanations.

The streets are filled with men, dogs, cars, cows, rickshaws and carts. On the footpaths human beings and animals eat, sleep and defecate, alongside each other. Others live in gutters. The continuous clamour of horns and shouts, and the stink of poisoned air, shake the very fundamentals of reason and no logic can put together any piece of this dramatic puzzle (that is even here) called life. In the courtyard of the temple of Kali, one of the most sacred temples in India, a crowd, calling out feverishly, watches the sacrifice of a small black goat, a symbol of the devil. As soon as the poor creature is beheaded, the crowd lunges forward to dip the right index finger in its blood; while rows of beggars wait crouched on the floor outside, their empty bowls before them.

It is here that Mother Teresa set off on her path to care for the lonely and the dying in 1952. She had just left the Order of the Nuns of Loretto, that she had been a part of when she arrived in India in 1928. This is where she founded her first shelter, the one which she is still profoundly tied to.

The idea is elementary. Give to those who don't have anything to eat or to wear, someone to take care of, a house in which to die, the touch of human warmth. An idea that is as simple as she is. On meeting her, as in the case of the Dalai Lama, it is exactly this that strikes you, her simplicity.

Mother Teresa is not an intellectual. The things that she says, specially now, her stories are often the same. But like parables, they plumb the depths of truth, seeking attention, igniting the imagination. 'One day I picked up a man from the street, his wounds were infected. It took me hours to take the worms out of the wounds. But he didn't complain.

'He smiled beatifically and said to me, "I lived like an animal, but now am dying like an angel."'

She has a simple idea, but it is strong and unshakeable. This is the foundation of her organization.

She would have passed unnoticed, like many others, if it was not for a newspaper in Calcutta that published her story. In 1969 the BBC commissioned a documentary on her. They sent a man to cover the story of this strange Western woman who cures people whom India had relegated to the sewers. A short time later a film team came over to document this story. The journalist Malcolm Muggeridge was a famous sceptic, aggressive and professional before he met her, but even he ended up believing in her. This documentary made her a star. Muggeridge wrote a biography titled, *Something Beautiful for God*, in which he was the first to talk of her as a saint and describe the miracle to which he had been witness. One morning filming in the house of the dying in Kalighat, there was not enough light. The cameraman said it was impossible to shoot. They shot anyway and when the film was developed, the entire hall, with its rows of beds seemed bathed in a magical light.

Mother Teresa became a symbol then, received by the powerful and visited by the VIP's of the world. In 1979 she received the Nobel Prize for peace. She soon became the most famous, some say, even the most powerful woman in the world.

Then came *Operation Debunking* in 1994. Criticisms on the management of the various Houses, on the tyranny of the order, of her links with the tyrants and the rebels of the world, began making the rounds. About the 'miracle', Hitchens wrote, that after twenty-five years, he went to meet the cameraman of the famous film, and he told him that the 'miracle' was a new type of film of Kodak.

Nevertheless, one just has to go to Kalighat to see the miracles occur daily. The first time I met the volunteers, there was a German, a bank employee, a lady from the fashion world in New York and some European students. They were cleaning the floors, bathing the sick, removing revoltingly odourous excreta, changing the blue mattresses of the beds. 'This is the most beautiful place in India,' said the German. The 'miracle' repeats itself day after day, with tens and thousands of Western students, who instead of spending their holidays sunbathing, work. Some only for a couple of weeks, some for a few months, in the various homes of the Sisters of Charity, without any remuneration, save her smile.

It is a miracle that this lady has set up an empire where people volunteer work and suppliers donate materials. In other words, a multi-national that works without computers, defying all norms of efficiency.

She has an empire of 3600 nuns and many homes for the poor. It is a multi-national run by nuns who reply to letters with the help of two old typewriters. One of the letters that they haven't replied to is the one asking them to return Keatings' money. You cannot enter her world doubting her accountability, with lawyers in tow, you cannot doubt her faith, and you cannot doubt her work, which is what she stands for. As for the medicines, 'We are not nurses. We are nuns,' she says repeatedly during her interview.

'But is it true that in your house, love is more important than medicines? And that prayer is more important than painkillers?'

'Yes, our centres are not hospitals, where people come for cure. They are homes in which people, whom nobody cares for, get a sense of belonging.'

'Once, Mother, you said that if you had to choose between the church and Galileo, you would choose the church. This is consistent with a lot of what you say and do, but this also seems like a refusal of modern science, which is the very basis of Western thought today.'

She did not let me finish. 'Then why does the West leave people to die on the streets? Why? It is our duty to open centres like these in Washington and New York, to give food to the poor. We give food, clothes, shelter. Most of all, we give love. Because to be refused by everyone, felt unloved by everyone, is worse than having been hungry and cold. This is the worst disease in the world today; even in the Western world.'

We talk about abortion and about the fact that Mother Teresa has defined it as 'the greatest threat to the peace of the world today'.

'It is a sin! It is a sin! Abortion is the greatest sin!' she interrupts. 'If a mother is capable of killing her own child, what prevents us from slaughtering each other? Nothing.'

'But don't you think that in a country like India, the increase in population is one of the causes of poverty, and of the suffering that you are trying to ease?'

She does not listen to reason. She says, 'Life is sacred and it is not for us to decide. A married couple can decide not to have children and use natural methods for family planning. I counter abortions with adoptions. I have given away more than 4000 children. They would have all been aborted. But today they live happily, each with a good family, peacefully.'

With regard to poverty, Mother Teresa has never promised to eliminate it with her work. 'What we do is a drop in the ocean. But if that drop was not there, the ocean would be smaller.' In her simple and direct way, she seems to have understood the nature of poverty better than many experts of economy and development. 'It is not God who has created poverty. He has created us, and we have created poverty. The problem of poverty will be solved when we give up our greed.' Like Gandhi, Mother Teresa does not believe that the problems of humanity can be solved by a social, political or a scientific revolution —but by a spiritual revolution.

Will her message, like Gandhi's, also be forgotten with her? 'The future is not my concern.'

Not even that of her organization? 'No, He will take care.' She says, lifting her eyes to the sky. 'He has chosen me, and in the same way, will choose someone else to continue the work.'

I want to tell you of a dream she repeatedly told me about. Mother Teresa went to St Peter and he, blocking the gates to heaven, says to her, 'Go away, go away! This is not a place for you. In paradise, there is no place for poor wretches and slum dwellers.'

'In that case, I will fill paradise with these people, so that even I will have the right to come here,' Mother Teresa says to St Peters.

'Now do you think you have sent enough people there to have acquired that right, Mother? Do you feel close?' I asked her.

'I'm waiting for Him to call me.'

'Are you not scared of Death?'

'No, why should I be? I have seen so many people die, none of them died in a bad way.'

It was late and the bell had already rung twice, a signal for the nuns and volunteers to collect in the chapel on the first floor for the evening prayer. She wanted to go and take her place, to kneel on a rag.

To look at her that last time in the midst of all her people, it seemed to me that all the qualms about her succession were superfluous. If the work that she and her nuns were doing was not 'theirs' but 'His', then that work will continue.

Believing, after all, seems like what counts the most.

~

Julian West

Benazir Bhutto: 'Power, Men and My Regal Style'

The Sunday Telegraph
2 February 1997

'WHY DO YOU think I'm regal?' asked Benazir Bhutto, kicking off her little black patent pumps and flopping back on the bed pillows. Pakistan's former Prime Minister gave a nasty hacking cough—an allergy to dust, and too many speeches—and croaked, 'Is it because people say I am?'

Earlier, in our interview, I had tried to broach the subject of Benazir's known autocratic style: suggesting that she was more like a queen than a Prime Minister. The question did not go down well at the time. But it had obviously remained in her head and now she seemed intrigued—and not entirely displeased with the idea.

There was of course no answer. Benazir is famously haughty: an Asian, aristocratic Mrs Thatcher. Her interviews are party political broadcasts. When I had tried switching to a more personal tack—

**Benazir Bhutto returned to Pakistan on 18 October 2007 after reaching an understanding with President Pervez Musharraf by which corruption charges against her were dropped. She was assassinated on 27 December 2007, two weeks before elections were due to take place.*

was she demoralized by her dismissal, her brother's death and her husband's imprisonment; was it true she might divorce him if he was charged—she had either ignored the question or, in the latter instance, ticked me off for impertinence.

So I was surprised and a little apprehensive at being summoned to see her privately. But Benazir switches roles like a seasoned actress. Now, having invited me for tea in the women's quarters of the house she was camping out in, in Larkhana, her home constituency in Sindh, she was in a chatty, girls' dorm mood.

Patting the crocheted bedcover beside her in invitation, she passed me a plate of little biscuits and took a finger-full of nuts. In real life Benazir is not as stunning as her photos. But at forty-three she is striking and immensely charismatic. Pakistan gossip claims half the National Assembly was in love with her. Taking the opportunity of our private chat, I tried to draw her out on this. 'Pakistani men are very flirtatious aren't they?' I said. She sniffed visibly. 'Well,' she said 'no one's ever tried to flirt with me.'

She took another nut. It is Ramazan—most of Pakistan seems to be fasting—and Benazir seemed to think it necessary to explain her lapse. 'It's all right to eat when you're ill,' she said quickly, giving another cough. She adjusted her dupatta: 'It's nice to have female company.'

Benazir is well known, even by her critics, for her charm. And now she was charming me. But I could also see what she meant. The days when Benazir travelled with a couple of girlfriends, to break the monotony of campaigning, seem to have gone and now she is surrounded by men.

Her aids are male; there are oceans of men at the rallies; and most of the reporters following her are men.

Benazir likes to think of herself as a populist. In every speech she tells the crowd, 'I'm your sister.' At rallies, fighting her way to the stage through the wall of humanity, she seems exhilarated, not repulsed, like other politicians, by the crush of the crowd.

But her education and background put her in another universe to even the women in her electorate. She is in Belgravia. They are in Pakistan. Even if this were not so, Pakistan's Muslim conventions and her status would inevitably isolate her.

As we whirred over the barren limestone escarpments of the Sindh desert and then the wheat fields of the Indus valley, she sat in solitude behind a makeshift pink and cream patterned purdah curtain, pinning off a corner section of the helicopter's rear. It was a peculiar arrangement. Under the circumstances, even a nosy female reporter seemed to be a relief.

Benazir is on a losing wicket. Last week the Supreme Court upheld President Farooq Leghari's dismissal of her government for corruption and various other crimes last November. At the time this was greeted with rejoicing in the streets. But although Benazir had predicted the verdict, she seems unable to see her government's unpopularity or to admit any mistakes.

When I asked her about conditions in Liyari, the Karachi slum where open sewage and rubbish runs calf deep between the houses, she said: 'Well it used to be worse.' (This is unimaginable.) 'They now have water for half the day.' Marie Antoinette could not have put it better. Liyari has consistently been a People's Party stronghold. Her husband, Asif Zardari won from there, last time; and so has she. But they are unlikely to vote her in this time.

Of the corruption charges, she dismisses them by pointing out the interim government has produced no proof. And she claims she is the victim of a conspiracy. In this, she may be partially right. Although tomorrow's polls are likely to be the fairest ever held in Pakistan, probably bringing in Nawaz Sharif as Prime Minister, analysts say no transition of power has ever happened without the approval of 'Them'. This is code for the army. With an estimated 40 to 60 per cent of the country's budget allocated to defence, the generals have had most to lose from Pakistan's tattered economy and rampant corruption. And 'They' have clearly had enough of Benazir.

In Sindh, the People's Party's traditional feudal power base, Benazir's convoy was showered with rose petals and her rallies drew the usual cheering crowds. But everyone knows rallies in Pakistan are deceptive. On closer inspection, her audience were mainly poor landless peasants, who now represent perhaps only half of the electorate. Many had come out of curiosity to see the most interesting show in town.

Electoral demographics mean Benazir stands to lose most from a low turnout tomorrow. Analysts say the electorate is so disillusioned with corrupt governments that barely a quarter will vote. Benazir cannot see this. She says she will not accept the election results as long as the interim government is in power. And she has hinted that, if she loses, she may take to the streets. 'Why does everyone say we're losing?' she suddenly asked me during our chat. 'We think we're winning.'

Benazir was educated at Oxford and Harvard, but she has never been an intellectual. Her literary references are standard schoolgirl fare: Julius Caesar, Macbeth, Byron and Shelley. And her reading is said to be Mills and Boon. Although she was head of the Oxford Union, she gives the clear impression that she does not welcome or enjoy any kind of debate. Even in her close circle, there seems to be no one, these days, who will tell her the truth.

'She's surrounded herself with flunkies who hang on every word,' said a childhood friend. 'As far as she's concerned, it's everybody else's fault. She's made no mistakes.'

Of her husband Asif Zardari, widely believed to be the most corrupt person in the country, and the main cause of her downfall, she is said to be very angry with him—she did not give him a ticket in tomorrow's elections—but to be too in love with him to separate. Although these days, she seems less vocal in his defence.

Benazir was not always so myopic and autocratic. She appears to have been genuinely idealistic when she first returned to Pakistan in 1986, leading massively popular demonstrations against General Zia ul-Haq, and eventually bringing her party to power. Childhood friends remember 'a very nice young woman', who listened to Joan Baez and took part in anti-war demonstrations while she was at Harvard. Benazir herself seems to remember that carefree era with fondness. She referred to it when we met.

One old friend believes she was indelibly scarred by the hanging of her father, Zulfikar Ali Bhutto, whom she adored, in 1979. 'I think the hanging must have changed her. That was her real grief and she's never got over it, which is not surprising.' Others believe her character was changed by her almost three years of house arrest in the late 70s; much of it spent in solitary confinement in Al-Murtaza, the Bhuttos' gloomy ancestral home in Larkhana, which is now occupied by her estranged sister-in-law and political rival, Ghinwa.

Still others believe there are two women doing battle inside Benazir. The Western-educated democrat and the monarch from a feudal dynasty, who believes 'making money from politics isn't wrong'.

'She's a split person,' said a Pakistani newspaper publisher. 'Her Western education enables her to gain sympathy overseas. But it's the toughly feudal Benazir who rules here.'

I asked Benazir if she would ever leave politics. Surprisingly, she said she had planned to move to the Senate in 1998, if her government had not been dismissed. 'I told Leghari "I'm after your job,"' she said. 'But now I've got to become Prime Minister again.'

There is a hope in Pakistan that the likely election of Nawaz Sharif, who represents the middle class, may usher in a new era of less autocratic and more representative political leaders. Is Benazir finished? Opinions vary. But unless she becomes less of a queen and more of a leader, there are signs the Pakistani electorate may say 'enough'.

~

David Loyn

The Taliban's One-Eyed Strongman Hides in His Lair

BBC

9 March 1997

Kandahar: MULLAH MOHAMMED OMAR, head of the Taliban and more controversially since last year the Amir ul Momenin (leader of all Muslims), is choosy about whom he talks to. German diplomat Dr Norbert Holl, who is leading a United Nations attempt to negotiate peace in Afghanistan, is becoming increasingly embarrassed by the fact that he has never met the man who now controls three-quarters of the country. And until now the Amir has had only one meeting with a journalist since founding the Taliban in 1994.

He agreed to a second interview with the same journalist, the BBC's man on the north-west frontier, Rahimullah Yusufzai, on condition that I stayed outside the room in the former governor's residence in the southern city of Kandahar.

I was rewarded at the end with a glimpse of a tall man with only one eye (he lost the other fighting against the Russians) but an otherwise distinguished appearance, a fair complexion and a Grecian nose. Wearing a European-style dark brown jacket over his traditional black shalwar and kameez, he climbed into a Toyota Land Cruiser and sped away, almost running over a man who threw himself in front of it in pursuit of a personal grievance.

When Rahimullah asked the Amir why he refused to meet any outsiders, surrounding himself with a cloak of mystery, his answer revealed the single-minded obsession that built a revolutionary student army out of nothing, conquering most of the country in less than three years. He said he had nominated others to do interviews. He did not want to meet anybody who was not 'helpful' to his cause.

By not meeting the UN negotiator, he confirmed the impression that in his view the UN peace initiative was not helpful. He said the war would only end when the Taliban had won. 'The end is only a matter of time.'

The gulf between the Taliban and the alliance of forces now defending northern Afghanistan widened when the Taliban launched a large-scale offensive immediately after a round of UN-brokered talks in the Pakistani capital, Islamabad, in January. It retook all the ground it had lost in October when it faltered after taking Kabul. It has now forced the northern leader, General Abdul Rashid Dostam, to retreat north of the strategic Salang Pass that crosses the Hindu Kush mountain range.

The Taliban is now close to control of the Shibar Pass, which gives access to the long way around the Hindu Kush. Dostam has launched a fresh attack in the deserts in the west, but his forces are demoralized and under severe pressure from the Taliban.

The interview was conducted while the Amir was meeting a dozen military commanders to discuss progress in the war. They sat cross-legged on carpets around the walls of the tiny room and the Amir lay on a bed with an assistant squatting at his feet.

Far from his chilling image as the spiritual head of the most fundamentalist Islamic movement in the world, he was relaxed throughout, laughing and joking with the commanders. He said the Taliban had no territorial ambitions beyond Afghanistan, denying Russian claims that it wanted to export its Islamic revolution north across the Oxus river to the central Asian republics of Uzbekistan and Tajikistan. He blamed the Russians for heightening border tension.

He denied that the Taliban was repressive towards women. He said that there were priorities in war and women's education could follow once the war was won. The Taliban closed down girls' schools when it took the capital, Kabul, last September.

The Amir was keen to correct what he called a number of wrong impressions in the West. He had never given an interview to a French magazine which claimed he said the Taliban raised taxes from the opium trade. He denied that the movement had been backed by Pakistan. 'It is a purely religious movement which has received no support from outside,' he said.

Despite the austere discipline demanded, this is a very informal movement. Talib fighters swarm around the governor's residence, eating huge communal meals and listening to whatever is going on, including the interview with the Amir. They came and went, even, through the dirty curtain hanging over the doorway into the Amir's room during the interview. At one point, when his assistant whispered in his ear, the Amir unlocked a box to give money to some fighters who had turned up in Kandahar without food or a bed for the night.

This informality makes it hard for the international community to come to terms with the Taliban, which has not been recognized as the legitimate government by any foreign country.

At one point last week I found that the man driving me through the mud of a barrack, past cannons left from wars with the British, was the minister of the government department I had just left, who wanted to sit in on my next interview. One foreign aid official threw up his hands in exasperation. He said there were no clear structures of government, 'no organograms'.

Some key government departments are still here, but most are now in Kabul, although incredibly the Amir confirmed that he had still not been to the capital since the Taliban took it in September and he had no plans to visit.

The Taliban is trying to address the problem of its international profile. I came to Kandahar principally to film a BBC interview with Mullah Waqil Ahmed, the most senior member of the government to agree to appear on television. Ahmed has just returned from New York, where he pressed the Taliban case for UN recognition. He has opened an office there; a London office will follow.

But this unprecedented television access came paradoxically in the same week that the Taliban renewed its restrictions on any filming of people. Television is seen as an evil influence. Two French aid workers have been held for more than a fortnight in Kabul; their crime appears to be no more than having cameras at a farewell party attended by Afghan women staff. Negotiations to secure their release have so far been fruitless, and the longer they are held the more likely it is that they will face a sharia court, the strictest form of Islamic justice.

Since it took power in Afghanistan, the Taliban has overseen the stoning of an adulterous couple and amputation of the hands of thieves. I quoted a saying by Deng Xiaoping to Ahmed. The late Chinese leader knew that when he opened the doors to the world 'a few flies would come in'. Ahmed said that Afghanistan was aiming to keep out the flies.

~

John Zubrzycki
Midnight's Orphans
The Anglo-Indians of India

The Weekend Australian
9 August 1997

HIDDEN IN THE jungles of the east Indian state of Bihar stand the haunted remains of a bygone era, the buried hopes of a rootless people searching for an identity and a place they could call home. Peeling paint on rusty nameplates, cobweb-covered gates, country lanes that lead to abandoned red-brick bungalows overgrown with creepers and bougainvillaea are the only reminders of the dream that suddenly faded fifty years ago.

McCluskiegunge was to be a homeland for the Anglo-Indians, the forgotten flotsam of crumbling empire, midnight's orphans set adrift by the British Raj when it abandoned India on 15 August 1947. Time and emigration have shortened the roll-call of those who made McCluskiegunge a thriving settlement in the 1930s and 40s, with its own shops, schools and an active social life that included fancy-dress balls and football tournaments.

With independence came exodus.

Afraid that their mixed parentage would lead to discrimination, tens of thousands of Anglo-Indians from McCluskiegunge and other parts of India left for countries such as England, Canada and Australia, most of them never to return.

The Allens, O'Neils, Potters, Kings and Castellaris have long since departed. The Nest, the Grange, Greenacres, Bonner Bhavan, the Beacon and dozens of other dilapidated bungalows stand vacant or have been sold to outsiders. Today fewer than twenty Anglo-Indian families remain in a community that once supported nearly 300.

Despite the decay there is no other place remotely like 'The Gunge' in India or, for that matter, anywhere else in the world. Set high on the Chota Nagpur plateau, where tigers and tribal insurgents stalk the hardwood forests that stretch westwards as far as the eye can see, it emerges from the landscape like a mirage, an imagined piece of England built by a people who had never seen its shores.

The original homestead of E.T. (Earl) McCluskie, the son of an Indian mother and an Irish father, still stands on a hill overlooking the railway line with a plaque in the garden commemorating him and the Colonization Society of India.

McCluskie and other members of the society believed that the Anglo-Indians were an orphaned community whose needs were being ignored by the British as they prepared India for independence.

'They wanted some place they could call home, where their own people could live all the time, like all other communities in India,' says Captain Don Cameron, president of the Anglo-Indian Association of Eastern India and a long-time resident of McCluskiegunge.

After months of searching, McCluskie finally leased in perpetuity 4050 hectares from the raja of Ratu on a branch line of the main railway link between Calcutta and Delhi. The original settlement was called Erin's Isle because its shape resembled Ireland. But the similarity stopped there.

When the first settlers arrived this was little more than an inhospitable tract of jungle.

'The Anglo-Indians worked in the railways, the police, post and customs services; they weren't farmers, they didn't know how to make a living off the land,' says Cameron, who has converted McCluskie's homestead into a school with half-a-dozen students and a guesthouse that rarely has any guests.

McCluskie died in 1936 without ever seeing his dream fulfilled. But his vision somehow took root in the fertile soil and within a few years more than 100 families had built homesteads, planted orchards and started small-scale businesses such as poultry farming and pig breeding.

'They came with big money, there was no wanting. They lived a lavish lifestyle and were very happy. Had the British rule remained, I think this would have succeeded very, very well and we would have had many such colonies in India,' laments Cameron, one of the few residents who still believe that The Gunge has a future.

Like many of the remaining Anglo-Indians, Cameron, sixty-eight, has strong links with Australia. His sister, the controversial former Greens senator, Christabel Chamarette, lives in Perth, while he owns property in Adelaide.

'Anglo-Indian culture has been maintained more strongly in Australia than it has in India,' says Cameron. 'The question is, how do we get people to come back to this place?'

A retired schoolmaster who made his money racing horses at the Calcutta Turf Club in the company of jockeys such as Lester Piggott, Cameron has mastered the art of self-promotion, becoming a self-styled ambassador for McCluskiegunge and the Anglo-Indian community at large.

The rare visitor to the Highlands Guest House is given a copy of his seven-page biography in which he describes himself as an 'eminent Anglo-Indian Educationist, social worker and businessman' and a 'high-profile contender' for one of two seats reserved for Anglo-Indians in India's federal parliament.

Cameron may share the vision of the settlement's founder, but The Gunge needed a revolutionary spirit like McCluskie to reunite and inspire the remaining residents to pull it back from the brink of extinction.

Although the Orchard Growers Association, the Citizens Committee, the Christian Burial Society and the Anglo-Indians Association still meet occasionally, deep divisions run through this marooned community, based on petty personal animosities whose origins have often been forgotten.

A kilometre or so up the road from the Highlands Guest House, past the peeling facades of the churches of St Anne and St Stephen, live Clement and Judy Mendonca, who have hardly exchanged two words with Cameron since they settled here nearly a decade ago.

'There is too much backstabbing going on here,' says Clement Mendonca, over a cup of milky sweet tea. 'But at least you can afford to keep a bearer and a servant. We couldn't do that if we had emigrated.' He served in the merchant navy for forty-five years, spending much of that time running coal ships between India and Australia.

'I was fascinated by that country,' he says. 'I loved the people there. They didn't have a superiority complex like the Indians.'

The Mendoncas have established a school on their property in direct competition with Cameron's and have surrounded their house with a high brick fence, something that would have been unheard of even a few years ago.

'Bihar is on the brink of anarchy,' says Clement Mendonca, who owns an impressive collection of vintage firearms.

'The law and order situation around here is out of control.'

Just a few kilometres from McCluskiegunge lies one of the main bases of the Maoist Communist Centre, a ragtag peasant militia that believes in the most primitive forms of justice to protect the interests of the poor and exploited tribal populations in the area.

'They have what is known as the six-inch law,' says Tom Robinson, who has driven down from his bungalow on the northern edge of McCluskiegunge for morning tea with the Mendoncas.

'If you don't heed their warnings, they will take a tape measure and cut your throat at the six-inch mark. I found three severed heads on my veranda one morning.

'They mostly target Hindu moneylenders who cheat the local tribals. But if you treat the tribals well, they'll leave you alone.'

Banditry is not the only problem keeping this faded utopia in a state of limbo.

McCluskiegunge is an isolated community. Only four trains stop here each day.

Ranchi, the nearest city with an airport, is a bumpy two-hour drive away. The power supply is erratic and the phones hardly ever work. There are no doctors or dispensaries and the rich social life has dwindled down to just a few events a year, such as the annual Founders' Day dinner and a children's Christmas party.

Enormous open-cut coalmines are gradually encroaching upon the surrounding forests and farmlands. Fly ash and coal dust cover orchards that once grew the best guavas, mangoes and citrus fruits in eastern India.

Brian Mendles, whose living room bookshelves are stuffed with 1960s paperbacks and memorabilia from the Queen's coronation, remembers a very different McCluskiegunge.

'The community spirit used to be very strong. That relationship was there as though they were one family. Everything was cooperative, everyone helped each other in whatever way they could. Every week there would be a picnic, a show and dances,' he recalls.

'We always used to carry our guns whenever we went out at night. The women would hitch up their ballgowns and run if they spotted a bear or a wild boar.'

The turning point for McCluskiegunge came in 1947, says Mendles. 'After Independence we thought we would get second-class citizenship. That is why people started going to England, Australia, Canada, America. Every day the [railway] platform would be packed from one end to the other with those who were leaving and those who'd come to see them off.'

It was an ungracious exit for a community that had slowly begun to find its roots and its own identity after nearly 300 years, and would soon give the world entertainers such as Cliff Richard (born Harry Webb in Lucknow) and Engelbert Humperdinck (born Gerald Dorsey in Madras).

The history of the Anglo-Indians goes back to the early days of the East India Company. The company's employees were encouraged to take native wives and mistresses because of the exorbitant cost of bringing women out from Europe.

By the second half of the nineteenth century the offspring of these liaisons outnumbered the British, but it was not until the census of 1911 that they were officially recognized as a distinct community. But that did little to remove the stain of racial prejudice. Indians refused to mix with them and, despite their loyalty to the Union Jack, the British kept them out of their clubs and made sure they would never rise above a certain level in the administrative posts they held.

At the time of independence there were about 600,000 Anglo-Indians scattered around the subcontinent, many of them living in railway colonies that still survive in large towns, such as Asansol and Jabalpur.

'The community itself was spoilt by the British. They did not teach them how to be independent. They made them into slaves doing menial or lower-grade jobs. They were not trained to do things on their own,' says Cameron bitterly.

'On the other hand, when they've settled abroad, they've gone into other trades and professions and they have succeeded. What they didn't do here they have done elsewhere.'

Although the community is divided over the future of McCluskiegunge, there is general agreement that it cannot survive as an Anglo-Indian enclave.

'There is nothing doing here and there is only a handful of us, and everyone is busy with their own affairs,' says Clement Mendonca.

Cameron, for once, agrees. 'It would be too far-fetched to think that you could operate this place with only people of British descent.

'But if we can build up a community of 200 or 300 families of like-minded people having the same sort of social mores, the same outlook on life, we could have a very good community which would be very rewarding to the people living here.'

It's a distant dream. But in many ways it is no more fanciful than McCluskie's original concept of a homeland for his community. As far as Cameron is concerned, he will stay on no matter what happens.

'If I go to Australia, I'll be just one of the crowd, a nobody, so to speak. I've given up all that just to have the dignity of being able to pass away my old days in a place like this.'

~

Andrew Whitehead
Eunuchs Bless His New-Born Son

BBC Radio
August 1998

WE KNEW THAT the hijras would come. They always do when a baby is born. To offer a blessing, and make away with as much money as they can.

They had been around once before, just after our daughter was born. That time, my wife had bartered with them for an hour or more. They sat on the steps of our flat and refused to leave. Eventually, she gave them Rs 2150—then worth about $70, I suppose—and they had delivered their benediction and departed.

Now, we had had a son—a much more auspicious event in this deeply patriarchal society. Now your family is complete, we had been told repeatedly by family, neighbours and even the nurses at the maternity home. The hijras would certainly hear of the birth. They would be round to demand their cut in the family's good fortune.

So it was one Saturday morning that the bell rang, and I took a peep through the magic eye in the door to see two women in gaudily coloured saris, more muscular and much less graceful than most Indian women.

That is all I saw of the hijras. Our bargaining strategy had been worked out. Just a glimpse of white skin would have made them more determined to hold out for a high price. So I sat out the encounter out of vision, but within hearing range, while my Indian-born wife engaged in a good half-hour of banter and badinage.

The hijra who did most of the talking was Tulsi. She—and I say she because hijras always use the female gender when talking about themselves—was courteous and dignified, dressed in a mustard and red cotton sari and wearing rather showy metal jewellery. By her side was Babita, bedecked in a sequined peacock blue sari which didn't say much for her dress sense. They did not beat around the bush. Give us Rs 11,000 and a piece of gold, they demanded, and we will bless you and your baby boy.

How hijras manage to find out about new-born babies is something of a mystery. The nursing home where our son was born is in a different part of Delhi. We had never taken him to the park or even put him in a pram. Their intelligence network is impressive. Each household of hijras—and they live clannishly as social outcasts often do—watches over a certain locality, picks up on gossip in the market, and keeps in contact with domestic cooks and maids.

They are mocked and ridiculed by most Indians. In a status-conscious society, they are about as low as it is possible to be. But they are also feared. No one wants to annoy a hijra. For a start, their curses are said to be as powerful as their blessings. For another thing, picking a row with a hijra means creating quite a scene—they have raucous voices, and a vulgar vocabulary. They are reputed sometimes to strengthen their bargaining power by threatening to strip and expose their genitals.

Not that Tulsi and Babita resorted to such crudeness. They simply insisted on getting their due.

'Why,' my wife asked Tulsi, 'do you want so much more money to bless a boy than a girl?'

'Because everyone in the world wants a boy and no one wants a girl,' she replied. A particularly telling comment coming from a hijra—someone who has, after all, crossed the boundary between genders.

Some hijras are hermaphrodites, born with genital abnormalities. Most are brought within the fold as young boys—they are runaways, or simply are befriended by hijras, initiated into their lifestyle, and sometimes at least doctored, castrated, to make them eunuchs.

Hijras have no prospect of paid employment. The live on what their blessings, and their dancing, bring in.

'This is our only livelihood,' Tulsi pleaded. 'I've got old hijras at home to feed. And we've got to demand a lot because we wont be getting any more money from your family until your son gets married in twenty years' time.'

Marriages are another auspicious event that attracts hijras—sometimes, indeed they are invited to sing and dance to bring good luck to the couple. Increasingly, hijras are also turning to prostitution to make a living. But Tulsi and Babita seemed, as hijras go, quite respectable. They were not menacing in manner. They knew they did not need to be. Turning away a hijra empty-handed is simply not an option.

So it was just a matter of agreeing a price. And eventually, the deal was struck. Tulsi and Babita were handed Rs 3150 and a new sari. A bit of a come down from their original asking price. But still more than a nanny or maid would earn in a month.

They delivered a blessing and left happy.

And if the truth be told, we are happy that they came—for an Indian birth would hardly be complete without the hijras.

~

Maseeh Rahman
Is Nothing Sacred?

Time
29 May 2000

New Delhi: MAHATMA GANDHI BELIEVED that a nation could be judged by the way it treats its animals. If that yardstick were applied to his own country today, India would be in the doghouse. Hindus venerate many of God's creatures, and the cow is considered especially sacred. But the international animal-rights group People for the Ethical Treatment of Animals (PETA) has exposed horrendous cruelty to India's cows as they are transported, illegally, to slaughter houses. Many arrive dead or badly injured after long and torturous journeys in trains and trucks or on foot. 'It is Dante's Inferno for cows and bullocks,' says PETA president Ingrid Newkirk.

India's livestock population, estimated at more than 500 million, is the world's largest. More than half are cows, buffalo and bulls. Once they become unproductive, many of the animals are sold by their owners, mostly subsistence farmers, and marched off to slaughter houses. Cow slaughter is permitted in just two provinces, the communist-ruled states of West Bengal in the east and Kerala in the south. Although it is illegal to transport the animals for slaughter across state borders, traders bribe officials to look the other way as they pack the cows into rail cars or trucks headed for West Bengal or

Kerala. The animals frequently gore one another or break their pelvises when forced to jump from the trucks. Some suffocate inside boxcars. Thousands of others are surreptitiously herded overland—often without food or water. If they collapse from exhaustion, herders break their tails or throw chilli pepper and tobacco in their eyes to make them walk again.

The campaign against the practice is attracting support from a number of animal-activist celebrities. Paul McCartney, Brigitte Bardot, Steven Seagal and Nina Hagen took part in an international day of protest two weeks ago in their home countries. 'My heart breaks for the misery endured by all the mother cows and their calves . . . who have become throw-aways in today's India,' McCartney declared. The $1.6 billion Indian leather export industry is feeling the pinch. Gap and its subsidiaries Banana Republic and Old Navy have banned the use of Indian leather in their garments. The British shoe company Clark's announced last week that it will review the purchase of products made from Indian leather. PETA's hit list also includes Florsheim, Nordstrom, Casual Corner and other retail chains. 'It's a wake-up call to India's leather industry,' says PETA's Indian campaign coordinator Jason Baker. 'If it doesn't do something soon to stop the cruelty against cows, there will be no leather industry left.'

India's leather barons are worried that the protests will cripple exports to the West. Nearly 4000 tanneries and leather-goods factories depend on the export trade. The industry employs around 1.7 million people, nearly a third of whom are women. 'The campaign is going to affect us, no doubt about it,' says Mohammed Hashim, chairman of the Council for Leather Exports. He feels his tribe is unfairly targeted. 'We're only scavengers,' he says. 'We take skins sold by slaughter houses.' Moreover, he adds, 90 per cent of the hides council members use are from buffalo, goats or sheep. His organization has appealed to exporters to use only leather from animals that have been killed humanely.

The government, though, shows no sign of moving against the illegal transport and slaughter. Before PETA's campaign, Indian animal-rights groups had been trying for years to stop the brutal cattle trail. It's a multimillion-dollar business, and the kick-backs to politicians and officials are thought to be huge. (The cow 'death trains' are operated by the state-owned railway.) Banning cow slaughter in West Bengal and Kerala probably wouldn't help, as it would surely lead to an increase in the number of illegal, backstreet slaughter houses. New Delhi may simply find it easier to respond to other demands by animal lovers, like creating a national authority for protecting cows or introducing tougher penalties for cruelty to animals (under existing law, the fine is only about $1).

A simpler solution would be to lift the ban on cow slaughter throughout India, to deter the deadly, illegal herdings across state lines. 'Villagers can't afford to keep unproductive cows. They're not saints,' says Bangalore animal-welfare worker Suparna Baksi-Ganguly. 'Slaughter has to be made more accessible—suppressing it causes greater misery to the animals.' But such a step would provoke the ire of cow lovers, and no political party is likely to risk that. So in a land that venerates them, cows will continue to pay a high price for their holiness.

~

Daniel Pearl
In Indian Quake, Death Haunts the Living

The Wall Street Journal
5 February 2001

Anjar: WHAT IS INDIA'S earthquake zone really like? It smells.

It reeks. You can't imagine the odour of several hundred bodies, decaying for five days as search teams pick away at slabs of crumbled buildings in this town. Even if you've never smelled it before, the brain knows what it is, and orders you to get away. After a day, the nose gets stuffed up in self-defence. But the brain has registered the scent, and picks it up in innocent places: lip balm, sweet candy, stale breath, an airplane seat.

The smell had become acute around Gujarat state's Kachchh province by Thursday. It was a pretty good gauge of how many bodies were trapped in any particular place. Numbers of dead are thrown about—25,000, 100,000—but nobody really knows. And it isn't just the number that explains why the world's media are here. AIDS will kill more Indians this year but get less coverage here. In India's Orissa state, reports are emerging of starvation from drought. In Afghanistan, refugees are freezing to death in camps. But an earthquake is sudden death, a much more compelling story.

The New Delhi fire department, working to exhume bodies at a collapsed apartment building in the town Gandhidham, assumes an actual corpse is what a journalist would want to see and photograph. 'Come closer, come closer, you can see the hand,' a firefighter says, beckoning. The spray the firefighters use to mask the smell doesn't really work, and an older member of the crew pulls away and gags. The department has a crane and a hydraulic extrication device, but for some reason, when it's time to search deep in a hole in the rubble, nobody has a flashlight. One firefighter produces a box of matches.

Ragendra Singh, manager of the Shiv Regency hotel in Gandhidham, is standing below a sagging beam that used to be above the second floor.

'Come on in, it's perfectly safe,' he says. After the earthquake, the second floor collapsed into the first floor. He points out the unbroken windows and says all the guests got out—luckily, there was nobody in room 113, which now has the kitchen from below sticking up through it.

'All the televisions were perfectly okay,' he marvels.

Five days after the earthquake, Mr Singh and his family resume sleeping inside their suburban home, which has a slight crack in each wall. The door is left open during dinner, and if anybody notices the death smell pushing inside, nobody says anything. The next morning, a faint whiff reaches the roof, where Mr Singh's father, a retired army colonel pressed back into service for quake relief, shows off his pet pigeons.

'Animals can tell when death is coming,' he says. 'They pray to the gods to take them instead of me.'

The earthquake victims weren't all poor people in mud-brick villages.

Gujarat includes some of India's richest businesspeople, even if they're not known for flaunting their wealth. The hotel billboards are still standing—'Entertain your corporate clients in style', 'Free bowling', 'For your hard day's night'—but the hotels are flattened.

Owner-occupied villas seemed to survive better than apartments. Temples seemed to survive better than student dormitories. Is it random?

Some Indians are pointing the finger at some builders, though the evidence is still circumstantial. 'When money-making is involved, they resort to cheap materials,' opines Shaukat, translator for this Gujarat assignment.

Even amid the rubble, some people are quietly trying to get on with their lives: A child plays on the remains of a wall. Businessmen set up a sidewalk desk with typewriters and phones salvaged from their shipping office. At the Razdip apartments in Gandhidham, where locals say forty people died, Ranjena Shah climbs through the top of a pile of rubble, under a slab that used to be her ceiling. Isn't that dangerous? 'I don't have any clothing. I'm trying to salvage what I can,' she says, pulling out a plastic clock.

The desperate ones are charitable organizations trying to get their work mentioned. 'Please flash this to the world. It will be very good for us,' says a white-bearded Nirmohananda Avadhuta, with a neatly typed handout about the international religious organization Ananda Marga's work digging up corpses and sheltering survivors at its ashram. 'When can we meet? When?' Mr Avadhuta pleads, at a busy news-stand.

Maybe everyone really just wants to help. But why does Mahantshree Devprasadji Maharajshree, eighth in a line of gurus of Shree Anandabava Seva Sanstha temple in Jamnagar, already have the photo album ready a day after his visit to the razed village of Jodia? Photos of the guru distributing water barrels and the guru talking with survivors are quickly posted on the website along with an appeal for funds. Later, a disciple of the guru phones asking for 'advice' on their efforts to 'adopt' Jodia. OK, why not send money to a big organization, instead of adding to the chaos among competing aid groups? 'Yes, but we don't want to be one of these organizations that tries to do everything everywhere and ends up doing nothing.' Seconds later, he talks about expanding from Jodia to other villages. That requires money. Publicity would help.

The ride around the shore of the Gulf of Kachchh, from Gandhidham to Jamnagar, usually takes three hours, but now it's nearly doubled: The bridges have cracks, and white rocks have been laid out to confine vehicles from both directions to a single lane. Clothes lie piled up by the side of the road. Some trucks stop by the side of the road and unload their cargo to whoever gets there first. Kids sell donated bags of water to passing drivers. And that smell: It wafts in from nearly every village now. It sticks around, even days later, in the shoes, the camera bag, the computer bag, the notebooks.

~

Peter Popham
Darkness and Horror in Gujarat

The Independent
28 January 2001

IN THE DEVASTATED town at the earthquake's epicentre thousands are dead—and the rescue effort seems non-existent.

Last night the town of Bhuj in Gujarat, western India, was a place of darkness and stark horror. No electricity, no water supply, hospitals in ruins, the old city—which until yesterday drew crowds of tourists—reduced to piles of rubble. Some say the shocks lasted three to four minutes. When they subsided the town was in ruins.

It is forty-eight hours since the huge earthquake—7.9 on the Richter scale—shattered this historic desert town, but for the thousands rendered homeless the nightmare continues.

'We were at the front desk preparing bills,' says Ajay Bora, a receptionist at the Prince Hotel, Bhuj's best, 'when the desk started shuddering under my pen. I thought it was a big cracker—sometimes the army lets off these things over in the hills. Then the whole building began lurching from side to side and everyone started screaming and we ran out into the street.'

The maze-like lanes of the old city look as if they have been pounded by hundreds of artillery rounds. The 400-year-old Aina Mahal (Glass Palace), home to a celebrated museum of the ruling family's heirlooms, still stands, but lumps of masonry litter the grounds and no one has yet ventured inside to assess the damage to the collection. Outside a

**The Gujarat earthquake killed at least 19,700 people in India and caused damage in neighbouring Pakistan. The quake affected 15.9 million people in 7904 villages.*

body lies covered by a sheet; nearby a dead cow lies on its side, its belly inflating. No rescue work is in progress here.

On a pile of rocks, Pravina Abla stands in tears, pleading with a solitary soldier to help remove the tons of rock that entomb her eight-year-old daughter, who was trapped in the house. Until yesterday afternoon, we are told, her faint cries could still be heard.

Bhuj was the epicentre of Friday morning's quake; it rocked the entire subcontinent, but until we reached the Gulf of Kutch, 75 miles south of Bhuj, there was little sign of its destructive power. Then we crossed the bridge that brought us into the Rann of Kutch—a huge salt marsh that fills with seawater in the monsoon and turns Kutch practically into an island—and the change was instantaneous and startling.

Villages were reduced to stones. Small cement structures lay toppled on their sides. Newly built brick or concrete houses sprawled in devastation. One cement building had shattered into pieces, leaving intact a desk and chair standing inside. And every few minutes we saw lines of villagers stolidly fleeing their stricken homes, filing along the road with babies in their arms and water pots or sacks of grain on their heads, moving in the direction of food, water and shelter.

Yet out here in the countryside the relief effort seems nonexistent. In the morning one military plane after another left the encampment in Ahmedabad, bringing food and medical supplies to Bhuj, but none of it that we could see had reached the devastated villages. Relief brought in by road was insignificantly small—a couple of ambulances, a Jeep or two with medical supplies on the roof.

In the old town of Bhuj, as Mrs Abla stood weeping for her buried daughter, not one hand moved to lift the heaps of stones. It was uncanny. An army officer arrived on the scene, alerted perhaps by Mrs Abla's complaint. 'We are working on the multi-storey building near our base,' he said. 'The town administration tells us where to go and what to do. We are not without equipment—we have earth shifters, metal cutters and so on.' Was the administration doing a good job? He smiled wryly but declined to comment.

Organized relief in the town, such as it is, is concentrated in a broad, dusty open space called Jubilee Ground. Here in a crammed, squalid, dusty tent Dr Mehendra Goswamy, a local surgeon, works with negligible resources, giving first aid and sending serious cases to a real hospital 25 miles away.

'Yesterday we local doctors were working on our own,' he said. 'Today forty doctors were flown in from as far away as Bombay and Delhi and we have seen 800 or 900 patients. There are enough ambulances and medicines. Nobody can say for sure, but perhaps 2000 people have died in the city itself.'

Outside the first aid tent, the families who have lost their homes prepare to bed down for a second night under flimsy shelters in the cold desert air.

~

Daniel Lak
The Royal Massacre in Nepal

BBC
2 June 2001

At least eight members of the Nepalese royal family have been shot dead at a dinner in the main palace in the capital, Kathmandu. First reports from usually reliable sources say the dead include King Birendra, the Queen, and several of their children and close relatives. The gunmen is said to be the king's eldest son, Crown Prince Dipendra who himself is in a critical condition in hospital.

Kathmandu: HIGHLY PLACED SOURCES have told the BBC about this unthinkable massacre. One was at the hospital where the bodies and the wounded were taken. Another is in close contact with the Royal Nepal Army, which has been placed on high alert in the aftermath of the killings. Both give similar accounts of the killings at a regularly scheduled family dinner. They say about twenty-four people were gathered in the billiards room of the main, Narayanhiti Palace in central Kathmandu last evening, Friday. King Birendra was standing with several male relatives when his son, Crown Prince Dipendra came into the room carrying a machine gun. He opened fire, gunning down his father and a number of other people including his sister, Princess Shruti. His mother Queen Ashwariya was not there at the time. Later, her body was discovered in the courtyard, along with her youngest son. Both were lying dead at the foot of the stairs to Dipendra's second floor bedroom. The Crown Prince was nearby, a bullet wound in his head, alive but barely breathing. Survivors and the dead have been taken to the Royal Nepal Army's military hospital on the outskirts of the capital, and Dipendra is being treated for his wounds although he's said to be in a deep coma. There have been no official announcements from the Nepalese government. Local radio and television are playing solemn music but giving no information. Internet news sites and the international media are broadcasting the story of this massacre but it's the middle of the night here and most people are still sleeping. The streets are quiet but there are reports that police and army units are taking up positions in the city, in anticipation of trouble tomorrow. Diplomatic sources have told the BBC that a meeting of the Privy Council—the body that approves the succession to the throne—is to take place in the morning. In theory, Crown Prince Dipendra is next line to be king, but the question of a comatose killer on the throne is not addressed in the constitution. Nepal's elected politicians are not returning telephone calls and the Prime Minister, G.P. Koirala is said to have rushed to the military hospital to be briefed by doctors. This country is a parliamentary democracy but most people venerate their constitutional monarch and his family. If all the details of this massacre are confirmed, there's likely to be immense grief and anger. With the nation already in the grip of a Maoist rebellion that has left thousands dead and paralysed normal life across much of the land, Nepal is about to enter into perhaps the most dangerous period of its turbulent history.

~

Daniel Lak
After the Nepal Massacre

The South China Morning Post
9 June 2001

'A COMBINATION OF Shakespeare, Ruth Rendell and Quentin Tarantino.' That's how a foreign aid official here describes events in the eight days since the Nepalese royal family was massacred on the first of June. His perception, in part, comes from the groundswell of media coverage of events in the palace over a week ago.

Before the killings, Nepal could advertise itself as a tranquil Shangri La, a Himalayan zone of peace in a turbulent region. It's appeal to tourists was more than Mt Everest, it was the friendly smiling people with pristine mountain cultures and an ancient way of life, little changed down the years. Or so the government tourist board brochures had it.

Now the world sees this Hindu kingdom as a place of regicidal and maniacal princes, or hardened communist rioters and a confused, self-deluding public who cannot come to terms with the truth. That's how newly arrived foreign correspondents have presented Nepal over the past week, covering first the massacre, then the bizarre notion of a comatose king accused of killing his parents and a people who believe cooked up conspiracy theories rather than the accounts of eyewitnesses to the royal carnage earlier this month. Nepalis have been brutally ripped from their cultural moorings of king and temple and thrust blinking into the merciless glare of globalization's shock troops—reporters and camera crews from the newspapers and television channels of the world.

'Just lean a little lower darling,' urged the British tabloid photographer, trying to get an attractive young female mourner to inadvertently offer his lens a peak down her cleavage as she laid flowers by a shrine to the late king Birendra. A reporter for one of the rapacious British popular papers was heard to wonder, 'If the current king dies, then we've got the perfect headline, "What the Four King Hell is going on?"' There were scrabbling rushes for Britons married into the Royal family (there are two of them) and the accounts of British tourists stranded by rioting and curfews.

The Spanish were little better. A huge Spanish media contingent fought each other constantly for interviews and time on the hotel internet link. It turns out that they were covering the Nepalese royal tragedy because their own Crown Prince, Felipe, has a similar problem to the late Dipendra. He too is in love with someone that his mother does not approve of. Time will tell if he takes similar steps to deal with his difficulties.

The cynical press corps found Nepalis welcoming at first, eager to have someone force their authorities to tell them what had happened.

The journos took full advantage. A very highly regarded reporter from one of the leading newspapers in the United States spoke to two senior editors of Nepal's top publications, and then quoted them extensively as eyewitnesses to the killings. A shaken local press corps started to clam up.

Nepalis now regard the foreign media's unsympathetic scrutiny of their most sensitive matters—the royal family, a son killing his father, the future of their country—with suspicion and scepticism. The fact that eyewitnesses to the 1 June massacre in the Royal Palace spoke first to international television channels detracts from their account of things, even though Nepalis got their early news of the carnage from the BBC and CNN.

'Why do they talk to you?' asked a young man of a BBC correspondent at a communist rally in the city of Patan, near Kathmandu. 'It's because they know you'll believe their lies. No true Nepali could kill his father or mother. It is a lie, perpetuated for a political end.'

It's easy to blame this sort of reaction on grief, or confusion arising out of scanty official information from the government. But it's a widely held view, and the Nepali public is very much at loggerheads with its elite, including local journalists. This is a nation refusing to accept that a Crown Prince could kill a king, a son murder his father, whatever it reads or sees on international or local media. It's a nation deep in denial but perhaps also disgusted by the most basic principle of freedom of information, that getting the truth out is more important than the negative impact it might cause. Editor and activist Kanak Mani Dixit, one of Nepal's leading champions of press freedom and journalistic ethics, writes in a cutting column in the *Nepali Times*, 'It's not just the paucity of official information. Vacant minds easily ingest rumour and this is the case for the Kathmandu intelligentsia, whose members have so little respect that they are willing to impute their own worst motives to others.'

Nepal has seen itself in the full glare of international scrutiny and it doesn't like it what it sees. Uncomfortable truths about violence and repressive behaviour among the royal elite have gone beyond gossip. Like the royal Windsors of Britain, and yes, the Bourbons of Spain, Nepal's Shaha family and what could be its tragic and bloody denouement are now part of international media legend. Nepal has some dreadfully challenging days ahead, and a rapacious global press pack will be there, howling at its heels.

~

Daniel Pearl

Smuggling in Afghanistan Helped to Fill Coffers of Taliban and Manufacturers

The Wall Street Journal
9 January 2002

Peshawar: DURING THEIR FIVE years in power in Afghanistan, the Taliban raged against modern culture and values. But the regime profited from traffic in Sony televisions, Gillette shaving cream and Marlboro cigarettes, among other products.

None of these consumer goods from the West and Asia is made in Afghanistan, and under the Taliban government, they didn't have much of a market there. Watching television, for instance, was banned.

But for decades, whoever has run Afghanistan has exacted tolls on smugglers who ship foreign-made goods through the country and then illegally move the merchandise over the border to Pakistan. The products end up in places such as Peshawar's sprawling Karkhano market, where vendors' shelves are packed with cartons of smuggled Marlboro and Dunhill cigarettes and sidewalk carts offer bright Korean fabrics. Stacks of mud-stained cartons of Sony Trinitron televisions line courtyard after courtyard.

By smuggling these items through Afghanistan, traders evade Pakistan's stiff taxes and duties on foreign goods. This allows consumers at Karkhano and other markets to enjoy large discounts compared to legally imported products.

Boosting Sales

Smuggling also effectively boosts Western and Asian manufacturers' sales volume by allowing goods to be retailed at lower prices in

Pakistan, a poor nation overall, but one with 140 million inhabitants and a substantial consumer class. The manufacturers all condemn smuggling but say they can't stop it once products leave their direct control. But a close look at the behaviour of one major manufacturer, Sony Corp., reveals that some company representatives appear to have tolerated smuggling as part of Sony's marketing strategy in the region.

The fees the Taliban collected on shipments of goods manufactured by Sony and other foreign companies provided one of that harsh regime's biggest sources of earnings. A United Nations study released last year estimated that 'unofficial' exports from Afghanistan to Pakistan in 2000 totalled $941 million, with merchandise worth another $139 million moving illegally from Afghanistan to Iran. The UN estimated the Taliban's annual take at $36 million. The World Bank, in a 1999 report, said it was $75 million.

The prospect of exacting similar tolls on the smuggling business helps explain why the Taliban's successors are now wrestling for control over Kandahar, Jalalabad and other cities that are important transit points on smuggling routes. US bombing and poor security have discouraged smuggling for the last three months, but it is expected to resume as relative calm returns.

Employment Opportunity

Beyond providing potential revenue to those in charge, smuggling offers employment to poor inhabitants of tribal areas along the Afghan border. That is one reason Pakistan—eager for stability in that area—has made only feeble attempts to compel vendors at Karkhano to pay taxes.

Smuggling economics are simple: A smuggled 21-inch Sony Wega TV typically costs the equivalent of about $400 in Pakistan. The same legally imported television costs the equivalent of $440, after duties and taxes. Sony receives the same payment—about $220—from the distributor either way. Manufacturers thus have little financial incentive to crack down on smuggling.

During most of the 1990s, Sony imported few TVs through legal channels into Pakistan and assembled no sets locally, according to Sony Gulf FZE, Sony Corp.'s wholly owned subsidiary and sales office in Dubai, United Arab Emirates. But that doesn't mean Sonys were unavailable. The Pakistan Electronics Manufacturers Association, a trade group that includes local TV assemblers hurt by sales of smuggled goods, found in a 1996 survey that 500,000 televisions were smuggled into the country that year. At least 70 per cent, or 350,000, of them were Sonys, the survey found.

Today, Sony TVs remain one of the most prominent consumer-electronics products in Pakistani smuggled-goods markets. Sony Gulf's authorized distributor in Dubai sells sets to traders who often ship them to the Iranian port of Bandar Abbas. From there, some of the goods head north-east to the Afghan border near Herat, then south-east on the highway to Kandahar, on to Jalalabad, and then typically enter Pakistan illegally along the Khyber Pass near Peshawar.

Twice a month, Khalid M. Khan, a manager with Sony Gulf, visits the Karkhano market in Peshawar, which is widely known as a major retail centre for smuggled goods. He says he makes the trips merely to see which models are popular and should be supplied legally by the local assembly plant in Pakistan that Sony opened in 1999. Mr Khan acknowledges, though, that none of the locally made Sonys are sold in Karkhano. All of the TVs he sees changing hands here have been smuggled from Afghanistan, he says.

Dealers in the Karkhano market who acknowledge they sell smuggled TVs say that for years they have routinely ordered Sony products from the traders in Dubai who obtain the goods from the authorized Sony distributor there, Jumbo Electronics Co. One of the Karkhano dealers, Abdul Basir Khan, manager of Muslim Electronics, says Sony Gulf's Khalid Khan (no relation) 'doesn't come here to book orders, but he gives ideas'. For instance, the Sony Gulf man points out that 'such-and-such model is available', Abdul Basir Khan says. The Muslim Electronics shop is filled with Sony Trinitron TVs and has a large Sony sign above the door. 'Khalid usually presses us hard to dispose [of inventory] as quickly as possible,' Abdul Basir Khan says.

No Apology

For his part, Khalid Khan makes no apology for telling black-market dealers here that certain Sony models are available in Dubai or Singapore. 'There is no harm in this encouragement,' he says. 'They are making our brand popular in the country.'

But he denies promoting smuggling in any way. He says that when Sony Gulf discovers traders selling through unauthorized channels, it threatens to punish them. The company has fined one trader and briefly cut off another one, he says. Smuggling hurts sales of the Sony televisions assembled in Pakistan, he says. But, he adds, smuggling is 'beyond our control'.

Ram Modak, a spokesman for Sony Gulf, also denies his company has knowingly shipped any goods intended for Pakistan through Afghanistan. He says, 'Sony Gulf is not aware of the routes the [Dubai-based traders] use for their shipments to Pakistan.' Kei Sakaguchi, a spokesman at Sony's headquarters in Tokyo, says the parent corporation has nothing to add to Mr Modak's comments.

Vishesh L. Bhatia, director of Jumbo Electronics, says his company isn't allowed by Sony Gulf to sell goods directly in Pakistan, and it often can't control what traders do. 'Duty barriers always encourage smuggling,' he notes.

Minoru Kubota, Japan's ambassador to Pakistan from 1997 through early 2000, says he heard complaints from Pakistani businessmen during that period about the smuggling of Japanese goods. But he says the smuggling issue 'is a business matter', not a concern of governments. 'If trade shrinks, it will not benefit anyone,' he adds.

Smugglers have operated across the Afghan–Pakistani border since Pakistan became independent in 1947. In the 1980s, huge amounts of US money flooded the region, as the Central Intelligence Agency used Pakistani proxies to fund the Mujahedeen resistance to Afghanistan's Soviet-backed government. Smuggling of electronics, tires, crockery and textiles gave some Mujahedeen commanders a way to enrich themselves and keep supporters employed. For its part, 'the government of Pakistan encouraged people to invest in this business', even supplying telephone and electricity connections for the Karkhano market, recalls Rafique Shinwari, a longtime distributor of smuggled goods in Peshawar who says he now imports only legally.

Shipping TVs

In 1994, after the Soviets had left Afghanistan and the country was divided among rival commanders, Abdul Haq, an ex-Mujahedeen Afghan leader living in Peshawar, approached Sony Gulf about distributing TVs in Afghanistan. Sony Gulf's Khalid Khan says he negotiated a deal under which Mr Haq's company, Khyber–Afghan International, began sending televisions by his family's airline from

Dubai to Jalalabad, in eastern Afghanistan. 'Whatever he did [with the TVs] inside Afghanistan, we don't know,' Mr Khan says.

Black-market dealers in Pakistan say Mr Haq's family was prominent in the cross-border television trade in the mid-1990s. Mr Haq was killed in October trying to organize anti-Taliban forces. His nephew, Abdulrahim Zalmai, says, 'The family itself was not involved by any means,' in smuggling. But he says that traders in Jalalabad who bought TVs from his uncle may have smuggled them into Pakistan.

Pakistani officials say they haven't cracked down aggressively on smuggling markets such as Karkhano. 'We have been working over the last two or three years to start curtailing smuggling,' says Abdul Razak Dawood, Pakistan's commerce minister, but 'through economic means rather than coercion'.

Pakistan has been reducing import duties to diminish the price advantage of smuggled products. It has also ended duty-free access through the Pakistani port of Karachi for Afghanistan-bound goods, such as TVs, that often end up being smuggled back into Pakistan. Smugglers responded to the new obstacle in Karachi, however, simply by shipping through Iran and then across Afghanistan.

Traversing Afghanistan is by no means a simple trip. During the country's civil war in the early 1990s, various Mujahedeen set up more than a dozen checkpoints along the country's major roads. Truckers had to pay small fees at each stop, and sometimes had their whole cargo expropriated by fighters or roving bandits.

The Taliban first gained prominence in Afghanistan in 1994 by eliminating most of the highway checkpoints and robberies. Afghan traders based in Dubai and Singapore poured money into the Taliban's coffers, as the regime extended its control from Herat to Jalalabad and enforced more orderly transportation, according to Pakistani officials who were also assisting the Taliban at the time.

Simplified Fees

After conquering Kabul in 1996, the Taliban simplified the fees for passage through Afghanistan, exacting a single payment determined by weight and other factors. For example, the Taliban sometimes imposed fees equivalent to roughly 5 to 10 cents a kilogram, regardless of the merchandise, says one Dubai-based freight forwarder. 'These guys didn't want to use calculators,' he says. The 1999 World Bank study estimated that televisions worth $367 million were smuggled into Pakistan from Afghanistan in 1997.

Traders say they quickly adjusted to the Taliban's spiritually motivated rules. To get around the ban on packages with depictions of humans or living animals, traders put boxes in larger, blank cartons or simply reminded Taliban authorities that the packages were moving on to Pakistan.

The smuggling of American-made goods was hindered in July 1999, when former President Clinton signed an anti-terrorism executive order prohibiting US companies from exporting any goods, except for humanitarian aid, to Afghanistan. But Pakistani traders say they still could obtain products smuggled from Afghanistan—such as Gillette shaving cream, Head & Shoulders shampoo and Marlboro cigarettes—if the goods came from distributors outside of the US.

Manufacturers of these goods say they discourage any smuggling but can't always control it in distant lands. 'It is obviously something we don't sponsor or endorse,' says Eric Kraus, a spokesman for Gillette Co. Linda Ulrey, a spokeswoman for Procter & Gamble Co., maker of Head & Shoulders, says the company lacks specific information about smuggling through Afghanistan.

A spokesman for Philip Morris Cos., which makes Marlboros, says the company can't comment because it doesn't do any business in Afghanistan. British American Tobacco PLC, maker of Dunhill cigarettes, says in a written statement that it doesn't condone or encourage smuggling.

~

Alex Perry
Battlefields in the Garden of Eden

Time
3 June 2002

Srinagar: THERE'S A DELICIOUS secret shared by veteran journalists reporting on Kashmir. It's called Butt's Houseboats. The chance for a correspondent to return to Gulam Butt's stately pine-panelled cabins on the shores of Dal Lake, gaze up at the snowy Himalayas and feast under chandeliers on minced goat curry, spiced spinach and cardamom tea, has for years helped keep the conflict near the top of the news agenda. The guest book, filled with enraptured reporters' reviews, contains some of the most earnest writing many of these war hacks have ever produced. 'Once more, an island of sanity and calm in a sea of trouble,' rhapsodizes a journalist from the Washington Post. 'Gulam Butt led me from his tree-shaded office through a well-tended rose garden onto an immaculate houseboat,' swoons National Geographic. 'Birds singing in the beautiful garden, majestic trees towering above boats gliding silently on a shimmering lake . . . wonderful souls of human kindness,' gushes a German TV correspondent.

Yet you rarely find this sort of balladry in dispatches from the front. Kashmir may be beautiful, but war is sickeningly ugly and any seasoned journalist knows he'll only confuse the reader if he writes: 'Rebels today slaughtered thirty-one women and children in a savage attack beside a babbling brook in a meadow of wild irises, daisies and tiny pink anemones.'

The thing is, wars are rarely fought over dumps. Nepal's countryside, now being made a hell by vicious, marauding Maoists, is simultaneously a picture of bucolic paradise, rivalled perhaps only by Afghanistan's northern mountains in springtime. Cambodia's civil war raged against a backdrop of some of the world's most stunning architecture, Angkor Wat and its surrounding Khmer temples, while the battlefields where 65,000 people have died in two decades in northern Sri Lanka are lush jungles of palms and ponds alive with kingfishers, green parrots and black and yellow longtails. Kashmir in May, as the snow pulls back through the damp pine forests and ponies wander through flower-filled grasslands, is perhaps the most beautiful war zone of all. 'Sometimes you wish it was just a little less pretty,' sighs Omar Farooq, Kashmir's young spiritual leader and leading moderate separatist. 'Maybe then not so many people would want it.'

For the correspondent too, all this beauty comes tainted. Listening to Nepalese Maoists explain how they torture and kill at will is all the more troubling when heard in a pastoral idyll. It is difficult to imagine the age-old, sun-drenched rice terraces as the execution grounds where the rebels say they machete their enemies, civil servants, anybody with a job and shatter their legs over wooden blocks. Sometimes beauty can even seem obscene. No journalist I know ever takes a day off in Afghanistan partly because there's a terrible guilt, an abhorrence, about enjoying the scenery in such a desert of destruction.

But perhaps most disturbing is the manner in which those who live in war zones often seem barely to notice the blood and destruction. I've rarely felt less comfortable than I did when turning up at the scene of a massacre of 300 Taliban in Mazar-i-Sharif last November, I was greeted warmly by the Afghan perpetrators, offered tea and, as the gagging stench of rotting bodies filled the air, asked with a combination of Afghan politeness and pride how I was enjoying my stay in the jewel of northern Afghanistan.

And yet maybe there's some hope here. That even killers can lyricize is perhaps a reassurance that behind their battle-narrowed eyes lies a soul. The dreamy pride that Tamil suicide-bomb squad commanders take in their mined and cratered hometowns is at once odd and oddly comforting. It speaks of murderers who can move on, who can see beyond conflict and chaos to a future of peace and picnics. A tranquil Eden is never going to be the first thing that comes to mind when I think of Kashmir. And with an average death toll of thirteen people a day, it'll be difficult to find room to mention the scenery in my dispatches. But in these fearsome days of violence, terror and nuclear brinkmanship, I take some solace from the notion that when a Kashmiri thinks of peace and beauty, he thinks of home.

~

Celia W. Dugger
Religious Riots Loom over Indian Politics

The New York Times
27 July 2002

Ahmedabad: HERE IN THE adopted hometown of Mohandas K. Gandhi, the great apostle of non-violence, Hindu mobs committed acts of unspeakable savagery against Muslims this spring.

Mothers were skewered on swords as their children watched. Young women were stripped and raped in broad daylight, then doused with kerosene and set on fire. A pregnant woman's belly was slit open, her foetus raised skyward on the tip of a sword and then tossed onto one of the fires that blazed across the city.

The violence raged for days and persisted for more than two months, claiming almost 1000 lives. It was driven by hatred and sparked by a terrible crime: a Muslim mob stoned a train car loaded with activists from the World Hindu Council on 27 February, then set it on fire, killing fifty-nine people, mostly women and children.

The carnage that followed here in the western state of Gujarat has become a festering political sore because of widespread allegations that the Bharatiya Janata Party, the Hindu nationalist party that leads India and Gujarat, and the World Hindu Council were complicit in the attacks on Muslims. The party and the council—both part of the same Hindu nationalist family—deny the charges.

But official statistics provided in June by the police department, now under new administration, show that the state of Gujarat—the only major one in India governed solely by the Bharatiya Janata Party—failed to take elementary steps to halt the horrific momentum of violence.

The day after the train attack, police officers here in Ahmedabad did not arrest a single person from among the tens of thousands who rampaged through Muslim enclaves, raping and looting as well as burning alive 124 Muslims.

Police officials and survivors said in interviews that workers and officials of the party and the council were complicit in the attacks and, in some cases, instigated the mobs.

'This was not a riot,' one senior police official said angrily. 'It was a state-sponsored pogrom.'

Party officials who lead the national government, while publicly condemning the attacks, dispatched soldiers to restore order but resisted opposition calls for a forceful assertion of the Central government's authority to halt the violence.

Fathoming what happened here in the first major outbreak of Hindu–Muslim violence in almost a decade is critical for India. The spectre of such violence has shadowed the country since its birth.

India, a secular democracy, and Pakistan, an Islamic nation, were hacked apart when they won independence from Britain in 1947. The furies of religious hatred were unleashed, and about a million people died.

The use of religion for political gain is an enduring theme in both India and Pakistan and a wellspring of violence that vexes the subcontinent even today.

Senior national leaders of the Bharatiya Janata Party, including Prime Minister Atal Bihari Vajpayee, have maintained that India's tolerant Hindu ethos has helped guarantee religious freedom for India's billion-strong population, which includes 820 million Hindus and 130 million Muslims.

Until the violence in Gujarat, the party, which has led the national government since 1998, had proudly pointed to the absence of Hindu–Muslim violence during its years in power as evidence of its secular credentials.

But many influential Indians are once again questioning whether the party can be trusted to ensure that Hindus and Muslims live together in peace and to resist the temptation of exploiting religious divisions to reap Hindu votes.

Gujarat, a state of fifty-one million people, has over the past decade become the country's laboratory for Hindu nationalism. That ideology has long depicted Muslim and Christian Indians as converts to foreign religions who must accept the primacy of Hindu culture. Gandhi's assassin was an extreme adherent of this view.

In the recent carnage in Gujarat, most of those killed were Muslims. Among the survivors, 100,000 became refugees in their own country.

More than 20,000 homes and businesses were damaged or destroyed, along with 360 Muslim places of worship.

The events have inspired an anguished outpouring from many Indian intellectuals.

'Gujarat disowned Mohandas Karamchand Gandhi long ago,' Ashis Nandy, one of India's leading social thinkers wrote in *Seminar*, a monthly magazine that addresses domestic and international problems in India. 'The state's political soul has been won over by his killers.'

In an interview in June, the state's chief minister, Narendra Modi, offered no consolation to the state's Muslims and expressed satisfaction with his government's performance. His only regret, he said, was that he did not handle the news media better.

'We have 18,600 villages,' he said in his office, where a photograph of Gandhi hung on the wall. 'Ninety-eight per cent of Gujarat was peaceful. Is it not a credit for the administration, the government?'

Mr Modi was a longtime party organizer and *pracharak*, or preacher, from the source of the Hindu nationalist movement, the Association of National Volunteers. He was handpicked less than a year ago by the Bharatiya Janata Party's high command to turn around its fading fortunes in the state.

[Mr Modi dissolved the state assembly on 19 July to bring on elections. In the usual practice, he resigned and was named caretaker chief minister while he led the party's political campaign.]

At the national level, too, hard-liners in the party appear to be on the upswing. Lal Krishna Advani, India's home minister, who represents Gujarat in Parliament, was elevated recently to be India's deputy prime minister and is expected to succeed Mr Vajpayee as the coalition's standard-bearer.

Mr Advani led a movement to build a Hindu temple in Ayodhya, on the site of a sixteenth-century mosque said to be the birthplace of the Hindu deity Ram.

That movement was critical to the party's rise to power and culminated in the mosque's demolition by Hindu zealots in 1992, igniting the last major spasm of Hindu–Muslim violence, which left more than 1100 people dead, most of them Muslims.

Mr Advani said he regretted the mosque's destruction, just as he has decried the violence in Gujarat. Still, he stood by Mr Modi, and at a recent news conference, said that Mr Modi's government had generally performed well.

Others disagree. The National Human Rights Commission, headed by a retired chief justice of the Supreme Court, concluded that the state's efforts were 'a comprehensive failure'.

The commission released a confidential report on 12 June that named officials from the Bharatiya Janata Party who have been accused by survivors and witnesses of instigating the violence. It noted that many politically connected people were yet to be arrested.

'These are grave matters indeed,' the commission wrote, 'that must not be allowed to be forgiven or forgotten.'

An Attack and a Vengeful Mob

The train that pulled into Godhra station at 7.43 a.m. on 27 February was packed with more than 1500 volunteers of the World Hindu Council, who were returning from Ayodhya, where they had agitated once again for construction of a temple on the site of the demolished mosque.

Roused by religious fervour, hundreds of devotees poured out of the train at Godhra station, which is in the middle of a densely packed Muslim slum.

A Muslim vendor was ordered to say 'Hail Ram' and refused. The Hindu activists yanked his beard and beat him, said a state police investigator.

As the train pulled out, an angry Muslim crowd pelted it with stones. No one seems certain why, but the mob's fury focused on coach S6. Stones crashed through the windows. A flaming rag soared inside, landing on a synthetic leather seat that caught fire. Police investigators say that as many as 16 gallons of gasoline were poured onto the floor. Fifty-nine people were killed.

Fury over the atrocity came fast. Within hours, a Muslim driver was pulled from his rickshaw and killed with a cricket bat. Hindu mobs burned down shops in the city and threw stones at a mosque.

Rumours fed anger. Giriraj Kishore, a national leader of the World Hindu Council, said in an interview that day that Hindu girls had been abducted by Muslims and raped, an account the police later said was false. The World Hindu Council called a general strike for the following day, 28 February, to protest the killings. Senior police officials say the ruling Bharatiya Janata Party's endorsement of the strike made violence virtually inevitable.

Mashiha Qureshi, an eleven-year-old Muslim girl, and her family fled to the safety of Juhapura, the city's largest Muslim ghetto. The family's house was gutted by fire. She is now afraid to live among Hindus.

'Somebody might catch me, kill me, throw me under a train,' she said.

'There are good people. There are bad people. Some save you, some kill you. But how do you know which is which?'

The chief minister, Mr Modi, said he gave clear instructions that the police were to deal with any violence firmly.

But in a country where authorities routinely round up suspects to head off Hindu–Muslim violence, the Ahmedabad police did not make a single preventive arrest the day of the train attack, city police officials said.

P.C. Pande, who was city police commissioner at the time, and C.K. Chakravarthi, who heads the state police, refused repeated requests for interviews.

Other senior police officials—sickened by what happened, but unwilling to be quoted by name—contradicted Mr Modi. One official said the chief minister directed that the police 'should not come down harshly on the Hindus tomorrow'.

As a result, they said, no clear orders were given.

Two large massacres took place on 28 February in Ahmedabad, a gritty city of 3.5 million people, as the police stood by or, according to some witnesses, aided the mobs.

Thirty-nine people were killed at the Gulbarg Society, a walled compound that was home to Muslim families in the midst of a largely Hindu neighbourhood.

The mob started gathering in the morning. By early afternoon, more than 10,000 Hindu men assembled, many armed with stones, iron rods, tridents, swords and homemade bombs, screaming: 'Beat them! Burn them! Cut them!'

Muslim women and children in the neighbourhood had gathered in the home of Ehsan Jafri, a Muslim and a former member of Parliament from the Congress party. They believed he could protect them.

Through the day, witnesses said, Mr Jafri made increasingly frantic calls to the city police commissioner and other powerful people, among them Amarsingh Chaudhary, who was the state Congress party president and a former chief minister of Gujarat.

Mr Chaudhary said he, in turn, called the heads of the city and state police forces. The third and last time Mr Jafri called, he wept, begging:

'Kindly help me. They will kill me. My society is burning.'

The police arrived in numbers only large enough to take on the mob at about 4 or 5 p.m.—too late to save the women and children, who burned to death with Mr Jafri, survivors said.

The next day, the smell of roasted flesh still hung heavy in the ruins of the residential complex. K.G. Erda, a senior police inspector, was standing outside, watching as people carried on with their looting.

He said the few officers who had been there the day before had stayed in the traffic intersections, only firing at the mob when it stoned the police. He and other officers had called for reinforcements, he said, but none came. In fact, he said, ten policemen, including two high-ranking officers, were called away.

'What can two or three policemen do when confronted by 20,000 people?' Mr Erda asked.

The second massacre of Muslims unfolded in a poor area called Naroda Patia, where eleven-year-old Mashiha and her family lived.

Many survivors accuse people from Hindu nationalist groups, among them Bipin Panchal, known to many as Bipin Bhai, of leading the mob.

A man in the World Hindu Council's front office confirmed that Mr Panchal was a council worker. Days after the atrocity, Mr Panchal said his shop had been damaged by fire and looted. The Muslims had attacked, he claimed, and he had only defended himself.

'They live here in India and pray for Pakistan,' he said contemptuously.

'They only deserve one treatment. They should pack their bags and board the train to Pakistan. There should be no Muslims here.'

He denied even belonging to the World Hindu Council.

Mr Panchal has since been charged with being a leader of the mob and is said to have absconded. However, an official at the Naroda police station said the police knew where he was but had been instructed not to arrest him.

On the day these two massacres took place, 28 February, no one was arrested for participating in the violence. The next day, fifty-five people were killed, but only ninety-three arrests were made.

State officials would later point to the large number of Hindus arrested to prove the police were vigilant. Here in the city the police have arrested more than 3500 people—but those arrests came belatedly, after the carnage had already gotten out of control.

Asked about the failure to make arrests early on, Mr Modi, the chief minister, asserted that the police had fired into the mobs to halt the violence.

Yet in the three days after the train attack—when Muslims were overwhelmingly the victims of violence—the police killed more Muslims than Hindus, twenty-two to fourteen, in what was ostensibly an effort to stop attacks on Muslims.

An alliance of non-profit groups surveyed almost 2800 Muslim families who accused the Bharatiya Janata Party or affiliated Hindu nationalist groups of involvement in the violence. But Mr Modi dismissed the charges. 'Not a single complaint has been registered like this,' he insisted. Instead of rooting out those who may have been complicit, Mr Modi used his authority to penalize officers who enforced the law, senior police officials say. They cite what they describe as punitive transfers of four police superintendents in March.

Mr Modi called the transfers a 'purely administrative decision'. But several officials confirmed that Mr Chakravarthi, who heads the state police, wrote a letter protesting the transfers and commending the men for their handling of the violence.

The transferred police officials told dramatic stories of confronting mobs.

Himanshu Bhatt recalled arriving at a Muslim village surrounded by a Hindu mob of 15,000 that was brandishing swords and scythes. Already, fourteen Muslims had been killed. Mr Bhatt immediately gave the order to fire. A deputy headman from a neighbouring Hindu village was killed, and the mob ran away.

Mr Bhatt said he took great pride that all the Muslim inhabitants were home cooking dinner by the next evening.

Rahul Sharma, another officer, described rescuing 400 children, ages six to fourteen, at an Islamic school that was surrounded by a mob of 8000 armed with swords, pipes and soda bottle bombs.

'We fired tear gas, but the wind was against us and it blew back on us,' he said. 'So we fired three rounds of musket fire. Four or five were injured. The entire crowd vanished.'

'I don't think any other job would have allowed me to save so many lives,' he said. 'That is a bank balance for a lifetime.'

As the violence in Gujarat continued into April, the political and civic outcry across the country rose, as did pressure on the Central government.

Mr Modi's role became an issue, with even some of the Bharatiya Janata Party's own allies calling for his dismissal. After a bruising debate in Parliament, the Central government finally dispatched a senior retired police officer, K.P.S. Gill, to advise Mr Modi.

Mr Gill arrived on 3 May and within days, the city's three top police officials were replaced. K.R. Kaushik, the new police commissioner, said he immediately issued orders for the police to arrest anyone gathering in a mob. By the evening of the next day, 11 May, he said, the violence was under control.

Unapologetic, Separate, Hopeful

Today, there is no more apt symbol of the divide between Hindus and Muslims in Ahmedabad than the road separating Juhapura, the Muslim ghetto where so many sought refuge during the carnage, from neighbouring Hindu areas.

The Hindu houses back up to barbed wire fences and high brick walls topped with jagged shards of glass. The windows in virtually every house on both sides were shattered in the rock throwing that accompanied the violence.

It is as though the Muslims of Juhapura and the Hindus in adjacent neighbourhoods live in separate nations. They refer to the road that divides them as a border. It looked like a war zone that has come under heavy shelling.

But as desolate as the road looks today, it ends on a green field, called Unity Ground, where Hindus and Muslims used to play cricket together.

Days after her husband, the former Muslim parliamentarian, was burned alive by a mob, Zakia Jafri, sixty-five, still clung to the idea of an India where Hindus and Muslims lived in peace. For years, she and her husband resisted their children's entreaties to leave their majority-Hindu neighbourhood.

Mrs Jafri, haggard and grief-stricken, vowed to go home.

'That is my husband's memory and dream,' she said. 'I will not abandon it.'

But Mrs Jafri said recently that none of her Hindu neighbours ever came to her to express sorrow that they could not save her husband. She asked, 'How can I go back to such a place?'

~

Françoise Chipaux
A Pakistani Returns from Guantanamo

Le Monde
9 November 2002

MOHAMMED SANGHIR, A missionary preacher with the Tablighi Jamaat, a non-political organization for the propagation of Islam with several million adherents around the world, returned to his village in Pakistan last November after more than a year's imprisonment in the US base at Guantanamo in Cuba.

The first Pakistani to be released, he still wears the green plastic bracelet that bears his 'American' ID: US 9PK 0001 43 DP, plus his age (fifty-one), height, weight and a photograph.

Sanghir had been in Afghanistan around three months when war broke out and was taken prisoner in the chaos of the battle for Kunduz. 'Together with around 250 people, fifty of whom died,' he was loaded into a container to be taken to Uzbek leader General Rashid Dostom's notorious Sheberghan prison.

'They were screaming for water, they were banging their heads against the walls and there, right there beside me, they died,' says Sanghir of his companions. After forty-five days in Sheberghan 'they turned us over to some US soldiers who blindfolded us and took us by helicopter to Kandahar'.

There he was finally interrogated. 'There was an American and a translator. They asked me where I was from, why I was in Afghanistan, if I had links with Al Qaeda, if I knew people from Al Qaeda, if I'd ever seen Osama bin Laden and if I'd be able to recognize him.'

After this one summary questioning, a doctor called for Sanghir. 'He took my fingerprints and one earprint,' he says. Eighteen days later, they came again. 'They shaved my head, my beard and my moustache, put a blindfold over my eyes and put me in a tent where I waited for two or three hours with some other people.

'Before they shaved us, an American woman who spoke a little Urdu said: "We're taking you to a place where you'll have better facilities and you'll be more comfortable."'

The soldiers, he says, completely ignored his attempts to save his beard, which has religious significance. 'I protested physically, but they weren't having any of it and they just said, "It's not allowed."'

For the twenty-two-hour flight to Cuba, Sanghir was tied to his seat, gagged, blindfolded and had earplugs in his ears.

'A woman gave us apples twice, and some bread and water,' he recalls. The arrival at the Guantanamo base was rough. 'While we still had our hands tied behind our backs and our eyes blindfolded, I was thrown outside and beaten by some soldiers,' Sanghir says, showing his cheek.

He was to spend the next three and a half months, dressed in red overalls, in a cage open to the winds, 'to the millions of mosquitoes and to the heat,' and without even a minute's privacy.

'We were like animals. If we were men, why put us in a cage? In the beginning, they didn't let us pray or speak to each other, but after two days of hunger strike a superior officer came, allowed us to pray and gave us half an hour for lunch.

'Twice a week they took us out to walk, and they gave us a clean uniform once a week,' Sanghir explains, adding that a doctor was always on hand. After three and a half months, he was transferred to a new, more comfortable cage, with running water and a WC in the corner.

Over the ten months he spent at Guantanamo, Sanghir was interrogated around twenty times.

'The questions were always the same, just presented in different ways. First, they showed me photographs of members of Al Qaeda to find out if I knew them; then they asked me if there were any Al Qaeda members around me; they wanted to know if I'd met bin Laden and if I'd be able to recognize him. The photos were of people who looked like Afghans or Arabs.'

Sanghir maintains he did not recognize anyone. The only people whom he saw at Guantanamo—'once, during a move'—were Mullah

Mourners attending the state funeral of former Sri Lankan prime minister Sirima Bandaranaike grab for posters of the late political matriarch whose daughter, Chandrika Kumaratunga, served as President between 1994-2005. Mrs Bandaranaike died shortly after casting her vote in parliamentary elections in October 2000. Photograph by John MacDougall/AFP.

Police stand guard outside the Indian Parliament following a suicide attack on the building on 13 December 2001 by Islamic militants. Among the dozen people killed were the five assailants. No members of Parliament were hurt. Photograph by Kamal Kishore/Reuters.

Hindus riot in the smoke-shrouded streets of Ahmedabad in the western Indian state of Gujarat in 2002. Nearly a thousand people, mainly Muslims, were killed in clashes following the burning to death of fifty nine Hindu pilgrims in a train in February that year. Photograph by Arko Datta/Reuters.

An American soldier stands over a hooded detainee in eastern Afghanistan. The man was one of a number taken prisoner during Operation Dragon Fury, part of the United States' War on Terror in June 2003. Photograph by David Orr.

At Cuddalore in the southern Indian state of Tamil Nadu, a woman mourns the death of a relative killed by the tsunami that hit many coastal areas of South and South-East Asia on 26 December 2004. Photograph by Arko Datta/Reuters. (World Press Photo of the Year 2004.)

Earthquake survivors cross a damaged bridge near Muzaffarabad, Kashmir, in November 2005. The 7.6 magnitude quake that struck on 8 October, killed more than 70,000 people. Photograph by Asif Hassan/AFP.

A shepherd takes his goats across the dry bed of the Himayatsagar reservoir, the second largest reservoir in Hyderabad in the southern Indian state of Andhra Pradesh in 2005. Photograph by Mustafa Quraishi/AP.

Tribals at a meeting called by Maoist rebels in the Abujh Marh forest of Chhattisgarh in 2007. Over the past four decades insurgents have taken control of huge swathes of the countryside in central India. Photograph by Mustafa Quraishi/AP.

Abdul Salam Zaeef, the ex-Taliban ambassador to Pakistan handed over to the US by Islamabad, 'who looked very weak'; Khairallah Kwaiwa, ex-governor of Herat, arrested in Chaman on the Afghan–Pakistan border; Mullah Fazl, ex-commander of Kunduz; and another commander, Mullah Abdel Raouf.

'One day, a new general came and said to me, "You're going to have some good news next week,"' Mohammed explains, recalling his release. He is still shocked that not one US official expressed even the slightest remorse at the year he had lost and the humiliation he had suffered.

'They just said, "You are innocent." No one apologized.'

Sanghir plans to claim damages from the US. 'At Guantanamo, the soldiers told me I would get US$400 for each month's detention, but I only got US$100 when I arrived in Islamabad.'

Sanghir makes his living using a machine for cutting wood, highly prized in this isolated and mountainous region. 'For a year, my family had to borrow in order to survive, and now, how am I going to repay the money?' he asks, indicating how his machine has rusted from lack of maintenance.

'What can I do against the United States? It is a great power,' he says, resignedly, when asked how he feels about the Americans.

His fellow citizens, in this highly conservative region, are not always so reserved. Painted in black on the wall of the village school two Kalashnikovs frame an unambiguous call to arms: 'Jihad on those who deny the Quran.'

~

Phil Reeves

Living in Poverty and Abandonment, the Barely Functioning State that Trusted Its Saviours

The Independent
24 February 2003

Kabul: THE DETAILS ARE so compelling. The snowman, for instance, that someone built on a roundabout in the middle of this battered city.

This was clearly meant to represent Osama bin Laden, for his name was written on his midriff. He also had a long scraggy beard made of grass and a Taliban head-dress.

A little joke, a dash of black humour to take the mind off the oppressively cold weather and dismal poverty? Or was it an act of scorn at a defeated oppressor? Or an expression of support? And what about the blizzard of propaganda leaflets flung into the streets from a passing car the other night?

That was the first time the 'night letters'—regularly distributed in provincial cities—have appeared in the capital, threatening jihad against the foreign soldiers and their allies. Are these the desperate death throes of defeated Islamist extremists, or a sign that they are rallying anew?

And what of the persistent whispers that Al Qaeda and Taliban elements have secretly slipped back into Kabul? These were considered serious enough by the United Nations security analysts for them to issue a kidnapping warning to staff on Thursday.

Now, remember, this is Kabul, a city protected by nearly 5000 international peacekeepers, and the safest, quietest place in Afghanistan. Yet anxiety is gripping it like winter flu.

These unsettling little tremors, possible signals of a more dangerous faultline, are not all. A more basic issue is in play: a deep concern in Kabul that the international community is losing interest even though the task of repairing the wreckage of war—let alone, the even more massive job of nation-building—has just begun.

People remember Tony Blair's pronouncement that the world 'will not walk away from Afghanistan, as it has done so many times before'. But Afghans have also listened with astonishment as Americans portray their country's experience since the overthrow of the Taliban as a 'success'.

Now the United States is priming its laser-guided bombs anew, and the attention of the world's media has swivelled to the deserts and oilfields of Iraq. Few in Kabul seem convinced by the repeated assurances—from the US government and its military, from the UN and Britain—that they will not be forgotten or allowed to lapse back into the bloodshed that prevailed after the occupying Soviet forces were driven out by the CIA-funded and CIA-armed Mujahedin in 1989.

There are plenty who dislike the presence of the Americans and their allies sweeping around their pot-holed streets in shiny new four-by-fours or army jeeps. This is a city that still has a deeply conservative strain—despite all the trumpeting about the liberation of women, many of those on the streets still wear burqas—and one whose capacity for trust has been corroded by past international betrayals. But a fear of abandonment—or at least a sharp fall-off in international support—is palpable and encompasses many international aid agency workers as well as residents. One agency official, a veteran of several previous conflicts, told the *Independent*: 'The Pentagon and the White House have absolutely no policy on Afghanistan.'

You find the anxiety in the squalid little shack where Ilal Mohammed adds a few dollars to his $30 monthly income as a government worker by renting out DVDs of women's wrestling and vaguely raunchy Hindi movies—unthinkable in the Taliban days. Feeding his five small children is hard and conditions at home are miserable. But, he says, it was worse before.

You find it over the road in the grubby hut where Hazrat Shah, a gnarled seventy-five-year-old Pashtun, is selling firewood—a thriving business in a city routinely plagued by power cuts and freezing weather. He has seen it all—Soviet invasion, civil war, the rise of the Taliban, the arrival of the Americans after 9/11. There is at last a measure of relative stability, he says. But these are 'very risky times'.

And it is there in the outdoor money-changers' market, where a local surgeon called Dr Ali—he was fearful of giving his full name—is investing in a few greenbacks. He spelt the position out better than anyone. 'If the Americans attack Iraq and leave here, we will lose everything. We have already been through that once before, and we don't want it to happen again. The international community is our only hope, the only way that we can stand on our two feet one day.' That day is still a very long way off. The brave new world promised in the aftermath of the Taliban's ousting has yet to dawn. The country is not remotely close to becoming a functioning state, with a viable infrastructure and control over its territory. And the US-led war against Al Qaeda is not over, even though the world's attention has drifted elsewhere.

A year ago, the impromptu church service held this month for a small group of US infantrymen in the mountains of south-eastern Afghanistan would have made TV news bulletins worldwide. We would all have seen Capt. Jimmy Nichols, battalion chaplain for 2-504 Parachute Infantry Regiment, lead his soldiers in a gruff rendering of the hymn 'Keep on the Firing Line'. Dressed in full combat gear, he launched into a sermon about Samson, turning to the wrathful pages of the Old Testament to fire up his men before they resumed their efforts to kill or capture a small group of armed zealots. Samson was, the chaplain declared, the 'original tough guy, long before Rambo', whose 'super-strength' was a gift from God. 'God has given us also gifts. You see, the reason that Samson is such a good story for folks like you and me in the military is that Samson is you—Samson is me.'

On the front line, fundamentalism is used to fight fundamentalism.

But, fifteen months after the fall of the Taliban, the American Samson has yet to prevail. According to Col Roger King, the US military spokesman at the Bagram air base outside Kabul, there are 'probably several hundred' Taliban and Al Qaeda forces around Afghanistan and 'maybe a larger number' over the border with Pakistan. Some of these forces appear to have forged links with Gulbuddin Hekmatyar, a militiaman who once pocketed CIA funds to fight the Soviet Union before joining the civil war, earning a reputation for extreme brutality. He is marching under the banner of a self-declared jihad against the Americans and their allies.

The head of the Hezb-i-Islami party, he is suspected in Kabul of involvement in numerous rocket attacks and a car bomb that killed thirty in September. Last year he narrowly missed being killed by a missile fired by a CIA Predator, an unmanned aircraft.

There are other ominous signs. Some 400 rockets have been fired at American forces in ten months.

They find two or three caches of arms, often 107mm Chinese rockets, each week. 'This place is a 100 times more dangerous than Iraq,' said one US reserve officer at Bagram, a veteran of Operation Desert Storm in Iraq in 1991. 'Here they are liable to toss a grenade under your vehicle at any time.' A fortnight ago the Taliban issued what is thought to be its first communiqué since being removed from power. It named two senior figures—Mullah Obaeidullah and Mullah Biradar—as commanders in a new campaign to oust the Americans.

And the international effort to help establish a meaningful Central government under Hamid Karzai is also incomplete. Many of the building blocks of a viable nation-institutions capable of imposing law and order, health services, power supplies, a road network, communications, education—are often absent.

In the first six months of the Karzai interim administration, two ministers including the first vice-president were assassinated. The President came close to being killed in Kandahar last September.

Some international agency workers report that there is outright anger and frustration in the provinces over the slow pace of reconstruction and the lack of security, a sense that the Karzai government has done nothing for them. Ethnic rivalries are crucial: dissatisfaction is said to be particularly strong among Pashtuns, who believe that the interim government is dominated by the light-skinned, sandy-haired and often green-eyed Panjshiris.

The Karzai transitional government has been unable to assert its control over most of the country.

Until it does so, the free-and-fair elections required next year by the Bonn Agreement will remain a pipe dream.

The UN and Hamid Karzai have tried to persuade the international community to tackle the resulting 'security vacuum' by extending Kabul's peace-keeping force, the International Security Assistance Force (ISAF), to key provincial cities—exporting the relative stability that they have created within the capital.

These efforts failed. The Pentagon has proposed a cheaper option: dispatching reconstruction teams of eighty to 100 dominated by US reservists to provincial centres. But this has met strong opposition from international aid agencies.

In the meantime, Afghanistan is awash with hundreds of thousands of weapons, many supplied by the West after the Soviet invasion. Much of this arsenal, including tanks, is in the hands of rival warlords who are still feuding over control of key trading routes. Though several have taken senior jobs and most have expressed verbal support for the Karzai government, they have yet to relinquish their private armies.

The lack of money has dogged Afghanistan from the start. A year ago, the World Bank estimated $10.2 billion (£6.4 billion) was needed over five years. International pledges were about half that sum. And, according to Care International, an NGO monitoring international aid, the money actually spent per capita last year in Afghanistan was under half that of post-conflict Rwanda, Bosnia, Kosovo and East Timor. The CIA has spent some of that paying warlords and militias for help in the 'war on terror'—strengthening rivals to the Central government.

So what does this tell us about the fate of Iraq after the Americans have taken it apart?

It is not hard to find international aid workers who see that the problems of Afghanistan will be repeated in Iraq. 'There is a real question over whether the international community is prepared to take on the burden of rebuilding Iraq over the long term,' said Paul O'Brien, advocacy co-ordinator for Care in Afghanistan.

Another Western observer summed up his views more acidly. 'If the Americans think this is success, then outright failure must be pretty horrible to behold.'

~

Manjeet Kripalani
Asking the Right Questions

BusinessWeek
22 August 2003

THE MAIN HALL of the Science & Technology Museum in Shanghai was packed. More than 150 top executives of multinational companies had arrived at the invitation of IBM chief Sam Palmisano to participate in IBM's Business Leadership Forum, a high-level conference held on a different continent every May for the past three years. On the dais, Palmisano introduced the day's speaker: Sunil Mittal, chairman and CEO of India's premier mobile-services provider, Bharti Tele-Ventures Ltd. This company, said Palmisano, 'is on a rocket to the moon'.

Why would IBM's chief be in China lauding an Indian telco that few outside India had even heard of a short time ago? It's not just because Bharti did a ten-year $750 million IT-outsourcing deal with IBM. It's also because Bharti—one of the world's fastest-growing telcos and the most capital-efficient—is one of the many Indian companies proving to be visionary in their fields. We're not talking about the champions of Bangalore, innovative as they are. These trendsetters range from telco newcomers such as Bharti to established giants like the $18 billion Tata Group and even former state-run players like ICICI Bank. All are rethinking the way they manage assets, distribute products, and use technologies to create new services. India's 'rapid, incremental innovations', in the words of John Hagel III, a business-strategy consultant and author of a recent book on India and China, *The Only Sustainable Edge*, can provide lessons to companies everywhere.

What characterizes the best of the Indian outfits? They've learned to question the basic concepts of their industries, an attitude born of collective experience. For decades after achieving independence in 1947, India imposed severe restrictions on the capital private companies could tap, the technologies they could import, and the foreign exchange they could hold. So the best ones learned how to devise ingenious, low-cost solutions to their problems and even reimagine industries such as software services.

Since Indian industry was unshackled from state strictures in 1991, it has accelerated the process of innovation to stress affordability and quality. Bharti is the largest mobile operator in India, with twelve million subscribers and a 22 per cent market share. It earned a net profit of $330 million on sales of $1.8 billion for the fiscal year ending 31 March. CEO Mittal, forty-eight, likes to tell investors that Bharti charges just 2 cents a minute for phone calls on its Airtel service—and pockets 1 cent of that.

Mittal realized that the Western model for mobile-phone businesses—building and maintaining huge, expensive cellular networks—wasn't for Bharti, which wanted to keep costs down in any way possible while providing reliable service. So in February 2004, Bharti became the largest telco in the world to try something truly radical. It outsourced its entire cellular network to its three existing equipment suppliers: Ericsson, Nokia and Siemens—a $725 million, three-year deal. The move to 'deep outsourcing' was revolutionary. Networks are as crucial to telecom players as engines are to auto makers. But it worked, and the effect on Bharti was profound. With executives no longer focused on managing the network, Bharti has turned its attention to marketing and customer service. In a year it has added six million subscribers—one-fourth of India's annual subscriber growth and by far the fastest sign-up rate in India's history. 'It's a big transformation, and it's becoming a global model,' says Erik Oldmark, who runs marketing strategy worldwide for Ericsson. On 8 August, Bharti took its model one step further by outsourcing its call-centre operations.

Cars on Demand

Bharti was able to tap outside expertise to remake its business. The $18 billion Tata Group relies on outside knowhow as well—but in this case, it's the traditional skills of India's working class. Tata, a conglomerate, has long made sturdy trucks. But four years ago, Chairman Ratan Tata plunged into the passenger-car business despite much scepticism. The result was India's first indigenously designed, developed, and produced car—the $6600 Indica. Tata used all of India's low-cost engineering skills to develop the car, at 60 per cent of the usual cost of launching a new model. Now he has put his team to work on his dream project: a car that will sell for only $2200. 'I wanted to change the rules of the game,' Tata says. 'I wanted to change the way business is done.'

The 'people's car' will use a combination of steel and composite plastic for its body, put together with industrial adhesive along with nuts and bolts. But what's the business changer? Tata will attempt to do away with the traditional model of manufacturing solely in a factory and distributing exclusively through established dealers. The plan is to make the basic components of the car in Tata plants—and then to send the car off the company's assembly line much like a bicycle, in a knocked-down kit form. These will be shipped across the country to Tata-trained franchisees. Some of them will be Tata Motors car dealers. But other franchisees may be any of India's thousands of roadside garages.

The mechanics will keep the kits in their garages and assemble them on demand for customers—then service them as needed. 'It will give an opportunity to young, capable people to create an enterprise,' says Tata. But the move will also save an estimated 20 per cent of an auto's production, experts say. 'Tata's plan makes the car a commodity,' says Kumar Bhattacharyya, director of Warwick Manufacturing Group at the University of Warwick in Britain.

If Ratan Tata's plan works, he will have stripped away a layer of distribution and manufacturing costs. Other Indian companies are tackling different kinds of distribution costs—and blowing away traditional assumptions in the process. In the case of Indian Tobacco Co. (ITC), managers are aggressively seeking ways to eliminate the exploitative middlemen who buy, transport, and market Indian farmers' produce.

Calcutta-based ITC is best known as a hotelier and as India's largest producer of cigarettes. But it also sells fertilizer to farmers and buys their grain to make processed foods. For years, ITC conducted its business with farmers through a maze of intermediaries, from brokers to traders. So ITC's head of international business, S. Sivakumar, thought of using e-commerce as a way to break the unhealthy hold of traders over the supply chain. In the initial experiment—begun four years ago in the central Indian state of Madhya Pradesh—Sivakumar set up computer kiosks in twenty villages and hired a well-known local farmer to run each kiosk. He and other farmers would access the company's intranet—dubbed e-chaupal, for electronic 'town square'—twice a day to check ITC's own offer price for produce, as well as prices in the closest village market, in the state capital, in New Delhi, and on the Chicago commodities exchange. The site relayed daily weather conditions and educated users about new farming techniques worldwide. In the evening, the local children took free lessons on the computer. In return, the farmers would usually give ITC first dibs on their crops, thus eliminating the middlemen.

Rising Incomes

How well the model works can be seen in the life of farmers such as thirty-eight-year-old Gulab Singh Varma. His two-room house is well-appointed by the standards of Bhaukhedi, the village of 3000 where he lives in Sehore district, Madhya Pradesh. In pride of place, next to a bright-red velvet sofa, is the e-chaupal computer, complete with speakers, printer, a satellite connection, and two sets of solar-powered batteries.

Before e-chaupal was set up, he says, farmers would spend three days travelling to the nearest market to sell their produce and never got a fair price. Then they would buy fertilizer and pesticides at premium rates and return home feeling cheated. 'Now it takes a few hours to make a sale in the local market,' Varma says, 'because we know the prices a day ahead of time, and we negotiate with the local market on the website.' Selling produce to ITC, thanks to the direct connection, nets the farmers 5 per cent to 15 per cent more than in the traditional marketplace. ITC is now building large, rural Wal-Mart-like supermarkets where farmers come to sell their produce and buy everything they need, from tractors to cell phones. 'Since e-chaupal began, the farmers' incomes have increased by 25 per cent to 30 per cent,' estimates Varma.

Through 2010, when ITC hopes to reach its goal of 100,000 villages participating in e-chaupal, the company will spend $100 million a year on developing this network. None of the competition, including US rival Cargill Corp., can match this head start. Consultant Hagel worries that Western companies are 'far too complacent about the changes and won't have the capabilities to respond' to such business models.

Will Western multinationals find themselves confronting model Indian companies outside India as well? For now, Indian companies are venturing overseas more slowly and cheaply than their state-backed Chinese counterparts. The Indians are making $1 million to $100 million acquisitions to learn about foreign markets or to tap capabilities for their own operations.

But that doesn't mean there won't be surprises. 'Companies out of India and China will be disruptive business models, coming at you in ways you can't anticipate,' says Jayant Sinha, author of a recent McKinsey & Co. study of globalizing companies from the developing world. Already, India's ICICI Bank, with $42 billion in assets, is adapting the outsourcing model to finance. It has turned itself into a low-cost consumer bank by building its own high-tech back office and is expanding in rural India by setting up automated teller machines in villages.

Now, ICICI is using that technological edge abroad, opening up a wholly owned bank subsidiary in Canada. By operating its low-cost back end in India, the bank is passing on those benefits to locals who bank through the Internet in the form of interest some thirty-five to seventy-five basis points higher than what's available at other Canadian banks. The product has been so popular that the bank already has 22,000 customers, with 1500 new ones signing up every week. Indian companies like ICICI can successfully take their models overseas because they are firmly anchored to their home market. A home market that is constantly being reinvented.

~

Simon Long

Sonia—and Yet So Far

India's New Government

The Economist
22 May 2004

THE COMPARISONS THAT have been drawn with the Buddha and Mohandas Gandhi seem a bit overblown. But India reveres renunciation, and the decision by Sonia Gandhi (no relation to the Mahatma) to forgo the chance to become India's Prime Minister has mightily enhanced her stature. It has probably also been good for her party, Congress, and the prospects of the government it will lead under Manmohan Singh, her anointee, who was due to be sworn in on 22 May.

The party itself found this hard to accept. Its members of Parliament seemed to think they had wandered into a production of 'King Lear', a less happy tale of renunciation. In an emotional—nay, hysterical—meeting on 18 May they hectored, cajoled and begged Mrs Gandhi to change her mind and take the job. The unbridled sycophancy was a reminder of the party's feudal attachment to the Nehru–Gandhi dynasty, and fear that, without her as a neutral figurehead, its kingdom will fall apart.

Mrs Gandhi was swayed neither by them nor by the several hundred equally high-pitched party activists gathered outside her front gate, some of whom felt genuinely cheated. They had worked hard to help her achieve the election result announced on 13 May, bringing a Congress-led coalition back to power against all expectations. They had rooted for her right to be Prime Minister despite being born in Italy. Some argued, incredibly, that if she was unwilling to serve, then her son Rahul, a thirty-three-year-old first-time MP, should step in. Others complained she was yielding to a xenophobic campaign that should have been confronted.

That may indeed have been one factor in Mrs Gandhi's decision. The Bharatiya Janata Party (BJP), the former ruling party, and its coalition partners had said they would boycott her swearing-in, though the BJP's leader and former Prime Minister, Atal Bihari Vajpayee, would attend. One former BJP government minister, Sushma Swaraj, and her husband were to resign their seats in the upper house of Parliament in protest at the 'national shame' of installing an Italian-born Prime Minister. Similarly, another senior BJP leader, Uma Bharti, had resigned as chief minister of the state of Madhya Pradesh. After Mrs Gandhi's sacrifice though, Miss Bharti, a sanyasin, or religious renunciate, looked rather silly.

Other groups linked to the Rashtriya Swayamsevak Sangh (RSS), the Hindu-nationalist mass organization that spawned the BJP, had already taken this campaign to the streets. Ram Madhav, an RSS spokesman, blamed the BJP's electoral defeat in part on its failure to find 'any real national-level emotive or ideological issue'. There was a risk that Mrs Gandhi's Italian origins might fill that void and prove the dominant theme of the new government's early days. Rahul Gandhi and his sister Priyanka were also said to oppose their mother's taking office, fearing for her life, though Rahul denied this. Their father, Mrs Gandhi's husband Rajiv, and grandmother, Indira, both former Prime Ministers, were each assassinated.

Mr Madhav claims that even some Congress voters were uneasy about being ruled by a native Italian, and he probably has a point. She speaks Hindi, wears sarees and says she prefers naan to pasta. But her foreign birth would always have been a stick to beat her with. Her party's mandate in the election was hardly a clear-cut endorsement either of its policies or its leader. Congress gained just under 27 per cent of the national vote, about 1.5 percentage points less than in the last election in 1999. Its coalition won almost exactly the same share of the votes, about 36 per cent, as the BJP's.

Mrs Gandhi herself had always been careful not to promote herself as a prime-ministerial candidate. During the campaign, this was seen as a shrewd tactic to stop the BJP turning it into a presidential-style contest between an untested, foreign-born novice and the popular, statesmanlike Mr Vajpayee. It now seems that Mrs Gandhi all along saw her duty as limited to rescuing her late husband's party from its recent slump and, in her words, to providing India with 'a secular government that is strong and stable'; but not leading it.

Outside the Congress hot-house, some were relieved at that. The political drama in Delhi was played out against the distant thud of a crashing stockmarket. The Mumbai exchange suffered its worst-ever day on 17 May, at one point having fallen by more than 17 per cent. The next day, news that Mrs Gandhi was thinking of stepping aside helped spur a recovery.

One reason for the market's cheer was the assumed identity of Mrs Gandhi's replacement. Having attributed to her the wisdom of the Buddha it was inevitable that Mrs Gandhi's parliamentary colleagues would ask her to nominate one. Her choice, Manmohan Singh, is popular with investors as the author of India's economic liberalization. An academic economist, he was Congress's finance minister in 1991, when, in response to a balance-of-payments crisis, the government launched a package of reforms, beginning the dismantling of the 'licence raj' of state planning, import controls and excessive regulation that was Nehru's legacy.

So his presence is heartening for investors who have two worries about the new government: first, that it will be hostile to business and reluctant to continue or accelerate the liberalization Mr Singh began; second, that it will be unstable and short-lived. The fears stem partly from its status as a minority government. Not only will Congress rely on a coalition—to be known as the United Progressive Alliance (UPA)—but the UPA will itself be a minority, relying on the 'outside support' of other parties, of which much the biggest is a 'Left Front' dominated by the Communist Party of India (Marxist), or CPI (M).

Playing the Red Card

The CPI (M) has been in power in the state of West Bengal since 1977, and like ruling communist parties elsewhere, has become pragmatic in office. Once notorious for red tape and strikes, the state has recently been hard-selling its attractions as a destination for inward investment in information technology and services such as call-centres. The communist chief minister, Buddhadeb Bhattacharjee, boasts of its success in promoting enterprise: exporting roses to the Netherlands, and housing potato-processing facilities for PepsiCo. It has even, with the help of British government aid, been closing down some of its loss-making state enterprises.

But during the election, Mr Bhattacharjee said that the CPI (M) could never join a Congress-led coalition, because of differences on economic policy. Mr Singh, whom the communists are now happy to accept as a Prime Minister, was 'the first torch-bearer for the IMF'. One cause of the stockmarket crash was a suggestion by a communist spokesman that the disinvestment ministry, which oversees India's privatization programme, should be abolished (not a bad idea in itself, but he appeared to want to abolish privatization as well).

The possibility of an end to the 'disinvestment' of state enterprises, which in recent months helped fuel a surging stockmarket, is a specific fear of investors. A broader concern is that all economic policy will likewise be hostage to the populist demands of Congress's coalition partners. A number of the reforms that economists argue are most needed will probably not make much headway. Labour laws, for example, which make it hard to shed staff without state government permission, are unlikely to be tackled.

The same is true of the reform that Arun Shourie, the outgoing BJP disinvestment minister, believed the most important of all, to the system by which funds are allocated to government departments and states. He argued that these reward poor performance—'the bigger the deficit, the bigger the grant'. But tampering with this system may not appeal to state leaders whose support Congress needs, such as Laloo Prasad Yadav of Bihar, a state notorious for economic underperformance.

However, fears that reforms are about to be shelved, and the markets' reaction, seem excessive. The reform process has always involved more stops than starts, and Congress may be no worse placed to pursue it than was the BJP. Surjit Bhalla, of Oxus Fund Management, a hedge fund in Delhi, says that, since 1991, every government that has taken power in India has accelerated the reforms, and he expects this one to be no different. The Left, he says, is to Congress as the RSS was to the BJP, minus the RSS's communal tendencies. Just as the BJP had to resist the protectionist 'self-reliant' economic tendency within the RSS, so Congress will be fending off leftist conservatism.

The markets are now awaiting the 'common minimum programme' Congress and its partners are drafting. To the extent that this mirrors Congress's own manifesto, it will differ little from the BJP's approach, though privatization is to be 'more selective', and not pursued, in Mr Singh's phrase, 'as an ideology'.

The national vote was too evenly split, and too driven by local factors, to be interpreted as a clear mandate; much less, despite some attempts to do so, could it be seen as a national indictment of the reforms. But it has been taken as a slap in the face for the BJP from the mass of Indians who live in poverty in the countryside. Every new government pays them lip-service. This one, relishing the shock of victory, knows better than most how much it needs to concentrate on agriculture and rural infrastructure. That, however, is itself an argument for accelerated reform.

Stability Pacts

The other fear about the new government is that it will prove shaky. Because it tends to be a competitor for power at the state level with its potential partners, Congress has in the past found it hard to forge national coalitions. Many UPA members have a price: one wants a new state carved out of Andhra Pradesh; another demands the ditching of harsh anti-terrorist legislation. Others, notably the Left parties and the Samajwadi ('Socialist') Party, which won thirty-six seats in India's largest state, Uttar Pradesh, are not actually joining the coalition: a form of power without accountability. Not having the responsibility that goes with cabinet seats, they could blackmail the government on issue after issue, and risk turning policymaking into a saga of serial brinksmanship.

Power in Indian politics is a great adhesive. Having touched it, the Left will be loth to let it slip. But managing such a complex and potentially fissile arrangement will demand great political skill. Mr Singh is, in this respect, untried. He is much admired as a kind, courteous and clever man. As a Sikh, he is India's first non-Hindu Prime Minister and living testimony to its secular traditions. But he sits in the upper house of Parliament and has never won a direct election.

His first challenge will be to form a government that satisfies his coalition partners without sacrificing his policy goals. He is fortunate in being able to fill most jobs from Congress ranks. Besides the economic portfolios, much interest focuses on the foreign ministry and the post of national security adviser.

The next stage in the peace process with Pakistan—talks on measures to build confidence about the two countries' nuclear arsenals—is due next week. In August, foreign ministers are to meet, and by then the two sides should have begun to discuss the hardest issue, the status of Kashmir. Congress has supported the peace initiative Mr Vajpayee launched last year.

But it may find it harder to negotiate on Kashmir than would the BJP, whose Hindu-nationalist background makes it less vulnerable to attack from chauvinists. The peace process was to be Mr Vajpayee's claim to a place in history. It would be good if, in opposition, he ensured that it enjoys bipartisan support. But his party's willingness to stoke racist antipathy to Mrs Gandhi, and his own silence as it did so, do not bode well for restraint.

~

Edward Luce

Supply and Demands
What Has Water to Do with Politics? In India, Everything

Financial Times Weekend Magazine
24 July 2004

INDIA'S PRINCIPAL MONSOON begins in late May at its south-west tip in the lush and beautiful state of Kerala. Six weeks and several heart-stopping pauses later, the annual rains will—with luck—reach Rajasthan in India's arid north-west. Its progress, sometimes relentless, other times half-hearted, has been celebrated by every poet to have been touched by India—Rudyard Kipling and Rabindranath Tagore included. The sentiment is always traditional: if the rains fail, darkness descends.

Nowadays, however, Indians seem to have banished that fatalism with which, we are told, ordinary people were once so afflicted. The rain gods may or may not fail (India has had two severe droughts since 1987). But it is humans who are held to account.

India's recent general election (in May), in which the ruling, Hindu nationalist-led coalition was voted out—in the midst of the most rapid phase of economic expansion in years—was no exception. The election took place in the aftermath of last year's generous monsoon, which boosted spending in much of rural India.

But India's voters are restless. Nowadays they have a sharper awareness of their political clout, in a spirit that runs counter to the traditional passivity of village society. In spite of last year's good rains, much of that restlessness stems from the continuing lack of 'Bijli, Sadaak, Paani' (electricity, roads, water) for many of the 700 million people still living in villages, and the 200 million or so who constitute the urban poor (from a total population of 1.03 billion, according to the 2001 census).

India's sophisticated metropolitan elite periodically pays attention to these deficiencies—though it doesn't suffer much from them itself. But the urban middle classes were too much in thrall to the ruling party's hubristic mantra of 'India Shining' to anticipate the recent electoral shock. In its wake, the masses' growing impatience for the basic needs of life has come centre stage again.

Most Indians have extremely limited and unreliable access to what they need most. Around three-quarters of the population have no public sanitary facilities (such as toilets). More—about 80 per cent—have no access to safe drinking water. They experience a daily crisis. Many even die from it: every year more than one million Indian children are killed by microbes in their drinking water.

Living like this means unremitting labour. At dawn each day, tens of millions of women walk for miles to collect water. In states such as Andhra Pradesh, abysmal irrigation means the crops keep failing. The state is known as one of India's leading software magnets, yet, away from the air-conditioned, dark-tinted offices, some 500 of Andhra Pradesh's farmers have committed suicide this year alone, often by drinking the deadly pesticide that was purchased with debts they cannot repay. Even in Hyderabad, the gleaming state capital, municipal water comes only every other day.

The Indian (and Nobel Prize-winning) economist Amartya Sen famously observed that famines do not happen in democracies. That theory, tested by widespread hunger in Rajasthan in the last four years, is upheld by India's democratic record since 1947. But India also shows that democracy's record of providing the most basic social services, such as water, cannot be taken for granted.

It is no use pointing vaguely to the skies. In essence India's water crisis is about how the country is governed. 'If you look at data for the last 100 years, there has been absolutely no change in the pattern of India's monsoon,' says Onkari Prasad, director of India's meteorological office. 'Our problems are man-made. You cannot blame the weather.'

Thus, amid an indifferent monsoon this year, the new Congress-led government, headed by the reticent economist Manmohan Singh, who launched India's liberal reforms in 1991, inherits an impatient public mood. Singh knows his coalition too will fall victim to the electorate's record of 'anti-incumbency' unless it changes the quality of people's lives. Its performance on water will be the most important measure of all.

Over tea in his New Delhi office, Mani Shankar Aiyar, a leading Congress politician and now cabinet minister for local government, puts the challenge in perspective: 'We live in a system where the poor throw out whatever government they have at whatever level whenever they get the chance.' Aiyar, a graduate of Oxford University, says his elite background is a handicap in a democracy that suffers from what he sees as the curse of paternalism. 'In between elections we forget the poor and diligently consult the urban middle classes to discover the state of "public opinion". It is time we got our hands dirty. Do any of us really know what it is like to worry about where your next pail of water will come from?' Aiyar doesn't, but many voters in his constituency, in the drought-prone state of Tamil Nadu in the south, certainly do.

The people of western Rajasthan, which is blanketed by the beautiful Thar desert that stretches into neighbouring Pakistan, spend much of their lives thinking about water. Or rather, the women do. Although collecting water is back-breaking, it is the women's backs that break in Rajasthan—as in most parts of the developing world.

Last December the thirty million voters of the state also ejected their government—which, at the state level, was Congress. In a movement which was a mirror image of what happened the following May, they elected in its place a Hindu nationalist BJP administration. India's state governments are feeling the brunt of anti-incumbency more sharply than at the federal level, since it is state capitals that are accountable for providing water, power and other basic amenities under India's federal system.

Although the Congress-led alliance won the national polls in May, its parliamentary vote share declined sharply in the states it governs. Conversely, the BJP lost power in New Delhi but captured the bulk of the national vote in states such as Rajasthan, where the provincial BJP government had come to power too recently to fall victim to anti-incumbency.

In other words, India's election was an agglomeration of local votes—its outcome a mathematical accident. National issues, such as peace talks with Pakistan, secularism versus Hindu nationalism, or how to manage the country's record foreign-exchange reserves, played only a marginal role in the polling booths. It is only by visiting India's villages that one can get a sense of why.

Jaisalmer is a heart-breakingly beautiful fort-town that peers down upon the desert below. There are no flights to Jaisalmer since it is close to the border with Pakistan and airspace is monopolized by the Indian military. So, to get there, I take a five-hour car journey across the desert.

The landscape I drive through is littered with man-made ponds, 'tanks' (large catchment areas), medieval stepwells, which served as caravanserai stops for traders on the ancient silk route to China, and a taxonomy of structures that draw on different types of groundwater. In the same way that Eskimos have dozens of words for different types of snowflakes, Rajasthanis could fill a small dictionary with their rich appellations for water.

Although western Rajasthan has the lowest rainfall in India—an average of just 150 millimetres a year—Jaisalmer has not suffered a full-blown famine for centuries. This is because of a deeply ingrained culture of harvesting every raindrop that falls from the skies to recharge the underground supply for the dry season.

But in the last few decades the villagers of Rajasthan have had to contend with something new: a government that insists it will provide the water instead. And they have learned that this is often less reliable than self-reliance. In the transition from self-sufficiency to dependency, much of the highly sophisticated local knowledge has been lost.

Amb Singh, the fifty-eight-year-old headman of Keeta, a village 20 miles from Jaisalmer, explains what has happened. We are seated on the floor of his hut—a bamboo structure held together with cow manure that hardens like concrete under the desert sun. He hands me a glass of water, an offering reserved for fortunate guests. Most get milk.

'When the government laid down water pipes to our village we started changing our habits,' says Singh, who, like his neighbours gathered around, wears a traditional Rajasthani turban and a bristling handlebar moustache. 'The young have no clue where to find natural sources. But often government water doesn't come. So we are stuck in the worst place between the old and the new. We are no longer in control.'

Singh and his friends tell me about a permanent tug-of-war with the local water engineer, an important post in India's district bureaucracy. The engineer is often absent, which means the nearby tubewell, from which the village receives its water, stops its supply.

'Whenever we complain to the chief engineer he passes our complaint to someone else,' says one. 'We have been to Jaisalmer to see the collector (the most senior bureaucrat in the district). He sent our complaint back to the chief engineer. The complaint then returns to the local engineer. Nothing happens.'

Last year's bumper monsoon seems beside the point. It is the everyday wranglings with aloof and often inaccessible bureaucrats that chiefly preoccupy Singh's village. Later that day, I visit the collector, P.L. Agarwal, a member of the elite Indian Administrative Service (IAS), at the ramshackle district headquarters in Jaisalmer.

Agarwal says politicians are to blame for the farmers' plight—irrigation supply is as intermittent as drinking water. Agarwal is the tenth collector for Jaisalmer in fewer than eight years. Every time a collector stands up to the local politicians, he is transferred to another district.

Agarwal argues that politicians should be held to account for the failure to complete the Indira Gandhi canal—a project to supply Rajasthan with the plenteous waters of Punjab, India's best-irrigated state (its name means 'five rivers' in Hindi). The canal extension, which would ease western Rajasthan's constant thirst, is fifteen years behind schedule. 'As civil servants we have no power to do anything,' he says. 'Knowing that you will probably be transferred in six months, there is no incentive to take any long-term initiatives.'

I tell Agarwal what the villagers have said to me—that they rarely get to see the collector or his underlings and it is not often of much use when they do. He has heard this before. 'The villagers can always come and see me. I will always listen. But you must understand that most of these people are illiterate. They don't always understand water problems.'

Surely, I interrupt, they understand their own water situation better than anyone else? Agarwal gives me an avuncular smile. But I sense he is irritated. 'Water is a very technical issue. If you want to write about it you should visit the chief water engineer and the chief irrigation engineer in Jaipur (the state capital, 250 miles away). Villagers always complain.'

Sita Kanwal, a thirty-year-old mother of five, says her husband gave up complaining long ago. At first she had been too shy to talk to me. I am apparently the first male stranger she has permitted into her house. She drapes her veil in front of her face in typical Rajasthani style and giggles whenever I ask a question.

Kanwal lives in a hamlet a few miles from Singh's village. Every morning she rises at four to pound the wheat for breakfast. Her three daughters, aged eight, ten and twelve, leave home just after dawn on a 5 kilometre walk to the nearest well. They trudge this journey twice a day, balancing two pots, one on top of the other, decorously on their heads. All told it takes six hours. Naturally, like their mother, they are illiterate. 'There is no time for them to go to school—but even if there was time, the teachers are not often turning up,' says Kanwal, having finally dropped her veil to reveal a charming but prematurely wrinkled face. Out of courtesy I drink the water she has offered, although with strong misgivings about its quality.

Her husband has repeatedly requested the district authorities to lay a pipe from the well to the hamlet. Sometimes he hires a camel-pulled water cart for Rs 150 to give his daughters a rest. This is big money in a country where one-third of people live on fewer than Rs 50 a day. Kanwal has never met a government officer. 'Nobody has ever asked me about these things before,' she says.

But getting a pipeline would not necessarily put an end to her woes—as Singh was earlier keen to point out. 'If there is electricity then the water can be pumped to the village,' he says. 'But the government officers never know when there is going to be electricity. Sometimes we have to bribe him to switch on the pump even when there is electricity.'

I ask to speak to the women (a request not always entertained). They tell me that they have enough water to wash about every four days. They change their clothes every two weeks. They have complaints about the bad road and absentee teachers. But when I ask what they most want to change about their lives, they drop their veils and yell: 'Paani! (water)' It takes me a while to recover from the sudden increase in decibels. Then one woman adds quietly: 'And we don't like building houses with cow manure.'

I cannot resist asking the men if they share these priorities. 'You shouldn't listen to everything women say,' says Singh. 'Even when they are collecting water they are always talking and shaking their heads from side to side (he does a mocking Indian headshake).' The women laugh uproariously. In Keeta, the battle of the sexes evidently comes second to the collective struggle against bureaucracy.

Before leaving I ask a final question, about politics. 'Politicians are all blood-suckers,' says Singh. In May, they all voted BJP. The time before they voted Congress. Next time, no doubt, they will switch again.

Back in Delhi I arrange lunch with T.S.R. Subramanian, former cabinet secretary of India—the most senior job in the civil service. Earlier this year, Mr Subramanian published his memoirs: *Journeys Through Babudom and Netaland*. 'Babu' is a derogatory term for bureaucrat, as is 'neta' for politician.

Many in India's elite civil service write memoirs (they never really retire—they join think-tanks). But this one stood out. The book concludes with four iron laws of India's bureaucracy, of which the most scathing is: 'The administration only takes decisions that benefit administrators.' This would explain why, according to India's new government, upto 85 per cent of development spending does not reach the poor. It is either absorbed by the 'delivery mechanism'—the consultants, advisers, their equipment and studies—or pocketed.

'People complain about corruption as if it is a minor nuisance,' Subramanian tells me over mutton kebabs at the well-watered Delhi Golf Club. 'What they haven't yet grasped—but will do so gradually—is the link between corruption and maladministration. At the moment their only real power is to vote out governments.' Subramanian's formula explains why India's administration can build large dams but is unable to maintain rural irrigation systems, why it can launch satellites but not build public toilet facilities, why it can pave multi-lane highways but not simple all-weather roads to its villages. (The lack of passable roads is why more than half of all vegetables grown in India rot before reaching a market.) 'You must understand that India's bureaucracy is not remotely accountable—unlike the politicians, we are unsackable,' he says. 'The decisions it takes are about creating money-making opportunities. There is no money in providing drinking water or roads or education to people who have no money.'

We discuss the outlook for Manmohan Singh, who has said his government will be judged on its ability to deliver basic services to all Indians. Prime Minister Singh, whose reputation for integrity is unquestioned, has made it plain this can only be accomplished by reforming the administrative system 'at every level'. In saying this, the new Prime Minister has set himself the hardest task imaginable—far more difficult than building nuclear weapons or capturing software markets in the west.

Nobody believes Singh would jeopardize the unity of his twelve-party coalition by putting an end to the job-for-life culture of the civil service. Furthermore, all of the issues on which he says he will be judged are powers reserved for the states. The capital can, of course, give states more money. But money, as a senior foreign aid official explains, is virtually irrelevant. 'What is the point of putting more water into the bucket if it is already leaking so badly? The problem is not lack of money. It is the accountability of those who spend it.'

My next visit is to Kerala which—geographically and meteorologically—is at the other end of the scale to Rajasthan. The densely forested and mountainous state receives an average of 3000 millimetres of rain a year—almost thirty times Rajasthan's quotient, and three times that of rain-sodden Britain. Last year Kerala's rainfall was 2700 millimetres—still a fantastical amount by Rajasthani standards. But enough to cause a drought.

'We get piped water every other day for about an hour,' says A. Achyuthan, a much-respected elder of the People's Science Movement—a social environmentalist group that does tireless battle with bureaucracy. We meet at his leafy residence in the balmy port of Calicut on Kerala's Malabar coast. Achyuthan explains why such a verdant, rain-blessed state should be suffering what has been dubbed the 'wet drought'. He laughs: 'It's like that poem—"Water, water everywhere, nor any drop to drink." It is nothing to do with the amount of rainfall—enough falls on Kerala to supply half of India.'

Kerala receives an average of 10,000 litres of rainfall per person a day. The United Nations says each person needs 30 to 50 litres a day for his needs, so all Kerala would need to 'harvest' is 0.5 per cent of what falls from the skies. That, apparently, is beyond the powers of government. In May, Kerala's voters ejected every single sitting Congress MP in favour of the main opposition communists (Kerala's state government is Congress). Next time the pendulum will probably swing back.

I drive to the district of Palakkad up in Kerala's central highlands, which is suffering from its first drought in memory. After the failure of the winter crop, some paddy farmers have taken the same route out of misery as their counterparts in Andhra Pradesh—they have committed suicide, bowed down by their inability to repay usurious moneylenders (for India's poor, it is as hard to get credit from state-owned banks as it is to get irrigation from state water boards).

The scenery is like the Garden of Eden. We drive pass fecund plots of tapioca, plantain, cardamom and rubber tree. Tropical butterflies flap lazily across the fields. Women are unveiled. Small children, girls and boys, march to school in neat, starched uniforms. Kerala is almost 100 per cent literate. Nobody complains about lack of household water. Everywhere you look there is a small well. But, as in Rajasthan, and almost everywhere else in India, the groundwater level is dropping sharply because nobody is replenishing it. 'People are pumping water from the ground because the government is not providing it to them,' says Sunita Narain, head of the Centre for Science and the Environment, and one of India's most effective activists. 'But they have lost the art of replenishing ground water—it is a dying wisdom. Either they wait for the government to change its ways, or they take responsibility for their own water, as communities did in the past. The state has failed them.'

In some ways this is a bleak diagnosis. Maintaining rainwater harvesting systems is not for the romantic: desilting ponds, clearing feeder channels and digging tanks is heavily labour-intensive. Yet, in the absence of good government, many in Kerala are responding to this logic. 'For the first time in years I know my crops will be irrigated,' says R. Prakash, a farmer in Palakkad, who has renovated derelict local ponds with the help of his neighbours. He points disdainfully to a ditch that is clogged up and dry. It is the government's irrigation network. Prakash's ponds are full. His crop did not fail. I ask what his dream scenario would be—expecting him to request a government that provides reliable water supply. He ignores my hint, even after repeated promptings. 'I have what I need,' he pronounces finally. A government that provides reliable irrigation is beyond his imaginings.

Nearby, I visit Ambika Vijaykumar, a housewife and something of a local celebrity. She welcomes me into her sparse living room, its walls decorated with chintzy pictures of beribboned kittens. She is a stout lady with the voicebox of a prima donna. I begin to understand how she defied the netas and babus. Vijaykumar rallied a group of housewives to take control of the local water supply. They raised their own money and qualified for a grant from an international agency. With this they dug a well, linked pipes into the houses, and built receptacles for rainwater on their roofs. They all happily pay a weekly rate for their water, even though government-supplied water is free.

'We used to queue at the municipal tap for hours. There was only one tap. The government never told us what time of day it would come. So we could never go out,' Vijaykumar says to murmurs of agreement from the others. 'You should have heard the names the local politicians were calling us when we started the project,' she says, thumping the table. 'Now we laugh in their faces.'

I don't envy the local politicians. But it is hard to feel sympathy for them in Kerala, or anywhere else. There are sharp ideological differences between India's parties, particularly on whether India should be a secular or a Hindu majority state. But when it comes to reform of India's mostly abysmal public services, barely a chink of light can be detected. All are wedded to the idea that water should be free. In practice this means that the poor get no water and are forced to pay astronomic rates to private water providers—the so-called water mafia—to deliver their needs by truck. Hypocrisy is too mild a criticism for those who defend this system in the name of the poor.

'Time and again it has been shown that the poor are happy to pay for water if they get it,' says Narain. 'Proof of this is that they don't get it and have to pay private water mafia a multiple of what they would pay to the government if it actually arrived.'

India's rapidly expanding capital of fifteen million people provides the starkest example of the power of the water mafias. People (including me) who live in the pleasant housing complexes of colonial New Delhi receive water twenty-four hours a day at less than 10 per cent of what it costs the Delhi Water Board to deliver it. Consumption is unmetered so there is no incentive to conserve. As a result the middle classes of New Delhi use roughly triple the volume (300 litres a day) of their counterparts in Copenhagen or Sydney.

The seven million or so who live in Delhi's illegal slums get on average 30 free litres a day from the Delhi Water Board's tankers, for which they wait endlessly with buckets, jerry cans, empty Coke bottles and anything else at hand. Water fights often break out in the scramble for the hose. It is rarely enough. So they resort to the water mafia, who charge the same for a day's supply as the monthly bill of an average middle-class household. And when they do get free municipal water it is sometimes unfit for consumption.

Khatija Khatoon is one of almost 200,000 people who were forcibly evicted from their central Delhi slum in March and relocated to the government-built slum of Bawana about 20 miles outside the city. Her house, like the 10,000 others in the 'colony', has been constructed from jute and is covered by tarpaulin. The open drains have been built on high ground, which means that whenever it rains, their huts are flooded with sewage. Aid officials report several child deaths a day from cholera, typhoid and dysentery—courtesy of the government's free water and sanitation services.

Three months ago Sheila Diskhit, New Delhi's popular Congress chief minister, visited Bawana to check on conditions. 'For two days before she arrived, municipal workers worked day and night to clean everything up,' says Khatoon. 'She promised us she would get our drains fixed within a week. Nothing has happened.'

As is so often the case, there is an electoral moral to Khatoon's grim tale. She and her neighbours were evicted on the order of Sri Jagmohan, India's former minister of tourism, who was also the BJP candidate for south Delhi, where their former slum was located. The voter list had not yet been transferred. Jagmohan, who had plans to beautify the area for tourism, lost his seat by a wide margin. 'We all made sure we went back to vote against him,' says Khatoon. In ordinary circumstances, the forcible eviction of 200,000 people with no right of appeal ought to have caused a scandal. But with one or two exceptions, India's media, under whose noses it took place, did not cover the incident. The story in March was about how India's 'feel-good' economy would bring Jagmohan and his colleagues a second full term in office.

It would be wrong to give the impression India does not have many honest and conscientious public officials (or that large parts of India's economy are not booming). As a former civil servant, who has headed dozens of departments, Prime Minister Singh knows India's system of government better than almost anyone, and he hasn't shrunk from diagnosing the problem. But in comparison to the peaks he scaled in the 1990s—when he dismantled India's dirigible 'Licence Raj' and helped lift annual economic growth to an average of 6 per cent a year—his next challenge is Himalayan.

In the 1990s Singh won the admiration of India's chronically over-regulated private sector. This time round he needs to satisfy hundreds of millions of people such as Khatoon, Prakash and Vijayakumar. Unlike in the west, where the poor generally vote in lower proportions than the middle classes, in India they turn out in much higher numbers.

India's political elite has taken a long time to grasp this. But the message is seeping through. 'India's poor may be powerless in other respects but on polling day they are starting to use what little they have ruthlessly,' says Aiyar, whose plans to decentralize more power and money to village councils is an important element in the new government's agenda. But, even if decentralization is the right strategy, it will take time to show results—longer, certainly, than the normal electoral cycle.

Brief as our interaction was, I cannot stop thinking about Khatoon, a semi-literate woman, with no home or assets, to whom life (and government) have dealt the worst possible hand. 'We have not seen one municipal officer since we were moved here—not one,' she says. Egged on by a small gathering of equally beleaguered neighbours, Khatoon gives vent to an infectious anger. Her horizon is undeniably gloomy. But there is no trace of passive acceptance. Khatoon knows her rights. It is hard to miss the silver lining.

~

Simon Long
The Pursuit of Happiness

The Economist
16 December 2004

ONCE UPON A time, in the high hills far away, was a magic kingdom with a secret. The people were poor, but, thanks to the secret, they were happy. They loved their forests and fertile valleys, their snow-capped mountains and gurgling rivers, their white-washed temples and red-robed monks. And they loved their king, for he was good and wise, and kept the secret well.

Since they were far away, not many people knew of their happiness. But the king in his goodness and wisdom decided this had to change. This made the people uneasy. And he wanted to give up many of his powers, which made them afraid. The king was married to four beautiful sisters and had many children. But he worried that future kings might not be as good and wise as he. So he wanted the people to rule themselves. To help them, he bequeathed the secret of his golden rule. And he gave it a name: Gross National Happiness.

Shangri-La-Di-Da

The Himalayan kingdom of Bhutan is not in fact an idyll in a fairy tale. It is home to perhaps 900,000 people—estimates vary wildly—most of whom live in grinding poverty. It is grappling, like most other countries, with the boons and curses of globalization, trying to preserve its own traditions while opening its doors to prosperity.

Bhutan, however, is different in ways that draw both foreigners and the Bhutanese themselves into romantic flights of fancy about the country.

First, few places have been so romanticized as Shangri-La, or remained so backward and so isolated for so long. Serfdom was abolished only in 1956, by the third king in the present dynasty. After China's crushing of an uprising in neighbouring Tibet in 1959, he went beyond the freeing of the serfs to embark on a tentative opening up. The fate of other Himalayan Buddhist kingdoms and theocracies—Sikkim (absorbed by India), Mustang (Nepal) and Tibet itself (China)—was warning enough of the perils of isolation. Bhutan, squeezed between two giants, agreed in 1949 that its policy would be 'guided' by one of them, India. It still has no diplomatic relations with the other, China.

Bhutan's first paved road dates only from 1961. Before 1968 it had no banks. Until 1999, there was no television and no access to the Internet. Thimphu still advertises itself as the world's only national capital without a traffic light.

Second, Bhutan has taken unusual steps to safeguard its heritage. Most visibly, weaving and costume are protected by rules making traditional dress compulsory in public places. Men wear a gho, a long one-piece robe belted and hitched up at the waist, leaving a big pouch in the upper folds. It looks a little like a dressing gown, but is typically worn with knee-length socks and sturdy lace-ups. Women wear the kira, a floor-sweeping straight dress topped with a blouse and short jacket.

Both are elegant. Traditional architecture, too, is promoted. Even new houses are traditionally painted—white with ornate decorated window-frames, and the occasional mural, such as a big flying phallus, a symbol of a popular Tantric master, known as the Divine Madman, who made good use of his.

Third, there is Gross National Happiness. When, in the 1970s, Bhutan's fourth and present king said that he cared more about this than about Gross National Product, it seemed something of a throwaway remark. King Jigme Singye Wangchuk, who succeeded to the throne in 1972, is a modernizer like his father, but this seemed a simple statement of the obvious: that economic growth alone does not bring contentment. Over the years, however, the idea has taken hold. At home, Bhutan's rulers find it a handy excuse for some of their quirkier policies. Abroad, some development theorists have latched on to the idea as an alternative to the globalizers' creed of growth-oriented market economics.

So a new set of initials—GNH—is now used to abbreviate a small academic industry. At an international conference on GNH in Thimphu last February, sixty papers were tabled. Then, in June, Bhutan's Prime Minister, Jigme Thinley, based his annual report on the government's performance on the tenets of GNH.

Even in Bhutan, however, opinions differ about GNH. For its adherents, it offers a guide to policy that will enable Bhutan to pick and choose in the globalization supermarket, modernizing on its terms alone.

Bhutan's experiment, in this view, also offers important lessons to other poor countries.

For critics, however, GNH is at best an empty slogan—one that risks 'including everything and ending up meaning nothing', in the words of Dorji Penjor of the Centre for Bhutan Studies, the think-tank that held the conference in February. At worst, say some foreign observers, GNH provides ideological cover for repressive and racist policies.

Some of GNH's exponents, such as Mr Thinley, seem a bit bemused by the vogue. He is no longer prime minister, a post that rotates each year among five of the ten-member cabinet. But, as home minister, he still sits in his gho and orange ministerial shawl in Thimphu's seventeenth-century dzhong, a fortress that serves as both monastery and government office.

It is a suitable seat from which to expound on merging tradition with modernity.

Happiness Has Four Legs

Mr Thinley is suspicious of efforts to turn GNH into a science, or to devise indices measuring happiness along the lines of the UN Development Programme's human-development index (which ranks Bhutan 134th out of 177 countries). Yet he has done more than any other government minister to underpin the king's insubstantial aphorism.

He says there are four 'pillars' to GNH. The first is 'sustainable and equitable socio-economic development'. Revealingly, some at the conference modified this to 'economic self-reliance'. Bhutan's economy is tiny, and its foreign links tinier still. Subsistence farming still sustains some four-fifths of the population. The priority remains road-building. Even the main 'highway' from Thimphu to Paro is in many places only wide enough for one car. Mr Thinley boasts that motorable roads now connect all but one of Bhutan's twenty districts, though many villages can still be reached only on foot.

In 2003 Bhutan's total exports, almost all of which went to India, were worth just 5700 million Bhutanese ngultrums (about $120 million). Electricity generated from Bhutan's rivers accounted for about half the exports.

The other sources of foreign exchange were, and are, aid—especially from India—and tourism. About 7000 tourists visit each year. They are charged at least $200 a day, shared cosily between the government and private travel agents. The only foreign investment of note is in two smart resorts.

Yeshey Zimba, the trade minister, says the government no longer limits the number of visitors. It regulates itself, thanks to the difficulty of getting to Bhutan. Mr Zimba is, by local standards, an ardent supporter of globalization: 'There is nothing we can do to prevent it.'

Indeed, Bhutan is embracing it, and trying to join the World Trade Organization. Nobody seems quite sure why. Mr Zimba argues that it is like the United Nations, which Bhutan joined in 1971: 'Everybody is a member.'

The second pillar is the pristine environment. Bhutan is one big, mountainous forest. Only 16 per cent of its land is arable, so there is pressure to fell trees and sell timber. Ministers worry that logging could swiftly turn the fragile ecology into a 'mountain desert', and a law requires the proportion of tree cover to be kept above 60 per cent. In fact, the tree cover is spreading, having increased from 64 per cent to 72 per cent of the country in the past ten years, says Mr Thinley.

Similarly, few of Bhutan's mineral resources—coal, possibly tungsten, and limestone suitable for cement—have been dug up. The hydropower projects are mostly 'run-of-the-river' schemes with far less impact on the environment, and far less human displacement, than huge dams would have.

This wonderful record has a cost, of course, and, as a guide to policy, it is where GNH parts company from GNP. Yet it is in the third pillar—the 'preservation and promotion of Bhutan's culture' that things start getting really tricky, and one group's GNH starts looking like another group's grief. Nobody could quarrel with Bhutan's wish to preserve its unique cultural heritage. But what is it?

For most Bhutanese, the cultural inheritance is dominated by a strain of Tibetan Buddhism. Bhutan was unified in the seventeenth century by a Tibetan lama. It has thousands of temples, an 'altar room' in every home, and many boys still become monks for life. Officially, the number is actually growing.

Bhutan, however, has many ethnic groups, some of them migrants. Though Hindu Nepalese started migrating to the fertile south of Bhutan in the late nineteenth century, the big influx of economic migrants came in the 1960s and 1970s. Then, in the late 1980s, the government started pushing 'one nation, one people' as a principle. The dress rules appeared. Nepali, which was taught as a third language (after the national tongue, Dzhongkha, and English) in some schools, was dropped from the curriculum. Nepali-speaking southerners had to produce documents to prove their citizenship. Some protested. Some were expelled. Others fled.

Between 1988 and 1993, thousands of Nepali-speakers left Bhutan, many ending up in refugee camps in Nepal, which now house about 100,000 people, a tenth of whom were born there. A further 20,000-

30,000 are believed to be in India. Efforts to agree with Nepal on the fate of those in the camps are subject to endless delays and bickering.

The issue has been costly for Bhutan. Its image is dented. Shangri-La seems less alluring if its bliss relies on keeping an eighth of the 1990 population in a grim exile. Some aid donors, such as the Dutch, have turned off the tap in protest.

Many of the 'refugees', claims the government, were recent illegal immigrants; some had never been in Bhutan; most had emigrated of their own accord and forfeited citizenship, for which they would have to reapply. Of the 12,000 in the camps whose status has been 'verified', Bhutan admits only that 297 were expelled. Some 75 per cent, it claims, left voluntarily and the rest were non-Bhutanese.

Many north Bhutanese insist the government had to act. The country risked being swamped, they say, by Nepalese who could wander over the open border with India and occupy Bhutan's most fertile land. In their camps the Nepali-speakers may hang portraits of Bhutan's king. But, it is said, once they are securely in Bhutan, the portraits are those of the king of Nepal. Some foreigners in Thimphu, while not defending the government's means, have some sympathy for the ends. Others deplore continued the discrimination against Nepali-speakers.

And Now, Traditional Television

Mr Thinley insists the idea of GNH is inclusive. Nepali is spoken in the National Assembly. The one newspaper, *Kuensel*, a weekly, appears in English and Nepali as well as Dzhongkha. But, besides 'preserving and promoting' Bhutan's culture, the government is also defining, limiting and sometimes even inventing it. Some 'traditions', such as the requirement that everybody should wear a long shawl (whose colour denotes the wearer's status) when visiting government offices or temples, are fairly recent discoveries. In September it was decreed that any women wearing their scarves draped over one shoulder were flouting a two-shoulder custom. Last year the Dzongkha Development Commission coined 400 new words to help a liturgical language cope with the modern world.

Who controls the past, as Big Brother knew, controls the future. Bhutan is a friendly and engaging place but there is an Orwellian tinge to its government. Last month it became the first country to ban tobacco.

Citizens must return to their village each year to obtain their identity card. Those who travel abroad surrender their passports on return and can reclaim them only by going to Thimphu.

All that could perhaps change with the building of the fourth of Mr Thinley's pillars, good governance. Democracy, for now, is of the trickle-down variety. In 1981 the king introduced twenty district committees, elected by households. Ten years later decentralization was extended to 201 committees representing 'blocks' of villages, elected by individual voters. Reform is now to be entrenched in a new constitution. In January the king will tour the country, drumming up support for this—a document that will take away much of his power.

Sonam Tobgye, the chief justice and chairman of the drafting committee, admits many are uneasy about the changes—especially the replacement of the king's role as ombudsman, to whom everybody has the right of appeal, with a supreme court. Some in the Thimphu elite fear electoral democracy, worrying that it may one day threaten their interests in favour of the poor rural majority. They also fear the emergence of political parties, which may form along ethnic or regional lines. Some hope that party politics can be avoided in favour of civilized debate and continued consensus. Mr Tobgye, though, is adamant: 'Democracy can't work without parties.'

The chief justice is also an optimist, arguing that you 'must trust human beings; with friction there is energy'. Until recently, Bhutan's rulers showed little such trust. Like over-protective parents, they shielded their people from evil influences.

The big exception is television. Until 1999 there was none, except for a lucky few with secret satellite dishes or video-players. Then, when Bhutan started producing its own, very limited, television programmes, it also opened up to cable operators. In an unusual big bang for such a cautious regime, viewers suddenly had access to a full forty-six channels, offering everything from news to near-naked fashion models to wrestling.

Sok Sian Pek, who conducted a 'media impact study' for the communications ministry, says television has wrought huge changes in the towns. People adjust meal-times for their favourite programme. Most popular are Indian soap operas (understanding of Hindi is spreading fast). Ms Pek scoffs at those who blame television for rising crime, but does detect concern at the changes in family life it has brought.

Similarly, Karma Phuntsho, a Bhutanese scholar of Buddhism at Cambridge University, laments the consumerism sweeping Bhutan. People, he says, are becoming restless and materialistic. 'The invisible culture is at stake.' In Thimphu's bars, young people are glued to Spanish football matches, or listen to pop music (performed by young men in ghos), or play video games in a dingy arcade. Many carry mobile phones, introduced last year. The shops are small, but full of imported goods.

Traffic lights will surely come. In its capital at least, Bhutan, sad to say, is becoming more like everywhere else.

GNH, in one sense, is an expression of that nostalgia, and an appeal for alertness about what might be lost under the incoming tide of modernity. But an eighty-year-old woman in a village near Paro has a different perspective. Asked about the changes she has seen, she can think of nothing bad to say about them: electric light, which came ten years ago, is better than a smoky kerosene lamp; taking a bus up the new asphalt road, down which all those evil influences roar, is better than walking along a muddy path. The good old days? Bah.

~

John Lancaster
Outracing the Sea, Orphans in His Care

The Washington Post
30 December 2004

Navalady, Sri Lanka: TWO HUNDRED YARDS from the beach, in the orphanage he had built, Dayalan Sanders lounged in his bed early Sunday morning. He was thinking, he said, about the sermon he was due to deliver in the chapel in half an hour. A few yards away, most of the twenty-eight children under his care were still in their rooms, grooming themselves for services.

**More than 230,000 people were killed by the Asian tsunami of 26 December 2004, along the coasts of Indonesia, Sri Lanka, Thailand and India, triggered by a 8.9 magnitude quake off the coast of Sumatra.*

Then he heard the pounding of feet in the corridor outside his room, and his wife burst through the door, a frantic look on her face.

'The sea is coming!' she said. 'Come! Come! Look at the sea!'

But the children did not die. Thanks to quick thinking, blind luck and an outboard motor that somehow started on the first pull, the orphans and their caretakers joined the ranks of countless survivors of the epic earthquake and coastal disaster that so far has claimed over 100,000 lives in Sri Lanka and eleven other countries. This is their story.

It is also the story of their chief rescuer, Sanders, a Sri Lankan-born missionary and US citizen whose mother and siblings live in Gaithersburg, where he once owned a townhouse. A member of the country's Tamil ethnic minority, Sanders, fifty, studied to be an accountant before founding a missionary group and moving to Switzerland in the 1980s. He worked with Tamil refugees displaced by fighting between Tamil rebels and Sri Lankan government forces, both of which have been observing a cease-fire since 2002.

In 1994, Sanders founded the Samaritan Children's Home in Navalady, a small fishing village that occupies a narrow peninsula on Sri Lanka's economically depressed eastern coast, about 150 miles east of Colombo, the capital. He built the orphanage with donations and money from the sale of his Maryland townhouse, he said.

With ocean on one side and a lagoon on the other, the four-acre orphanage was a strikingly beautiful place, set in a grove of stately palms. The children—some of whom had lost their parents in the civil war—lived four to a room in whitewashed cottages with red tile roofs and attended school in the village nearby. Bougainvillaea spilled from concrete planters.

'People used to come and take photographs of the flowers,' said Sanders, a handsome, youthful-looking man who speaks precise idiomatic English and peppers his conversation with scripture. 'They used to say it looked like Eden.'

It was a busy, happy time at the orphanage. On Friday, the children sang, danced and performed the Nativity scene at their annual Christmas pageant, followed the next day by Christmas services and dinner for 250 guests, many of them Hindus from the nearby village. Sanders was so exhausted by his duties as host, he said, that he went to bed early on Saturday night. He also forgot to check, as he usually does, on whether the outboard motor had been removed from the orphanage launch, as it was supposed to be each night as a precaution against theft.

It proved to be the luckiest mistake he ever made.

'A Thunderous Roar'

On Sunday morning, Sanders said, he rose at his customary hour of 4 a.m. to wander the grounds and pray, then went back to bed. He woke up again about 7.30. He recalled the stillness. Not a breath of air stirred the surface of the sea. Small waves rolled listlessly onto the beach, then retreated with a gentle hiss.

'It was so calm and so still,' he recalled. 'The surface of the ocean was like a sheet of glass. Not a leaf moved.' Two young men on his staff wandered down to the ocean for a swim.

It isn't clear who saw the wave first. Sanders's wife, Kohila, said she was alerted by one of the orphans, a girl who burst into the kitchen as Kohila was mixing powdered milk for her three-year-old daughter. Kohila ran into the brilliant sunshine and saw the building sea. Even the colour of the water was wrong: It looked, she said, 'like ash'.

Kohila ran to inform her husband, who told her not to panic, he recalled. 'I said, "Be calm. God is with us. Nothing will ever harm us without His permission."' Wrapped in a sarong, he ran outside and looked toward the ocean. There on the horizon, he said, was a '30-foot wall of water', racing toward the wispy casuarina pines that marked the landward side of the beach.

With barely any time to think, let alone act, he ran toward the lagoon side of the compound, where the launch with its outboard motor chafed at a pier. By then, many of the children had heard the commotion and run outside, some of them half-dressed. Sanders shouted at the top of his lungs, urging them all towards the boat.

Desperate, he asked if anyone had seen his daughter, and a moment later one of the older girls thrust the child into his arms. Sanders heaved her into the boat, along with the other small children, as the older ones, joined by his wife and the orphanage staff, clambered aboard on their own. One of his employees yanked on the starter cord and the engine sputtered instantly to life—something that Sanders swears had never happened before.

'Usually you have to pull it four or five times,' he said.

Crammed with more than thirty people, the dangerously overloaded launch roared into the lagoon at almost precisely the same moment, Sanders said, that the wall of water overwhelmed the orphanage, swamping its single-story buildings to the rafters.

'It was a thunderous roar, and black sea,' he said.

As the compound receded behind the boat, Sanders said, he watched in amazement as the surging current smashed a garage and ejected a brand-new Toyota pickup. 'The roof came flying off—it just splintered in every direction,' he recalled. 'I saw the Toyota just pop out of the garage.'

The vehicle bobbed briefly on the surface, collided with a palm tree—the mark of its impact was clearly visible on Wednesday—then slid over the edge of the compound in the torrent before slipping beneath the rapidly rising surface of the lagoon. Another vehicle, a maroon van, was smashed against a palm tree. A three-wheeled motorized rickshaw parked on the property whirled around as if it were circling a drain, Kohila Sanders recalled.

A Narrow Escape

The orphans' ordeal did not end when their boat pulled away from the shore.

Not only was water cascading over the lagoon side of the peninsula but it was pouring in directly from the mouth of the estuary about two miles away. Sanders feared the converging currents would swamp the small craft. At that point, Sanders said, he recalled a line from the Book of Isaiah: 'When the enemy comes in like a flood, the spirit of the Lord shall raise up a standard against it.'

He raised his hand in the direction of the flood and shouted, 'I command you in the name of Jesus—stop!' The water then seemed to 'stall, momentarily', he said. 'I thought at the time I was imagining things.'

As the launch then headed away from the mouth of the lagoon, he began to worry that waves would overtake them from behind, swamping the small boat. Reasoning that it was better to hit the waves head on, he said, he ordered the helmsman to reverse direction and head back toward the open ocean.

But that manoeuvre carried its own risks. As it made for the mouth of the lagoon, the boat was broadsided and nearly capsized by the torrent pouring over the peninsula. 'The children were very frightened,' recalled Kohila Sanders, thirty. 'We were praying, "God help us, God help us."' As the waters began to roll back out to sea, the turbulence subsided. It was then, Sanders and his wife said, that they became aware of the people crying for help as they bobbed in the water nearby. They were villagers who had been swept off the peninsula. The passengers rescued one young man, who was 'howling for his missing wife and daughters', Kohila Sanders said. But they had to leave the rest behind. There wasn't any room.

'People were crying, "Help us, help us,"' Kohila said. 'Children were crying.'

Eventually the boat made it to the opposite shore, about a mile and a half distant in the city of Batticaloa. Sanders and his wife, their daughter and perhaps a dozen of the orphaned and now-displaced children have found temporary refuge in a tiny church; the rest have been sent elsewhere.

The city is short of food and water, and on Wednesday afternoon, corpses were being burned where they had been found at the edge of the lagoon. With more than 2000 people dead in Batticaloa district, local officials say that they lack the means to dispose of the bodies properly and that residents are burning them as a precaution against disease.

The scene at the orphanage was one of utter devastation. The grounds were covered by upto three feet of sand. Several buildings, including the staff quarters, were entirely wiped away, and the others were damaged beyond repair. A body burned near the ruined chapel.

Surveying the wreckage, Sanders broke down and cried. 'Twenty years of my life put in here, and I saw it all disappear in twenty seconds,' he said between sobs. The orphanage had no insurance.

But at other moments, Sanders was philosophical about his loss. 'If there was anyone who should have got swept away by this tidal wave, it should have been us,' he said. 'We were eyeball to eyeball with the wave.'

~

David Orr
Wodehouse Mania

The Sunday Telegraph
13 February 2005

Delhi: IT IS HARD to know what P.G. Wodehouse would have made of the Indian world of information technology. Like the butler Jeeves when confronted with one of his master's more garish suits, he would probably have found it 'a trifle too bizarre'. About the 'high tech' community's view of the author, however, there can be no doubt—India's 'techies' are in the throes of an obsession with all things Wodehouse.

'This fascination has really grown because of the internet,' says Ranga Nathan (twenty-nine), a software marketing specialist and a member of 'Wodehouse India', a web group whose mostly Indian membership also includes fans from the UK. 'I get about forty or fifty e-mails a day from other members and I reply to about half a dozen. I've made so many friends this way. Wodehouse has really become a big thing in the "IT" world.'

This most English of writers has always had a strong following in India. Scratch any Indian with a reading habit, they say, and you will find a Wodehouse fan underneath. What is surprising, however, is that the author—once regarded as 'The Master' and now widely seen as 'outdated' in his native land—should have gained such a fan base among the computer whiz kids of India's IT industry.

Every large Indian city has its Wodehouse club or discussion group but the southern city of Bangalore has become the centre of Wodehouse mania. The subcontinent's fastest-growing 'cyber city', Bangalore has a huge population of IT workers who are well-read, well-off and quite Westernized.

'At college, I thought there were only a couple of others like me but when I moved to Bangalore, I discovered there were lots of people far crazier than me about Wodehouse,' says Deepak Misra (forty), a manager in one of the city's leading multinational IT companies. 'I'd say we're a pretty progressive, liberal lot drawn together by our love of this writer.'

As well as exchanging Wodehouse lore on the Internet, Mr Misra and other members of the online group meet up in a restaurant every month or two for discussions about 'Plum' and his oeuvre. When they travel, they contact Wodehouse fans in other cities. Towards the end of last year, they attended a Wodehouse quiz evening at the British Council library in Bangalore and hope to organize more such events. Each member has adopted the name of a character from the novels.

'I can tell you, we get some pretty curious looks from other diners when we address each other by our nicknames,' says Mr Misra, known to his peers as J. Hamilton Beamish. 'This is a character from my favourite novel, *The Small Bachelor*. He's an efficiency expert with a very logical mind and can talk on any subject under the sun.'

One subject often discussed by 'Wodehouse India' members is why the author should be so popular in India. Rashmi Rao (thirty-eight), a business analyst who goes by the name of 'Claire Lippett', believes it has something to do with the country's colonial past. Ramakrishnan Gangadharan (twenty-eight), a software engineer known as 'Psmith', believes the author's use of language is crucial. Ranga Nathan ('The Crumpet') agrees.

'Indians love playing with words and transposing them from one language to another,' says Mr Nathan who speaks Tamil, Hindi and English. 'We can really appreciate his rich use of language. I think we also relate to the strong social hierarchy found in the novels. This is something we can understand even if we don't have retinues of servants ourselves. And then there's the cricket . . .'

Wodehouse's works are sold on Indian railway station platforms and airport bookstalls alongside the latest blockbusters. At British Council libraries in the main Indian cities, demand for Wodehouse reputedly outstrips that for any other author. Questions about Bertie Wooster and the Empress of Blandings remain staples of every Indian TV quiz.

'It was the writer Malcolm Muggeridge who remarked that the Indians are now the last Englishmen,' says Shashi Tharoor, Under Secretary-General for Communications at the United Nations. 'That may be why they love such a quintessentially English writer.'

Whatever the reason, as a new generation of Indians forge their way into cyberspace, there is every sign that the love affair with 'Plum' will go from strength to strength.

~

Simon Denyer
Fear Rules in Nepal's Maoist Heartland

Reuters
21 March 2005

Kasala, Nepal: A BOY IN green combat fatigues emerges at the trailhead. The child, scarcely taller than the rustic rifle he is carrying, stops to take a rest. Around his head, a scarf from the movie *Titanic*.

He looks little more than ten years old.

Half a dozen boys follow, all with guns. Then comes a stream of girls, perhaps a little older, most carrying rifles, one with a guitar sporting a Union Jack sticker on its side.

This is the village militia of Nepal's Maoist revolutionary force.

'They are not fighters,' insists a nervous Maoist cadre, Comrade 'Adiga', parrying the unspoken charge that the revolution might employ child soldiers. 'They take care of the village, simple policing, and just keep watch.'

This is the heart of Maoist-controlled Nepal, the Himalayan foothills where the rebels draw recruits to fight a nine-year insurgency

**On 24 April 2006 Nepal's King Gyanendra bowed to weeks of street protests, reinstated the country's dissolved Parliament and handed over power to a multi-party government. Seven months later, the government and the Maoists signed a peace accord under which the rebels gathered in camps under UN supervision and kept their weapons under lock and key. Of 31,000 fighters in the camps, the UN later found that nearly 3,000 were children under the age of eighteen. In December 2007, the mainstream political parties and the Maoists agreed to abolish the 239-year-old monarchy and turn Nepal into a republic.*

that has cost 11,000 lives and brought the country to the brink of a humanitarian catastrophe.

Last month King Gyanendra sacked the government and seized power in Kathmandu, pledging to crush the Maoist rebellion. Here, though, among the ripening wheat fields, remote mountain terraces and forests, the king and his army seem a world away.

'Let's enter the first phase of the strategic offensive and raise the process of revolutionary transformation to a new height,' proclaims a banner over the dusty mountain trail near the village of Kasala in the western district of Rolpa.

A red hammer and sickle flutters in the breeze.

At a rocky trail-side rest stop, a young man smartly dressed in a black shirt and jeans, Chinese Goldstar sneakers on his feet, a black Nike baseball cap on his head, pauses for a chat.

Six years ago, he sat with four friends in the isolated mountain village of Gumchal, bemoaning the lack of development, electricity, opportunity. The police burst in, accused them of being Maoists and beat them with rifle butts.

The next day he ran away to join the 'People's Liberation Army'.

'The army calls us terrorists, but we are fighting for the country and people,' he said, giving his party name, Comrade Sunil.

'The government has no interest in the problems of ethnic minorities and the poor. If the government was sincere in providing health, education and transport, we would have no need to shed our blood.'

Sunil is on his way home to see his family, on a week's leave after a successful attack to burn down government offices in nearby Agarkhanchi district.

Four girls walk past in the opposite direction, on their way to rejoin the rebel army after their week's leave. Their hair freshly cut in bobs, some with fresh nail polish, the only giveaway a pistol which one conceals beneath her T-shirt.

'We are fighting the reactionary army,' says one, smiling and friendly. 'But we cannot say more, we are not allowed to give interviews to anyone who meets us on the trail.'

The Call of the Revolution

Rolpa is one of the poorest districts in one of the world's poorest countries. Thatched clay houses sit amid green and yellow wheat fields on the steep mountain terraces, the scenic beauty concealing an ugly reality.

The average income here is less than $100 a year, easily less than half the national average. There is just one government-built road, a bone-jarring dirt track which snakes along the sides of the steep ravines to the district capital, Liwang.

Healthcare and education are poor or non-existent. Development money almost never reaches the remote mountain villages where the minority ethnic Magar group make their homes.

It is easy to see why many young men and women here heed the call of the revolution.

Fifteen years of chaotic and corrupt multi-party democracy ended when Gyanendra seized power on 1 February. Sunil has little affection for the parties, still less for the monarch, who he describes as 'selfish'.

The king's power grab, he says, has left the Maoists in a head-on fight with the king, a fight they think they can win, on the path to a communist republic.

'All the politicians did was build high-rises in Kathmandu,' he said. 'That is why we think the multi-party system has no future.'

His calmness and sincerity shine through as he chats for more than an hour about his vision for the country's future, as a small crowd gathers. For a while, the wheat fields go untended.

In just nine years the rebels have gone from a small band of unarmed militants to a force that runs much of Nepal's countryside. But today the movement stands at something of a crossroads.

Militarily, they are almost impossible to dislodge from their remote rural strongholds. But they lack the firepower to challenge Nepal's army directly or take a district capital for more than a few hours.

They have another problem too, and that is to sustain the revolutionary fervour that has brought them this far. For the passion of the cadres cannot obscure an ugly side to the revolution.

They may claim to be fighting for the poor, but it is fear not fervour that rules these mountainsides.

The rebels demand at least one person per household work for the party. Many end up in the Maoist army.

'You cannot refuse them,' said a teacher in one village. 'Anyone who is fourteen could be asked to go.'

Younger children are not spared. Many are taken from school for a few months to join the militia ranks and indoctrinated in the party's ideology, said a local aid worker. Some work as porters and messengers.

After falling behind their classmates, many do not want to return to the education system.

'Parents are in a panic,' said a local health worker. 'They want to send their children away before they are taken by the Maoists.'

Rebel soldiers, unpaid by the movement, demand food, shelter and taxes from people who have scarcely enough to survive. Several days a month, villagers are forced to leave their fields and attend unpopular indoctrination sessions.

'Maybe only thirty or forty per cent of people here support them,' said a local aid worker. 'The rest only support them out of compulsion.'

'Martyrs' Road'

The Maoists are trying to win the hearts and minds of the people they claim to represent, building what they are calling 'Martyrs' Road', a 90 kilometre (55 mile) dirt road winding through pine and rhododendron forests.

Near the small village of Triveni at the head of the road, a steady stream of women and girls plod up from the river bed, each balancing a heavy stone on her head.

Above them, teams of workmen chip away at a rock face with pick axes.

'The government calls us terrorists but we want to prove we are capable of mobilizing hundreds of thousands of people in a cause that benefits them,' said a leading regional official, Comrade Surya, his name the Nepali word for sun.

Surya said the rebels were making history by being the first insurgent movement to undertake large-scale development while still fighting a war. Two bodyguards stood close by, red cloth stuffed in their rifle barrels to keep out the dust.

But is this really a 'historic' case of revolutionary development, or simply a sinister example of forced labour on a massive scale?

None of the people working on this road are paid or even fed. Some are Maoist cadres who have 'volunteered' their labour.

Many are locals who are simply expected to contribute to the cause.

An army helicopter buzzes far overhead, scanning this 'enemy' road, a calculated insult to the fading power of Nepal's state. Shortly after construction began last November, there was a lone raid. Since then the army has left the Maoist labour teams alone.

The rebel authorities in Rolpa have asked every family to contribute one person's labour for ten days to help build the road. So far, 60,000 people have taken part, Surya said. Some have to walk several days to get here.

At the end of a hard day's work, dozens sit by the roadside to watch a three-hour video about the 'People's War'. Before they finally return to their villages, they will also be treated to a cultural programme and political discussions.

It could take three years to reach the road's final destination at Thawang, a small village the rebels consider their symbolic capital.

Some, like local woman Sita, say they are happy to contribute to a road that could bring the development they crave. Many, though, are scared the army could one day mount a major attack, and some have fled.

Others are unhappy to be treated as forced labour, or to be taken from their field for regular indoctrination.

'People are scared,' said the keeper of a barely stocked local shop. 'People are forced to work. They cannot say no. They cannot oppose the Maoists.'

There is a suffocating atmosphere in the small village of Triveni and nearby Nuwagaon, around the uncompromising rebels whose rule is law. As the day drew on, a child shouted noisily.

'Keep quiet,' his mother scolded. 'Otherwise the Maoists will come and take you away.'

Alcohol, gambling and prostitution are outlawed in Maoist-controlled Nepal, crime rare. 'People's courts' dispense swift judgements.

Maoist officials say criminals are not locked up, but sentenced to work on community projects or are assigned as house help.

Human rights groups say those who dare to criticize rebel rule often end up dead. Maoist officials reject the charge.

'We only execute people who inform on us to the police and army and get our people killed,' said Comrade Current, a local area chief. 'If they get thirty or forty of us killed, then what is wrong with executing two or three of them?'

~

Amy Waldman
India Accelerating

The New York Times
4 December 2005

New Delhi: IN THE MIDDLE of the old Grand Trunk Road a temple sits under a peepul tree. The surrounding highway is being widened to four lanes, and vehicles barrel along either side. But the temple and tree thwart even greater speed, and a passing contractor says they soon will be removed.

Kali, Hindu goddess of destruction, thinks otherwise. She is angry, say the colourfully garbed women massing in the holy tree's dappled shade. As evidence, they point to one woman's newly pockmarked face and other mysterious ailments recently visited on their nearby village, Jagdishrai. They have tried to convince Kali that the tree and temple devoted to her must go, but they have failed. Now they have no choice but to oppose the removal, too, even if they must block the road to do it.

Goddess versus man, superstition versus progress, the people versus the state—mile by mile, India is struggling to modernize its national highway system, and in the process, itself.

The Indian government has begun a fifteen-year project to widen and pave some 40,000 miles of narrow, decrepit national highways. It amounts to the most ambitious infrastructure project since independence in 1947 and the British building of the subcontinent's railway network the century before.

The effort echoes the United States' construction of its national highway system in the 1920s and 1950s. The arteries paved across

America fuelled commerce and development, fed a nation's auto obsession and created suburbs. They also displaced communities and helped sap mass transit and deplete inner cities.

For India, already one of the world's fastest-growing economies and most rapidly evolving societies, the results may be as radical. At its heart, the redone highway is about grafting Western notions of speed and efficiency onto a civilization that has always taken the long view.

Aryan migration, Mogul conquest, British colonialism—all shaped India's civilization over centuries. Now, in a span of less than fifteen years, capitalism and globalization have convulsed India at an unprecedented rate of change.

The real start came in 1991, when India began dismantling its state-run economy and opening its markets to foreign imports and investment. While that reform process has been fitful, leaving the country trailing its neighbour and rival, China, India has turned a corner. Its economy grew 6.9 per cent in the fiscal year ending in March. India has a new identity, thanks to outsourcing, as back office to the world, and the new highway is certain to jump-start its competitiveness.

To grasp that transformation, and India's transition, a New York Times reporter and photographer spent a month this year driving the first stage of the highway project, which has been dubbed, in awkward but bullish coinage, the Golden Quadrilateral.

More jagged than geometric, the four- and six-lane quadrilateral's 3625 miles run through thirteen states and India's four largest cities: New Delhi, Calcutta, Chennai, formerly Madras, and Mumbai, formerly Bombay. The journey along the highway offered a before-and-after snapshot of India, of the challenges of developing the world's largest democracy, and of how Westernization is reshaping Indian society.

To drive east from New Delhi to Calcutta is to travel through flat fields, almost primeval forests, lush rice paddies—and some of India's poorest, roughest states, where contractors have battled violence and corruption to get the road built.

To move south from Calcutta, alongside the Bay of Bengal, through palm-covered hills, then up the west into Rajasthan's desert, is to see the highway as a conduit for the forces moulding the new India. Ever-flashier cars, evidence of a frenzied new consumerism, leave bullock carts in the dust. Truckers slow at night for roadside sex workers, each of them potential carriers of HIV. Farmers' sons make a beeline for swelling cities that are challenging the village as the centre of Indian life.

The highway itself brings change. For a nation inured to inefficiency, the improved interstate saves time—for Kailash Pandey, a milk-seller, one-third off a ninety-minute commute to market; for Imtiaz Ali, fifteen, half off the bike ride to school; and half off the travel time for Sarjeet Singh, a trucker.

These micro gains make for macro benefit: some $1.5 billion a year in savings, by one World Bank estimate, on everything from fuel costs to faster freight delivery. More intangibly, the highway may turn India into a society in a hurry, enslaving it to the Western notion that time equals money.

Nationalists also hope the highway will further unite a country that is home to twenty-two official languages, the world's major religions, a host of separatist movements, and thirty-five union territories and states, many more populous than European nations.

But coherence may bring collision. Since 1991, India's population of poor has dropped to 26 per cent from 36 per cent, yet the poor seem poorer than ever. India now juxtaposes pre- and post-industrial societies: citizens who live on dirt floors without electricity and others who live like twenty-first-century Americans, only with more servants. The highway throws these two Indias into jarring proximity.

Outside Jaipur, young men virtually bonded into labour hack with primitive tools at old tires. They work in an archaic assembly line beside the highway, chopping the tires into pieces and loading them onto trucks so they can be burned as toxic fuel at a brick kiln. The tent camp they call home splays out in dirty disarray behind them. A brutish overseer verbally whips them to work faster.

'Please take me out of here,' Rafiq Ahmed, twenty-one, whispered as he bent in the darkness to lift another load. 'My back hurts.'

On the revamped road next to him, the darkness has been banished by electric lights overhead. Auto-borne commuters race along six silky lanes toward the Golden Heritage Apartments, the Vishal Mini-Mart, the Bajaj Showroom featuring the New Pulsar 2005 with Alloy Wheels, all the while burning rubber that will eventually fall to the young men, hidden by night, obscured by speed, forgotten by progress, to dispose.

Driving in India has meant more stops than starts, necessitating braking for sacred cows, camel carts, conversational knots, tractors and women balancing bundles of wood on their heads.

The new highway, then, is nothing short of radical, which becomes clear after Agra, where large stretches are already complete. An American-style interstate unfurls through villages where mud-brick buildings rarely rise above two stories and women still cook with buffalo dung. The highway is smooth, wide, flat and incongruous: an ambitious road amid still-humble architecture, a thoroughfare from this century amid scenery from a previous one.

To drive it is to gain momentum, to not want to stop, and not have to. Drivers no longer pass through towns, but by them, or where the highway soars into the air, over them. The rural landscape, formerly painted in pointillist detail, becomes a blur, an abstraction—a vanishing trick that may portend things to come.

Building a highway is by nature a violent act, since everything in its path must yield. So the project has cut a swath of destruction, swallowing thousands of acres of farmland, shearing off the fronts of thousands of homes. Smashed walls and piles of bricks line the route like broken teeth.

In the village of Kaushambi, in Uttar Pradesh, Anil Kumar, a thirty-four-year-old shopkeeper, watched truck traffic speed by on the widened highway and explained how the artery's revamping had reconfigured long-held local geography.

Because vehicles rarely travelled at more than 25 miles an hour, village life had always happened on both sides of the road. The two-lane highway inhabited space, but did not define it. The railway station and village hand pump were on one side, the school and fields on the other. Women roamed across the land, indifferent to whether soil or asphalt was beneath their feet, gathering wood, water, the harvest.

In India roads have been public spaces, home to the logical chaos that governs so much of life. They have been commas, not periods, pauses, not breaks.

The redone highway has challenged that, trying to impose borders and linearity, sometimes controlling pedestrian (and bovine) access to ensure drivers' speed. For many rural Indians, insulated from the Westernizing of urban India, the highway is the most dramatic change in their lifetimes. All along the route, the disorientation showed in the faces of uncomprehending pedestrians who darted out in front of cars coming fast enough to kill.

The highway was bifurcating Kaushambi, too. Villagers had begun pressing district officials for a second hand-pump so women wouldn't have to keep crossing for water.

'It is almost like two villages now,' Mr Kumar said.

Service with a Smile

In a perky blue uniform, thirty-four-year-old Pradeep Kumar stepped forward to pump gas with a smile. He had reason to: he had been coached on American-style, customer-comes-first service, and in an area of north India with rampant unemployment, he was thrilled just to have a job. That it made little use of his bachelor's degree in political science was of secondary concern.

Where crops once grew along the Golden Quadrilateral, gas stations are sprouting. Mr Kumar's employer near Allahabad—Reliance Industries Ltd, one of India's largest private conglomerates and a petroleum giant—is planning 5000 stations. Perhaps more than any company, it has grasped the highway's commercial potential.

Commerce along the American interstate system began with quirky roadside establishments. Over time it evolved toward deliberately homogenized chains—McDonald's, Motel 6—whose signs meant familiarity in unfamiliar terrain.

Reliance has leapfrogged that process, making itself the Golden Arches of the Golden Quadrilateral. Its British-designed gas stations are identically bright and streamlined, with computerized billing and clean, airy dhabas, or restaurants.

The growth of gas stations suggested the way India's agricultural society is yielding not to an industrial economy, but a service one. Fifty per cent of India's gross domestic product is now in the service sector, compared with 25 per cent apiece for manufacturing and agriculture.

In twenty-first-century India, the $50 a month that Mr Kumar, the attendant, was earning was still more than farming would pay.

Bureaucracy and Bandits

In the shade of a makeshift shelter at the border crossing between Uttar Pradesh and Bihar, two truckers were killing time on string cots. They wanted to move from one state to another, but given India's cumbersome, often corrupt interstate bureaucracy, they might as well have been trying to pass to Pakistan.

It was noon, and they had been waiting five hours, their trucks among hundreds parked in endless lines. They figured they would pass by nightfall, after paying a bribe on top of the interstate tax.

The improved highway was already easing their passage and saving them time, the truckers said, cutting their drive from New Delhi to Calcutta to three days from five. They relished the new ease of the ride.

But the improvements had not addressed other obstacles. Petty extortion by officials was common at many border posts. In the north, bandits, or dacoits, robbed truckers on the highway.

'In Bihar, they'll cut off your neck and leave you six inches shorter,' said Rajesh Sham Singh, thirty.

Feats of Engineering

At night on a floodlit bridge in Bihar, a chain of women moved in graceful tandem, hoisting buckets of cement onto their head and hurrying to pour before it hardened. Imported from southern India, they were living in a meagre shanty camp next to the highway, earning less than $40 a month.

Such mingling of primitive methods with the mechanization mostly being used to construct the Quadrilateral fascinated the Korean engineers ensconced 12 miles down the road, in a camp near the town of Aurangabad. Employed by Ssangyong, a construction giant in South Korea, they came to the state of Bihar to work on the highway with an Indian company, Oriental Structural Engineers Pvt. Ltd. 'We in Korea have never seen people putting cement on their heads,' said M.S. Won, a planning engineer. 'We only use machines.'

His boss, Noh Sung Hwan, was a cheery man who spoke a smattering of Hindi and had taught his Indian cook to make kimchi. Having arrived with an appreciation of India's rich engineering history, he was soon well versed in its current challenges.

They had far less to do with building the highway than with the forces circling it. This stretch of Bihar was home to often violent local mafias, some tied to a Maoist insurgency that has spread through at least eleven states.

Some three years ago the Maoists attacked a construction plant for the highway, and fractured the bones of a project manager with rifle butts and sticks. The Maoists occupied the plant for months while negotiations dragged on over how much it would cost to buy their cooperation.

'India is very fantastic,' Mr Noh said. 'Just a little bit risky.'

A Study in Limits

For four years, the Indian project managers and engineers of Oriental Structural had been living in enclosed camps next to the highway, serenaded nonstop by truck horns.

In the camp near Aurangabad, Bihar, eighteen families and some thirty single men found their entertainment in a volleyball and badminton court, television and cold beer. Most of them were from Punjab or southern India. Bihar was as much of a foreign country to them as it was to their Korean counterparts, a country they could not wait to leave.

The sociologist Yogendra Yadav calls Bihar a metaphor: for the rest of India, it represents being poor. Bihar offers a reflection at which ascendant India recoils.

Bihar is home to more than eighty-two million people and some of India's most storied history. Bodhgaya, where Buddha achieved enlightenment, is only a few miles off the highway. The area was once a centre of democracy and learning, and of India's freedom struggle against the British.

Today, Bihar is a study in democracy's limits. Villagers depend on doctors who are quacks, schoolteachers who siphon government grain meant for children, policemen who charge businesses to provide security.

Bihar, by most measures, is India's poorest state. Migration to other states for work is epidemic. Only 5 per cent of rural households have electricity.

Biharis did not want the road, one engineer asserted, because they preferred a potholed one that would make it easier to rob passing trucks.

Farther east along the highway, near the town of Mahapur, dozens of armed guards patrolled another camp where more Oriental Structural employees had bunkered down. Its chief project manager, P. Nageswara Rao, grey-haired, and on this project, usually grim-faced, never left camp without an armed escort.

Buddha preached ahimsa, or non-violence, in the area, 'but the most crime is here', he said. 'For nothing they will kill the people.'

His camp operated under an even greater threat of violence. What appeared to be an armed robbery nearby took the life of a government engineer working on the project; it took seven months to fill his shoes. Government had all but melted away here. From the highway, the Maoists extorted money and, for followers, jobs.

The Maoist movement had begun with a 1968 agrarian peasant uprising in West Bengal. In the years since, Naxalites, as the rebels are known, have flourished, penetrating, with arms and ideology, the many corners where prosperity has yet to reach.

Mahapur, Bihar, is one such corner.

Poverty and Promise

In a gilding morning light on the margins of the Grand Trunk Road, a fight broke out over wet concrete.

A hailstorm the night before soaked the ground before the concrete could finish drying. So scarecrow-like scavengers had come out to scrounge the wet muck. An emaciated Bishnuji Bagwan, at least ninety and wearing little more than rags, had brought his wife, children and grandchildren to collect enough of it to shore up his dilapidated house. Malti Devi, mother of four, married to a man she called useless, wanted to smooth her floor.

One family accused another of greed, and the fight began. Ms Devi shrugged off the finger-pointing, hoisted a load atop her head, and headed across the highway.

'It's my share of concrete,' she said. 'If someone takes it, won't I fight?'

She called the highway a 'blessing', and said she had never seen anything like it. And it holds promise for Indians like her, with data showing that proximity to a real highway could alleviate poverty.

For now, the villagers living along the route rarely had bus fare to reach nearby Mahapur. For them, the highway was more spectacle than utility.

An American Dream

As Ms Devi was lugging wet concrete into her mud house, Mr Rao, the project manager, was counting the days until he could take highway, train and plane, and escape for a holiday in America.

He had three daughters living there, one a computer engineer, the other two married to computer engineers. Most of his engineers—almost all, like him, from the southern state of Andhra Pradesh—had relatives in America, too.

If Bihar was enemy territory for the professionals roosting in rugged camps to build India's dream highway, America was the promised land. India's traffic with America has never been higher; sending a child there had become a middle-class 'craze,' in one engineer's word.

The founding elites of India were British-educated. Today, the ambitious young pursue degrees from Wharton and Stanford, with some 80,000 Indian students in the United States. Two million Indians live there, working as doctors, software engineers, and motel owners along America's highways.

No surprise, then, that America has shaped the ideas of what India's highway can be. Mr Rao's deputy, B.K. Rami Reddy, also with a daughter in America, was nearly breathless as he described one stretch of finished roadway in southern India: 'You really feel like you are in the US, it is so nice. When you go on that road, you feel you are somewhere else.'

~

Padma Rao

'A Few Seagulls, Tarzans and Man Fridays' Britain's Dirtiest Secret

Der Spiegel 5 December 2005

Port Louis, Mauritius: *'J'ai quitté mon pays, J'ai quitté mon petit île, J'ai laissé ma famille, J'ai ausssi laissé mon coeur.'* A small group of people will chant the elegiac ditty outside London's Royal Courts of Justice on Thursday this week. They will be singing about paradise and heartbreak—but also about Britain's dirtiest and most well-kept secrets.

How Her Majesty's government 'sanitized' the tiny Chagos archipelago in the Indian Ocean of almost 2000 native islanders—its own subjects—whom it dismissed as 'some few Tarzans and Man Fridays' not in a bygone era of slavery, but just thirty years ago.

How British officials terrified the Chagossians by first starving them, then gassing their domestic pets to death in front of their children and finally forcing them into the holds of ships to be dumped four days later, on the docks of Seychelles and Mauritius, 2000 miles away.

And how, for US$14 million disguised as a discount on Polaris nuclear missiles, Britain leased Diego Garcia, the Chagos' largest island to the United States to build its most important overseas military base in 1973, assuring them and the United Nations that the atolls were uninhabited, insignificant specks of British territory in the Indian Ocean.

The saga began in the early sixties when the Americans were looking for strategically-located overseas bases in the Indian Ocean to contain

**The Royal Courts of Justice turned down the Queen's Order-in-Council in 2006 and again recognized the Chagossians' right to return to their homeland. To date, and other than organizing yet another 'junket' to the neighbouring islands and back, the British Foreign Office has shown no signs of compliance. Bancoult and the Chagossians are tired and are now speaking of 'taking matters into their own hands and setting sail for their home, come what may'. For now, the British Foreign Office has organized yet another trip for a select group of Chagossians to the Chagos archipelago to clean up the graves of their ancestors.*

Iran, the Soviet Union and China. For a lease on any of several islands still under the British Crown—thought most, like Mauritius, to which Chagos then belonged, were clamouring for independence—Washington turned to London for help.

Aldabra in the southern Seychelles and not Diego Garcia, was the US' first choice, but the island was also home to a rare breed of giant tortoises and the British reared the wrath of animal rights activists.

Evidently, Chagos stirred no such qualms. British and US officials began arriving on island-hopping trips and their visits are well-documented on archival film footage.

For five generations and since their forefathers were first brought here in the late 1700s as slaves from Madagascar, Mozambique, Senegal and southern India by French and later British colonists, Chagossian islanders had pressed *copra*, or desiccated coconut for oil to light the lamps of neighbouring Seychelles and Mauritius. Chagos came to be known as the Oil Islands, and living conditions for the labourers who were paid in commodities like rice and milk, were good.

There was a church, a school and even a small railway line. For husking and crushing 700 coconuts per person, per day, from 7 a.m. to 12 noon—and perhaps in return for devotion to the church (all Chagossian were devout Christians), the plantation-owners ensured housing and basic medical facilities on the three largest islands, Diego Garcia, Peros Banhos and Salomon.

There were ponies and donkeys, pigs, poultry and house pets. In the afternoons, there was ample fishing in the lagoons that fringed the islands. It was a simple, fulfilled life, and the islanders showed off their loyalties by flying the Union Jack and the Chagossian coat-of-arms of three turtles, from the lowest tin-roofs.

The US approved of Diego Garcia—the largest island—but asked for it to be first 'swept clean'.

The British Foreign Office, as aware of the presence of the sizeable native population on Chagos as the visiting US navy personnel but worried about the questions the United Nations (UN) would inevitably raise about their welfare, began to weave an elaborate web of deceit.

A flurry of communication and footnotes flew between London and the British mission at the UN.

First, there was a suggestion to pass off the Chagossians as mere 'transient workers' from Mauritius or Seychelles. But when Office's own new survey of the Chagossians' ethnicity proved this absurd, it was decided to keep the matter hidden from the world body altogether.

'I would advise a policy of quiet disregard—in other words, let's forget about this one till the United Nations challenges it,' advised one civil servant in an internal memo.

Mauritius soon strained for independence, and Britain saw its opportunity. The former got its freedom but at a price: Chagos.

While countries across the world were shaking off European colonial rule, Britain declared a fresh colony: The British Indian Ocean Territory (BIOT) of Chagos.

Finally, it was going to be possible to evict the islanders in a covert operation and declare the islands as 'uninhabited', if later required by the UN.

In August 1966, Permanent Under-Secretary at the Colonial Office Peter Greenhill—later Baron Greenhill of Harrow in the House of Lords—had his secretary, Patrick Wright dispatch a note to the British mission at the UN.

'We must surely by very tough about this,' wrote Wright. 'The object of the exercise was to get some rocks (Chagos) which will remain ours, there will be no indigenous population except seagulls.'

In a footnote, Greenhill lent his own wit.

'Along with the Birds go some few Tarzans and Man Fridays . . . who are being hopefully wished upon Mauritius,' he added.

The sequence of nefarious deals begun in 1965 and in violation of every tenet governing human rights in the UN charter, reached its conclusion after the forcible deportation was completed in 1973.

Since then and swelled in exile to more than 5500, the Chagossians live in shantytowns and on the fringes of society: 4500 in ten poor neighbourhoods of the Mauritian capital Port Louis, 650 in Seychelles, and some 300 housed near Gatwick Airport in London. The Creole-speaking islanders are plagued by squalor, poverty, drugs, alcoholism, prostitution, a high incidence of HIV, unemployment and social discrimination.

By the mid-eighties, the British government had paid each islander a total compensation of UK£3000, and tried—illegally again—to get as many of them as possible to place their thumbprints on a document relinquishing their rights over Chagos, in exchange for the money.

A judicial struggle began in 1998. As poor subjects of the Crown, the Chagossians could access British legal aid. They also received support from sympathetic British MPs—both Labour and Tory, the Mauritian government—itself keen to restore its sovereignty over Chagos—and left-wing Mauritian groups that wanted the US base on Diego Garcia closed altogether.

Importantly, the British High Court granted the Chagossians' legal term—headed by Nelson Mandela's own advocate Sir Sydney Kentridge—access to classified documents in the British Records Office. The secret correspondence and handwritten footnotes exchanged by Britain's top civil servants under then Prime Minister Harold Wilson over Diego Garcia, provided the final, clinching evidence.

In a historic judgement, the British High Court in 2000 declared the eviction of Chagossian islanders 'illegal' and ordered the British government to ensure their return home.

But thirty years after acquiring it, Diego Garcia, or 7 00 S, 71 30 E, as the US navy refers to it, had now become its most 'indispensable' overseas platform.

This is where B-52s and Stealth bombers headed for Afghanistan and Iraq had taken off, this is where Camp Justice to interrogate Al Qaeda suspects is located.

There are two runways, jetties and piers, a natural lagoon and a deep harbour for thirty war ships. There are weapon ranges and training areas, there are dumps for oil, petrol and aviation fuel. From Diego Garcia, the United States effectively polices the oil routes across the Indian Ocean and keeps an eye on China. This is where more than 4000 servicemen and casual contract workers—drawn from Sri Lanka, Philippines but none from Diego Garcia itself—are stationed.

'Diego Garcia is continuously experiencing rapid growth and change . . . to meet both your professional and personal needs,' exclaims the US navy webpage. 'Living and working conditions are outstanding. Recreational opportunities are numerous and we are constantly expanding facilities to make life more comfortable.'

There are bars, a cinema, restaurants and water sports in the translucent lagoons. The Chagos islands are a palm-fringed utopia tourists would pay thousands of dollars to escape to, and yet remain off bounds to all except a British Representative and the visiting families of US army personnel.

In June 2004 and compelled to respond to the High Court verdict, the British Foreign Office promised it would organize a brief visit for the exile Chagossians to all other islands except Diego Garcia, and cited various obscure reasons for doing so.

On the other hand, Washington warned that it had no intention of ever leaving Diego Garcia, not now or even when its lease expired in 2016. Nor was it going to allow the former coconut plantation workers back onto even just the neighbouring islands, as they could introduce 'surveillance, monitoring and electronic jamming devices' that could 'place at risk vital military operations'.

British diplomats went into a fresh huddle to invent new tactics to delay the permanent return of the Chagossians as ordered by the High Court.

Soon, they announced that a 'feasibility study' had found it was going to be too expensive for the British taxpayer to rebuild infrastructure in Chagos and repatriate the islanders.

'I've got sympathy . . . but this is today, almost forty years after the event,' argued British Foreign Office Minister, Bill Rammell, in *Stealing a Nation*, a gripping television documentary containing archival footage by award-winning British journalist John Pilger, that shocked British viewers last year. 'The government and the British taxpayers have to choose whether to finance that (Chagos), or . . . help poor people throughout the world.'

The Chagossians' attorney, Richard Gifford points that the minister himself had earlier estimated the cost of rebuilding to be £5 million. 'That's peanuts—it's the cost of one embassy building in London.'

As pressure mounted from both the Chagossians urging the implementation of the High Court order and the United States to not do so, the British Foreign Office ran out of excuses and went for the jugular.

In a move once again befitting a totalitarian state, it got Queen Elizabeth II to initial a rarely invoked 'Order in Council', essentially a royal decree circumventing parliamentary scrutiny and overruling the High Court judgement.

In June 2004 and on Election Day when her subjects were preoccupied with the future of their own country, Her Majesty banned the islanders from ever returning to their homeland.

With the last remnants of their dwindling British legal aid, the islanders' trip to England will this week challenge the Queen and therewith the ancient medieval law that gives British governments such extraordinary powers to bypass public scrutiny, once again at the Royal Courts of Justice.

'Was Her Majesty given an opportunity to read what she was signing?' asks Oliver Bancoult, an electrician by day and the Chagossian groups' leader by night. 'Did she remember how Britain sent entire fleets to defend the rights of 2000 Falkland islanders, but will strip us 2000 Chagossians of ours, even though we all are all loyal to the same Crown?'

Like Bancoult—whose three brothers died of alcoholism and drug overdose and whose sister killed herself in exile, Chagossians have been riddled with drugs, disease and suicides over the past thirty years in exile. But they still insist that their greatest killer has been '*chagrin*', Creole for sadness.

On the walls of the Chagos Refugee Group's small office in the poor Port Louis neighbourhood of Cassis hangs a framed photograph of Bancoult with Nelson Mandela, who along with Mahatma Gandhi, remain a shining inspiration for the peaceful Chagossian struggle. There is also a lithograph of the Magna Carta of 1215, whose promise of the 'right of all Englishmen to live in their homeland without fear of removal', was instrumental in winning the Chagossians the historic judgement of 2000. And occupying pride of place in the middle is a weathered map of the Chagos atolls, scattered like tiny pearls across a aquamarine swathe of velvet sea.

The print on the old map may be fading, but in the narrow lanes of Cassis' shantytown and astonishingly so, faith in the British sense of 'fair play' still lives on.

'I was born in Diego Garcia, my children were born here but our accents and shabby clothes still give us away as the *llois* from Chagos,' says factory worker, Rita Baptiste, fifty-six, as she runs her hand over the coconut scythe and small wooden box she was allowed to bring in the stifling hold of the ship all those years ago. 'I am sure the Court will understand that and return us to our home soon.'

The small tin shack is cluttered with disparate objects but there is the ubiquitous portrait of the Duke of Edinburgh as also a poster of Manchester United on an asbestos partition.

For others like truck driver Norbet L'Emclume of Salomon Island, memories of Chagos are bitter sweet. Tears roll down his cheeks as he remembers his first wife and two children who lie buried there.

As the sixty-five-year-old dangles his thin, useless legs—paralysed in an accident—at a rickety table with his head bowed in hazy memory, chickens cluck, his second wife hangs clothes on the cramped courtyard, teenagers stare vacantly into space and rattle a mindless rhythm with pebbles inside an empty can. Babies play on old mattresses, the only bedding for the family of twelve, piled up across an open drain and supported by cardboard boxes.

'We didn't know money or need it,' says L'Emclume, wiping his rheumy eyes with sudden vigour as though to catch a glimpse of those better days. 'It was a good life, another life.'

Chagossian leader Bancoult and his lawyers have also appealed to courts in the United States and as British-EU citizens, to the European Court of Justice in Strasbourg. 'Europe has such a good record of human rights,' says Bancoult. 'So it's important they know what the current EU chair and the champion of human rights in his election manifesto of 1998, Mr Tony Blair, has been doing to us.'

The islanders' struggle is no romantic quest for a Paradise Lost, nor are they asking the United States to withdraw from Diego Garcia. They are well aware that they will remain British, eager to develop their islands into tourist havens but also grateful for any civilian employment at the US base.

'We are a small people with no blue eyes, blond hair or an education,' says Bancoult. 'But we beg the world to respect our dignity and help us go home.'

~

Somini Sengupta

In India, Maoist Guerrillas Widen 'People's War'

The New York Times
13 April 2006

Bhanupratapur Forest Reserve: THE GREY LIGHT of dawn broke over the bamboo forest as the People's Liberation Guerrilla Army prepared for a new day.

With transistor radios tucked under their arms, the soldiers listened to the morning news and brushed their teeth. A few young recruits busied themselves making a remote-control detonator for explosives.

The company commander, Gopanna Markam, patiently shaved.

'We have made the people aware of how to change your life through armed struggle, not the ballot,' said Mr Markam, who is in his mid-forties, describing his troops' accomplishments. 'This is a people's war, a protracted people's war.'

Mr Markam's ragtag forces, who hew to Mao's script for a peasant revolution, fought a seemingly lost cause for so long, they were barely taken seriously beyond India's desperately wanting forest belt. But not anymore.

Today the fighting that Mr Markam has quietly nurtured for twenty-five years looks increasingly like a civil war, one claiming more and more lives and slowing the industrial growth of a country hungry for the coal, iron and other riches buried in these isolated realms bypassed by India's economic boom.

While the far more powerful Maoist insurgency in neighbouring Nepal has received greater attention, the conflict in India, though largely separate, has gained momentum, too. In the last year, it has cost nearly a thousand lives.

Here in central Chhattisgarh state, the deadliest theatre of the war, government-aided village defence forces have lately taken to hunting Maoists in the forests. Hand in hand with the insurgency, the militias have dragged the region into ever more deadly conflict.

Villagers, caught in between, have seen their hamlets burned. Nearly 50,000 are now displaced, living in flimsy tent camps, as the counter-insurgency tries to cleanse the countryside of Maoist support.

The insurgents blow up railway tracks, seize land and chase away forest guards. They have made it virtually impossible for government officials, whose presence here in the hinterland is already patchy, to function. Police posts, government offices and industrial plants are favoured targets. Their ultimate goal is to overthrow the state.

Today the Communist Party of India (Maoist), which exists solely as an underground armed movement with no political representation, is a rigidly hierarchical outfit with toe-holds in thirteen of twenty-eight Indian states. It stretches from the tip of India through this east-central state to the northern border with Nepal, where the Maoists have set off full-scale civil war.

Estimates by Indian intelligence officials and Maoist leaders suggest that the rebel ranks in India have swelled to 20,000, though the number is impossible to verify. One senior Indian intelligence official estimated that Maoists exert varying degrees of influence over a quarter of India's 600 districts.

The top government official in one of Chhattisgarh's rural Maoist strongholds, Dantewada, acknowledged that the rebels had made some 60 per cent of his 6400-square-mile district a no man's land for civil servants.

Not that there are many civil servants. His district's police department has a vacancy rate hovering around 35 per cent; in health care, it is 20 per cent.

A Durable Rebel Movement

The Maoist insurgents are also known in India as Naxalites, after Naxalbari, the town north of Calcutta where an armed communist rebellion first erupted thirty-eight years ago. It was quickly put down, then quietly reappeared.

Local police forces, with their feeble jeeps and outdated guns, have been largely unable to stanch the rebellion. Nor, students of the conflict argue, is that rebellion likely to vanish soon.

Rather, they say, the Maoists may pose at least as great a challenge to the country's health as the far more talked-about Islamist insurgency in disputed Kashmir.

India offers a most fertile ground: a deep sense of neglect in large swaths of the country and a ballooning youth population, set against the backdrop of economic growth rates of up to 8 per cent elsewhere.

The Maoists, meanwhile, survive niftily by extorting taxes from anyone doing business in the forest, from bamboo merchants to road construction companies.

'It is one of the most sustainable anti-state ideologies and movements,' argued Ajai Sahni, a security analyst and executive director of the New Delhi-based Institute for Conflict Management.

'Unless something radical is done in terms of a structural revolution in rural areas, you will see a continuous expansion of Maoist insurrection.'

Attacks have become more brazen and better coordinated.

Last June, an apparently synchronized set of nine attacks in Bihar state left twenty-one people dead as Maoists robbed two banks and looted arms from a police station.

In November, also in Bihar, hundreds of Maoist troops orchestrated a jailbreak, freeing more than 300 prisoners and executing nine members of a private militia raised by upper-caste landlords.

In February, here in Chhattisgarh, rebels attacked a warehouse of a state-owned mining company, killing nine security officials and making off with 19 tons of explosives.

Later in February they set off a land mine under a convoy of trucks on a remote country road, instantly killing seven and then, according to wire reports, butchering several others. All told, twenty-eight civilians were killed.

So far this year, the conflict has killed nearly two Indians a day.

The People Fight Back

Chhattisgarh, home to many of India's indigenous people, or adivasis, is most gripped by the war.

Sitting at the bottom of the Indian heap, the adivasis here make a living selling items of value that can be found in the forest: bamboo, leaves to make hand-rolled cigarettes, flowers to distill into country liquor.

They also bear some of the country's worst rates of poverty, health and malnutrition.

But there are riches here, too. Chhattisgarh is negotiating roughly $1.8 billion in private Indian investment, mostly in mining industries, which the insurgents violently oppose. In the heart of the state, in thick forests of valuable sal trees and bamboo, terror has now spawned terror. Last summer, an anti-Maoist village defence movement was born, calling itself the Salwa Judum, or Peace Mission.

The group has coaxed or hounded thousands of people out of their forest hamlets and into the squalid tent camps, where suspected Maoist sympathizers are detained.

The camps are guarded by police officers, paramilitary forces and squads of local armed youths empowered with the title 'special police officer'.

The Delhi-based Asian Centre for Human Rights, in a report in March, found children in the ranks of the Salwa Judum. The centre also accuses the Maoists of recruiting child soldiers. It calls the conflict 'the most serious challenge to human rights advocacy in India'.

Baman, a resident of a village called Kotrapal, who like many adivasis uses one name, narrated the story of how life had sunk so low.

Last summer the Salwa Judum called a meeting in a neighbouring village, where they threatened to beat Baman and others if they did not divulge the names of Maoists and their sympathizers. Baman said he was scared. He named names. He did not care for the Maoists anyway.

Two days later, he was summoned to another meeting, this time by the Maoists. There, he was beaten. Had he refused to attend, Baman said, the Maoists would have simply come to his house and thrashed him.

They had already executed a village priest whom they suspected of being a government informant; Baman said his killers had cut off the priest's ears and left him along the road.

Last September the Salwa Judum, backed by the local police, swept through Kotrapal with a clear message: Move to the camps or face the Salwa Judum's wrath.

'We finished off the village,' said Ajay Singh, the Salwa Judum's leader in a nearby town, Bhairamgarh. Then he clarified: 'People were excited. Of course they destroyed the houses.'

Baman and his clan moved out. Today, Kotrapal, an hour's walk from the nearest country road, is an eerie shell of a village.

Baman pointed out the charred remains of several homes. One was burned by Maoists because they suspected the owner to be a police informant, he said.

Another was burned by the police because they suspected its owner to be the brother of a Maoist.

The school was shuttered. The community hall's doors lay open to the wind. The only signs of life were a few women and children, who were gathering flowers from the forest floor to sell to the country liquor maker.

Before nightfall, they would all to go back to their tent camps.

Salwa Judum leaders say they have waged their campaign with a singular goal in mind: to clear the villages, one by one, and break the Maoists' web of support.

'Unless you cut off the source of disease, the disease will remain,' is how the group's most prominent backer, an influential adivasi politician named Mahendra Karma, put it. 'The source is the people, the villagers.'

There is little doubt that in carrying out its agenda, the Salwa Judum enjoys government support.

State governments are 'advised to encourage the formation of local resistance groups', the Indian ministry of home affairs states in its latest annual report.

The Chhattisgarh government has begun to allocate land and money to villagers who agree to abandon their forest homes and build new houses along the road to Bhairamgarh.

It also supports the 'special police officers' who work arm in arm with the Salwa Judum.

So far, 5000 have been trained, given uniforms and offered what counts here as a generous salary, about $35 a month.

As it lapses deeper into an undeclared state of emergency, Chhattisgarh is now poised to enforce a stringent new law that would allow the local police to detain anyone who belongs to or aids 'an unlawful organization' for up to two or three years, without facing a court of law.

A Forced Enthusiasm

Mr Markam and his Maoist forces appear undaunted. They drill in their forest redoubts. They haul villagers to propaganda meetings.

They build their own weapons, including crude pistols and mortars.

To see them in their jungle camp, sleeping on tarpaulins, armed with antiquated rifles and pistols, with no real territory under their full control, it is difficult to fathom how they have maintained their movement for so long, let alone expanded it across such a wide swath of the country.

They sustain themselves on food given by the villagers, plus a share of the annual rice harvest. To speak to people who live in the area is to realize quickly that they have little choice but to comply.

As the forest woke up on this recent morning, the rebels prepared for the next phase of their revolution. Birds began to chatter. A dozen young people practiced song-and-dance routines for an afternoon rally, like cheerleaders marooned in the Indian forest.

A boy in a fighter's uniform, who looked no older than twelve, horsed around with a homemade rifle. Mr Markam said the boy was just visiting.

By late afternoon, with the rally about to get under way, long rows of villagers came up the dirt paths, accompanied by armed Maoist cadres.

Under the wide arms of a mango tree, the cheerleaders sang a version of *The Internationale*. They danced with bells around their ankles, promising 'people's rule'. They denounced the Salwa Judum, chanting 'Death to Mahendra Karma'.

The audience for the most part sat still, some breaking into giggles only as the People's Liberation Guerrilla Army began military drills, at one point charging ahead with weapons pointed as a hapless chicken scurried across the field.

One man, Maharishi, who was among those who had come on the long afternoon march, said his village had been informed of the rally the night before.

Yes, he said, speaking reluctantly to a stranger, everyone from his village had come. Yes, everyone always comes. 'They say you have to come,' he said.

~

Peter Foster

The Forgotten Victims of India's Drive to Success

The Daily Telegraph
2 May 2006

IT IS THE forgotten face of a new and prosperous India, and it belongs to a little sparrow of a child who is emaciated almost to the point of death.

Her name is Devki and—were it not for the intervention of a local health worker—she would almost certainly have joined the 1.2 million Indian children who die every year from the side-effects of malnutrition. She still might.

While Africa hogs the headlines, the celebrity endorsements and the crisis summits the reality is that half of the world's 146 million under-nourished children live in just three countries—India, Bangladesh and Pakistan.

A report to be published by the United Nation's Children's Fund (Unicef) tomorrow will offer some sobering statistics about the world's failure to tackle extreme poverty and hunger.

To the outside world, India is striding towards greatness, with an economy growing at 8 per cent and potential markets for foreign investors that made India the star of the show at this year's World Economic Forum in Davos.

However in Devki's village of Sersai Khurd in the central Indian state of Madhya Pradesh 270 miles south of Delhi, the benefits of the emerging India seem a very long way off.

A health worker has arrived to check on Devki's weight, and see whether her mother, Gangawati, has been keeping up with the breast feeding programme that she was given to try to nurse her baby back to health.

The child is unwrapped to reveal a pitiful little bag of bones whose skin hangs off her like an old man's, but soon she is suckling gratefully at her mother's breast.

The causes of her condition—Devki was born weighing 5 pounds but within six weeks her weight had fallen to 3 pounds 8 ounces—are as much cultural as they are due to the grinding poverty of Indian village life.

While Devki guzzles, her twin brother, Rahul, sleeps contentedly on a charpoy, his limbs positively plump by comparison with his sister—stark evidence of the social preference for boys that still rules in India.

The reality, explains a Unicef official, is that when resources are limited—Devki's family farm just five acres of unproductive land—boys get preferential treatment, even if that means that girls starve to death.

Back in Shivpuri, the nearest large town, an eight-bed emergency feeding centre is filled with babies like Devki who mew and cry in the midday heat. It could be a scene from an African famine.

One little girl, eighteen-month-old Kiran, weighed just 9 pounds 8 ounces—less than half the recommended weight of a healthy one-year-old (22 pounds)—when she was brought to the centre a few weeks ago.

Her mother, Gyan Bai already has two boys and is almost eight months pregnant with her next child. She has made clear that she must return to her village, even if that means the death of Kiran. The new child must take priority, particularly if it's a boy.

Children as starved as Devki and Kiran are just the tip of an iceberg of poverty that, for all the Mercedes Benz dealerships and new mobile telephone connections, continues to hold back India.

While not starving, almost half of India's children are malnourished, suffering from anaemia and vitamin deficiencies which render them unable to defeat infections that cause pneumonia, diarrhoeal diseases and often death.

India's new middle classes are often insulated from the poverty in which the great majority of Indians still live, however research shows that failing to tackle poverty will leave everyone worse off.

A recent World Bank report estimated that failure to tackle nutritional issues could negatively impact productivity by up to 5 per cent of GDP.

The contrast between India and China is huge. In China the prevalence of underweight children almost halved between 1990 and

2002—from 19 to 8 per cent—while in India the annual rate of reduction since 1990 is less than 2 per cent.

Tackling nutritional issues will be key to whether India's wider population enjoy the fruits of economic growth in the decades to come.

Stories have always trumped statistics when it comes to conveying the essence of a problem, and this particular story, which occupied a few column inches of my morning newspaper, said more about India at sixty than all the heaps of dust-dry numbers to which discussions on the future of this great country so often revert.

It concerned a twenty-year-old girl called Phusi, who lived with her parents in a village in rural Rajasthan, a few miles outside the great princely city of Jodhpur. This girl was desperate to go to school but her parents, who were poor, could not afford to buy a bicycle so she could ride to the nearest school 4 miles away.

However, Phusi cajoled and nagged her parents until, at last, her mother could bear it no more. Blind with rage, Phusi's mother picked up her 'belan'—a rolling pin used for making chapattis—and beat her daughter unconscious. Fearing she had killed the child, she hung Phusi from the ceiling of their house and rushed outside, claiming suicide.

Later, she confessed to her terrible crime. In mitigation, her husband explained that the family had borrowed a small fortune—Rs 28,000 (£350)—after her mother developed complications at Phusi's birth and they were still paying off the debt. 'How much could we spend on her?' said the despairing father. 'It was not possible to buy her a bicycle.'

And then, the killer coda. Two years ago, the paper reports, the local government had announced a laudable scheme to provide free bicycles to all school-age girls in the state, but, as so often in rural India, the promised bicycles had never reached Phusi's village.

It is a story that illustrates in so many ways the predicament of India sixty years after Nehru announced that a free nation was finally fulfilling its 'tryst with destiny'.

Note first the little girl's ambition. She desperately wanted to go to school; even in her isolated rural village, she had realized that, without education, she could never progress in the 'new' India.

The sad truth, however, is that, if Phusi had ever made it to school, she would have been lucky to find a teacher. A UN report this week put India above only Uganda when it comes to teacher absenteeism. The result is that 40 per cent of Indians still cannot read and write.

And for those without skills, India in 2007 offers precious little opportunity. While China has created millions of manufacturing jobs, India's growth story has been largely jobless. It's worth remembering that India's much-vaunted IT sector employs just 1.3 million people from a workforce of 400 million.

And yet, if Phusi had been lucky enough to make it through to college, modern India would have offered her opportunities that even middle-class families could not have dreamt of a generation ago. The twin boons of the Internet and cheap telephony have enabled Indians to sell their skills in the global workplace, earning the salaries that are fuelling the domestic economy.

India is full of ambitious children like Phusi. Or like the two young entrepreneurs from modest backgrounds I met last week, who gave up safe, salaried jobs to start an Internet business. They work 100 hours a week and they burn to succeed. The tragedy is how few Indians ever get the chance.

Why? Phusi's story contains the answer. Her father was in chronic debt after he borrowed the equivalent of three years' wages to save his wife in childbirth. India's public health system is disastrous and woefully inadequate for the task of keeping 1.1 billion people productive, happy and healthy.

For millions of Indians, paying for private healthcare—too often there is no other option—is still the biggest reason to get into debt. And once in debt the unskilled—who earn 50 pence a day if they are lucky—have no way out.

The result is a country that is nothing short of a public health disaster. Almost half of children under six are malnourished. They don't receive the basic number of calories required to develop their bones and their brains so they can play a part in India's new, brain-intensive economy.

India's public policy makers should be scared by the statistics. Gordon Brown, when he visited the subcontinent shortly before becoming Prime Minister, praised India for lifting '100 million people' out of poverty in the past decade. He was only half-right.

The truth is that in large swaths of north India, many of the key health indicators are going backwards despite a decade of eight per economic growth. As a report published last week by the Asian Development bank confirmed, while urban India booms, many millions are being left behind.

All this is well known to India's leaders and—for all the self congratulation of recent days—there have been many voices urging that India's 800 million very poor people are not forgotten amid all the global partying.

But understanding India's chronic development deficiencies is not the same as doing something about it. The politicians of Phusi's local government knew that girls like her needed bikes to get to school, they forged an eminently sensible solution to that problem, but somehow, as so often in India, the precious, life-giving gift of bicycles never came to pass.

It is those triple failures of poor health, education and ineffectual government, all so graphically illustrated by Phusi's story, that threaten to blight the next sixty years of India's story.

Visit any sizeable Indian city and the evidence of change lies all about—new wealth, new spending and new opportunities. But step into any government office, places heavy with lassitude and decay—and it's as if the new India had never been born.

India knows all this. Hardly a day goes by when the Prime Minister doesn't make a wonderful, perspicacious speech about 'what needs to be done'. But what Phusi needed, and what hundreds of millions of poor Indians now need, is action, not words.

~

Amelia Gentleman

The Flashy Cars of a Maharaja for Modern Times

International Herald Tribune
25 October 2006

Pune: JUST AS MOST people don't waste their time counting up trifling possessions like, say, underwear or socks, Poonawalla has no interest in taking stock of his car collection. He has a large number of them but certainly not yet enough.

'I've lost count. Anyway, I know I've got eight Rolls Royces,' he concludes, casually gesturing somewhere beyond the veranda of his mansion, past the three cages of brightly-plumed parrots, (imported from Latin America), past the lemon yellow Lamborghini, past the waiting line of uniformed chauffeurs, to a cluster of shining vehicles.

Since he took possession of the first new Rolls Royce to be sold in India in five decades, Poonawalla has become a poster boy for a new era of conspicuous consumption here. Featured on the front of society magazines dangling the keys to his new $940,000 Phantom from fingers heavy with diamond-encrusted jewellery, his style is that of a modern maharaja, a man with no reserve about flaunting his money.

A multimillionaire through his family business—which encompasses pharmaceuticals, hotels and horse breeding—he devotes both his cash and his spare time to nurturing a lifelong obsession with expensive cars.

Fifteen years ago, India's closed economy made it impossible to bring cars into the country, and the austere tastes of a socialist-leaning nation meant it was hard to indulge in such frivolous displays of ostentation. Now, with its 83,000 dollar-millionaires (an elite club that grew by 19.3 per cent last year), India is becoming familiar with the eccentricities of a growing class of super-rich who live to buy cars. Vintage car rallies are held in Delhi and Mumbai annually and new showrooms for Porsche and BMW are thriving.

Still, it's not easy to be a car collector in a country where the dreadful state of the road system is seen as one of the most pressing obstacles to economic development.

And it's a particularly peculiar passion to have in a city like Pune—a quiet, emerging software centre in southern India—where the roads are truly abysmal, and where expensive cars are such a rarity that the locals go into a frenzy of excitement every time they see one.

Poonawalla finds driving in these conditions so nerve-racking that he has pretty much given it up. 'I don't like driving any more; I no longer find it fun,' he says mournfully. 'The traffic is bad. The roads are bad. You have to worry about cows and dogs coming the wrong way up the street. It's very, very stressful and anyway I have high blood pressure.'

Luckily he has a team of drivers to step in. When he bought the Phantom last year, he sent six of his chauffeurs to Mumbai for a specialist driving course with Rolls Royce staff who had been sent to India from Britain. (The family's other twenty or so drivers are not allowed to get behind the wheel of the Phantom).

Being rich in India's smaller cities remains a lonely affair and there's not much opportunity in Pune for flashing one's wealth—the occasional wedding, the odd party. On the rare instances he decides to drive himself in one of his most treasured automobiles, perhaps to take his wife out for a drink in the city's best hotel, Le Meridien, he is followed by a chauffeur driving a lesser vehicle ('My BMW maybe, or a Porsche') to ensure that no one smashes into the back of the really valuable car, and to make sure that there is a trained chauffeur on hand to help with parking.

Poonawalla, thirty-four, is scrupulous in pointing out the details that he believes justify the Phantom's price tag. The words 'Custom Built for Poonawalla' are embossed in silver on the doorsill, at about the spot where you might stamp a muddy foot stepping into the car. There are two telephones, a couple of televisions, an array of walnut panelling, the letter 'P' stitched and embossed at prominent spots in and outside the car, a button that slowly closes the door for you (saving the wearisome labour of stretching out your arm), another button that pulls black curtains across all the back windows for total privacy, long black umbrellas that slot ingeniously into the door panels, with built-in drying systems so that raindrops don't mildew.

He demonstrated how the silver figure at the helm of the car, the flying lady, sinks inside the hood if anyone tries to steal it—although under the circumstances this is a rather redundant feature. The guards in pearl grey uniforms with gold-trimmed red sashes around their waists who stand beneath the cast-iron stags looming over his front gates ward off any potential thieves, and the car is never left unattended.

Poonawalla pauses to consider whether it was really worth the money. 'Was it a good investment? No. The day you take it out of the showroom its value drops 30 per cent. But I was looking for a nice car. This car offered a lot in terms of road presence, comfort and prestige,' he says. 'People ask me where I plan to drive these cars, what I'm going to do with them. But driving them is not really the point. My passion is just for spending time with them on Sunday morning. I like to check they've all been cleaned nicely, and that my chaps are not lazing around.

'It is a lot of money, but if you love cars, then that's a lot of car. These cars are all about attracting attention.'

Grabbing attention in Pune is not difficult. If residents of India's biggest cities are becoming blasé when faced with displays of exceptional wealth, the novel thrill of big money is still intense in small-town Pune.

When he takes out his $450,000 Lamborghini (a present for his wife in May) to demonstrate the hysteria it causes, people on motorbikes swerve to follow him and passengers fumble to take pictures with their mobile phones. As it races along shady roads, beneath the long, dangling trellises of banyan trees, every head turns to look at a car painted the same yellow and black as the local three-wheeled rickshaw, but otherwise an alien phenomenon.

Strangely there are no number plates on the vehicle, but the chauffeur driving the car behind Poonawalla explains that his boss doesn't need to worry about that kind of detail. 'Mr Poonawalla is a big man. Nobody in the police would touch him. He's royalty here.'

When the Lamborghini stops at the lights for a minute, dozens of beggars holding skinny, half-naked babies beeline for the car and start tapping on the window.

Poonawalla is undismayed. In a country where around 300 million people earn less than $1 a day, he claims he encounters no malice or envy. 'Even though we live in such a poor country there is no resentment. You will always see a smile on a poor person watching the car go by,' he insists, and drives away, offering no alms.

He finds it harder to keep his cool a few minutes later when there is a terrible crack as the low slung car drives at speed over a pothole.

Dust flies everywhere, the car struggles on and Poonawalla makes a brave attempt at feigning indifference.

~

Peter Wonacott

India's Skewed Sex Ratio Puts GE Sales in Spotlight

The Wall Street Journal
18 April 2007

Indergarh: GENERAL ELECTRIC CO. and other companies have sold so many ultrasound machines in India that tests are now available in small towns like this one. There's no drinking water here, electricity is infrequent and roads turn to mud after a March rain shower. A scan typically costs $8, or a week's wages.

GE has waded into India's market as the country grapples with a difficult social issue: the abortion of female foetuses by families who want boys. Campaigners against the practice and some government officials are linking the country's widely reported skewed sex ratio with the spread of ultrasound machines. That's putting GE, the market leader in India, under the spotlight. It faces legal hurdles, government scrutiny and thorny business problems in one of the world's fastest-growing economies.

'Ultrasound is the main reason why the sex ratio is coming down,' says Kalpana Bhavre, who is in charge of women and child welfare for the Datia district government, which includes Indergarh. Having a daughter is often viewed as incurring a lifetime of debt for parents because of the dowry payment at marriage. Compared to that, the cost of an ultrasound 'is nothing', she says.

**In December 2006, the Hyderabad High Court dismissed the case against GE–Wipro, saying the machine was sold to the clinic, cited by prosecutors, before the legislation became operative.*

For more than a decade, the Indian government has tried to stop ultrasound from being used as a tool to determine gender. The devices use sound waves to produce images of foetuses or internal organs for a range of diagnostic purposes. India has passed laws forbidding doctors from disclosing the sex of foetuses, required official registrations of clinics and stiffened punishments for offenders. Nevertheless, some estimate that hundreds of thousands of girl foetuses are aborted each year.

GE—by far the largest seller of ultrasound machines here through a joint venture with Indian outsourcing giant Wipro Ltd—has introduced its own safeguards, even though that means forsaking sales. 'We stress emphatically that the machines aren't to be used for sex determination,' says V. Raja, chief executive of GE Healthcare South Asia. 'This is not the root cause of female foeticide in India.'

But the efforts have failed to stop the problem, as a growing economy has made the scans affordable to more people. The skewed sex ratio is an example of how India's strong economy has, in unpredictable ways, exacerbated some nagging social problems, such as the traditional preference for boys. Now, some activists are accusing GE of not doing enough to prevent unlawful use of its machines to boost sales.

'There is a demand for a boy that's been completely exploited by multinationals,' says Puneet Bedi, a New Delhi obstetrician. He says GE and others market the machines as an essential pregnancy tool although the scans often aren't necessary for mothers in low risk groups.

Earlier this month, prosecutors in the city of Hyderabad brought a criminal case against the GE venture with Wipro as well as Erbis Engineering Co., the medical-equipment distributor in India for Japan's Toshiba Corp. In the suits, the district government alleges that the companies knowingly supplied ultrasound machines to clinics that weren't registered with the government and were illegally performing sex-selection tests. The penalty is up to three months in prison and a fine of Rs 1000.

Both companies deny wrongdoing and say they comply with Indian laws. A GE spokesman said yesterday the company hadn't received court notification but its legal team would be looking into the charges.

Vivek Paul, who helped build the early ultrasound business in India, first as a senior executive at GE and then at Wipro, says blame should be pinned on unethical doctors, not the machine's suppliers. 'If someone drives a car through a crowded market and kills people, do you blame the car maker?' says Mr Paul, who was Wipro's chief executive before he left the company in 2005. Mr Paul is now a managing director at private equity specialists TPG Inc., formerly known as Texas Pacific Group.

India has been a critical market to GE. Its outsourcing operations have helped the Fairfield, Conn., giant cut costs. The country also is a growing market for GE's heavy equipment and other products. The company won't disclose its ultrasound sales. But Wipro–GE's overall sales in India, which includes ultrasounds and other diagnostic equipment, reached about $250 million last year, up from $30 million in 1995.

Annual ultrasound sales in India from all vendors reached $77 million in 2006, up about 10 per cent from the year before, according to an estimate from consulting firm Frost & Sullivan, which describes GE as the clear market leader. Other vendors include Siemens AG, Philips Electronics NV and Mindray International Medical Ltd, a new Chinese entrant for India's price-sensitive customers.

India has long struggled with an inordinate number of male births, and female infanticide—the killing of newborn baby girls—remains a problem. The abortion of female foetuses is a more recent trend, but unless 'urgent action is taken', it's poised to escalate as the use of ultrasound services expands, the United Nations Children's Fund said in a report this year. India's 'alarming decline in the child sex ratio' is likely to exacerbate child marriage, trafficking of women for prostitution and other problems, the report said.

The latest official Indian census in 2001 showed a steep decline in the relative number of girls aged 0–6 years from ten years earlier: 927 girls for every 1000 boys compared with 945 in 1991. In much of north-west India, the number of girls has fallen below 900 for every 1000 boys. In the northern state of Punjab, the figure is below 800.

Only China today has a wider gender gap, with 832 girls born for every 1000 boys among infants aged 0–4 years, according to Unicef. GE sells about three times as many ultrasound machines in China as in India. In January, the Chinese government pledged to improve the gender balance, including tighter monitoring of ultrasounds. Some experts predict China will be more effective than India in enforcing its rules, given its success at other population-control measures.

Boys in India are viewed as wealth earners during life and lighters of one's funeral pyre at death. India's National Family Health Survey, released in February, showed that 90 per cent of parents with two sons didn't want any more children. Of those with two daughters, 38 per cent wanted to try again. While there are restrictions on abortions in this Hindu-majority nation, the rules offer enough leeway for most women to get around them.

GE took the lead in selling ultrasounds in the early 1990s soon after it began manufacturing the devices in India. It tapped Wipro's extensive distribution and service network to deliver its products to about 80 per cent of its customers. For more remote locations and lower-end machines, it used sales agents.

The company also teamed with banks to help doctors finance the purchase of their machines. GE now sells about fifteen different models, ranging from machines costing $100,000 that offer sophisticated colour images to basic black-and-white scanners that retail for about $7500.

To boost sales, GE has targeted small-town doctors. The company has kept prices down by refurbishing old equipment and marketed laptop machines to doctors who travelled frequently, including to rural areas. GE also offered discounts to buyers inclined to boast about their new gadgets, according to a former GE employee.

'Strategically, we focused on those customers who had big mouths,' said Manish Vora, who until 2006 sold ultrasounds in the western Indian state of Gujarat for the Wipro–GE joint venture.

Without discussing specific sales tactics, Mr Raja, of GE Healthcare South Asia, acknowledges the company is 'aggressive' in pursuing its goals. But he points out that ultrasound machines have broad benefits and make childbirth safer. As the machines become more available, women can avoid making long trips into cities where health care typically is more expensive, he says.

Indian authorities have tried to regulate sales. In 1994, the government outlawed sex selection and empowered Indian authorities to search clinics and seize anything that aided sex selection. Today any clinic that has an ultrasound machine must register with the local government and provide an affidavit that it won't conduct sex selection. To date, more than 30,000 ultrasound clinics have been registered in India.

GE has taken a number of steps to ensure customers comply with the law. It has educated its sales force about the regulatory regime, demanded its own affidavits from customers that they won't use the machines for sex selection, and followed up with periodic audits, say executives. They note that in 2004, the first full year it began implementing these new measures, GE's sales in India shrank by about 10 per cent from the year before. The sales decline in the low-end segment, for black-and-white ultrasound machines, was especially sharp, executives say. Only last year did GE return to the sales level it had reached before the regulations were implemented, according to Mr Raja.

Complying with Indian law is often tricky. GE can't tell if doctors sell machines to others who fail to register them. Different states interpret registration rules differently. GE also is under close scrutiny by activists battling the illegal abortion of female foetuses. Sabu George, a forty-eight-year-old activist who holds degrees from Johns Hopkins and Cornell universities, crisscrosses the country to spot illegal clinics.

The criminal case in Hyderabad against Wipro–GE, a company representative, three doctors and an ultrasound technician followed an inspection in 2005 that found one clinic couldn't produce proper registration and hadn't kept complete records for two years. A team of inspectors seized an ultrasound supplied by Wipro–GE. The inspection team's report said it suspected the clinic was using the machines for illegal sex determination.

The owner, Sarawathi Devi, acknowledged in an interview that her clinic, Rite Diagnostics, wasn't officially registered at the time of the 2005 inspection. She said the ultrasound machine was owned by a 'freelance' radiologist who had obtained proper documentation for the Wipro–GE machine, but wasn't there when the inspectors had arrived. She denied the clinic has conducted sex determination tests. Later in 2005, Dr Devi's records show she registered the clinic with the government and bought a Wipro–GE machine, a sale the company confirms.

The court case was part of a wider dragnet spearheaded by Hyderabad's top civil servant, District Magistrate Arvind Kumar. During an audit last year, Mr Kumar demanded paperwork for 389 local scan centres. Only 16 per cent could furnish complete address information for its patients, making it almost impossible to track women to check if they had abortions following their scans. Mr Kumar ordered the seizure of almost one-third of the ultrasound machines in the district due to registration and paperwork problems. A suit also was lodged against Erbis, the Toshiba dealer.

GE's Mr Raja says that, in general, if there's any doubt about the customer's intent to comply with India's laws, it doesn't make the sale. 'There is no winking or blinking,' he says.

A Wipro—GE representative is scheduled to appear 7 May at the Hyderabad court. An Erbis spokesman said he was unaware of the case in Hyderabad. A court date for Erbis hasn't been set.

A visit to the clinic in Indergarh, a town surrounded by fields of tawny wheat, shows the challenges GE faces keeping tabs on its machines. Inside the clinic, a dozen women wrapped in saris awaited tests on GE's Logiq 100 ultrasound machine. The line snaked along wooden benches and down into a darkened basement. On the wall, scrawled in white paint, was the message: 'We don't do sex selection.'

Manish Gupta, a thirty-four-year-old doctor, said he drives two hours each way every week to Indergarh from much larger Jhansi city, where there are dozens of competing ultrasound clinics. He said even when offered bribes he refuses to disclose the sex of the foetus. 'I'm just against that,' Dr Gupta said.

But he is not complying with Indian law. Although the law requires that clinics display their registration certificate in a conspicuous place, Dr Gupta's was nowhere to be seen. When Dr George, the social activist, asked for the registration, he was shown a different document, an application. But the application was for a different clinic: the Sakshi X-ray centre. Dr Gupta said the proper document wasn't with him, adding: 'I must have forgotten it at home.'

Asked by the *Wall Street Journal* about the clinic, the local chief magistrate of Datia district called for Dr Gupta's dossier later in the day. When a local official arrived, 'Sakshi X-Ray centre' had been crossed out on the application. In blue pen was written the correct name, 'Sheetal Nagar', the part of Indergarh where the clinic is located.

It's not clear how Dr Gupta procured the GE machine. Dr Gupta said he bought it from a GE company representative, but he declined to show documents of ownership. GE says it doesn't comment on individual customers.

Like the rest of India, the Datia district government has taken a number of steps to try to boost the number of girls in the district. For girls of poor families, the local government provides a place to live, free school uniforms and books. When they enter ninth grade, the government buys bicycles for them. Yet the low ratio of girls born hasn't budged much over the past decade, according to Ms Bhavre, the district government official.

Ultimately, says Mr Raja, head of GE Healthcare in South Asia, it's the job of the government, not companies, to change the prevailing preference for boys. 'What's really needed is a change in mindsets. A lot of education has to happen and the government has to do it,' he says.

India's ministry of health, which is now pursuing 422 different cases against doctors accused of using ultrasounds for sex selection, agrees. 'Mere legislation is not enough to deal with this problem,' the ministry said in a statement. 'The situation could change only when the daughters are not treated as a burden and the sons as assets.'

~

Matthew Rosenberg
Sri Lanka Seen Heading Back to Civil War

Associated Press
4 May 2007

Klinochchi, Sri Lanka: DAY AND NIGHT, warplanes roar over this rebel-held town as the steady thump of artillery echoes from afar—a preview, many fear, of a military showdown in Sri Lanka that could leave thousands dead.

'All we hear is war,' says Tavakumar, a forty-three-year-old rebel who only uses one name, patrolling a road a few miles from the front. 'I'm ready to fight.'

Five years after a cease-fire brought a measure of relief to Sri Lanka, a ferocious ethnic war is again raging between the government dominated by the country's predominantly Buddhist Sinhalese

**The six-year-old cease-fire between the Sri Lankan government and Tamil Tiger rebels formally ended on 16 January 2008, two weeks after the government gave notice it was withdrawing from the agreement.*

majority and the Tamil Tigers, separatists seeking a homeland for the largely Hindu Tamil minority.

The signs of a deepening conflict are everywhere: soldiers in full battle gear patrolling Colombo, the increasingly fortified capital; sandbagged bunkers and trenches going up all over the rebel-held north.

Both sides claim to be observing the truce, which remains officially in place. But clearly it has left neither side satisfied, and now it has completely collapsed. The rebels are mounting renewed attacks, including a bus bombing last June that killed sixty-four people, and Sri Lankan forces are pushing farther into rebel territory, with officials openly saying they aim to militarily crush their enemy.

'We want to destroy them, the Tiger bases, all these things,' Defence Secretary Gotabhaya Rajapakse told the Associated Press in an interview. Rajapakse, brother of President Mahinda Rajapakse, survived a Tamil suicide bombing of his motorcade in December.

Amid the spiralling violence, the AP secured permission to cross the front lines and make the first visit by foreign journalists to insurgent territory since the war reignited in August.

In Kilinochchi, the main rebel-held city, the cease-fire seemed a distant notion as a pair of warplanes dropped flares to light up a rebel mortar position in the jungles beyond town. Farmers and insurgents scrambled into dank, makeshift bomb shelters as the jets dropped their bombs, obliterating a rebel mortar position.

Nineteen years of suicide bombings, jungle clashes, torture and village massacres, from 1983 until the truce was signed in 2002, took an estimated 65,000 lives on this West Virginia-sized island of twenty million people off India's southern tip.

Since August, about 3000 more have been killed and 160,000 displaced, most in eastern Sri Lanka where the government has plowed through relatively lightly defended rebel territory.

Next up, officials say, is the rebels' heavily fortified northern heartland, a would-be Tamil state of about 500,000 people with courts, traffic cops, a forestry department and a legal code that bans adultery and pornography.

It's territory the rebels say they'll defend with everything they've got.

'The fighting in the north is going to be more intense and the (rebels) probably won't withdraw,' as they did in the east, said Jehan Perera of Sri Lanka's National Peace Council, a think tank. 'Battlefield losses will be heavier.'

There's also growing concern about the rise in human rights violations. The rebels and government allied militias are both alleged to have abducted and in some cases killed hundreds of civilians, and there are well-documented cases of top government officials threatening critics of the war, especially journalists.

The roots of the conflict stretch back to the years after independence from Britain in 1948, when the government gave Buddhism a prominent role and declared Sinhala the sole official language.

The result was widespread discrimination against Tamils, until war broke out in 1983.

The 2002 cease-fire negotiated by Norwegian diplomats raised hopes which were reinforced two years later by a belief that the Indian Ocean tsunami would force the warring sides to work together for national recovery. But by late 2005, sporadic shootings and bombings were back. Most—such as a bus bombing that killed sixty-four people in June—were blamed on the Tigers, who many believed were trying to force the government to make concessions at the negotiating table.

If that was their strategy, it backfired spectacularly.

Mahinda Rajapakse had been elected president in late 2005 in part by Sinhalese hard-liners who viewed the cease-fire as a betrayal. In August, he opted for all-out war, while claiming to be honouring the cease-fire and only responding to rebel provocations.

He is being cheered on by hard-line Buddhist monks who see themselves as guardians of the island's Sinhalese culture, and, increasingly, by many ordinary Sinhalese. A recent poll by Colombo's respected Centre for Policy Alternatives found nearly 60 per cent of the Sinhalese supported a military solution.

It highlights the changing mood in a country that a few years ago was hoping to ride the coattails of India's economic boom and nurture its own blossoming tourism and garment industries.

But while any glitch in India's rush forward is apt to be felt internationally, Sri Lanka's war rages away from centre-stage.

There are no peacekeepers—just a team of cease-fire monitors from Nordic countries with no powers to intervene. The US and European governments regard the Tigers as terrorists but are pressuring the government to stop attacking rebel territory, pressure that has largely been ignored. India, the regional power, is loath to repeat its disastrous military intervention in the war in the late 1980s.

The not-an-inch attitude of the government and its growing ranks of supporters is evident at a well-heeled dinner party in Colombo, where Jaya Dayananda, a Sinhalese housewife, tells a guest: 'These Tamils, you must understand, only know how to kill.'

'We tried peace. They didn't want peace,' she says. 'War is our only solution.'

That war is a day's drive north.

At the last checkpoint in government territory, a post that once bustled with people and commerce, a soldier warns of recent shelling in the area and advises: 'You can get killed up there. We can do nothing.'

On the other side, visitors are welcomed to 'Tamil Eelam', made to fill out an immigration form, and are thoroughly searched for guns, porn and booze.

Kilinochchi, the rebels' de facto capital, is another hour up a bumpy road patrolled by farmers and labourers who have been armed and trained to fight.

The rebels, formally known as The Liberation Tigers of Tamil Eelam, assign minders to accompany visitors almost everywhere. There's little opportunity to speak with ordinary people or venture beyond the crumbling main strip of Kilinochchi, a town of one- and two-story buildings hemmed in by bush and jungle, to see their preparations for war.

The air raids are 'the one thing we're afraid of', says a twenty-six-year-old who gave only her nom de guerre, Sita. 'There's nothing we can do against them.'

It's hard to gauge the sentiments of ordinary Tamils, but the government's push against the Tigers appears to be strengthening their support for the rebels.

'It's not that we don't have problems with the Tigers—we do,' says Father James Pathinathan, a Tamil Roman Catholic priest in nearby Mullativu, another rebel town.

'But if you look at the whole picture, people here know they have more to gain from supporting the Tigers,' he continued. 'So many Tamils are being killed by the government.'

Fresh graves of rebels are filling the cemeteries and every able-bodied adult—along with quite a few children, say aid workers—is being trained to fight.

'There's no difference now between the political cadres, the military, the regular people,' says Maran Rajdurai, a former fighter with a deep bullet scar on his left arm.

These days, he works in the rebels' development secretariat, but says: 'Everyone will fight if they have to.'

The Tamil Tigers are now thought to have more than 10,000 men and women in their cult-like army, a force in which fighters aren't allowed to marry until their mid-20s and carry cyanide capsules to kill themselves if captured.

They bested Sri Lanka's army in conventional battles and waged guerrilla campaigns before the cease-fire, which has given them an opportunity to dig in and rearm.

The rebels have carried out more than 240 suicide bombings; their victims include a Sri Lankan President and a former Indian Prime Minister. The bombings have led the United States and European Union to label the rebels as terrorists.

In March they launched their first air strike, using a single-propeller plane to drop bombs on an air force base next to the international airport in Colombo, killing three airmen.

The attack sent shivers through the tourism industry, prompted warnings of a new phase in the war, and clearly boosted Tamil morale at a time when stresses are showing in the rebel enclave.

During the cease-fire, buildings went up, banks opened and markets filled with biscuits and soft drinks shipped in from the south.

Nowadays fuel is scarce, power supplies are virtually nonexistent, and even Coca-Cola is hard to come by, jobs even harder.

'Living like this, it's very difficult,' said a man who gives his name only as Francis.

The fifty-nine-year-old, wearing only a soiled cloth around his waist, makes about a dollar a day carrying loads for other people. 'It's not enough,' he says.

Nonetheless, in a rare conversation with no minder listening, Francis says he'll settle for no less than a Tiger victory.

'We are asking for our freedom from the Sinhalese people,' he says. 'We should live apart.'

~

Peter Foster
Why the Tiger's Future Is Far from Bright

The Daily Telegraph
30 August 2007

THESE ARE DARK days for the Royal Bengal tiger, lord of the Indian jungle and without doubt the most mesmerizing of all the great beasts of the forest. As new census figures indicate, in a few short years—perhaps a decade, maybe two—it is likely that the tiger as a truly wild animal will become extinct.

They won't all die, of course—a handful of docile and inbred examples will survive in protected forest reserves for the benefit of foreign tourists in the their safari 4x4s. But the animal that Blake used to symbolize his vengeful and pitiless God will essentially have become a tame thing, something to be gawped at in zoos and fenced-off national parks. Not real tigers, just big kitties with stripes.

How has this happened? Until quite recently, India's tigers were cited as one of the world's great conservation success stories. After India's then Prime Minister, Indira Gandhi, launched 'Project Tiger' in 1973, tiger numbers rose steadily, from a low of 1200 in the early 1970s to more than 3500 a decade ago. The tiger, it seemed, was back from the brink.

It now transpires that this was a false dawn. Today, tiger numbers are back down to—at their lowest—1300, with leading conservationists such as Valmik Thapar predicting that the inexorable downward trend will continue.

A decade of administrative neglect—40 per cent of Indian forest guard positions are currently vacant—and years of forest administrators cooking the books to cover up poaching losses and the endless encroachment of villages on to protected land, have put the tiger into irreversible decline.

Is it really too late? Probably, even though it seems at least that India's government has finally woken up to the crisis being faced by its national animal. Manmohan Singh, the Prime Minister, is now backing a new 'Project Tiger', doubling the tiger conservation budget, creating a new National Tiger Conservation Authority and a dedicated Wildlife Crime Bureau to tackle the poachers head on.

It would be comforting to think all this government action will bear fruit, but there are several reasons to think that Mrs Gandhi's great solo effort of thirty-five years ago cannot be replicated by Mr Singh. The fear among India's conservation community, based on the bitter experience of the past decade, is that all the new bureaux, authorities and Central government directives will turn out to be paper tigers, not real ones. The reasons are twofold.

Since Mrs Gandhi's day, the population of India has doubled from 560 million in 1972 to 1.1 billion today. In another thirty-five years, that figure will be 1.5 billion. Put simply, there just isn't enough forest—the tiger's natural habitat—to go around. For most of India's rural poor, every day is a battle to survive. Competition for resources—land, water, forest—is intense and will only become more so.

The effects of this human population pressure on the tigers are already visible: India now has only three viable tiger habitats. Even more worrying is that outside India's twenty-eight dedicated tiger reserves—where 60 per cent of India's tigers were estimated to be living in 2002—it was found that there simply wasn't enough prey to sustain the tigers. Day by day, the overwhelming pressure of people is driving the big cats into smaller and smaller parcels of land.

The second major reason for gloom is political. While Indira Gandhi was a political demi-god, commanding vast electoral majorities and unquestionable authority, Mr Singh's position at the head of a minority coalition is altogether more mortal. Modern Indian politics is increasingly factionalized, with regional king-makers draining power from the centre every day.

It is therefore encouraging to hear that the Prime Minister has written personally to all of India's chief ministers, demanding they fill those forest guard vacancies; but rather less encouraging to know that three identical letters have been dispatched from New Delhi in recent times, all to no effect.

The truth is that, for all the brave talk of saving India's national animal, whether by politicians in New Delhi or by conservationists around the world, the plight of the tiger holds little sway in the places where it actually lives.

No Indian politician ever won re-election by saving a tiger. And while reserves do bring in tourist dollars, far too much of that money disappears into the pockets of the big hotel chains and the local political elite. For tribal people, scratching a living on the land, there is all too little reason to turn down the poacher's shilling.

The Indian tiger is heading rapidly towards extinction thanks to a new breed of wealthy Tibetans who prize the skins as trimming for their traditional costumes, an investigation has shown.

Until recently it was tiger bone used in Chinese medicine that was thought to be driving the escalating poaching trade, but it is now clear that Tibetan fashions are stoking demand to unparalleled and unsustainable levels.

This year alarm bells sounded in India when it emerged that one of the country's most prestigious reserves, Sariska in Rajasthan, had been completely emptied of tigers by poachers.

Hearing rumours that the new Tibetan trend for skins was behind the rapid increase in poaching, a team from the London-based Environmental Investigation Agency went to Tibet and the Sichuan and Gansu provinces in China.

In New Delhi yesterday, Belinda Wright, of the Wildlife Protection Society of India, who was part of the undercover team, said the time for scaremongering was over.

'This is it. The end is now in sight for the Indian tiger. The sheer quantities of skins for sale is beyond belief. As the Sariska scandal so clearly showed, the Indian tiger is now being systematically wiped out.'

At horse festivals in Tibet and Sichuan, dancers, riders and spectators wandered about, openly wearing the traditional chuba, generously trimmed with tiger and leopard skin, while organizers and local officials joined in.

Traders said demand for the skins was coming from the newly monied classes who had made small fortunes from selling a local caterpillar fungus (*Cordyceps sinensis*) used in Chinese medicine.

Demand for the fungus has rocketed since two Chinese Olympic athletes attributed their success to its stamina-building powers. A rare mushroom is also fetching high prices, according to local people.

The skins are smuggled along well-established Nepali trading routes into Tibet where they are sold openly in shops in the capital, Lhasa.

Using hidden cameras Ms Wright, who has devoted the last thirty-five years to saving the Indian tiger, toured the centre of old Lhasa posing as a buyer.

She said: 'In ten shops we found twenty-four tiger skin chubas, most of them decorated with great swathes of skin, and all openly displayed for sale.

'In twenty other shops we recorded fifty-four leopard skin chubas. The dealers categorically told us that they had come from India. When we asked we were shown three fresh tiger skins and seven fresh leopard skins in four different locations—again, all from India.'

Wildlife experts accuse the Indian and Chinese governments of seriously underestimating the scale of the problem and, through a mixture of corruption and bureaucratic inertia, failing to address it.

According to Indian government census figures there are 3624 wild tigers left in India but that figure is now widely acknowledged to be a gross over-estimate. Some wildlife campaigners put the figure as low as 1500.

The Indian government has recently set up a new Tiger Taskforce to try to staunch the flow of big cat losses but, the experts say, the commercial poaching interests are better funded and more determined than the state.

Perhaps most depressing of all for the investigators was the apparent lack of concern among Tibetans wearing the tiger and leopard skin chubas, many of whom had clearly not stopped to consider the implication for tiger populations.

In Litang, in Sichuan province, Ms Wright talked to a twenty-one-year-old as he sat in his tent, swathed in a large fresh tiger skin that had cost his father about £6700.

'He said that he would wear it just twice a year—during the Tibetan New Year and at the annual horse festival—even though he said he didn't particularly like it.

'I asked him how wearing a dead animal's skin could be compatible with his Buddhist religion, but he had no explanation, except to say "I didn't kill the tiger."'

There was worse to come when the group travelled onward through the mountains to Linxia in Gansu province.

In a single street, Ms Wright said, there were sixty snow leopard skins (from China and India) and 163 whole, fresh leopard skins hanging in the doorways and on the floors and walls. More skins were rolled up in the backs of the shops for cleaning and tanning.

All were captured on camera by Ms Wright who, accompanied by another female investigator, posed as a Muslim woman out on a shopping spree with her 'niece'.

'People have taken great risks to obtain this footage,' she said. 'We hope it confronts everybody, including the Indian and Chinese governments, with the stark reality of this dreadful trade. We need action, and we need it now.'

~

Jo Johnson
Inequality Threatens India's Economic Boom

Financial Times
1 November 2007

IT IS A fair bet that when the ruling elite of a poor developing country ignores a non-violent protest by 25,000 desperate citizens, it will soon face a violent one. When a 25,000-strong army of landless workers, indigenous tribespeople and 'untouchables' from the bottom of Indian society marched 320 kilometres to Delhi to highlight the growing divide between haves and have-nots, they were met with crushing indifference. Admittedly, their timing was bad: Mumbai's Sensex index on Monday punched through the 20,000 mark for the first time, triggering orgiastic self-congratulation by the English language media and eclipsing all other national news.

'The first 10,000 took over twenty years. The next came in just twenty months. Superpower 2020?' rhapsodized the front-page headline of the *Economic Times*, the cheerleader for a phenomenon it calls the 'global Indian takeover'. In their excitement, several other newspapers double-counted the value of all Mukesh Ambani's stakes in various listed Reliance entities and erroneously concluded that he had overtaken Bill Gates and Carlos Slim to become the wealthiest person in the world, with investments valued at $63 billion (€43.6 billion). Although that joyous moment may not be far off—the elder Ambani is worth nearer $50 billion—it has not come yet.

As first-world India cheered the stockmarket, there was scarcely mention of the visitors from third-world India who had camped overnight in the old city. Feet swollen, mouths parched and hair matted, the protestors were physically detained in a gated enclosure throughout the day, denied the satisfaction of completing the symbolic last leg of their march down Parliament Street. The city's police force had instructions to keep the capital spruce for visiting dignitaries, among them Angela Merkel, the German chancellor, Henry Paulson, US Treasury secretary, and dozens of chief executives in town for a lavish conference organized by *Fortune*.

The chief executives cocooned in the sandalwood-scented splendour of the Imperial Hotel would have learnt far more from the marchers than from the predictable fare on offer at the conference. From the stunted and wasted frames of the landless, they would have observed how malnutrition rates, already higher than in parts of sub-Saharan Africa, are rising in many places, as wages lag behind soaring food prices. They would have learnt how the 120 million families who depend on the land for subsistence agriculture, generating no marketable surplus from one season to the next, live in terror of expropriation by state governments operating land scams in the name of development.

Fobbed off with promises of a committee to discuss land reform, the Gandhian leaders of the protest march sent a warning to the government: advocates of non-violent struggle are losing the argument to those with more radical ideologies. 'Forty per cent of Indians are now landless and 23 per cent are in abject poverty,' said P.V. Rajagopal, vice-chairman of the Gandhi Peace Foundation, which co-ordinated the rally. 'Such conditions have bred Maoist insurgency in 172 of India's 600 districts and farmers are killing themselves in 100 other districts. So we want to ask the government: where are the fruits of the reforms in these districts?'

It is in interests of western investors to listen. The capacity of Naxalite groups to disrupt the India growth story, by deterring investment in vast, resource-rich swathes of the country, is real. Posco, the South Korean steel group, knows from experience. Its plans to invest $12 billion in a new plant in the Naxalite-infested state of Orissa, potentially the largest foreign direct investment in Indian manufacturing, have been stalled by protests for nearly four years: four of its officials were even kidnapped by locals deeply sceptical of promises of compensation and rehabilitation. They have been released, but the company is no nearer to taking possession of the several thousand acres needed.

Posco's story highlights a much deeper crisis. It should raise important doubts about whether India will be able to attract the investment required to sustain its recent growth rates of more than 8.5 per cent. Investment as a share of gross domestic product has indeed risen sharply over the past three years, but it is skewed towards services. Attempts to start an industrial boom have backfired: a plan to promote Chinese-style special economic zones degenerated into a real estate racket. It displaced hundreds of thousands from their land, many of whom went uncompensated. The protests are becoming more violent: two people were shot this weekend as they fought plans for a chemical plant on 9000 acres in West Bengal.

As no image-conscious investor wants blood on their hands, it is hardly surprising that FDI in Indian manufacturing has recently been declining. During the twelve months to January 2007, it fell to just $1.5 billion from $1.8 billion the previous year, according to Morgan Stanley. Manufacturing, notwithstanding pockets of excellence, is struggling to become globally competitive and failing to play its traditional role as a sponge for surplus rural labour. It is a vicious circle: until the hundreds of millions who eke out a subsistence existence in the villages are given reason to believe they will receive fair compensation for the loss of their land and incomes, and not just hot air, they will fight tooth and nail for the status quo, miserable as it is.

~

Peter Wonacott, Matthew Rosenberg, Yaroslav Trofimov and Geeta Anand

India Security Faulted as Survivors Tell of Terror at Tourist Haunts and Train Station, Swiftly Launched Assault Overwhelmed Police; Home Affairs Minister Steps Down

The Wall Street Journal
1 December 2008

Mumbai: AS WAITERS STARTED setting dinner buffets in Mumbai's luxurious hotels, the killings that would ravage this Indian metropolis began out of sight, in the muddy waters of the Arabian Sea.

In the dusk hours of Wednesday, fisherman Chandrakant Tare was sailing his boat about 100 yards from a fishing trawler when he spotted young men killing a sailor on board. He says he saw them toss the body into the engine room. Assuming he had stumbled upon pirates, Mr Tare says, he sped away.

Hours later, at least ten terrorists, having arrived by small craft on the shores of Mumbai, began to sow death and destruction at will across India's financial capital.

Pieced together from interviews with dozens of witnesses and officials, this account of the three days of the battle for Mumbai shows just how a small but ruthless group of skilled militants, attacking multiple targets in quick succession, managed to bring one of the world's largest cities to its knees. The human toll—currently at 174 fatalities, including nine terrorists—was exacerbated by the Indian authorities' lack of preparedness for such a major attack. But the chain of events also points to just how vulnerable any major city can be to this type of urban warfare.

Niraj Sheth in Mumbai and Krishna Pokharel in New Delhi contributed to this article.

Authorities are still questioning the one captured terrorist, a twenty-one-year-old Pakistani named Ajmal Qasab, who they say has confessed to training with outlawed Pakistani militant group Lashkar-e-Taiba. The investigation remains in its very early stages, and the identities of the killed militants remain unclear.

Around 8.30 p.m. Wednesday, one dinghy with half a dozen young men landed at a trash-strewn fishing harbour near the southern tip of the Mumbai peninsula, witnesses say; a second arrived nearby shortly after. Mostly in their early- to mid-twenties, the men came ashore wearing dark clothes and hauling heavy bags and backpacks, according to fisherman Ajay Mestry, who saw one of the landings. The group he saw split up and raced toward the shimmering city.

When one young man with a bulging bag jogged up from the beach, Anita Rajendra Udayaar, the keeper of a roadside stall full of recycled plastic bottles, asked where he was heading. 'Mind your own business!' he shouted back, she recalls.

Mumbai's attention that night was focussed on one of the country's favourite sports: cricket. India was playing against England, and beating its old colonial master. In the open-air Café Leopold, a popular people-watching spot near the landing site, customers—many of them foreign backpackers—were watching the match.

At about 9.30 p.m., two gunmen with assault rifles appeared on the sidewalk, witnesses said. One stood at the entrance, the second to his left. Then they started firing.

Minutes later, they walked away, leaving more than a dozen casualties behind amid upturned, bloodied tables.

At about the same time, two other gunmen arrived at a Bharat Petroleum gas station at the corner of a small alley that leads to Chabad House, also known as Nariman House, the local headquarters of the Brooklyn-based Chabad-Lubavitch Jewish movement.

With its small, faded sign, the five-story Chabad House—which served as a guesthouse and source of kosher food for the many Israeli backpackers who travel through India—is so hard to find that most visitors ask for directions at the gas station. But the militants knew their way, a station attendant says: without stopping, they threw a hand grenade into the gas station, and walked into the alley.

Alarmed by the explosion, Chabad House's rabbi, Gavriel Holtzberg, called the Israeli consulate. The two gunmen burst into his building, taking a number of Israelis, a young Mexican Jewish woman, and the rabbi and his family hostage. It appears that they quickly shot dead one of the guests, an Israeli kosher ritual inspector, whose body would be found badly decomposed at the end of the siege.

The explosion and gunfire attracted the attention of neighbours. Some young men started throwing stones towards the building. Manush Goheil, a twenty-five-year-old tailor, stepped outside the family's shop to get a better view. His brother Harish watched from the shop as a gunman shot him dead with a well-aimed bullet fired from the Chabad House's top floor.

Around the same time about one mile north at Chhatrapati Shivaji Terminus, Mumbai's monumental colonial-era train station, two gunmen in dark T-shirts and hauling heavy backpacks walked down Platform 13, which opens into a large hall fringed by Re-Fresh Food Plaza, a fast-food outlet.

Throwing a hand grenade into the crowd of travellers, they unloaded volleys of gunfire. Bullets flew through the window where the station's manager, D.P. Chaudhari, observed the hall; he ducked down and survived. A colleague, S.K. Sharma, was cut down as he crossed the concourse. One bullet lodged in the stomach of Re-Fresh Plaza manager Mukesh Aggarwal. The gunmen peppered a bookstand at the back of the hall with bullets, shattering the glass next to a copy of *Complete Wellbeing* magazine, according to vendor Sarman Lal, who quivered on the floor saying his last prayers.

The two gunmen moved along two separate paths towards the station's main entrance, firing as they walked. They met virtually no resistance, even though several dozen police officers are usually deployed at the station. 'They were killing the public, and the police just ran away,' says Ram Vir, a coffee vendor whose stand is near Platform 8.

B.S. Sidhu, head of the Railway Protection Force for the Mumbai region, says that while some officers tried to fight back, there was little his force could do. Most police officers at the station—as they are throughout India—were unarmed or carried only bamboo sticks known as lathis. More than forty people, including three police officers, were killed in just a few minutes, authorities said. The wounded survivors screamed for help amid acrid smoke, piles of slumped, bloodied bodies and spilling suitcases.

By then, shooting had begun in two other spots: Mumbai's most luxurious hotels, symbols of the city's prosperity that were packed with tourists, visiting executives, and the local elite out for dinner. The historic Taj Mahal Palace & Tower and a complex housing both the Oberoi and Trident hotels rise high above the sea on opposite sides of the southern tip of Mumbai.

At about 9.45 p.m., two gunmen, slender and in their mid-twenties, ran up the circular driveway at the entrance to the Trident. They shot the security guard and two bellhops. The hotel had metal detectors, but none of its security personnel carried weapons because of the difficulties in obtaining gun permits from the Indian government, according to the hotel company's chairman, P.R.S. Oberoi. The gunmen raced through the marble-floored lobby, past the grand piano into the adjoining Verandah restaurant, firing at the guests and shattering the windows.

At the end of the lobby, they burst into a bar called the Opium Den, shooting dead a hotel staff member. Then they ran after a group of guests who tried to escape through a rear service area. They killed them, too.

The gunmen returned to the Verandah, climbed a staircase, dashed down a corridor lined with jewellery and clothes shops, and stopped in front of the glass doors of Tiffin restaurant, a swanky restaurant with a sushi bar in the Oberoi hotel.

They killed four of six friends who live in south Mumbai and had just settled down at a table near the front door. One member of the group, a mother of two, threw herself to the ground and shut her eyes, pretending to be dead. The men circled the restaurant, firing at point blank range into anyone who moved before rushing upstairs to an Indian restaurant called Kandahar.

Restaurant workers there ushered guests closest to the kitchen inside. The assailants jumped in front of another group that tried to run out the door. 'Stop,' they shouted in Hindi. They corralled sixteen diners and led them up to the twentieth floor. One man in the group dialled his wife in London and told her he'd been taken hostage but was okay. 'Everybody drop your phones,' one of the assailants shouted, apparently overhearing. Phones clattered to the floor as the three women and thirteen men dug through their purses and pockets and obeyed.

On the twentieth floor, the gunmen shoved the group out of the stairwell. They lined up the thirteen men and three women and lifted their weapons. 'Why are you doing this to us?' a man called out. 'We haven't done anything to you.'

'Remember Babri Masjid?' one of the gunmen shouted, referring to a sixteenth-century mosque built by India's first Mogul Muslim emperor and destroyed by Hindu radicals in 1992.

'Remember Godhra?' the second attacker asked, a reference to the town in the Indian state of Gujarat where religious rioting that evolved into an anti-Muslim pogrom began in 2002.

'We are Turkish. We are Muslim,' someone in the group screamed. One of the gunmen motioned for two Turks in the group to step aside.

Then they pointed their weapons at the rest and squeezed the triggers.

A few minutes later they walked upstairs to the terrace. Unbeknownst to the terrorists, four of the men were still alive; one of the survivors later provided the account of the shooting to the *Wall Street Journal*.

At the vaunted Taj hotel across the peninsula, two terrorists arrived from their attack on Café Leopold by about 9.45 p.m., broke down a side door and entered the building, according to a police officer investigating the attacks.

Two others entered the hotel's modern lobby, opened fire and threw grenades. As guests dashed for cover, the two pairs united. They would keep Indian police and commandos at bay for another sixty hours as they rampaged through the building.

Uptown, the two gunmen who had attacked the train station—recorded by the station's surveillance cameras—reached the nearby Cama Hospital for women and children, authorities said, shooting dead two unarmed guards at the entrance and racing up the stairs. By then, news of the attacks had spread in the neighbourhood. A number of policemen ran into the hospital as nurses herded expectant mothers into one room and locked themselves inside, a duty doctor says.

On the top floor, the terrorists and the police traded fire near a poster that reads 'Mother's Milk Is Best for Babies'. The policemen were badly outgunned. The gunmen killed one officer and escaped down the stairs, into a narrow alley that separates Cama Hospital from another hospital called GT.

In the alley, the state of Maharashtra's anti-terrorism chief, Hemant Karkare, sat in a police SUV packed with fellow officers, trying to coordinate a response to the mayhem engulfing the city. Creeping up, the two militants sprayed the vehicle with gunfire.

The officers appear to have died before any of them had a chance to fire back. The wall and metal blinds behind the van's spot are riddled with bullets. Not a single bullet mark could be seen by a reporter in the area from which the terrorists fired.

Dumping three of the officers' bodies on the ground and taking the others with them, the two militants jumped into the SUV and sped towards the Metro Big Cinemas multiplex. As they passed a crowd of journalists and onlookers, the SUV slowed down, a gun barrel emerged from the window, and bullets started to fly. Then, the vehicle sped on, with another police vehicle in hot pursuit. At one point, the gunmen ditched the SUV and hijacked a Škoda, police said, cruising through southern Mumbai—possibly looking for an escape route. Two hours later, they ran into a large police roadblock erected on a key road leading out of south Mumbai, at Chowpatty Beach.

Skidding to a halt 30 feet away from the roadblock, the Škoda's driver blinded the police with high beams and, flipping wipers, began spraying fluid on the windshield so that officers couldn't see into the car, said Sub-inspector Bhaskar Kadam, one of the officers manning the roadblock.

The three policemen armed with guns drew them. The nine others waved their bamboo sticks. Revving the engine, the car tried to U-turn but got stuck on the median. The man in the passenger seat rolled out and started shooting, killing one officer and wounding another. The surviving baton-wielding officers jumped on him, knocking him unconscious. Policemen with guns shot the driver dead.

This pair's killing spree was over. Police later identified the gunman taken alive as Mr Qasab, from the Punjab region of Pakistan, who they say is providing details of the plot.

Back at the Taj Mahal Palace, staff members had been calling room after room, advising hundreds of guests to lock the doors, switch off all the lights, and hide, guests and staff said.

At about 11 p.m., K.R. Ramamoorthy, the sixty-nine-year-old non-executive chairman of ING Vysya Bank, heard men in the corridor knock on his sixth-floor room, he says. 'Room service,' one of them called out in English.

Silence.

'Shoe polish,' the same voice called out.

Mr Ramamoorthy moved to the bathroom, accidentally banging the door. The two gunmen blasted the room door's lock open and entered. They tied Mr Ramamoorthy's hands and feet, he says, using his long Indian top known as a kurta, and his pajama bottoms. Then they ordered him to kneel on the ground. 'I'm sixty-nine years old. I have high blood pressure. Please let me go,' he recalls begging.

'We'll leave you, we'll let you go,' one of the men replied, he says. They turned him over so he lay face down on the floor.

Over the next hour or two, the two men spoke on their mobile phones in his room, seeming relaxed and happy, Mr Ramamoorthy says. He couldn't tell much of what they said but made out the word 'grenade' several times, he says. They ate some snacks from the minibar. Then, two more gunmen showed up in the room, dragging four other hostages—all uniformed hotel staff.

'What are your names and occupations?' the men asked the five hostages.

'I am Ramamoorthy from Bangalore,' Mr Ramamoorthy says he replied.

'What is your work?' one of the assailants asked in Hindi.

'I am a teacher,' he replied.

'No way can a teacher afford to stay here,' shouted the gunman, he recalls. 'You better tell us the truth.'

'I work for a bank,' Mr Ramamoorthy admitted.

The assailants were distracted by calls on their mobile phones. Minutes later, pushing the five hostages in front of them, the gunmen descended the staircase to a fifth-floor room. They shoved the hostages inside, laid them face down on the floor, and left.

Mr Ramamoorthy says he managed to free his hands and untied the others. By now, a fire possibly started by a grenade explosion was spreading through the sixth floor of the Taj hotel. As the choking smoke from the blazing fire enveloped the room, one of the four hotel staffers ripped off curtains and bedsheets, creating an improvised rope. The staffers used the rope to shimmy down the balcony outside to the third-floor ledge.

Certain he didn't have the physical strength to follow suit, Mr Ramamoorthy backtracked and descended via the smoke-filled staircase to the third floor. Some time later, he noticed the glare of searchlights. He opened the window and waved and shouted. Firefighters saw him and lifted a ladder to the window. 'You are safe,' he says they told him. He looked at his watch. It was 6 a.m. Thursday.

As the fires set by the militants burned through the hotel during the night, the general manager, Karimbir Kang, was busy shepherding hotel residents like Mr Ramamoorthy to safety. Mr Kang didn't manage to rescue his own wife, Neeti, and two young children: they died in the blaze.

In the other hotel complex taken over by the militants, the Oberoi-Trident, gunmen returned to the twentieth floor at around 6 a.m. Thursday. They pulled out their mobile phones and filmed the sprawled bodies of executed diners. The four injured men who survived the firing line there—one squashed under two bodies—were still playing dead, trying not to move.

'We'll booby-trap the bodies with bombs,' one of the gunmen said into the phone. As soon as the two terrorists left, the four injured men crept out to a terrace and hid behind a cooling tower, says one of the men. For more than twenty-four hours, they didn't move from their hiding place, drinking small amounts of red liquid inside the cooling system to soothe their thirst, the man says.

Authorities had asked the Mumbai-based Marine Commandos to help at the Taj in the first hours after the takeover of the hotels. But the so-called MarCos struggled to figure out the entrances and exits in the hotel and found it hard to match the gunmen who moved with ease through the building and seemed to know the structure inside out. The gunmen also were accustomed to operating in darkness, a commander on the force said.

At 6.30 a.m. Thursday, commandos from India's National Security Guard finally arrived—after they first waited for hours while authorities located a plane to pick them up at New Delhi, then waited for transportation from Mumbai's airport to the hotels under attack. The NSG commandos had proper equipment and training. They surrounded both the Taj and the Oberoi complex and a prolonged siege began.

The terrorists moved frequently through both buildings to confuse their pursuers and create the impression of greater numbers. Still, two of them found time on Thursday to call a local TV station to rant about India's mistreatment of Muslims.

As the fighting went on, new fires broke out at both the Taj and the Oberoi in the evening, sending plumes of smoke into the sky. 'Every time the terrorists were in a corner and under stress . . . they set fire to the curtains,' said J.K. Dutt, director general of the NSG.

By Friday morning, the NSG began to achieve real progress. At roughly 9 a.m. that day, Bill Bakshi heard a knock on his nineteenth-floor room in the annex section of the Taj. A diabetic who was running low on insulin, he peeked through the eyehole in hope of rescue and saw three uniformed men with assault rifles, he says. 'They wouldn't say who they were,' says Mr Bakshi, a sixty-three-year-old who owns a textile company. 'They were scared, too—they didn't know who was inside, either.'

Mr Bakshi opened the door. The next thing he knew, he says, he had three gun barrels thrust in his face. It took a couple minutes to convince the NSG men that he was not a terrorist, he says.

By late Friday morning, the NSG cleared out the annex section of the Taj, freeing hostages there. It also succeeded in storming the Oberoi, killing one gunman in a corridor and another in a bedroom. As they combed the hotel room by room, bringing out to safety the four injured men hiding behind the cooling system, the commandos found thirty-two other bodies inside.

At the Taj and the besieged Chabad House, the fighting continued. Two militants holed up inside the Jewish centre had blown off the doors of the elevator on every floor, and used the shaft to hide whenever NSG commandos fired back.

It appears that they executed their hostages one by one as the commandos closed in. Two young women guests, their wrists tied with white plastic rope, lay on the same bed, bullet holes in their heads, according to a photograph taken later at the scene. The terrorists shot Rabbi Holtzberg and his wife, who fell next to each other. As darkness fell, NSG commandos blasted a wall with explosives and finally penetrated the building. They killed the gunmen.

At the Taj, the battle raged into Friday night, with one of the gunmen opening fire from a window and shooting at the hundreds of journalists who gathered to cover the siege on the plaza outside. None were hit.

By Saturday morning, however, the commandos had taken over most of the building. They set a fire to smoke out three surviving terrorists, cornered in a restaurant called Wasabi, up a spiral staircase from the lobby. Two of the gunmen were shot dead. The third was hit with bullets as he tumbled backwards out of a window and on to the plaza outside. 'After that,' said Mr Dutt, the NSG chief, 'There was no more shooting.'

~

James Astill
In the Face of Chaos

The Economist
21 February 2009

Islamabad and Lahore: IN A ROOFTOP restaurant overlooking the old Mogul city of Lahore, Richard Holbrooke dined on 11 February with a group of liberal Pakistani businessmen, human-rights campaigners and journalists. He had come, midway through his inaugural tour as America's special representative for Afghanistan and Pakistan, with a heavy question. Against a rising thrum from the narrow streets of the red-light district below, Mr Holbrooke asked: 'What is the crisis of Pakistan?'

Well might he ask. Pakistan, the world's sixth-most-populous country and second-biggest Muslim one, is violent and divided. A Taliban insurgency is spreading in its north-west frontier region, fuelled partly by a similar Pashtun uprising against NATO and American troops in Afghanistan. Some 120,000 Pakistani troops have been dispatched to contain it, yet they seem hardly able to guard the main road through North-West Frontier Province (NWFP). On 3 February NATO briefly stopped sending convoys through Pakistan—which carry some 75 per cent of its supplies to Afghanistan—after Pakistani militants blew up a road bridge in NWFP. A related terrorism spree by the Pakistan Taliban and allied Islamists, including Al Qaeda, whose leaders have found refuge in the semi-autonomous tribal areas of the frontier, has spread further. Pakistan has seen some sixty suicide-bomb blasts in each of the past two years.

Parts of Pakistan's vast and thinly populated western state, Baluchistan, are also in revolt. And fears for the security of Karachi, a rowdy port city of 15 million, from which a militant group close to the army, Lashkar-e-Taiba (LET), launched an amphibious assault on Mumbai last November, are rising. Faced with these threats, the Central government in Islamabad, a coalition led by the Pakistan People's Party (PPP), and presided over by its leader, President Asif Zardari, is struggling. Cobbled together a year ago, after an election that swept the former army-backed government from power, it is short on competence and dogged by allegations of corruption. It has no one deemed fit to be finance minister. An unelected banker, Shaukat Tareen, holds the job, pending his expected election to Pakistan's upper house, or Senate, in March. Another unelected friend of Mr Zardari runs the interior ministry.

After a decade of army rule, it was inevitable that the new civilian government would take time to bed down, even if the times were less troublesome. Yet unfortunately, as always during Pakistan's bouts of civilian rule, the government has been beset by feuding. In a popular move, Mr Zardari pitted himself last year against the country's former army ruler, President Pervez Musharraf, forcing him to resign last August. Almost at once, Mr Zardari and his erstwhile ally, Nawaz Sharif, who leads the Pakistan Muslim League (Nawaz) party, or PML(N), fell to blows. Mr Zardari has been leaning on the country's Supreme Court to disqualify Mr Sharif from contesting any elections, because of a conviction some years ago on a hijacking charge. In the same throw, the judges may force his brother, Shahbaz Sharif, to step aside as chief minister of Punjab.

Mr Zardari, who inherited the party from his murdered wife, Benazir Bhutto, and fears that he too will be assassinated, is almost as unpopular as the detested Mr Musharraf. A survey released by the International Republican Institute in December found that only 19 per cent of Pakistanis wanted him for their leader; 88 per cent thought the country was heading in the wrong direction. It is, though

Mr Zadari is mostly not to blame. After two years of political turmoil and spreading violence, the economy is moribund. The textiles industry, which accounts for about half of Pakistan's industrial jobs and foreign-exchange earnings, has been pole-axed by gas and electricity shortages. A third of the textile factories in Punjab are said to have been shut down. In November, faced with the prospect of defaulting on its external debt, Pakistan had to return to the International Monetary Fund for a $7.6 billion bailout.

The Taliban insurgency is a particular worry. It is fiercest in the tribal areas, which the Taliban more or less rule, but is spreading throughout NWFP and touching Punjab in places. On 16 February NWFP's government, which is led by the Pashtun-nationalist Awami National Party, vowed to implement sharia law in the district of Malakand, where over 1,000 civilians are reported to have been killed recently by army shells or by beheading at the hands of the local Taliban. This may or may not placate the militants' leader, Mullah Fazalullah. His black-turbaned gunmen already control most of the area, including its lovely tourism region of Swat. Fittingly, Pakistan's tourism ministry is currently held by the Jamiat Ulema-e-Islam-Fazl (JUI-F), an Islamist party that has sown hundreds of radical madrassas across NWFP. The ministry has vowed to correct the 'immoral practices' of foreign tourists in Pakistan, assuming it can find any.

Holding Back the Tide

In Lakki Marwat, a district close to two thoroughly Talibanized tribal areas, North and South Waziristan, a hereditary Pashtun chief, Anwar Kamal, describes his efforts to hold back the militant tide. He and other chieftains have deployed a tribal army of 4,000 bearded Marwats along their 110-kilometre (70 mile) Waziristan frontier. In recent weeks they have fought several battles against the forces of Baitullah Mehsud, a Taliban commander who controls much of South Waziristan and is alleged to have supplied the killers of Ms Bhutto. Mr Kamal, who is also a senior member of Mr Sharif's party, says: 'We are heavily loaded with heavy weapons, from top to toe with anti-aircraft guns, anti-tank guns and mortars. It is the fashion these days, heavy weapons.' And yet, with perhaps 15 per cent of his tribesmen openly supporting the Taliban, 'For how long can I control my area?'

Security in Peshawar, NWFP's always-wild capital, home to

gunrunners, dope peddlers and, during the days of the anti-Soviet jihad in Afghanistan, Osama bin Laden, is deteriorating. Taliban bosses and bandit gangs—the Islamists' fellow travellers—are said to be renting houses in the city. Accordingly, wealthy Peshawaris are moving out. Fugitives from the frontier—where over half a million are estimated to have been displaced—have descended on the city. Two Afghan diplomats and one Iranian were recently abducted in Peshawar; the American consul was lucky to survive a murder attempt there last year. Last week a Taliban gang from Khyber circulated a video of an abducted Polish engineer, Piotr Stanczak, having his head sawn off with a butcher's knife. They had taken him hostage in Attock, a district of Punjab only 80 kilometres from Islamabad. On the day of his dinner in Lahore, Mr Holbrooke had also visited Peshawar—and a member of NWFP's government had been killed there by a roadside bomb.

Foreign diplomats in Islamabad sound increasingly despondent. One says: 'The more effort we've put into this place, the worse it's got.' The rate at which Mr Musharraf's few achievements have crumbled to dust is shocking. Bolstering the economy, mismanaged by Mr Sharif, was one. An ambitious package of local government reforms, establishing elected mayors to run the district-level bureaucracy, was another. In NWFP this system, perhaps unfairly, has been blamed for ushering in the Taliban, and is now being hobbled. Other provinces are expected to do likewise.

More depressing is the demise of Mr Musharraf's biggest triumph, a detente with India. A bilateral peace process, launched in 2004 by Mr Musharraf and Atal Behari Vajpayee, India's then Prime Minister, had brought the two countries closer than at any time in their painful history. Even a settlement of the dispute over divided Kashmir seemed possible. But in 2007 Mr Musharraf's attention wandered to crushing his democratic opponents, and the initiative drifted. In November, after the attacks in Mumbai in which over 170 were killed, India put it on hold.

On 12 February Pakistan's government admitted, for the first time, that the atrocity in Mumbai was LeT's doing. It also vowed to try the plot's ringleaders, including six LeT members already in its custody. This was encouraging. But it is much less than the eradication of anti-India militancy that India demands.

The Generals' Game

With all this bad news, it is tempting to wonder whether Pakistan could be heading for a meltdown—a Taliban takeover, perhaps. Even Mr Zardari has admitted that the militants hold 'huge amounts of land'. Yet the headlines give a distorted picture of the place. Most Pakistanis are moderate. That is why, in last year's unusually unrigged election, a coalition of Islamists, including JUI-F, did miserably, losing power in NWFP and Baluchistan. And though Punjab, where 60 per cent of Pakistanis live, is LeT's heartland, it is more orderly than several big Indian states, and richer.

To revert to Mr Holbrooke's question, Islamist militancy is not the only crisis of Pakistan. In fact, as America's envoy was emphatically told over his dish of spicy lentils, it is partly a consequence of the country's abiding affliction: the refusal of Pakistani generals to abandon a national-security policy that they have presumed to dictate, with disastrous consequences for Pakistan and its region, for six decades. It was founded on a belief that Hindu India is Pakistan's mortal enemy, and on an ambition to drive India from Kashmir. For a rear-base—or 'strategic depth'—against the threat of an Indian invasion, the army has sought to control Afghanistan; thus it helped propel Mullah Omar and his turbaned friends to power there in the 1990s. In fact, Pakistan's generals have consistently employed Islamist militants as proxies, from 1947 onwards.

By toppling Mr Sharif in 1999, Mr—then General—Musharraf followed a long tradition of army coupsters seizing power to 'save the nation'. However, by turning his back on the Taliban in 2001, he promised a new track. And in extending his hand to the Indians, he seemed to show that he was serious. At America's request, Mr Musharraf shifted troops from the eastern border to secure the north-west frontier. At the same time—and especially after Islamist assassins twice tried to kill him in 2003—he vowed to eradicate militancy in Pakistan, including some forty-odd jihadist groups with links to the army's Inter-Services Intelligence (ISI) agency. For this reason, liberal Pakistanis who were sceptical of Mr Musharraf's other promises—to improve Pakistani democracy, for example—supported him. Yet there were always reasons to doubt that a genuine policy shift was under way. Banned militant groups, including LeT, re-emerged under new names. Militant leaders, such as LeT's Hafiz Saeed, remained at large. After Mumbai, alas, these doubts have proliferated.

The alacrity with which the Pakistani army rushed to embrace the threat of an Indian military reprisal was remarkable. In fact, India did not explicitly threaten any such thing. And Mr Zardari, as a conciliatory gesture, offered to send the head of the ISI, Lieutenant General Ahmed Shuja Pasha, to Delhi. Yet Pakistan's generals, having scotched that offer, leapt to battle stations. They shifted several thousand troops from the north-west to the eastern border. Pro-army media commentators, spewing anti-India propaganda, whipped up the nation for war. In a briefing to Pakistani journalists, a senior ISI officer said that the Taliban had assured the army of its support in the event of a war with India. He referred to their leaders, including Mr Mehsud, the alleged killer of Ms Bhutto, and Mr Fazalullah, as 'patriotic Pakistanis'.

Tensions have since eased. But a senior ISI officer, giving a rare interview to the *Economist* last week, says he still regrets that a 'strike division', trained to punch into India, had been posted to the north-west frontier: 'Never in my lifetime will we ever have peace with India.'

Hapless on the Frontier

Doubts about the army's commitment to securing the north-west have also been persistent. In the aftermath of America's 2001 invasion of Afghanistan, Pakistan arrested over 600 Al Qaeda fugitives, but did nothing about the Taliban, who poured into Baluchistan and the tribal areas. From the start, the army believed America and its allies would swiftly withdraw from Afghanistan, opening the way for its former proxies to return to power. When America's attention wandered to Iraq, the generals became doubly convinced of this. To hasten the Westerners' departure, they are alleged—especially in Kabul—to have helped the Taliban launch their ongoing insurgency in Afghanistan. Around the same time, after entering the tribal areas to hunt down Al Qaeda, the Pakistanis found themselves fighting a billowing Pushtun insurgency of their own.

To pay for its campaign costs, the army has received some $10 billion from America. Yet its efforts have been so hapless that many accuse it of not really trying. It has lost over 1500 men, for little obvious gain. The civil administration along the frontier, which was always weak, has collapsed. The tribal elders whom the government had used as interlocutors have been murdered by militants (who are mostly youngsters; Messrs Mehsud and Fazalullah are in their early thirties). The army seems demoralized. Designed to fight tank battles against Indians, it is ill-equipped to take on Pashtun guerrillas in their mountainous terrain. Its troops are disinclined to kill their Muslim countrymen in a war that few Pakistanis support. This is a serious problem. It also means Pakistan feels bound to keep collateral damage to a minimum. The army claims that an operation against Mr Mehsud's men in South Waziristan was ended last year after the militants corralled themselves in a thickly populated area. Instead of scattering the militants, the army made a deal with them.

In return for their promise not to fire on the troops garrisoned among them, not to play host to Al Qaeda and not to fight in Afghanistan, Mr Mehsud and his confrères in North Waziristan have been left with the run of their areas. The army aims to make similar deals with militants in Bajaur and Mohmand, where it has been fighting fierce battles in recent months. That would leave it free, it hopes, to launch further operations in Orakzai, a pristine Taliban haven, and Khyber. But piecemeal operations of this kind have merely shunted Al Qaeda and other militants around the tribal areas. And the army's ceasefire deals have often been flouted; Mr Fazalullah has torn up at least two of them. Worse, suspicions that the ISI, or at least some of its officers, are still in cahoots with their jihadist enemies persist. Last year America, whose trust in the Pakistani army's good faith was almost a testament of its belief in the war on terror, began launching frequent missile strikes on the tribal areas. At least thirty people were said to have been killed in a strike in the Hurram tribal area on 16 January.

This strategy is reported to have been effective. By one—possibly wishful—estimate, American missile strikes in Pakistan have killed eleven of Al Qaeda's twenty commanders in the past six months. But they have also boosted anti-Americanism among Pakistanis, especially within the army. Senior ISI officers attribute most of their troubles in the tribal areas to anger over the American strikes. They also accuse India of giving 'significant' support to their Taliban enemies there. On both counts, this seems unlikely. Moreover, recent reports allege that the unmanned drones being used in the strikes are in fact based inside Pakistan, which would suggest a certain Pakistani complicity in the ploy. Nonetheless, as a symbol of America's mounting mistrust of its vital Pakistani allies, the policy needs better management. One suggestion is that a joint Afghan–Pakistani–American counter-terrorism agency might be set up to do it.

Presumably this is one of the problems that Mr Holbrooke has been hired to solve. His brief is certainly daunting. Unless Pakistan's army can be persuaded to undergo a 'strategic renaissance', in the phrase of Lieutenant General Talat Masood, a Pakistani military pundit, it may be unwilling or unable to deny the use of its north-west frontier to the Afghan and Pakistan Taliban. It will not, in a month of Fridays, be bulldozed into complying with America's demands. 'You can't insult a country into cooperation,' says General Masood. Besides stern words, Pakistan's army will therefore require even more American money and equipment, especially counter-insurgency kit, such as helicopters and night-vision gear, which it has long demanded. It will also require America to allay the army's fear of encirclement by a pro-India regime in Afghanistan. Meanwhile, America needs to stand up for Pakistan's democratic leaders, who are on its side. Mr Zardari and Mr Sharif both say they want peace with India and an end to ruinous militancy. Neither is a friend to the army.

Finally, America and NATO must convince the Pakistanis that they mean to stick it out in Afghanistan until the fledgling state can stand up for itself. Some ISI officers concede that NATO will remain in Afghanistan longer than the army had expected ('maybe another fifteen to twenty years'). But none seems to believe it can stabilize the place; and this remains NATO's improbable task. Without better help from Pakistan, it may not succeed. But even with this help, as the Pakistanis know, NATO may fail.

~

Emily Wax

Death of Rebel Leader Marks 'End of an Era' in Sri Lanka

After Years of Fighting, Questions of Reconciliation

The Washington Post
19 May 2009

Colombo, Sri Lanka: ONE OF THE world's most ruthless and elusive rebel leaders, Tamil Tiger chief Velupillai Prabhakaran, was reportedly killed Monday by Sri Lanka's military in a firefight that signalled the effective end to one of Asia's longest-running military conflicts.

It was a day many Sri Lankans thought would never come, after more than a quarter-century of sporadic fighting, ceasefires and failed negotiations. Top military commanders bearing bouquets of flowers met the country's President, Mahinda Rajapaksa, in his living room to deliver the news that the war was over. The Tamil Tigers, who had been fighting for a separate Tamil homeland, were officially defeated, they said, and the entire island for the first time in nearly thirty years was under one flag.

'We can announce very responsibly that we have liberated the whole country from terrorism,' Sri Lanka's army chief, Lt Gen. Sareth Fonseka, said on television, as rickshaw drivers honking in celebration passed dozens of sandbagged checkpoints in central Colombo where normally serious soldiers in flak jackets smiled their approval. Some

**Prabhakaran was confirmed dead on 19 May 2009, and the twenty-six-year war officially ended that day, with Sri Lankan President Mahinda Rajapaksa claiming that the rebels were finished 'forever'. That left hundreds of thousands of Tamils pushed off their lands and guarded in what human rights groups called 'internment camps' which, at the time, were locked and off-limits to journalists and to human rights and political leaders. Rajapaksa and his government said they would start a long-term peace process to meet Tamil demands but, by July 2009, Tamil anger was growing inside the camps at the lack of any sign of meaningful reform.*

women cooked or purchased rice and handed out small congratulatory packets to euphoric soldiers.

By dusk, a group of children in one neighbourhood had raised a scarecrow-like effigy of Prabhakaran, who was vilified as a despot across much of southern Sri Lanka. Young girls danced and cheered his death, as hundreds of adults lined the road, clapping and waving the country's flag of a sword-wielding lion.

After a two-hour firefight, officials said, Prabhakaran was shot along with two commanders from his inner circle: Tiger intelligence chief Pottu Amman and Soosai, the head of the 'Sea Tiger' naval wing, who used only one name. The three were killed as they were trying to flee the war zone in the country's north in an armoured van accompanied by a bus filled with armed rebels. The Sri Lankan government sent cellphone text messages to citizens across the country announcing that Prabhakaran and his deputies had been killed.

'It's the end of an era,' said M.R. Narayan Swamy, author of an unofficial biography of the rebel leader, who said the Tamil Tigers, formally known as the Liberation Tigers of Tamil Eelam, are 'finished . . . shattered beyond recognition'.

The government requested that shops and homes hoist the country's flag for one week as a show of unity and national pride in a country that has been splintered by conflict between the country's ethnic Tamil, mainly Hindu, minority and its Sinhalese Buddhist majority.

But the war's end—if it truly is the end—opens up new questions in a nation where armed conflict between Tamil rebels and mostly Sinhalese government troops has been the defining narrative for more than a generation.

A Tamil rebel website, however, reported that Prabhakaran was alive and in hiding. The government has denied such reports and is conducting a DNA test on the body to disprove those claims.

'The end of this war is something that we genuinely didn't think could ever happen,' said Rajinda Jayasinghe, twenty-seven, a civil society leader who is Sinhalese and works in the northern Tamil aid camps. 'With the death of Prabhakaran, the symbol of the divisions between Sri Lankan people is gone. The real question now is, will there be goodwill towards Tamils? Will Tamils feel the government has their best interest in their hearts?'

In Tamil areas of Colombo, Sri Lanka's capital and a city with a history of ethnic riots, the change in mood was stark, with streets eerily silent as residents seemed to stay indoors.

Prabhakaran was widely seen by Tamils as their only hope against the discrimination and alleged human rights abuses by the Sinhalese-dominated government.

'Actually, now we are fearing. I know that people are celebrating the end of the war, but what does it mean for us? No one knows,' said Jayea Baladhura, thirty-two, a Tamil and former worker for a German aid agency. She had to move her mother and sister from the country's embattled north to live with her in Colombo.

Sri Lankan authorities are still concerned about the capability of Tamil fighters to launch suicide attacks in Colombo, as the Tigers are known for sophisticated and dramatic comebacks after government gains. There is already fear that a new generation of Tamil militants could rise if Sri Lanka's government ignores Tamil grievances.

'Today we have enormous challenges before us to ensure that these sacrifices were not in vain. We must grab this opportunity to rebuild our country, to restore confidence and reintegrate all members of the community,' Foreign Secretary Palitha Kohona told reporters.

In Washington, State Department spokesman Ian Kelly said the end of fighting is an 'opportunity for Sri Lanka to turn the page on its past' and build a country that protects the rights of all people.

President Rajapaksa is expected to address the nation in a live speech from Parliament on Tuesday morning, and so far, many in his government predict his message will be one of reconciliation. They said he would seize the moment of triumph to unify the island by reaching out to the nation's Tamils, who represent about 15 per cent of the island's 20 million people. Billboards on nearly every street corner here show a smiling, white-robed Rajapaksa in a maroon scarf, along with the caption: 'One island, united against terror. Ready to build the nation.'

In some parts of the city, those who hailed Prabhakaran as a voice for Tamil emancipation discreetly mourned his death. Many Tamils feel that Prabhakaran and his Tiger fighters were the muscle behind Tamil politicians working with the mainstream government. Prabhakaran, a heavyset man with a bushy moustache, was an iconic figure across South Asia—reclusive and underground like Osama bin Laden but with the larger-than-life persona of Latin American revolutionary Ernesto 'Che' Guevara.

Prabhakaran consolidated power by killing off all potential rivals and many Tamil intellectuals and by leaving no apparent successor.

He was rarely seen in public, except for propaganda videos showing him firing an automatic weapon amid the coconut groves of the dense jungle. He would emerge each November to honour those young Tigers killed in battle or in suicide missions.

Long before Al Qaeda, the Tigers invented the suicide belt and pioneered the use of suicide bombings, recruiting hundreds of female suicide bombers. Followers were given vials of cyanide to wear around their necks in case of capture.

Prabhakaran allegedly orchestrated suicide bombings that killed a Sri Lankan President, six cabinet ministers and, in May 1991, former Indian Prime Minister Rajiv Gandhi. The United States has labelled the Tamil Tigers a terrorist organization.

Sympathy for the Tigers runs deep in the Tamil populations in Sri Lanka and abroad, where ethnic Tamils from the southern Indian city of Chennai to the streets of London championed Prabhakaran's cause.

The Sri Lankan government has been criticized by human rights groups for overstepping its powers. Officials marshalled public opinion to their cause by painting the conflict as a war against terrorism and courted China for weapons without restrictions on their use. They skirted dissent by journalists, aid workers and civil society groups, denouncing their scrutiny of the government and its war efforts as treasonous, rights groups said. 'There needs to be a look at the real causes of this war,' said Jehan Perera, executive director of the National Peace Council of Sri Lanka. 'Otherwise there could be a second Prabhakaran.'

The government also sealed the war zone, making independent observation by journalists and rights groups impossible. As the military campaign winds down, a humanitarian crisis is intensifying in the country's north, where as many as 300,000 mostly Tamil residents have been displaced by the fighting.

Many Tamils and aid workers say they are relieved the war appears to be over but are concerned about those left living in refugee camps.

'The lethal and cruel Tamil Tigers are gone,' said United Nations spokesman Gordon Weiss. 'The question is, at what cost?'

~

Notes on Contributors

James Astill has been *The Economist*'s South Asia correspondent since 2006. He was previously the magazine's defence correspondent, covering wars in Iraq, Afghanistan and Pakistan.

Arthur Bonner came to India as the first CBS correspondent in 1953 and stayed until 1961. He returned in 1962 to cover the war between China and India. After thirty years with NBC in America, he returned to the region as a freelance correspondent and to write books, two of which deal with Afghanistan and India.

Henry Bradsher was the Associated Press Delhi bureau chief between 1959 and 1964 and was FCA president (1962–63). Later, based in Hong Kong for *The Washington Star*, he reported from the subcontinent between 1970 and 1975. He covered the Bangladesh war and was among the correspondents expelled from what was then East Pakistan in 1971. He has written several books, two of them on Afghanistan.

Dean Brelis was *Time* magazine's South Asia correspondent from 1982 to 1985. He subsequently became the magazine's deputy bureau chief in New York and then South East Asia bureau chief based in Bangkok. He died in November 2006.

John F. Burns was *The New York Times*' South Asia correspondent from 1994 to 1998. He won the Pulitzer Prize in 1997 for his reports from Afghanistan, having won an earlier Pulitzer in 1993 for his coverage in Bosnia. After five years in Iraq, he is currently *The New York Times*' bureau chief in London.

James Cameron wrote for a variety of British and American newspapers and magazines, including *The Daily Mail*, *The New York Times* and *The Guardian*, and broadcasted on radio and television. He travelled extensively in the subcontinent from 1945 (in later years with his Indian wife Moni) till he died in 1985. His books include *An Indian Summer* (Macmillan 1974).

Françoise Chipaux has been *Le Monde*'s South Asia correspondent, based first in Delhi and now Islamabad, since 1997.

James Clad was *The Far Eastern Economic Review*'s South Asia correspondent from 1989 to 1991 and was president of the FCA in 1990–91. He is now US Deputy Assistant Secretary of Defence for South and South East Asia, and Australasia.

Barbara Crossette was *The New York Times*' South Asia bureau chief from 1988 to 1991. She is now the editor of *The InterDependent*, the magazine of the United Nations Association of the US, and teaches international affairs.

Simon Denyer has been Reuters' India and Nepal bureau chief since February 2004, after holding a similar post for two years in Pakistan and Afghanistan.

Edward W. Desmond was *Time* magazine's South Asia bureau chief from 1988 to 1991 and is now the president of Time Inc. Interactive.

Suman Dubey reported from Delhi for *The Wall Street Journal* and *The Asian Wall Street Journal* from 1976 to 1979 and from 1992 to 1995, when he became Dow Jones' chief India representative till his retirement in 2007. He was also editor of *The Indian Express* and managing editor of *India Today*.

Celia W. Dugger was *The New York Times*' South Asia co-bureau chief, with her husband, Barry Bearak, from 1998 to 2002. They are now co-bureau chiefs in Johannesberg, South Africa.

John Elliott was *Financial Times*' first South Asia correspondent (1983–1988). After a posting in Hong Kong, he left *Financial Times* and worked for the Hong Kong government. He returned to Delhi in 1995, writing mainly for *Fortune* magazine and *The Economist*. He is the current FCC president (2007–09).

George Evans was *The Daily Telegraph*'s roving correspondent in the subcontinent, Middle East and Africa from 1951 to 1961, having served in the Gurkhas from 1943 to 1946. He later became managing editor of *The Sunday Telegraph* and retired in 1986.

Adrienne Farrell was Reuters' correspondent in India between 1951 and 1960, and again from 1962 until 1970. She married Peter Jackson in 1954, and they jointly became Reuters' India team.

Mark Fineman was South Asia correspondent for *The Philadelphia Inquirer* from 1982 to 1986 and for *The Los Angeles Times* from 1986 till 1992. He died in 2003 in Baghdad.

Trevor Fishlock was *The Times*' South Asia correspondent from 1980 to 1983 and was FCA president (1982–83). The author of two books about

India—*India File* and *Cobra Road*—he is now an author and a freelance broadcaster.

Peter Foster was *The Daily Telegraph*'s South Asia correspondent and blog-writer from 2004 till January 2008. He now writes from New Zealand.

Edward A. Gargan was *The New York Times*' South Asia bureau chief from 1991 to 1994. After postings in Hong Kong and China, he now lives in Beijing where he is working on his third book.

Amelia Gentleman has been *International Herald Tribune*'s India correspondent since 2005.

Suzanne Goldenberg was *The Guardian*'s South Asia correspondent from 1995 to 2000. She is now the paper's Washington-based US correspondent and is the author of *Madam President: Is America Ready to Send Hillary Clinton to the White House* (Guardian Books 2007).

Michael Hamlyn was *The Times*' South Asia correspondent from 1983 to 1989 and subsequently became their correspondent in South Africa, where he now lives in Cape Town.

Selig S. Harrison was the Delhi correspondent first for the Associated Press (1951–54), and then *The Washington Post* (1962–1965). He returned to Washington to work with various policy institutes and wrote five books on Asia that include *India—The Most Dangerous Decades* (Princeton University Press 1960).

Erhard Haubold reported for the Swiss daily *Neue Zuercher Zeitung* in South Asia between 1968 and 1972. He later joined *Frankfurter Allgemeine Zeitung* as Asia correspondent, based in Singapore and later in Delhi. He retired in 2002.

Peter Hess was the South Asia correspondent of the Swiss daily *Neue Zuercher Zeitung* between 1968 and 1972. He reported, and wrote a book, on the Bangladesh war. He died in 1974.

David Housego was *Financial Times*' South Asia correspondent from 1988 to 1992 and was president of the FCC (1991–92) when the present club house was obtained. He now lives in Delhi where he has set up a home textiles company, Shades of India.

Olaf Ihlau worked in Delhi, among other places, for the Munich daily *Sueddeutsche Zeitung* and joined *Der Spiegel* in 1991. He retired in 2007 and lives in Berlin. A book on India, *Weltmacht Indien*, appeared in 2006, followed in 2008 by a study on Afghanistan, *Geliebtes, Dunkles Land*.

Bernard Imhasly was the *Neue Zuercher Zeitung* correspondent in Delhi from 1991 to 2007, and president of the FCC (1997–98). Earlier he was a Swiss diplomat, with a Delhi posting as his last assignment. His book *Goodbye to Gandhi* was published in 2007 by Penguin India. He now lives in Alibagh near Mumbai.

Peter Jackson was Reuters' Pakistan correspondent from 1952 to 1953 when he moved to Delhi, where he worked with, and married, Adrienne Farrell. Returning with her in the 1960s, he was for several years president of the Foreign Correspondents' Association (before it became the FCC).

Jo Johnson has been *Financial Times*' South Asia correspondent since 2005.

Ivor Jones arrived in Delhi as the BBC's correspondent in 1962, just before the India–China war, and stayed till 1966. He went on to a posting in Beirut and died in retirement in Wales in 1990.

Peter R. Kann was in South Asia as a roving reporter for *The Wall Street Journal* from 1969 to 1975 when he covered the Bangladesh war, winning a Pulitzer Prize in 1972. He subsequently became publisher and editor of the journal, then CEO and chairman of Dow Jones, retiring in 2007.

Manjeet Kripalani has been *BusinessWeek*'s India bureau chief, based in Mumbai, since 1998.

Daniel Lak was a BBC correspondent based in Islamabad, Delhi and Nepal from 1992 to 2004. He also wrote for other newspapers including *The South China Morning Post* and *The Economist*. He is the author of two books: *Mantras of Change* (Penguin India 2005) and *India Express* (Penguin Canada 2008).

John Lancaster was *The Washington Post*'s South Asia correspondent from 2002 to 2006. He is now a freelance writer based in Washington.

Simon Long was *The Economist*'s South Asia correspondent from 2002 to 2006. He is now their London-based Asia editor.

David Loyn was the BBC's South Asia correspondent from 1993 to 1997 and is now their international development correspondent. His book, *Butcher and Bolt*, a history of foreign engagement in Afghanistan, is to be published in September 2008.

Edward Luce was *Financial Times*' South Asia correspondent from 2001 to 2005, when he wrote *In Spite of the Gods* (Little, Brown 2006). He is now *Financial Times*' Washington bureau chief.

Arthur Max was with Associated Press in New Delhi from 1990 to 2000, and became the bureau chief in 1992. He is now AP's bureau chief in Amsterdam.

Neville Maxwell was *The Times*' Australian-born correspondent in India from 1959 to 1967. He was twice president of the FCA and broadened the name to Foreign Correspondents' Association of South Asia. His book, *China's India War* (Natraj Publishers 1970), became an academic bestseller. He ended his career as an Oxford don.

Sudip Mazumdar has been *Newsweek*'s South Asia special correspondent since 1984.

Tim McGirk was South Asia correspondent for *The Independent* from 1990 to 1996, and for *Time* magazine until 1998. He subsequently worked for *Time* in Latin America, the Far East and Pakistan. He is now the magazine's Jerusalem bureau chief.

Matt Miller opened *The Asian Wall Street Journal*'s South Asia bureau in 1985 and stayed until 1987. He is now senior writer with *Deal*, a New York-based group of financial publications.

David Orr has lived in Delhi since 1999. His articles and photographs have appeared in publications that include *The Irish Times* and *The Sunday Telegraph*.

Daniel Pearl was *The Wall Street Journal*'s South Asia bureau chief, based in Mumbai, from 2000 until his kidnapping and killing in Karachi in 2002.

Alex Perry was *Time* magazine's South Asia bureau chief from 2002 to 2006 and is now the magazine's Africa bureau chief based in Cape Town.

Peter Popham was *The Independent*'s Delhi correspondent from 1997 to 2002, since when he has been the paper's Rome correspondent.

Gerald Priestland came to India in 1954 when he was twenty-six as the BBC correspondent and stayed till 1958. After later postings in America and the Middle East, he became a newscaster and the BBC's religious affairs correspondent. He died in 1991.

Maseeh Rahman was *Time* magazine's South Asia correspondent from 1996 to 2001. He now writes from Delhi for *The South China Morning Post* and intermittently for *The Guardian*.

Padma Rao has been the South Asia correspondent of the German newsweekly *Der Spiegel* since 1998. She was FCC president from 2005 to 2007.

Phil Reeves was *The Independent*'s South Asia correspondent from September 2002 to January 2004. He is now National Public Radio's South Asia correspondent, based in Delhi.

John Rogers worked for Reuters, with Delhi as his first posting, from 1968 to 1971. He retired from Reuters in 2001, as head of the Americas desk in Washington, and now teaches journalism at universities in London.

Matthew Rosenberg has covered Pakistan and Afghanistan for *The Wall Street Journal* since October 2008. He was previously South Asia correspondent of the Associated Press, based in Delhi, from 2005.

Somini Sengupta has been *The New York Times*' South Asia bureau chief since 2005.

K.K. Sharma was *Financial Times*' Delhi correspondent from 1965 to 1992 and also wrote for *Time* magazine. He lives in Delhi.

Lewis M. Simons was *The Washington Post*'s bureau chief in Delhi for three years from 1972 till he became, in July 1975, the first foreign journalist to be expelled from India at the start of the emergency.

John Slee worked for *The Sydney Morning Herald* in Delhi as a correspondent between 1966 and 1971 and also wrote for *The Christian Science Monitor*. He remained with *The Sydney Morning Herald* for more than thirty years and has now retired and lives in Australia.

John Stackhouse was *The Globe and Mail*'s development issues reporter and South Asia correspondent from 1992 to 1999. He is now the paper's business editor.

William K. 'Bill' Stevens was *The New York Times'* New Delhi bureau chief from 1982 to 1984. Later he was on the paper's science desk, till he retired in 2000. He is the author of *Miracle Under the Oaks: The Revival of Nature in America* and *The Change in the Weather*.

Robert Stimson worked in India for twelve years, initially for *The Times of India*, and then from March 1947 as the BBC's first correspondent in India.

Tiziano Terzani covered Asia for *Der Spiegel*, and later for *Corriere della Sera*, based in Vietnam, Hong Kong, Beijing, Tokyo and Bangkok and then, from 1994 to 1997, in Delhi. The author of bestselling books, he died in July 2004 in his hometown of Florence, after recording how he faced fatal cancer in *The End Is My Beginning*.

Mark Tully was the BBC's South Asia correspondent from 1972 to 1994, but was expelled during the emergency from 1975 to 1977. He was president of the FCA (1974–75). He now lives in Delhi and has written several books, the latest being *India's Unending Journey* (Random House 2007).

Stephan Wagstyl was *Financial Times*' South Asia correspondent from 1992 to 1995. He is now *Financial Times*' Central and East Europe editor.

Amy Waldman was *The New York Times*' South Asia co-bureau chief from 2002 to 2005. She is now a national correspondent for *The Atlantic*, based in New York.

Emily Wax has worked for *The Washington Post* for over a decade and has been the paper's South Asian bureau chief, based in New Delhi, since 2007. Previously she was the bureau chief in East Africa, where she won the Medill Medal of Freedom for her coverage of the war in Darfur.

Julian West was *The Sunday Telegraph* correspondent covering South Asia, Afghanistan and Iran from 1996 to 2005. She has written a book on Nepal and a novel, *Serpent in Paradise* (Atlantic Books 2007). She is now based in Delhi and writes for *The Spectator*.

Charles Wheeler was for many years the BBC's longest-serving correspondent, having joined it in 1947. He worked in India between 1958 and 1962, before going to Berlin and other postings, and then back to London.

Andrew Whitehead was the BBC's Delhi correspondent from 1993 to 1997, and then editor, Hindi TV and country director, India, of the BBC World Service Trust from 2005 to 2007. He has written a history of the Kashmir crisis, *A Mission in Kashmir* (Penguin India 2007).

Peter Wonacott has been *The Wall Street Journal*'s senior South Asia correspondent since 2005.

John Zubrzycki was based in Delhi from 1994 until 1998, writing primarily for *The Australian*, *The South China Morning Post* and *The Christian Science Monitor*. He is now a senior writer at *The Australian*. His first book *The Last Nizam: The Rise and Fall of India's Greatest Princely State* was published recently.

Copyright Acknowledgements

Grateful acknowledgement is made to the following for permission to reprint previously published material:

Gerald Priestland: 'The Delhi Scene', 'With Nehru Around India' and 'Goa Showdown', extracted from *Something Understood* (1986). Reprinted by permission of Andre Deutsch (United Kingdom).

Arthur Max: 'Calcutta Today'. Used with permission of The Associated Press © 2007. All rights reserved.

Matthew Rosenberg: 'Sri Lanka Seen Heading Back to Civil War'. Used with permission of The Associated Press © 2007. All rights reserved.

Robert Stimson: 'Goodbye to India'. Reprinted by permission of BBC.

Charles Wheeler: 'Fast for Chandigarh'. Reprinted by permission of BBC.

Ivor Jones: 'India Mobilizes'. Reprinted by permission of BBC.

Mark Tully: 'Nehru Dynasty'. Reprinted by permission of BBC.

David Loyn: 'The Taliban's One-Eyed Strongman Hides in His Lair'. Reprinted by permission of BBC.

Andrew Whitehead: 'Eunuchs Bless His New-Born Son'. Reprinted by permission of BBC.

Daniel Lak: 'The Royal Massacre in Nepal'. Reprinted by permission of BBC.

Manjeet Kripalani: 'Asking the Right Questions'. Reprinted by permission of *BusinessWeek*.

Tiziano Terzani: 'Mother Teresa'. Reprinted by permission of *Corriere della Sera*.

James Cameron: 'The Death of Nehru'. Reprinted by permission of *The Daily Herald* (now *The Sun*).

James Cameron: 'The Trap! As Soon as Nehru said "FIGHT" He Had Lost the First Round'. Reprinted by permission of *The Daily Mail*.

Trevor Fishlock: 'Rebels Show Father New Pictures of His Kidnapped Son' and 'How an Assassin's Bullets Almost Ended Hostages' Hopes of Freedom'. Reprinted by permission of *The Daily Telegraph.*

Peter Foster: 'Why the Tiger's Future is Far from Bright' and 'The Forgotten Victims of India's Drive to Success'. Reprinted by permission of *The Daily Telegraph.*

George Evans: 'Indira Gandhi: "Why I Had to Clamp Down"'. Reprinted by permission of *The Sunday Telegraph.*

Julian West: 'Benazir Bhutto: "Power, Men and My Regal Style"'. Reprinted by permission of *The Sunday Telegraph.*

David Orr: 'Wodehouse Mania'. Reprinted by permission of *The Sunday Telegraph.*

Olaf Ihlau: 'Sai Baba: "Miracles Are Part of My Being"'. Reprinted by permission of *Der Spiegel.*

Padma Rao: '"A Few Seagulls, Tarzans and Man Fridays": Britain's Dirtiest Secret'. Reprinted by permission of *Der Spiegel.*

Simon Long: 'Sonia—and Yet So Far: India's New Government'. Reprinted by permission of *The Economist.* Copyright © The Economist Newspaper Limited, London (22 May 2004). 'The Pursuit of Happiness'. Reprinted by permission of *The Economist.* Copyright © The Economist Newspaper Limited, London (16 December 2004).

James Astill: 'In the Face of Chaos'. Reprinted by the permission of *The Economist.* Copyright © The Economist Newspapers Limited, London (21 February 2009).

James Clad: 'Towards a Hindu Raj: Religious-Based Party Sets Its Sights on Power'. Reprinted from *The Far Eastern Economic Review.* Copyright © Review Publishing Company Limited 1990. All rights reserved.

John Elliott: 'The Punjab: Gandhi's No-Go Area'. Reprinted by permission of *Financial Times.*

K.K. Sharma: 'Promising Start Down a Rocky Road'. Reprinted by permission of *Financial Times.*

David Housego: 'India's Financial Architect'. Reprinted by permission of *Financial Times.*

Stephan Wagstyl: 'The Child Victims of India's Slave Trade' and 'PSUs: Reluctant to Give Up Its Grip'. Reprinted by permission of *Financial Times.*

Edward Luce: 'Supply and Demands: What Has Water to Do with Politics? In India, Everything'. Reprinted by permission of *Financial Times*.

Jo Johnson: 'Inequality Threatens India's Economic Boom'. Reprinted by permission of *Financial Times*.

John Stackhouse: 'A Lesson in Village Democracy'. Reprinted with permission from *The Globe and Mail*.

Suzanne Goldenberg: 'Riding the Storm with the Wizard of Bihar'. Reprinted by permission of *The Guardian*. Copyright © Guardian News & Media Ltd 1996.

Amelia Gentleman: 'The Flashy Cars of a Maharaja for Modern Times'. Reprinted by permission of *International Herald Tribune*. Distributed by The New York Times Syndicate.

Mark Fineman: 'Nepal Maoists Kill Scores of Pro-Democracy Protestors'. Copyright © Los Angeles Times (7 April 1990). Reprinted with permission. 'Lynchings over Caste Stir India'. Copyright © Los Angeles Times (12 April 1991). Reprinted with permission.

Françoise Chipaux: 'A Pakistani Returns from Guantanamo'. Reprinted by permission of *Le Monde*.

Sudip Mazumdar: 'It Was Like Breathing Fire'. Reprinted by permission of *Newsweek*.

Barbara Crossette: 'In Kashmir Valley, Alienation Turns Deadly' and 'A Blast, and Then the Wailing Started'. Reprinted by permission of *The New York Times*.

Edward A. Gargan: 'Satyajit Ray Honoured: Without Profit in His Land' and 'Hindu Storm, Trust Is Torn: Police Role in Bombay Riots'. Reprinted by permission of *The New York Times*.

John F. Burns: 'The Fiercely Faithful: From Cold Wars, Afghans Inherit Brutal New Age'. Reprinted by permission of *The New York Times*.

Celia W. Dugger: 'Religious Riots Loom over Indian Politics'. Reprinted by permission of *The New York Times*.

Amy Waldman: 'India Accelerating'. Reprinted by permission of *The New York Times*.

Somini Sengupta: 'In India, Maoist Guerrillas Widen "People's War"'. Reprinted by permission of *The New York Times*.

William K. Stevens: 'Indian Army Goes into Nine Cities as Anti-Sikh Battling Flares: Throngs File by Gandhi's Bier'. Reprinted by the permission of *The New York Times.*

Peter Hess: 'In the Famine Region of North-East India'. Reprinted by permission of *Neue Zuercher Zeitung.*

Erhard Haubold: 'Model of a Guerrilla Revolt: How a South Indian Mountain Tribe Is Enticed by Maoists'. Reprinted by permission of *Neue Zuercher Zeitung.*

Bernard Imhasly: 'Destruction of the Mosque at Ayodhya: Violent Resolution of the Indian Temple Dispute'. Reprinted by permission of *Neue Zuercher Zeitung.*

Adrienne Farrell: 'Indian Government Promotes Tiger Hunting: Maharaja Organizes Shoot in Bundi' and 'India's Wildlife Is Disappearing: Indiscriminate Killing by Amateur Hunters'. Used with permission of Reuters Limited. Copyright © 2007. All rights reserved.

Peter Jackson: 'Model of Team Work Beat Everest'. Used with permission of Reuters Limited. Copyright © 2007. All rights reserved.

John Rogers: 'China Sets the Pace for India in Space Race'. Used with permission of Reuters Limited. Copyright © 2007. All rights reserved.

Simon Denyer: 'Fear Rules in Nepal's Maoist Heartland'. Used with permission of Reuters Limited. Copyright © 2007. All rights reserved.

Arthur Bonner: 'The Tragedy of Tibet'. Reprinted from *The Saturday Evening Post* magazine. Copyright © Saturday Evening Post Society 1961. (for further information, visit www.saturdayeveningpost.com)

Daniel Lak: 'After the Nepal Massacre'. Reprinted by permission of *The South China Morning Post.*

Arthur Bonner: 'India's Masses: The Public that Can't Be Reached'. Copyright © The Atlantic Monthly Group 2008, as first published in *The Atlantic Monthly*. Distributed by Tribune Media Services.

John Zubrzycki: 'Midnight's Orphans: The Anglo-Indians of India'. Reprinted by permission of *The Australian.*

Tim McGirk: 'Island Tribe Fights to Stay Alone in Dwindling Forest'. Reprinted by permission of *The Independent.*

Peter Popham: 'Darkness and Horror in Gujarat'. Reprinted by permission of *The Independent.*

Phil Reeves: 'Living in Poverty and Abandonment, the Barely Functioning State that Trusted Its Saviours'. Reprinted by permission of *The Independent.*

John Slee: 'The "Lion of Kashmir" Resumes His Fight'. Reprinted by permission of *The Sydney Morning Herald.*

Neville Maxwell: 'Tarnished Image of Mr Nehru'. Reprinted by permission of *The Times*. Copyright © Neville Maxwell, NI Syndication Limited (4 April 1963).

Michael Hamlyn: 'The Despot Who Rides a Hungry Tiger: *The Times* Profile—President Zia'. Reprinted by permission of *The Times*. Copyright © Michael Hamlyn, NI Syndication Limited (2 January 1986).

Dean Brelis: '"Dark Clouds and More Blood": Ethnic Riots Deal a Grievous Blow to a Struggling Democracy'. Copyright © Time Inc. 2008. All rights reserved. Reprinted from *Time* magazine with permission.

Edward W. Desmond: 'War at the Top of the World'. Copyright © Time Inc. 2008. All rights reserved. Reprinted from *Time* magazine with permission.

Maseeh Rahman: 'Is Nothing Sacred?' Copyright © Time Inc. 2008. All rights reserved. Reprinted from *Time* magazine with permission.

Alex Perry: 'Battlefields in the Garden of Eden'. Copyright © Time Inc. 2008. All rights reserved. Reprinted from *Time* magazine with permission.

Peter R. Kann: 'Dacca Diary' and 'Dacca Diary II'. Property of Dow Jones & Company, Inc. and used with permission. All rights are reserved by Dow Jones.

Daniel Pearl: 'In Indian Quake, Death Haunts the Living' and 'Smuggling in Afghanistan Helped to Fill Coffers of Taliban and Manufacturers'. Property of Dow Jones & Company, Inc. and used with permission. All rights are reserved by Dow Jones.

Peter Wonacott: 'India's Skewed Sex Ratio Puts GE Sales in Spotlight'. Property of Dow Jones & Company, Inc. and used with permission. All rights are reserved by Dow Jones.

Suman Dubey: 'The Indira Express'. Property of Dow Jones & Company, Inc. and used with permission. All rights are reserved by Dow Jones.

Matt Miller: 'Indian Phones Stuck in Primitive State' and 'Indian Firm's Success Stirs Controversy: Often Aided by State Licences, Reliance May